HAROLD NICOLSON
DIARIES AND LETTERS
1945-1962

Harold Nicolson in 1950

HAROLD NICOLSON

Diaries
and Letters
1945-1962

EDITED BY
NIGEL NICOLSON

THE BOOK
OF THE MONTH CLUB

This edition published by The Book of the Month Club
for members only

Printed in Great Britain
Collins Clear-Type Press
London and Glasgow

Dedicated to

BENEDICT NICOLSON

by his father and brother

Contents

CONTENTS

CONTENTS

CONTENTS

Illustrations

Introduction by Nigel Nicolson

The present, and final, volume of Harold Nicolson's diaries and letters extends between his sixtieth and seventy-seventh years. Even the latest were not years of relaxation. A man who pursues a normal career of appointments, promotion, postings and secondments usually knows long in advance the date of his retirement and the size of the pension which he will have earned. Not so a writer and politician. Harold Nicolson had not sat daily in an office since 1931. The table where he worked in London stood alongside the bed where he slept, and his bookroom at Sissinghurst overlooked the same patch of garden as his bathroom. The only schedule which bound him to his desk was imposed upon him by two weekly articles. The time-table for finishing his books was fixed by himself, and became a moral obligation. There was no easing of the pressure as he grew older, for the desire and facility to write both remained unabated, and he was obliged to earn. He had never saved money. Royalties on his past books did not bring him the equivalent of a pension. The only method by which he could afford his comfortable, varied life was by publishing two or three articles a week and a book every one or two years. As this was what he most wished to do in any case, the grindstone to which he held his nose was more stimulating than abrasive.

His capacity for hard work was always matched by a capacity for enjoyment. Although there might be nothing in particular to take him to London on a Monday morning, he never remained at Sissinghurst during the week, apart from 'holidays' during the summer, which were in fact periods of maximum output. He needed London as an Athenian needed Athens. He had a profound love of the countryside, both wild and cultured, but London was the place

15

where things happened, where people met and talked, where he recharged his intellectual batteries, where he maintained his political, diplomatic and literary friendships, and made new ones. Almost every evening his chambers at Albany, Piccadilly, were filled with people who dropped in unexpectedly and were always welcomed, men more frequently than women, men of all ages and different professions, who found there good talk, not very good drink ('He was the sort of man', Graham Greene was once saying about an acquaintance, 'who would offer you a glass of South African sherry', while Harold Nicolson had his back turned, pouring out for him a glass of South African sherry), and that ease which comes from shared conceptions of fun.

Harold Nicolson has been called a snob. This is a complete misunderstanding either of him or of the word. A snob is a person with an exaggerated respect for social position or wealth, who is ashamed of socially inferior connexions and tries to magnify his own importance by claiming an unfounded intimacy with the great. One has only to state this definition to see how inapplicable it is to the author of these diaries and letters. Breeding and money hardly counted with him, except as an indication of what to expect. What mattered was that his friends should be intelligent and share his own values. By intelligence he meant liveliness of mind. Knowledge was not an essential, nor culture, nor experience, nor background. But he did demand a certain inquisitiveness about general ideas, a capacity for understanding opposite points-of-view, and for relating generalisations to facts. By values he meant taste—an appreciation of excellence, rejection of the tawdry, the ability to praise without flattery and to mock without offence, and certain moral qualities, too, such as kindliness, truthfulness, modesty and tolerance. These are uncommon merits to find in the same person, but they have nothing to do with snobbishness. He felt ill at ease in the company of people who did not possess them in at least some degree, and he avoided the Ascot and the City sets just as he avoided the bar of the local pub, because he did not expect to find them there. In fact, he did what everybody does: he chose his friends for reasons that he thought important. But he was not a snob.

There has been a more tenable line of criticism: that he was 'superior'. Conscious that he belonged to an intellectual élite which was exacting in its demands but not exclusive, he took much the same view of society as had Edmund Burke two hundred years before. 'We are enlarged in our opinions', Burke once told the House of Commons, 'while the people are confined.' 'I hate uneducated people having power', wrote Harold Nicolson in the first passage from his diary printed in this volume, 'but I like to think that the poor will be rendered happy.' They must be protected. It was the same with Jews: he saw in them racial characteristics which he found unattractive, but he was always a strong supporter of Zionism and felt keenly the outrage of violent anti-Semitism. Or with coloured people: he warmly applauded Harold Macmillan's wind of change, because it was wrong to shoot people, and once you stop shooting them, you must free them. Or with Americans: he thought the great mass of the American people (like, indeed, his own) insensitive to the finer human qualities and resented the clumsiness with which they wounded the pride of older nations, but he had many American friends and looked forward to the day when the pattern of American thinking would change. In other words, he held an aristocratic, and hence a 'superior', view of the responsibilities of people like himself. But his categories of excellence were not limited. After all, there had been Asquith and Lloyd George, Curzon and Ramsay MacDonald, for which very different statesmen he had felt great regard. Now there was Ernest Bevin and Hugh Gaitskell, Eisenhower and John F. Kennedy. All of these he recognised as great leaders, not merely because they were on our side, but because they were all nurtured in the western tradition. It was this that mattered to him. For Khrushchev and Nkrumah or the more extreme British Trade Union leaders he had no time at all, because they did not think as he thought. This third volume should therefore be read as the attempt of a highly civilised man to come to terms with new men and movements wholly alien to him.

From the foregoing it might be assumed that he was more of a natural Conservative than he admitted. But there was another side of Conservatism which he found repulsive—the greedy and vulgar competition which it permitted and even encouraged, and its denial of that equality of opportunity which he thought was morally right and politically inevitable. There was, of course, a contradiction in his political thinking. 'I see the dawn of a new happiness for the world', he wrote in his diary for 1946, 'in which every man will at last have a chance equal to that of every other man.'[1] But then later: 'I do not like the masses in the flesh.'[2] His conscience led him to express views which his upbringing rejected. Equal opportunity simply means another form of competition, which would be no less vulgar for being universal, and if complete equality of opportunity were attained, the uneducated would gain power. I do not think that he ever sorted out this contradiction, possibly because it had not begun to emerge in its acutest form until after he had left active politics. When he took the decision in February 1947 to join the Labour Party, it was partly opportunism, because he saw in it the shortest way back to Parliament as a commoner or peer; partly because he had a genuine admiration at that moment (it was soon to fade) for Ernest Bevin; but mainly because of his 'cerebral Socialism', by which he meant his uneasiness about the social injustice which he saw around him and from which he had greatly benefited himself.

Having joined the Party, and having been half-promised a peerage if he earned it, he had little choice but to accept the invitation to fight the North Croydon bye-election as Labour candidate in March 1948. Between the lines of his diary later in that year there is an admission that he had made a mess of it, because he could never identify himself whole-heartedly with his supporters. The *Marginal Comment* which he wrote immediately after his defeat, and which is reproduced in full on pages 133–7, was an exposure of his dislike not only of the whole process of electioneering, but of the very people who had strained every nerve to secure his victory. The entire Labour movement deeply resented the implied assumption of that article that no Croydon man or woman was likely to read the *Spectator* or would understand it if they did. It was a main reason why he was never given a peerage. His political career was finished by 1,500 words which he typed, more out of amusement than pique, on an empty Sunday afternoon. Politics demands a convincing pretence that you enjoy all its manifestations, not merely the Chamber and the smoking-room, and of this deceit Harold Nicolson was incapable. It also requires ultimate confidence in the Party of your choice. This, too, eluded him. The habit of frequently transplanting

[1] p. 52. [2] p. 139.

his Party allegiances prevented the growth of political roots. When the Labour Government turned their back on Europe in 1950, he wrote, 'I am deeply distressed. How I wish I had not been such an impulsive fool as to join the Labour Party. It was certainly the cardinal error of my life.'[1] The only Party from which he never accepted support was the one to which he temperamentally belonged —the Liberal Party.

After the war, he never recovered the political influence which he had gained before and during it. Like Lloyd George, he did not feel 'well out of it': he just felt out of it. But there came a moment in 1956 when his conviction on what was right and wrong, wise and foolish, in British foreign policy revived with all the intensity of 1938. The Suez crisis would in any case have stirred him profoundly, for he believed that Britain's position in the world depended upon our talent for foresight, consultation with our friends, and the honourable observance of treaties. Suez was a denial of all this. The passion which the crisis excited in him was further stimulated by my own attitude and misfortunes. The reader must forgive me when he finds that I, the editor of this chronicle, emerge temporarily as a main actor in it. My father saw the Suez affair largely through my own eyes. He depended upon me for much of his Parliamentary information, and counselled caution when I felt only despair. The end of the crisis was the beginning of my personal disaster, for I was rejected by my Bournemouth constituents for having publicly opposed Anthony Eden in his hour of greatest need. This story, part of which I have written elsewhere,[2] is retold only in the barest outline in the present volume, but I have occasionally inserted passages from my own diary or letters to my father in order to give the gist of it, and to maintain something of the political continuity when he had left the House of Commons and I was still in it. My political career fizzled out, like his. We both possessed the stamina, but neither of us the dexterity, for survival.

If 1948 saw the end of Harold Nicolson's political activity, it also marked a fresh start in his literary achievement. He was invited to write the official biography of King George V. In the opinion of many people, his literary reputation will rest mainly on this book. He could not previously have been described as a professional

[1] p. 191.   [2] *People and Parliament*. Weidenfeld & Nicolson. 1958.

historian. His only venture into historical writing, apart from biography and semi-autobiography, had been *The Congress of Vienna*
(1946), and this had not been based on primary sources. *King George
V: His Life and Reign* was not as original as many of his other books.
How could it be? But it was in every sense his *magnum opus*. The
scale of the subject and its exposition was vast. That the book would
be of historical importance was predictable, since the events of King
George's reign were immense, and the bulk of the documents to
which he was given access had never been published before He
handled this mass of material with confidence and distinction,
combining his flare for historical balance with his gift for literary
embroidery. While his main theme was hammered out on the
deeper notes, his other hand was always running up the keyboard to
provide a lighter accompaniment. The book, he said, must be like
linen, presenting an equable surface in tone and style, and in this he
succeeded superbly. He laboured on *King George V* for three whole
years. He became, as a consequence, a Knight Commander of the
Victorian Order and an Honorary Fellow of Balliol.

Just as his diplomatic trilogy in the 1930's had cleansed his mind
and reputation after the disasters of Mosley and *Action*, so *King
George V* removed the stains of North Croydon. His literary success
exonerated his political incompetence. Implicitly it settled the
question which had been hovering over him since 1930: was he a
writer who dabbled in politics, or a politician who found solace in
literature? Even if he had been a younger man (he was nearly 66
when *King George V* was published), it is unlikely that he would have
returned to active politics, for he had already extracted from it
what it had to offer him and given it what he had to contribute. In
his older age he was happily occupied with his books—with *Benjamin
Constant*, *King George V*, *Good Behaviour*, *Sainte-Beuve*, *Journey to
Java*, *The Age of Reason* and *Monarchy*, which followed in succession
from 1949 to 1962, and with his weekly journalism, *Marginal
Comment* for the *Spectator* until the end of 1952 and his book-reviews
for the *Observer* from 1949 to 1963.

In 1955 he suffered, at an interval of eight weeks, two minor
strokes. Their effect upon him was both temporary and cumulative.
He was shaken by them at the time, psychologically more than
physically, and thought that he had not long to live. Then he dis-

covered that his mental powers had not been noticeably affected, and he managed, with astonishing resilience, to write one of his most light-hearted books, *Journey to Java*, eighteen months afterwards. The shock, however, was delayed. His last book, *Monarchy*, was his worst. This is partly because he wrote it from economic necessity and without much pleasure, but also because his normally acute sense of proportion had been upset by his strokes and advancing age. The book was superficial, mugged-up, hurried and misshapen. Its reception by the critics was cool, and although he started immediately on the research for *The Age of Romance*, he later abandoned it and repaid the royalties advanced.

II

During the period of seventeen years covered by this volume, the relationship between Harold Nicolson and V. Sackville-West was further deepened. As they grew older, and as we, their sons, left home to marry and have children of our own, their dependence upon each other became absolute. 'I am a bivalve', he wrote to her during one of her absences abroad, 'and don't function properly when I am forced to be unicellular.' To her he looked for consolation during his illnesses and political trials: to him she confided (as rarely before) her struggles with *The Garden* and *Daughter of France*, and sometimes, when she could not conceal it, her concern about her health. I commend to the reader's attention her letter of 4th December, 1956, in which she expressed to him in a short paragraph the feelings which she had nurtured so long. It is worth repeating here:

'I thought the other day, in the night, that you were the only person I have ever really loved. I thought this out rather carefully, and analysed my feelings, and came to that conclusion. I won't say that I haven't been *in love* with other people, but you are the only person that I have ever deeply and painfully loved. That is true. You know me well enough to know that people don't count very much with me. I love places (Sissinghurst, the Dordogne, Florence) far more than I care for people, and Rollo [her dog] probably means more to me than any of my friends. And of course Knole. .... but that is a separate thing I can't speak about. That goes too deep.'

While I have been editing these volumes, I have been haunted by the thought that she might not have approved the publication of her letters. She has stood behind my chair as La Grande Mademoiselle (the Daughter of France) stood behind hers. I was consoled by the discovery that she hoped that I might one day publish a selection of Harold Nicolson's letters to her,[1] although she made no mention of her letters to him. But it seemed to me that their marriage, if it was to be described at all, should not be described one-sidedly. It would not damage the memory of her to expose to view even the violently Conservative side of her nature, for she made no attempt to conceal it in her lifetime. The interplay of male and female characteristics in each of them, and in their relationship with each other, is the most absorbing aspect of their marriage. It could not be conveyed by his letters alone. But there was another reason. Some readers have found it difficult to believe that two such different people could have been happily married at all. If their affection was truly reciprocal, how could they have endured such long and frequent separations, even on holiday, even when one of them was seriously ill? V.Sackville-West's letters provide a complete answer to that question. Their odd mode of life was established first by necessity (his absence while he was in the Foreign Service and later in Parliament), then by choice (since he enjoyed public life and society, while she hated both), and finally by habit. She never felt lonely when alone, for she had her own occupations, and their daily correspondence was in a sense a more intimate link between them than constant companionship would have been. 'People often think that we are on the verge of divorce', she wrote in the letter which is reproduced in facsimile on page 372 of this volume. 'How wrong they are. How wrong!'

During the last six winters of her life, she and Harold Nicolson went on an annual cruise. They visited both coasts of each of the southern Continents except Australia. These journeys were mainly for the purpose of writing free from interruption. They resulted

[1] p. 358.

directly in two books, *Journey to Java* and *No Signposts in the Sea*, her last novel and one of her best, and indirectly in half-a-dozen others, for each would always return with a fid of manuscript written on board, in addition to the articles which both posted regularly to the *Observer* from their various ports-of-call. The interest of visiting places which neither had ever seen before, from Tokyo to Valparaiso, was so secondary that they came to dislike the interruption of the long ocean voyages by arrival at a port. Only Macao aroused in them the same intensity of delight that they had so often experienced on less ambitious journeys to Italy or the Dordogne.

Always present during these voyages was the nagging fear that one of them might fall seriously ill. Twice, at the end of 1957 and early in 1962, V. Sackville-West was bunk-ridden for nearly half the journey, and on her return to Sissinghurst in 1959 and again in 1960 she contracted virus pneumonia which kept her for two months in bed. She had a tough constitution, and her recovery from the first three of these illnesses was complete. But her exhaustion on board the *Antilles* in January 1962 was due to a more serious cause. She had a haemorrhage on the train while travelling to join the ship at Southampton. The two diaries of those days, hers and his, arouse all one's compassion when read side by side. She concealed from him what had happened. While he would record, 'Vita is taking a nap', she lay on her bunk in an agony of apprehension. She did not tell him the whole truth until their return, and then only because the specialist advised an immediate operation. The surgeon found cancer. It was from this that she died in Sissinghurst on 2nd June, 1962, at the age of seventy.

In the Introduction to the first of these volumes I mentioned that Harold Nicolson continued to write his diaries until 4th October, 1964, and that the third volume would contain extracts from all of them from 1945 onwards. When I came to read the diary of the last two years, I realised that this was not possible. His grief at her death can be imagined, but should not be laid bare. Nothing could adequately fill the gap which she left—not his many friends, not his • work, not even his family. He could not bring himself to revisit the places where they had been together, with the merciful exception of Sissinghurst itself, where I attempted to create a new happiness for him around my growing family. He travelled abroad—to Greece, to Paris, to New York, to Bergamo. For another year he continued to write his reviews for the *Observer*, never missing a week, not even the week of her death, but he resigned himself to abandoning his journalism and his last book, *The Age of Romance*, when he had a third stroke on 25th May, 1963. Two years later I persuaded him to leave his chambers at Albany to live permanently at Sissinghurst.

My mother bequeathed the castle to me, and other property to my brother, Ben. Soon after I began negotiations to make over Sissinghurst to the National Trust, and it became an accomplished fact on 13th April, 1967. Until the very last months of my negotiations I had not read the entry in her diary which is reproduced on page 268 of this volume. Although I was shaken by it, I do not think I would have acted differently if I had read it earlier. She had great respect and affection for the National Trust. She served for many years on its Gardens Committee, and Harold Nicolson was Vice-Chairman of its Executive. Her indignant rejection of the idea that Sissinghurst might pass to the Trust during her lifetime was not due to any hostility towards the Trust itself. It was due to her deep sense of family, privacy and ownership. Knole, she considered, had been wrested from her by antiquated laws of inheritance: it had then been 'taken' from the Sackvilles (though the Sackvilles gave it) and transferred to a public body. Sissinghurst was hers. She had bought it, rescued it, made it. Although she had opened the garden to the public for more than twenty years, no 'hard little metal plate at my door' should proclaim that Sissinghurst had gone the same way as Knole. To me it appeared differently. My main desire and duty was to save what she and my father had created, to preserve in perpetuity the garden which, together with her books, is the legacy of her imagination. Few private gardens of this size could survive in the economic conditions of our time. It was a choice between its gradual reversion to the fields and cabbage-patches from which it had emerged, and the surrender of the titular ownership to the National Trust. I chose the second alternative, without hesitation.

Here we now live, behind the metal plate, and here, I hope, my son Adam will raise a new generation after me. My father lives in the South Cottage, beside the red-and-orange garden which he first planned in 1930. He is now 81. His life is placid. He reads, but no longer writes. He enjoys occasional visits from his friends. He loves his grandchildren. He has read the typescript of this volume, and has found nothing which he wishes to eliminate or amend.

May 1968   *Sissinghurst Castle,*
                                                                  Kent

This Introduction was written in November 1967, and I have left it unaltered. Sir Harold Nicolson, who read it, died at Sissinghurst nearly six months later, on 1st May, 1968, a few minutes after midnight. The closing months of his life were eventless, but free from mental or physical distress. It became difficult to hold any prolonged conversation with him, and he could scarcely walk without assistance. His affection for his family and friends, however, remained undimmed, and he was gratefully aware of the beauty of the coming Spring. He died suddenly of a heart attack, as he was preparing for bed. His body was cremated two days later, and his ashes interred in the graveyard of Sissinghurst parish church.

Acknowledgement: The editor is greatly indebted to the following for reading the proofs of this volume: Sir Alan Lascelles, Mr John Gore, Raymond Mortimer, Kenneth Rose, Mrs Anthia Collins, Benedict Nicolson and Atheneum (New York).

1945

Reflections on the Labour victory – Hiroshima – President Truman – the Japanese surrender – errors of H.N.'s political career – Churchill in Berlin – Harold Macmillan on the future of the Conservative Party – Russian suspicion of the West – H.N. hopes for a peerage – V.S-W. on writing poetry – the delight of Greece – interview with Archbishop Damaskinos – advice to young Foreign Office officials – 'The Garden' – Churchill on the Russians and de Gaulle – leaving King's Bench Walk

On 26th July, 1945, the Labour Government came to power under Clement Attlee. In the Election, Harold Nicolson, who was then 58, lost his seat at West Leicester, which he had represented in Parliament for the last ten years. He was greatly depressed by his defeat, although it was not unexpected. At first he hoped to return to active politics by winning a bye-election or by elevation to the House of Lords; or, failing that, to be considered for the Chairmanship of the British Council. All these ambitions were disappointed. To Labour he appeared as a committed supporter of Churchill; to Conservatives, as an unreliable waverer. So neither a bye-election in a winnable Opposition seat, nor a peerage in the gift of the Government, came his way. Although his political interests remained as acute as ever and he still saw a great deal of his friends in Parliament, he was obliged to return for his living to literature and journalism.

During the period of the second phase of the Potsdam Conference, the dropping of the two American atom-bombs and the surrender of Japan, Harold Nicolson continued to write 'The Congress of Vienna' and his weekly article 'Marginal Comment' for the 'Spectator'. V. Sackville-West was finishing her long poem 'The Garden', and together they compiled their anthology 'Another World Than This'. For most of the week he remained in London, at King's Bench Walk, Inner Temple, where he had lived since 1930, but which, to his infinite sorrow, he now received notice to quit, as the chambers were required for practising barristers. He was still a Governor of the B.B.C., and became a member of the Executive Committee of the National Trust and a Governor of his old school, Wellington College.

His elder son, Benedict, (aged 31) had resumed his pre-war job as Deputy Surveyor of the King's Pictures. I (then aged 28) was writing the official war-history of my regiment, the Grenadier Guards, and was adopted as Conservative candidate for West Leicester, my father's old seat.

29

DIARY   *27th July, 1945*

I spend the morning analysing the Election results.[1] It is an amazing statement of public opinion, but I am not yet quite sure what it really means.

I feel sad and hurt, as if I had some wound or lesion inside. But I cannot make out what is the centre of this sadness. Naturally I much mind leaving the House and being outside public life. I also realise that I had counted upon my friends being returned, and half hoped that they would assist me, either to get back, or else to the House of Lords, or else to some job like Chairman of the British Council. But they will want any seat that they can get for their own front bench;[2] they will require every peerage possible; and the Labour Government will want someone far more left-wing than I am for the British Council. Therefore I see a denial of future opportunity.

But there is something else. It is not, I think, dread of the social revolution. I have expected this for a long time and do not fear it. It may be the conflict within me between the patrician and the humanitarian. I hate uneducated people having power; but I like to think that the poor will be rendered happy. This is a familiar conflict.

One thing I do mind is missing the appearance of the new House. I want to see how the new people fit in. I want to see how the brilliant Harold Wilson really does. He is only 22.[3]

Winston, it seems, has refused to go to Potsdam, and Attlee will fly there as a lonely little snipe tomorrow.

DIARY   *29th July, 1945*

Last Wednesday, the 26th, was indeed an unfortunate day. It was the day I lost my seat; and the Temple treasurer gave me notice that I must evacuate 4 King's Bench Walk by Christmas, as they cannot afford, owing to war-damage, to retain residential chambers for non-practising barristers. This is such a terrible blow that Vita had

[1] Labour had won 393 seats, the Conservatives' 213, the Liberals 12, and Independents 22.
[2] Among leading Conservatives who lost their seats were Harold Macmillan, Brendan Bracken, Duncan Sandys, L. S. Amery and Walter Elliot.
[3] Harold Wilson was in fact 29. He now entered Parliament for the first time as Member for the Ormskirk Division. He had been Director of Economics and Statistics, Ministry of Fuel and Power, 1943–44.

wisely kept it from me until I should have recovered slightly from my Leicester disaster. I am much depressed. I have lived there for fifteen happy years, and to leave it closes a further chapter in my life. I feel as if chapter after chapter was being closed, finished, put away.

DIARY   6th August, 1945

The 9 o'clock news announces that we have split the atom. A long statement, drafted by Winston, is read, explaining how the discovery was made. It cost £500,000,000 and took four years. They have used it today on a Japanese town [Hiroshima]. They cannot tell exactly what damage was done. It is to be used eventually for domestic purposes.

DIARY   7th August, 1945

The Press ring up to ask whether when I wrote Public Faces I knew about the atomic bomb.[1] This amuses me. I work hard at Chapter XVI [of The Congress of Vienna], and finish the book at 3.15 pm. Now comes the delicious period of revision, verification and notes.

Viti is thrilled by the atomic bomb. She thinks, and rightly, that it will mean a whole new era.

DIARY   8th August, 1945

David Scott[2] tells me that the Foreign Office are delighted with [Ernest] Bevin. He reads with amazing rapidity, remembers what he reads, cross-examines the experts, and having once mastered his brief, acts with vigour.

I have a talk with Tommy Lascelles.[3] He says that the King does not like the way the B.B.C. treat his constitutional position. Instead of saying, 'Mr Bevin was sworn in as Privy Councillor', they should say, 'The King held a Council. . . .' He tells me that when Truman came to Plymouth,[4] all went very well indeed. Truman is short, square, simple and looks one straight in the face. [James] Byrnes, the

[1] H. N.'s novel Public Faces, published in 1932, had foretold, by name and function, the atomic bomb. He had written that a single bomb, 'no bigger than an ink-stand', made of a new mineral discovered in the Persian Gulf, 'could by the discharge of its electrons destroy New York'. See Vol. I of his Diaries, p. 116.
[2] Sir David Scott, then Deputy Under-Secretary of State in the Foreign Office.
[3] Sir Alan Lascelles, Private Secretary to King George VI, 1943–52.
[4] On his way back from the Potsdam Conference on 2nd August.

Secretary of State, is a chatterbox. At luncheon in the *Renown*
Byrnes began discussing in front of the waiters the impending release
of the atomic bomb. As this was top-secret, the King was horrified.
'I think, Mr Byrnes', he said, 'that we should discuss this interesting
subject over our coffee.'

DIARY   *10th August, 1945*

After luncheon I go with Victor Cunard to buy some socks at
Simpsons in Piccadilly. I leave the shop at 2.20, and as we walk down
the street, we see some idiot girls leaning out of the window of an
office and sprinkling passers-by with torn-up paper. 'They think the
war is over', says Victor. 'No', I answer, 'I expect that they have
been demobilised.' We part outside Hatchard's, and I walk on and
bump into Harold Macmillan who is without coat or hat. He says,
'What a pity that we could not have kept on the old House and the
Coalition until today. Then we could have had a final celebration.'
'Is there any news? I have heard nothing', I say to him, feeling foolish.
'Yes', he answers, 'the Japs have surrendered.'[1]

Well, that is very odd. I have no feeling of elation at all. It seems
remote. I go to the London Library to check up on some reference
in Napoleon's correspondence. There is no sign of jubilation, and I
observe that the newspaper vendors have stacks of evening papers
unsold and unasked for. How different it all was on V.E. Day! On
going back to K.B.W. I meet a small procession of American
soldiers carrying Old Glory and followed by a very few urchins. It is
not inspiring at all.

I dine at the Travellers with Robin Maugham.[2] He tells me in
great detail how he visited Number 10 on the night of July 26th.
Clemmie had retired to her room with the migraine. He and Mary
[Churchill] were alone until Winston and Brendan [Bracken] came
in. Winston said, 'The new Government will have terrible tasks.

---

[1] The Japanese had accepted the Potsdam terms of surrender, but stipulated that
the Mikado's prerogatives should remain. There was further diplomatic negotiation on this point, and the actual ceasefire was not announced by President
Truman until 14th August. The final surrender was signed by the Japanese in
Tokyo Bay on 2nd September.
[2] The author, nephew of Somerset Maugham. He succeeded his father as second
Viscount Maugham in 1958.

Terrible tasks. We must do all we can to help them.' He said, as if to himself, 'It will be strange tomorrow not to be consulted upon the great affairs of State. I shall return to my artistic pursuits. Mary, get the picture I did the other day in France.'[1] The picture was brought. He was pleased with it. Not one word of bitterness; not a single complaint of having been treated with ingratitude; calm, stoical resignation—coupled with a shaft of amusement that fate could play so dramatic a trick, and a faint admiration for the electorate's show of independence.

H.N. TO N.N.   *30th August, 1945*
                                          4 King's Bench Walk, E.C.4

Read this letter in the train going up to Leicester.[2]

If you examine my political career you will admit that I muddled the logistics of the thing. It is true that I managed to acquire a certain reputation and influence, that I made some good speeches, and that I was almost always right. It is true that I became on terms of intimacy and confidence with most of the leading figures of all parties. But as a career the thing was mucked. I never became a Cabinet Minister and my presence on the front bench was only temporary and never effective. The reason was (apart from personal defects, such as lack of push and daring) that I was not part of a powerful organisation. When I look back I see that I made two fatal errors. The first was when I attached myself to Mosley; the second was when I joined National Labour.

Now why did I make these errors? People would say that it was due to 'lack of political experience and judgement'. That is not a sufficient explanation. It was due rather to the fact that I allowed myself to be influenced by personal affections and associations without thinking how these would operate at a later date. It happened that I had known Oswald Mosley for many years: it happened that I was a great friend of Cynthia Mosley: it happened that they seized hold of me and persuaded me at the time when I had not the knowledge of political factors to form an independent judgement. How

---

[1] Between the close of the Election campaign and the start of the Potsdam Conference on 15th July, Churchill had a short holiday at Hendaye.

[2] I was on my way to discuss with the Leicester Conservatives the proposal that I should become their candidate in place of my father.

came it that I joined National Labour? Partly because I knew Ramsay MacDonald, partly because of Buck [De La Warr]—purely personal considerations.

Thus the first thing to do, if you are not to follow my sad example, is to be tough and resistant about such things. One has a political connection, which is probably adventitious; one sees the door open; one enters it impulsively; and thereafter one finds that the door only leads to an anteroom, and that other doors are being opened all around through which one's friends pour in quite easily up the main staircase and into the ballroom. It is possible that there will never be a swing to the right comparable to the recent swing to the left. Unless such a swing occurs it will not be possible to win West Leicester from Labour. It is not a safe seat; it is not even a good seat; it is an almost hopeless seat. On the other hand you may feel that Leicester is an interesting and varied place, and that you would prefer a difficult seat with an admirable Chairman to an easier seat with a lot of old blimps and tabby cats to deal with.

H.N TO V.S-W.   6th September, 1945
                                    4 King's Bench Walk, E.C.4.

Arthur Salter told me that Winston had been marvellous in the House. By his speeches, and above all by his manner, he has driven away all bitterness and inspired the young Socialists with a sense of tradition and good behaviour. He says that Winston sits there listening to the dullest maiden speeches in order to encourage the beginners. 'Never', he said, 'has any man shown such superb magnanimity. He has recovered all his splendour.'

I went on to Pratt's. Randolph Churchill was there. He said that Winston had spoken again about the loss I would be etc etc. But that is all very well. I like these pleasant obituary notices, but I should have liked a little more appreciation while Winston and Eden were in power.

DIARY   12th September, 1945

Archie Clark Kerr[1] told me that when at Potsdam he lunched wit

[1] Sir Archibald Clark Kerr, later Lord Inverchapel, British Ambassador in Moscow 1942–46.

34

Winston, who was in a mood of extreme expansiveness. After luncheon Winston said, 'Come with me into Berlin'. The telephones got busy and the cars and motor-cyclists were assembled. Archie murmured to himself, 'Now remember; this is a great historic occasion. You must note down every word the great man says.' Off they started. Winston at his most exuberant. But when they got to Berlin he became suddenly quite silent. Not a word did he utter except to ask purely military questions to the Russian officer who accompanied them. In fact, the only remark he made was 'Mind your own business', and this was addressed to Mary Churchill when, as he was preparing to enter Hitler's bunker, she said to him, 'Don't go down the mine, Daddy'.

Harold Macmillan talked to me about his election.[1] It is not easy to know what line to take. One can no longer talk about Churchill and Eden and the Japanese menace; nor can one, since Bevin's success, indicate that the Tories alone can maintain our influence and prestige in the world. The only line to take is to preach Tory philosophy. Only by having a new idea (or rather by stating old ideas in a modern form) can one get away from opportunism or that foolish and even sinister optimism which supposes that Labour will collapse under its own difficulties, and that next time there will be a swing to the right. He does not believe in this. He believes that Labour will win the next two Elections, and that only gradually and with a great effort will the Tory Party recapture its hold on public opinion. But to do this their philosophy must be lucid, consistent and very incessantly formulated; and it must be directed away from big business to the ordinary habits of thought of the middle classes.

He shows me the draft of his election address, and we go through it point by point. It is almost entirely confined to principles. It will be very long indeed—in fact, a pamphlet. He will publish this pamphlet and sell it on the bookstalls. It will constitute the new Conservative manifesto.

DIARY   *16th September, 1945*

Michael Astor[2] says that there is a feeling among the young Tory

[1] A bye-election at Bromley, for which he was returned in November 1945.
[2] Conservative M.P. for the Eastern Division of Surrey, 1945-51. He was then aged 29.

back-benchers against Bracken and Ralph Assheton. They want to break the gang and start a new Conservatism. They feel that Winston is too old and Anthony [Eden] too weak. They want Harold Macmillan to lead them.

DIARY   25th September, 1945

I lunch at the French Embassy. M. Bidault,[1] General Catroux, the Lord Chancellor [Earl Jowitt] and Duff Cooper. They have all returned from the morning session of the Council of Foreign Ministers. They are in despair. Massigli[2] says to me, 'Imagine the most difficult and suspicious characters that you have ever known; multiply the first and treble the second—and you have some idea of what this Conference is like.' Bidault says to me, 'Ils nous haïssent.' The general depression is increased by the consideration that the Russians are so confident in their internal and external power that they omit all customary diplomatic proportions. They do not try to understand; they do not even pretend to conciliate; 'they lunge at us like wild boars'. If they are really afraid of a Western bloc, they have done everything in their power to create one.

H.N. TO V.S-W   28th September, 1945
                                                                      4 King's Bench Walk, E.C.4

We must have a conseil de famille upon my new little flag.[3] I am getting cold feet about it I dread the taking of my seat when I have to dress up in white fur and an Admiral's hat and bow three times to William [Jowitt]. I dread Hill [his manservant] calling me 'My Lord'. I dread Mrs Staples [the cook at Sissinghurst] saying, 'His Lordship is weeding in the nuttery' I am truly morbidly sensitive to ridicule, and I do not feel or look or think like a Lord. Anyhow it may come to nothing. I saw Hugh Dalton[4] yesterday, but he did not say one word about it· evidently he doesn't know.

[1] Minister of Foreign Affairs in the French Provisional Government.
[2] René Massigli, French Ambassador in London, 1944-55.
[3] The possibility that H.N. would be offered a peerage. He had written to Lord Jowitt indicating that he would be glad to go to the House of Lords, but would feel obliged to sit as an Independent.
[4] Chancellor of the Exchequer in Attlee's Government.

V.S-W. TO H.N.   *28th September, 1945*
                                                         Sissinghurst
I do hope quite absurdly that this idea of you going to the H. of L.
comes off. I wish I could analyse why. It certainly isn't for snobbish
reasons, although I would like the boys to be Hon. (isn't that odd?),
and it isn't because I would like to put 'Peeress of the Realm' instead
of 'Householder' on the various forms I have to fill in. (I would
much rather put 'Author' or 'Poet' instead of 'Householder', but
'Poet' is not a designation accepted by the authorities, and it is some
consolation to me to be able to put 'Householder' instead of 'Married
Woman'.) But above all I would like you to have a platform on
which to speak with authority, and not to have to worry about
elections or constituents. I am sure that if William [Jowitt] could have
his way, you would; but I don't trust Attlee to be so sensible.

DIARY   *30th September, 1945*
In the evening the boys abuse me for my literary style. They say that
I am so afraid of the obvious that I deliberately take refuge in the
recondite; they say that I so love extraordinary words that I introduce them without the slightest knowledge of their meaning. It is
a very agreeable conversation and I love them dearly.

There are troubles everywhere—in Saigon, in Java, in Bombay,
in Palestine, in Egypt. The whole world is simmering and seething
after the earthquake. The Russians think they have us on the run.

DIARY   *2nd October, 1945*
Lunch at the Beefsteak. Sit between the Belgian Ambassador[1] and
Lord Esher. Old Cartier is miserable because the *cuisine* in Belgium
is declining. This *cuisine*, he says, which was the finest in the world
and superior (as I agree) to the finest French cooking, was based upon
the lavish use of butter. Now they have to use margarine. The tone
in which the old boy used the word 'margarine' was replete with
all the loathing of the nineteenth for the twentieth century.

It was a crowded day at the Beefsteak, and William Jowitt,
coming in late, had to find a seat at the little side-table which serves
in extreme cases for the overflow. 'Observe that', said Cartier. 'In

[1] Baron Cartier de Marchienne, Belgian Ambassador in London since 1927.
He was then aged 73 and died in May 1946.

what other country in the world would a club like this allow the Lord Chancellor to take a seat away from the table? In what other country in the world would this happen quite naturally—without any of us regarding the occurrence as unusual?' 'In the United States', I say. 'Certainly not', he answers. 'If the Chief Justice came into a club in Washington, a place would be found for him at the head of the table.'

V.S-W. TO H.N.   *17th October, 1945*
                                                    Sissinghurst

You know, I do get so frightfully, frenziedly excited writing poetry. It is the only thing that makes me truly and completely happy. And then I feel that what I have been writing is so very poor—so wretched a reflection of what has been going on in my mind while I am at it. Why should one rise so high and then go so completely flop?

What worries me a bit is being so out of touch with poetry as it is being written today. I see that the influence of Tom Eliot and the Spender-Auden school is paramount, yet I cannot get into gear with it at all. It is just something left out of my make-up. I think perhaps that it is something to do with my dislike of politics, and by politics I don't mean party politics—I mean just a lack of interest in what must always be temporary things, things that in a thousand years' time will have become meaningless.

Oh dear, I don't know. . . . I wish I knew. I wish I could write some good poetry to add to the sum of English literature. I begin to wonder if I ever shall.

You quoted something the other day: 'My taste improves with age, but my genius is lost'. Not that I ever had genius—only a certain talent, which has now developed into a slick virtuosity. I loathe my present virtuosity—my skill—it is like a pianola reeling off. Why then should it make me so unbearably happy to write poetry, when I know that it is all out-of-date rubbishy words that mean simply nothing at all to Ben's generation? Will it ever mean anything to anybody's generation? I doubt it.[1]

On 25th October Harold Nicolson flew to Greece to give two lectures in Athens, one on Byron, the other on British democracy. His visit

[1] V.S-W. was then finishing her long poem, *The Garden*.

*coincided with a new crisis in Greek politics. Greece had had no
Government since the resignation of Admiral Voulgaris earlier that
month, and the Regent, Archbishop Damaskinos, was searching for a
new leader to stabilise the country politically and economically. Harold
Nicolson stayed with the British Ambassador, Sir Reginald Leeper,
whom Ernest Bevin was discouraging from intervening too openly in
Greek affairs, although it was mainly to the British that the Greeks
still looked for political, economic and military advice, the country
still being in occupation by British troops. From this delicate situation
Harold Nicolson sought relief by frequent expeditions to the Greek
countryside which he loved. He returned to England on 4th November.*

H.N. TO V.S–W.   *27th October, 1945*
                                             British Embassy, Athens

I felt stupid and deaf after my trip. One always feels after these vast
aeroplane journeys that one's brain has been left behind in Hampshire. It takes 24 hours for it to catch one up.

After luncheon the Leepers drove me out to Pentelikon. There are
Mediterranean pines and little Byzantine chapels and slim autumn
croci in the pine-needles. And a view such as only Attica can give.
The great sweep of the Attic plain and then the mountains of the
Peloponnesus and the islands. And below one Athens bathing in a
clear light. My God! I am not surprised that from this wonderful
air and setting should have come the greatest lucidity of mind.

As always, I find that the British here, who take their own politics
so calmly, catch some of the Hellenic fever in regard to Greek
politics. These, I admit, are somewhat tense at the moment. Even the
motor-cars blow their horns (and you know how Greeks love blowing horns) to the rhythm of a royalist slogan which means, 'We
want him back'.

H.N. TO V.S–W.   *29th October, 1945*
                                             British Embassy, Athens

There is no doubt at all about it—this *is* the loveliest country in the
world. I am drunk with its beauty and swallow great draughts,
I mean drafts (or do I?), of it, to find always at the base of my goblet
a little acid thought that I frightened you by coming and have no

39

right at all to enjoy myself. But you have no idea of the excitement and delight which is all around me. Hot it is, as never in England, with that light upon the marble hills which truly never was on sea or land. I brood over the definition of that colour. One says 'violet' or 'amethyst', but these words are meaningless. The beauty of Greece is the amazing fusion of sharpness with gentleness. Everything has an outline, and yet within that outline the shadows and colours are gentle and delicate. There is the sharp, sharp line of the sea, and the sharp outline of the mountains, and between them a curtain of gentle colour, from pink to orange, from blue to purple. I am entranced.

We went out to lunch with some nice young Greeks who have a cottage overlooking Euboea. It is some thirty miles away and the road was bad. But suddenly we came upon it—the great sweep of mountains and the vast sea like a lake between. All around the cottage were the sharp green Mediterranean pines, and the air was sparkling (that is the exact word I mean) with the smell of thyme and sage and gum-cystus. My God! My God! I shall hold that picture as tight in my mind as long as I can. The great mass of Euboea, the colour on the distant mountains, the lapis sea, the little bridge at Chalcis thirty miles below us, where Aristotle was drowned testing the currents which sway there.

We drove home as the sun set behind Parnes, and the whole of Attica suddenly became dark, and there shining above the purple plain was the Parthenon floodlit for the feast. One could see it ten miles away. Suddenly I realised that people ought not to do such things. One should not play Hollywood tricks with the Parthenon. I turned my eyes away.

H.N. TO V.S-W.   30th October, 1945
                                          British Embassy, Athens

The political situation is, I fear, bad. Everybody is frightened, and that makes them quarrelsome and irritable. They are frightened of the communists, frightened of the brigands, frightened of Tito and his Russian friends, frightened of the coming winter, frightened of inflation. Nor are these fears imaginary. They are all too real. I am terribly sorry for my dear Greeks. The tragedy is that after this long period of dictatorship and occupation, none of the younger men have had an opportunity for proving themselves in public life. And the older men are frightened or corrupt. I fear the situation is pretty hopeless.

H.N. TO V.S-W.   *31st October, 1945*
British Embassy, Athens

I went out with Osbert Lancaster[1] to a little inn in the village where Demosthenes was born.[2] When we got there it seemed deserted. Then shrill Mediterranean cries reached us from the olive trees, and a girl appeared and flung a cloth upon a table under the fig-tree, and in a trice there were wine and olives and little Aristophanic fish and an omelette consisting almost entirely of potatoes. Osbert talked and talked about the situation in Greece and about the rows between the Embassy and the military. When we had finished our luncheon he drove me back to Athens and dropped me at the Pnyx. I walked back through the old town, past the Tower of the Winds and the Choregic Monument to Lysicrates and through the palace garden. It was all very lovely.

Then in the evening I gave my lecture in the University—the first lecture, which is on Byron. The place was packed. I do not think they understood very much, but they were very polite.

DIARY   *31st October, 1945*
Athens

I have a discussion with Rex [Leeper], who is wondering what on earth he will do if, in reply to his telegram of yesterday, the Government authorise him to 'display greater activity'. At 10.55 I go to see the Regent [Archbishop Damaskinos] at his office. In the hall I meet Sophocles Venizelos[3]—very soft and dapper and silly, but he greets me warmly. I find the Regent sitting enormous with his back to shuttered windows. We have coffee and cigarettes. After compliments of a very high order the Regent tells me that the Royalists and the Liberals are meeting this afternoon to agree upon a joint programme. I ask who would be Prime Minister in such a fusion.

[1] He was attached to the British Embassy in Athens from 1944 to 1946.
[2] Liopesi.
[3] On the 29th October the Regent had asked him to form a Government, but he had been unsuccessful.

41

He says it would probably be 'a neutral'. I say that it would have to be a pretty strong neutral. The Regent says that the parties would be so evenly balanced that great strength would not be required. I say that the economic situation is far more urgent than the political situation. He makes a helpless gesture indicating, 'What would you?' He says that the communists are not worthy of being regarded as Greek citizens since they take their orders from abroad. It is not a really satisfactory discussion.

DIARY   6th November, 1945
                                                                          London

I go to see Hector McNeil[1] at the Foreign Office. He is being sent out to Athens to examine the situation and to 'assist Greece in her efforts for reconstruction'. I tell him that the economic situation comes before anything else, and that to my mind no existing Greek politician or group of politicians have the guts or the repute to apply to the situation the drastic remedies which it needs. The only thing to do is to choose the best Government we can, to assert that we wish to constitute a Government, and to assist it by appointing British advisers to the Ministries of Finance and Supply. Rather to my surprise, he absolutely agrees with this. He says that Ernest Bevin absolutely refuses openly to impose a Government on Greece. He adds that British troops will remain there for many years.

I dine with Ben at the Beefsteak. Hugh Sherwood,[2] who is there, attacks me for 'refusing' a peerage. I say that I have not done that. He says, 'But I know all about it. They approached you and you refused to accept the Labour Whip. I think you made a mistake.' I am amused by this, but a tiny bit uneasy.

DIARY   20th November, 1945

I lecture to the young men who have just passed into the Foreign Service under the new examination. What amuses me is that the lecture takes place in the former German Embassy [in Carlton House Terrace] which the F.O. have taken over. I talk about the qualities required by a member of the Foreign Service. I define the main quality as 'reliability', and analyse its five components as truthful-

[1] Parliamentary Under Secretary for Foreign Affairs, 1945-46.
[2] Lord Sherwood, formerly Hugh Seely M.P.

ness, precision, loyalty, modesty and a sense of proportion. They ask me good questions afterwards. One is: 'If a foreign official asks one whether some important fact is true, what should one reply?' I say that if one doesn't know, one should reply, 'I have no idea at all'. But if one does know, one should say, 'You ought not to have asked me that question'. Another young man asks what one ought to do if a foreign official says that he will tell one something interesting if one undertakes not to pass it on. I say that one should answer, 'If what you are about to tell me is merely a piece of gossip of secondary importance, I promise not to repeat it. But if it is of vital importance, I am bound to inform my Ambassador—so you had better not tell me'.

I dine with Sibyl [Colefax]. Others there are Harold Macmillan, T.S.Eliot, Cyril Connolly, the Kenneth Clarks, the Julian Huxleys and [Sir Pierson] Dixon of the F.O. Harold says that we shall only with the greatest difficulty convince the work-people of this country that they have got to work. They have no conception of the meaning of national wealth, and have been taught that it is merely the profits of the rich. They think that they can now be idle, and that in some manner the Government will provide. He says, and I agree with him, that France will become a prosperous Power long before we do.

DIARY   23rd November, 1945

I read Vita's poem *The Garden*. It does not contain passages of pure poetry as *The Land* did, but it is very deep and powerful, and beautifully constructed. It is most impressive.

DIARY   3rd December, 1945

I go with Guy Burgess to the Reform. He tells me (on what authority I don't know, but I suspect Hector McNeil[1]) that Bevin has turned me down for the post of Chairman of the British Council, and that in some way my peerage was involved in that appointment, so that this has also disappeared.

---

[1] Guy Burgess had now left the B.B.C. to work as Private Secretary to Hector McNeil in the Foreign Office.

V.S-W. TO H.N.   *5th December, 1945*
                                                      Sissinghurst

I am disturbed by Guy Burgess's remark. I do not mind so much about the British Council, for I feel that anything you write will be lasting, but administrative work dies with you. But I do worry about this Cranfield business.[1] I feel that owing to mistaken pride you may be queering your own pitch. With no loss of dignity whatever you could see William [Jowitt] and say you would like to know one way or the other exactly what Attlee said. It is now less than a month to the New Year, and you have been very patient.

I have been reading through my poem,[2] which I want to despatch to the publishers this week, and have been wondering what I should write next. I have turned down a lot of passing ideas, and now think that I will write another long poem called *Fire*. Do you think that this is a good idea?

H.N. TO V.S-W.   *6th December, 1945*
                                                4 King's Bench Walk, E.C.4

If you are really doing a poem about fire, I do hope that you will think hard (*la penseuse*) and not let the thing run away with you. I mean that the theme of life and death and the passage of time and the mutability of human fortunes has often been treated by many great poets. If you are to contribute to this theme, you must think it out in terms of modern transitions. I do not mind so much the transitions in the material world. I do not pretend to enjoy a socialist system, but I think it right and am prepared to make personal sacrifices for it. But what I do loathe and fear is the decline in spiritual values. Truthfulness is giving place to bigotry. Cruelty is replacing tolerance. And the sanctity of the individual is being blurred by mass emotions. I fear I have not got a communal mind.

DIARY   *19th December, 1945*

We drive to the French Embassy in a hired Daimler. Viti looks quite beautiful in diamonds and emeralds. The party consist of the [Sir]

[1] H.N., after considering several fanciful titles like Lord Sissinghurst, Lord Benenden, had decided that if he were offered a peerage, he would call himself Lord Cranfield, a defunct Sackville title.
[2] *The Garden*. The idea of *Fire* never matured.

44

John Andersons, the Kenneth Clarks, Lady Cholmondeley, the Oliver Lytteltons, a young man called Giles[1] who was Bevin's secretary, and Winston Churchill, Clemmie and Mary. The Churchills were the last to arrive and I was surprised to notice that when they enter, the whole room stands up as if they were reigning sovereigns.

Winston pays me lavish compliments on my speeches in the House and deplores my absence from it. He had, he said, been reading the speeches of Pitt and was amazed that any House could have stood such long, involved, empty and repetitive orations. 'It would not do today. The essence of our debates is the choice of prejudical points of attack.' He said that he had made friends with de Gaulle at last, whom he had found 'much mellowed'. He said that he had liked the Russians. 'The disadvantage of them is', he says, 'that one is not sure of their reactions. One strokes the nose of the alligator and the ensuing gurgle may be a purr of affection, a grunt of stimulated appetite, or a snarl of enraged animosity. One cannot tell.'

He is lively, happy, young. I have never seen him in better form. It was not so three days ago, when the Conservative M.P.s gave him a dinner. They put him beside some of their younger Members, and it had not been a success at all. Winston sat there scowling and silent. Afterwards he said to Malcolm Bullock,[2] 'They are no more than a set of pink pansies.' His passion for the combative renders him insensitive to the gentle gradations of the human mind.

H.N. TO V.S-W.   *21st December, 1945*
4 King's Bench Walk, E.C.4

This is the last letter I shall write to you from K.B.W I confess that I mind leaving it more than one ought to regret any material severance. It has seen such a large and important slice of my life from that moment at the end of 1929 when you met me and turned on the light outside the door. Much worry and much anxiety and so much

---

[1] Frank Giles, who left the Foreign Office to become *The Times* correspondent in Rome and later in Paris. He later joined the *Sunday Times*, becoming its deputy Editor in 1967. He married Lady Kitty Sackville, daughter of Lord De La Warr, in June 1946.

[2] Conservative M.P. for the Waterloo Division of Lancashire, 1923–50.

happiness these walls have seen. And now it will be turned over to people with hard hearts and heads who will not see the beauty of its ivory walls or know what privacy can really mean.

DIARY   *31st December, 1945*
                                              Sissinghurst

What a year it has been! For me (in spite of my defeat at the General Election and my failure to acquire a peerage) a happy year. The worst blow has been leaving K.B.W. But all this fades into a great surge of thankfulness that we have Nigel safe with us and Ben safe up in London. Never have I felt so acutely as in the last few days what a loving and united family we are. There is an underlying sense of harmony and love. It is perhaps the best thing that life can give. I thus embark with thankfulness and faith upon my sixtieth year.

1946

The problem of re-entering Parliament – 10 Neville Terrace – Goering and Ribbentrop in captivity – Senator Vandenberg – first meeting of the United Nations Assembly in London – Bevin on the Russians – 'The English Sense of Humour' – Grigore Gafencu – H.N. agrees to accept Labour Whip – he attends the trial of war-criminals in Nuremberg – and visits their cells – Eden on the diplomatic tangle – Smuts in brilliant form – H.N. broadcasts on the Paris Conference – Molotov and Byrnes – the Foreign Office regard Russia as the enemy – a long interview with Ernest Bevin – the reception at Versailles – the Nuremberg verdicts – end of the Paris Conference – Butler on Churchill – H.N. reaches the age of sixty – lectures at Burlington House – the garden at Sissinghurst

Harold Nicolson was still hoping by some means to re-enter politics. His name was not included in the New Year's Honours, but shortly afterwards the death of Eleanor Rathbone left vacant the Combined English Universities, the seat which he had fought as a New Party candidate in 1931. Here too he was disappointed. He did not find sufficient backing for his proposed Independent candidature. So, swallowing his pride and some of his prejudices, he told the Lord Chancellor that if he were to be offered a peerage, he would be willing to accept the Labour Whip. This too came to nothing, for reasons which were to remain veiled from him.

He left his chambers in the Temple to live with his two sons at 10 Neville Terrace, South Kensington, a Victorian house of unexampled hideousness which they christened Devil Terrace. Here and at Sissinghurst he busied himself with books, journalism and lectures. He wrote his long essay on 'The English Sense of Humour', began reviewing for the 'Observer' and the 'Daily Telegraph', and wrote a fortnightly article for the Paris 'Figaro'. His five-year membership of the Board of B.B.C. Governors ended in July.

Nationally and internationally, it was a period of winding-up and new beginnings—the period of the meeting in London of the first General Assembly of the United Nations, of the intensification of the Cold War and Churchill's Fulton speech, of the Nuremberg trials of major war-criminals. It saw the Labour Government's first steps in implementing the Beveridge Report and nationalising major industrial undertakings. There was a renewed fear of Communism in Britain. Demobilisation continued. So did rationing. It was bitterly cold.

H.N. TO V.S-W. *8th January, 1946*
10 Neville Terrace, S.W.7

I saw the Lord Chancellor last night. I said to him, 'William, what would you do if you were in my position and had been asked to stand for Eleanor Rathbone's seat?' He said, 'I should accept at once.' Then he explained the position as far as he knew it. Apparently, when he first wrote to the Prime Minister, the latter had replied in a manner which made him think that the matter was clinched. 'In fact', he said, 'I fully expected to see your name in the list published on January 1st.' But after getting Attlee's letter, he discovered that Lord Addison (who is the leader of the Labour Party in the House of Lords) did not like the idea at all. Lord Addison felt that the Labour Government should only give peerages to members of the Labour Party, and that to give outside peerages (apart from war honours) was not in accordance with their principles. William did not think that this was an unsurmountable obstacle, but still it was an obstacle.

Rather improvidently, perhaps, when asked what I intend to do, I have replied, 'Well, you see, it is rather difficult for me belonging to no party to find a seat. The only thing open to me is a University seat, and that really only means the Oxford seat or the Combined Universities. I can't stand for Cambridge. So it is all very difficult.' Then Eleanor dies, and I am faced with the very chance that I defined as unlikely; in fact an off-chance becomes an on-chance. I should look foolish if I just abstained from taking any action.

William sees this, but he sees something else. He says that if I were to stand and succeed, then that would be splendid. After a few more years in the Commons, I should have an added claim to go to the Lords. By then I might even have joined the Labour Party (I doubt this, and told him so). But if I stood for Eleanor's seat and failed to be elected, then my position would be worse than before. I did not quite see why myself, but he seemed to feel that having been beaten in Leicester and again beaten as an Independent in the Combined Universities, I should have a double failure on my shoulders, and for the Labour Party then to give me a consolation prize would arouse criticism among their supporters.

So you see what a jam your poor old tumbledown is in. What I have done is to make nothing but the most non-committal statements to the Press, and to write to the Vice-Chancellor of Leeds University asking him what one does if one wishes to put one's name forward, and telling him to keep my enquiry confidential.

So the Cranfield[1] gets further and further away. Why is it that I, who have such a simple attitude towards life, am so often involved in really difficult moral problems such as this? It is so absurd. I had

[1] See p. 44, note 1.

looked upon Cranfield at first as a *pis aller*, as a retirement, as a consolation prize. And now that it is being taken from me, I realise that I had come to desire the consolation prize even more than I desired the prize itself.

H.N. TO V.S-W.   *9th January, 1946*
                                          10 Neville Terrace, S.W.7

James [Pope-Hennessy] came in last night to see me. He found me sitting over the gas-fire in my greatcoat correcting my proofs [of *The Congress of Vienna*]. He said that the house was like a boarding house which had been turned into a reception centre for bombed-out Indian students. At any moment he expected to see a sleek black head looking over the banisters.

Nothing further yet about the Combined Universities.

DIARY   *9th January, 1946*

Ivone Kirkpatrick[1] told me about his experiences in Germany in June and July when he and Murphy[2] were representing the civilian side of the occupation. There were two concentration camps for the Nazi leaders, known respectively as 'Ashcan' and 'Dustbin'. He had visited them both. The former he had found to be a large hotel surrounded by barbed wire and sentries at lookout posts. All the Nazis were out on the terrace sitting in basket chairs. They had been told to stand to attention when he and Murphy arrived, and they did so obediently. Then after inspecting the kitchens and other accommodation, he went to see Goering who was in bed with bronchitis.

Goering was so bored that he was delighted to talk. He sat there for an hour. He was absolutely frank. Ivone asked him whether he thought the date chosen for the declaration of war was a good one. He replied that although he felt personally that Germany could get all she wanted without forcing us into war, yet, given that Hitler was determined on a general war, September 1939 was the correct date. Ivone asked him what was the greatest mistake that Germany made. He answered in a flash, 'Not invading Spain and North Africa

[1] Then Deputy Commissioner of the Control Commission, Germany.
[2] Robert D. Murphy, the American diplomatist, then political adviser to the American Military Government in Germany.

in 1940. If we had seized Gibraltar, we should have won the war.' He
also said that it was our bombing of the centres of communication
which brought on the final collapse. They could cope with the
destruction of railway lines etc, but what did them in was the
blocking of all cities by rubble and the destruction of all post-offices,
headquarters, telephone exchanges, central stores etc.

Thereafter Ribbentrop was brought in. He was not frank at all.
He denied everything. 'But', said Ivone, 'I heard you say this myself.
We have documents to prove it', and so on. Ribbentrop would
pass a weary hand over his eyes. 'You astonish me', he would say.
'You confound me. But I never wanted war.'

DIARY   *16th January, 1946*

I go to see Mummy,[1] who is sunk in gloom. 'I do not see one bright
spot anywhere', she says. I say that I see the dawn of a new happiness
for the world in which every man will at last have a chance equal to
that of every other man. She does not like that idea. She is a Victorian, bless her heart, and wants privileged classes with nice clean
Sunday-school discipline for the poor.

DIARY   *28th January, 1946*

I dine with the Camroses. Senator Vandenberg[2] is there. He tells me
that he had visited Roosevelt a week before he died and that 'the
shadow of death was already on him'. The Senator had asked him
whether, in view of his known anti-Russian attitude, it would not
be better if some less controversial figure went to San Francisco.
Roosevelt had replied, 'No, I want you, above all men, to go, and
for that very reason. At Conference after Conference I have been
forced to agree to things with which I did not agree, in fear lest
Russia should make a separate peace. She will now blackmail us
again by threatening to withdraw from U.N.O.' Prophetic words!

After the women went out, Vandenberg asked John Anderson
what England would do if Congress threw out the Loan to Britain

---

[1] Lady Carnock, who was then 85. Lord Carnock had died in 1928.
[2] Senator Arthur H. Vandenberg, who was U.S. Representative to the United
Nations at the San Francisco Conference in April 1945. He was the leading
Republican spokesman on foreign policy.

Bill.[1] There was some danger of that, since although they were glad to give us money, they could scarcely fail to offer similar advantages to Russia, and there was great antipathy to doing that. 'What would she do with the money, anyway? She would take it and retire behind her steel curtain.' There was thus a good chance that our loan would be refused. What would we do? Anderson thought for a few moments, and then said impressively, 'The Government would fall. There would be a Coalition Government as at the time of Dunkirk. That Government would be obliged to impose upon the British people a system of acute suffering. I say "suffering" and not "sacrifice", since suffering is what I mean. After three years of this, we would recover. All that would remain would be a passionate hatred of America.'

It was an agreeable dinner, and we had champagne.

H.N. TO V.S-W.   *31st January, 1946*
                                              10 Neville Terrace, S.W.7

I went to an enormous party given by the Port of London Authority for the U.N.O. delegates. It was a magnificent show, and will, I fear, give them the impression that London flows with milk, honey, sherry and liqueurs. What masses of people were there! What crowds of foreigners! The U.N.O. joke is that it is a misfortune to appoint as Secretary General a man of the name of Tricksy Lie.[2] Now, that is not a good joke, and I went into a corner and ate some chocolate cake and thought why it was not a good joke. There I was interrupted by A. P. Herbert who said that he thought it an excellent joke. Puns on people's names are never excellent, I said. But they are, said he. At which all conversation was hushed in contemplation of the really classic deformity of Eleanor Roosevelt's face.

---

[1] Lend-Lease to Britain was terminated in August 1945. This was a big shock to Britain's finances, and to replace it, an agreement was negotiated in Washington by Lord Keynes for credits of $3,750 million at 2%. This agreement had had a stormy passage through the House of Commons, and was not approved by the U.S. Congress until July 1946.

[2] Trygve Lie, formerly Norwegian Foreign Minister, was appointed first Secretary General of the United Nations earlier in January.

DIARY   *31st January, 1946*

I lunch at the Belgian Embassy. The guests include the Prince
Regent, the Attlees, the Ernest Bevins, the Anthony Edens and [Paul-
Henri] Spaak. I sit between Beatrice Eden and one of the Belgian
delegates to U.N.O. whose name I don't know. I talk across him to
Ernest Bevin. He regrets that the Americans should be so feeble in
the Azerbaijan controversy.[1] 'You can never, my dear 'arold, deal
with the Russians if you lie down and let them walk over you.'
He feels that the compromise reached yesterday represents a satisfactory solution. I remain silent. 'But what would you 'ave?' he
says. The Belgian next to me is impressed by the fact that these
politicians, having spent the whole of last night arguing with each
other and abusing each other, should meet on terms of the utmost
amity and intimacy.

DIARY   *4th March, 1946*

It is a horrible day darkened by snow and then by sleet. I work
almost all day at my English humour,[2] and get to page 22. That is
more than half. Before tea we drive to the village and record our
votes in the County Council election. Viti votes for the Conservative and I for the Labour man. I refuse to vote Tory.

In the evening we discuss the Russian situation. I say that there are
two views, the optimistic and the pessimistic. Under the former, the
Russians are just bluffing, trying to get as much as they can while
the going is good, but are really too exhausted and anxious to devote
themselves to reconstruction as soon as they have obtained security.
Under this view, all the trouble they are giving us in India, Egypt,
Persia and elsewhere is a mere manœuvre in order to force us to
make concessions to them in the Eastern Aegean, Trieste and the
Straits. The pessimistic view is that the pan-Slav and world revolution elements have gained the upper hand in Russia and that Stalin
has ceased to count; that they know that they possess a strong fifth
column in every capitalist country which would suffice to paralyse

[1] The Russian refusal to evacuate Azerbaijan, the north-west province of Persia,
was the first main business to come before the Security Council. The Russian
and Persian Governments were requested to solve their differences by direct
negotiations, and these succeeded in March.
[2] *The English Sense of Humour.* Dropmore Press, 1946.

our effort if we threatened war; that they believe that a war for world mastery between the U.S.A. and themselves is quite inevitable; and that meanwhile they are seeking to weaken us, regarding us an outpost of America in Europe. Therefore it is 1938 again on a far more dangerous scale, and this time we shall not have our own, or French, or American opinion united behind us in the conflict.

DIARY   *11th March, 1946*

I meet Robert Barrington-Ward[1] at the Beefsteak. His view is that our working people will not work, not because they are temperamentally lazy, not because they dislike income tax, but because they have nothing to buy with what they earn. Once there are things in the shops, then they will work well enough. I do not believe this. I believe that our lower classes are for some curious reason congenitally indolent; and that only the pressure of gain or destitution makes them work. When their profits are taken for income tax and they are insured against destitution, their natural indolence comes to the surface.

DIARY   *8th April, 1946*

I lunch at the French Embassy to meet Gafencu.[2] The Vansittarts are present and Oliver Stanley. Gafencu says he has derived much relief and refreshment from his visit to London. There is such exhaustion and defeatism in other countries that it is an amazing discovery to find a country which seems self-confident, active and calm. I am flattered but a little surprised by this description of poor old tired England. He says that we are faced by a very grave Russian danger, and that it is no use pretending that it is not a danger. Russia is determined to create a unitary system in Europe. She is assisted in this by the fact that although her theories appeal only to a minority in every country, it is a very active, ruthless and unscrupulous minority. In Germany our great difficulty is that Russia can claim that her system would not be worse than any other, and that it is only under communism that Germany can attain her unity. Thus the sense of national unity (which is strong in Germany) is identified

[1] Editor of *The Times*, 1941-48.
[2] Grigore Gafencu, former Foreign Minister of Rumania, then living in Switzerland.

with communism; social democracy implies the division into zones. To combat this we must provide an alternative ideal; the only possible ideal is a federal Germany in a federal Europe.

H.N. TO V.S-W.   *11th April, 1946*
                                                    10 Neville Terrace, S.W.7

I went to the *Contact* luncheon.[1] I sat next to Violet [Bonham Carter]. She talked about Shirley Morgan,[2] saying that she appeared to her one of the most competent and serene young women she had ever known. She is certainly very lovely. I made my speech and George Weidenfeld made his speech, and all went well.

DIARY   *16th April, 1946*

At the London Library I analyse *Punch* jokes from 1860 onwards.[3] I see a man opposite me looking on with disapproval. I can see that he is thinking, 'How strange that a man, obviously a man of education and even refinement, can spend a lovely afternoon like this sitting in a reading-room and poring over old volumes of *Punch*!'

I dine with Sibyl [Colefax], Michael Redgrave,[4] Terence Rattigan,[5] Ellen Wilkinson[6] and the Lord Chancellor, to say nothing of the French Ambassador [Massigli] and his charming wife. I sit between Terry and Ellen. She tells me that she once had a supernatural experience. She had just finished her exams for a scholarship and had been sleepless with anxiety about the result, knowing that her whole life depended on it. Then one morning, as she was polishing the bath-tap, she suddenly 'knew' that she had passed. She said sensibly that these experiences are only valid to oneself. But she is certain that it was something psychopathic, not supernatural, but just some faculty which one does not understand.

I have a talk with William Jowitt. I say, 'You remember that there

1 To launch the magazine *Contact*, of which George Weidenfeld was Editor. It was out of this magazine that the publishing firm of Weidenfeld & Nicolson developed.
2 The daughter of Charles Morgan, the poet and novelist.
3 For *The English Sense of Humour*.
4 The actor, then aged 38.
5 The playwright. His play *The Winslow Boy* was produced in this year.
6 Labour M.P. for Jarrow since 1935. In 1946 she was Minister of Education, but died in February 1947.

was some suggestion that I should go to the House of Lords as an Independent? You remember that you told me that Lord Addison did not like this idea and said that all Labour peers must be Labour peers? Well, I have thought it over and I would gladly accept the Whip.' He said he thought that a wise thing to do. I said I was heart and soul with the Government in its foreign policy and that I also agreed with its domestic policy. What worried me were the left-wing elements who seemed to me too revolutionary. 'They are what worry all of us', he said. I did not feel that all difficulties would be solved by my joining the Labour Party—nor did William. But anyhow I have taken the plunge and am rid (at some cost to my pride) of the incubus of being an independent. But no evasions will obscure the facts (a) that I have *asked* for a peerage; and (b) that when I found I could not get one as an independent, I changed my party coat.

On 30th April Harold Nicolson flew to Nuremberg for four days to attend the trial of the major Nazi leaders before the International Military Tribunal. The trial had started on 20th November, 1945, and sentences were pronounced on 1st October, 1946. The purpose of his visit, which was arranged by the Foreign Office, was to write about the trials for British and French journals, and while he was there, it emerged that it was also in the minds of the authorities to invite him to describe the trials in a book. This proposal did not mature.

H.N. TO V.S-W.   *25th April, 1946*
                                             10 Neville Terrace, S.W.7

I am afraid I have a nasty bit of news for you. It is now confirmed that I fly with George Clerk[1] to Nuremberg next week. I am sorry about this, as I know that it casts over you a cloud of anxiety. But I should always blame myself if I funked going to Nuremberg (which quite honestly I do), since it would be like having a chance to see the Dreyfus trial and refusing it. But I do dread it so. I know I am squeamish about this sort of thing, but I hate the idea of sitting all comfy in a box and staring at men who are certain to be hanged by the neck and who are in any case caught like rats in a trap. You know as well as I do that my feelings for Ribbentrop have always been cold

[1] Sir George Clerk, British Ambassador in Paris, 1934–37.

57

feelings. But I do not want to see the man humiliated. And Schacht[1] was a friend of mine. I do not want to see him like a prisoner in the dock. Nor really do I want to see Germany in its present state. But I should never forgive myself if I shirked this opportunity.

DIARY   *30th April, 1946*
Nuremberg

The colouring of the courtroom is dark brown relieved by heavy green marble surrounds to the several doors. The room is lit by slit-lights from above. It is far smaller than I had expected. The dominant note is silence. The proceedings are carried on almost in a hush.

My gaze turns to the dock. The defendants sit in the following order: Front row: Goering, Hess, Ribbentrop, Keitel, Kalten-brunner, Rosenberg, Frank, Frick, Streicher, Funk, Schacht. Second row: Doenitz, Raeder, Baldur von Schirach, Sauckel, Jodl, Papen, Seyss-Inquart, Speer, Neurath, Fritzsche.

They look drab, depressing, ill. They have the appearance of people who have travelled in a third-class railway carriage for three successive nights. It seems incredible that such a dim set of men should or could have done such huge and dreadful things. That is the first impression that they convey in the mass. But when one looks more closely, one observes differences between them. Goering is the dominant figure. Clad in a loose light uniform without badges of rank, he leans his pasty face upon a fat pasty hand, and at times he will place the fist against his chin in the attitude of Rodin's *Penseur*. For so vast a man, although he is now shrunken, his movements are alert, rapid, nervous, impulsive. Beside him sits Hess—bearing a strong resemblance to the Duke of Rutland—apparently not attending much, opening a book occasionally which he holds on his knees, but not reading it with any attention, just glancing down as if it were something he happened to be holding in his hand.

Ribbentrop is much changed; his face is grey and thin; his soft collar flops; he closes his eyes and adopts a mask; he seems inarticulate, utterly broken. Keitel, in *feldgrau* uniform stripped of all badges,

[1] Dr Hjalmar Schacht, Hitler's Finance Minister, had been President of the Reichsbank in the late 1920's when H.N. was Counsellor of the British Embassy in Berlin.

gives a different impression; he looks trim, tough, distinguished. Rosenberg[1] is much changed; he is no longer the handsome young man; he is a dim middle-aged creature with hanging head. Schacht at the end of the front row stands out from the others. He is completely unchanged; he still wears the high stiff collar that I remember; he does not converse much with his fellow-defendants; as he moves his face upwards, his pince-nez catch the ceiling lights and flash; he looks almost gay. Baldur von Schirach[2] is not what I expected; I had imagined a plump tough; he is a thin ascetic with a delicate sensitive face. Jodl sits there looking exactly like a reliable family coachman of Victorian days. Papen looks haggard and very untidy. Seyss-Inquart is younger than I imagined. Neurath, who was a solid and dignified man, has shrunk and aged; he also looks unbrushed. Fritzsche[3] seems less crushed than the others; he is lively and moves his face and hands. The others give the impression of sitting hunched and tired.

Dr Dix, the leader of the Berlin bar, is making a long, rambling and, to my mind, ineffective speech in Schacht's defence. *'Eure Lordschaft'*, he says, *'ich gestehe. . . .'* Schacht sits in the witness box opposite him. He is flanked by two young Americans in white helmets. Every hour, two other snowdrops appear from behind and silently take over from their comrades the white batons of office, stepping into their place. At 3.15 there is a short recess. The German counsel rise from their seats and talk to their clients in the dock. They are carefully watched by the snowdrops as they do so.

Then we begin again. Schacht is asked questions by his counsel. He answers in a loud clear voice. He is completely master of himself and of his dates and facts. 'Did you adhere to the Nazi *Weltanschauung?*' 'I reject every philosophy which is not based upon true religion.' 'What was your true opinion of Hitler?' 'A man of *diabolische Genialität* [diabolical genius]. A man who may at the start have had fine ideas, but who in the end became infected by the poisons which he instilled in the masses.'

[1] Alfred Rosenberg had been one of Hitler's earliest associates. He was the 'philosopher' of the Nazi Party, and Minister for the occupied Eastern Territories.
[2] The first Hitler Youth leader and later Gauleiter of Vienna.
[3] He was head of broadcasting in Goebbels' Propaganda Ministry, the least important of the war-criminals on trial. He was acquitted.

At 5 the Court rises. We drive back to Birkett's[1] villa. He is carefully guarded. He has a military policeman in his car and is followed by a jeep containing other red-caps armed with tommy-guns. He says that the Nazi leaders would never have allowed themselves to be taken alive had they known that we should find such utterly damning documents.

DIARY   *1st May, 1946*
Nuremberg

We have breakfast off trout. We then drive down with the judge. I gaze at the terrible destruction on the way. Houses tumble, bridges collapse, railway tracks are twisted, and the road here and there is diverted round craters—but the trees are immune. Great chestnut trees extend their candelabra across the rubble, and in calcined court-yards the lilac bushes burst into dim flame.

We enter the courtroom. This time we are in the Visitors' Gallery above the Press Gallery where we were yesterday. Schacht is again being examined. He sits there, benign, confident, a complete master of his own defence. He remarks that Ribbentrop was one of the most incompetent men he had ever known. The latter drops his strained mask for a second and shakes a weary head. They all look even scrubbier than yesterday. The head-phones disarrange their hair.

At 11.15 there is an adjournment and we gather in Birkett's room. Colonel Andrus, who is Commandant of the prison, comes to fetch us. The courts are connected with the adjoining prison by a long covered wooden passage which twists and turns and has a duck-board floor. Our feet resound upon this floor as if it were a xylophone. The defendants as they walk to the court must hear either their own feet or those of the guard echoing upon this duck-board. For those whose lives are spared that sound will echo till they die. Two-thirds of the way down this wooden corridor is a gate leading to an exercise yard. There are lilac bushes in flower and the grass is worn by miserable feet.

We enter a prison gallery, identical with those I have seen at Brixton and Wormwood Scrubs. The only difference is that the prison smell is absent; it is replaced by the smell of beans cooking in

[1] Sir Norman Birkett, one of the British judges at the trial.

tomato. The cells run along each side, and the names of the prisoners are attached outside: 'Goering, Hess, Ribbentrop, Keitel . . .' and so on. Andrus takes us into Sauckel's cell, and then into Ribbentrop's. They are made to clean the cells themselves and to fold their blankets. They have a bunk, a chair and a table. The latter is so flimsy that they cannot stand on it to reach the window. They have books and papers, and on their tables are pasted the photographs of their wives and children. In Ribbentrop's cell it was sad to see, not the accustomed prisoners' photographs taken at Margate, but Bond Street photographs of charming boys.

We saw the food, which was good. 'Ah yes', said Colonel Andrus, 'no mother has ever cherished her children as I cherish these men. I must keep them fresh for the last day.' But he is not a gloating man; he is a nice, clever man, and humane.

He takes us to see the depository where the prisoners' luggage is kept. It is pitiable luggage. Hoess,[1] who confessed with pride that he had caused the deaths of two million Jews, had only a carton which had once contained American rations. Schleicher, when arrested, had no luggage at all. A fat suitcase of imitation leather belongs to Goering. It contained his particular drug. 'We have suppressed that parcel', said Andrus, 'and friend Goering has never been so healthy in his life.' In a way, those waiting suitcases, gathered together as in the cloakroom at Victoria, were more expressive than anything else.

We return to the main building. As the door of the prison clangs behind us, I feel that it is indeed pleasant to have won this war and to be at liberty to drive through the May woods.

After luncheon we go for a short drive through the old city. It is difficult to convey any conception of the extent of the ruins. It is said that at least 10,000 corpses are still buried under the collapsed houses. When the work of clearing up has been accomplished, there will be a vast *terrain vague* where once stood the city of Nuremberg. Slowly and sadly we climb up to the Burg. The walls remain, but the turrets and roofing have been destroyed. We look down upon ruins decayed and jagged like some old jaw-bone of a camel in the desert. Beyond

---

[1] Rudolf Hoess, Commandant of the extermination camp at Auschwitz. In March 1947 he was hanged by the Poles in the same camp, but he was not one of those on trial before the Military Tribunal.

the grim dusty ruins of the city the country spreads itself in the May sunshine. It is very hot.

The court rises at 5. We have some tea in Birkett's room, and then drive with him to the *Heldenfeld*, or stadium, now called 'The Soldiers' Field'. I visit this scene of the great Nazi rallies with awe. It is a fine and vast erection, being a tremendous affirmation of the drama and power of the whole system. The huge eagle and swastika by which it was surmounted have been taken down, showing brick scars upon the stone plinth. The Americans have painted in huge blue letters underneath the tribune the words 'Soldiers' Field'. We mingle with the crowd, Birkett being accompanied by his military policeman and the tommy-gun. The people glance at us, realise that we are the conquerors, and then look aside as if we were not there. If I were a Nuremberger I should feel nothing but undying hatred for those who had destroyed my lovely city. We see no scowls; merely a pretence at ignoring us.

David Maxwell Fyfe[1] comes to dinner with Judge Biddle. Biddle is an agreeable, social type of American. He says to Birkett, 'Now, Norman, have you persuaded Nicolson to write the book you wanted?' Birkett evades the question with some embarrassment. I gather that they have some idea of my writing a book about the trial.

DIARY   *2nd May, 1946*
                                                          Nuremberg

Lord and Lady Lawrence[2] come to dinner. Lady Lawrence tells me that the most dramatic moment in the trial was when they turned on a film showing the trial by Nazi justice of some wretched young man who had been involved in an attempt on Hitler's life. The judge yelled at him, pointing accusing fingers, shouting, 'You beast! You brute! You traitor!' The sound of his objurgations echoed through the courtroom, rising in the end almost to a scream. Then the film stopped, the lights went up, and the gentle voice of Lord Lawrence intervened: 'Please continue your examination, Dr Dix'. The contrast between violence and calm was such that even the defendants moved uneasily upon their hard and narrow bench.

[1] Sir David Maxwell Fyfe, later Earl of Kilmuir, the Deputy Chief Prosecutor.
[2] Lord Justice Lawrence, President of the Tribunal.

DIARY

3rd May, 1946
Nuremberg

I have a talk with Birkett. He feels that it was a mistake to have included in the indictment the Organisations such as the S.S. It would be impossible to prove that all the thousands who formed part of such organisations were individually guilty. It was the Americans who had insisted upon their inclusion. He feels that the trial will not finish before November. He also says that he now thinks that the book to be written about the trial must be written by someone who was there the whole time.

DIARY

20th May, 1946

I dine with Baba Metcalfe [Lady Alexandra Metcalfe] in Wilton Place. There are Lord and Lady Halifax, Jim Thomas and Archie Clark Kerr. After dinner Anthony Eden comes in from the House. He is appalled by the diplomatic tangle in which we are involved. His one desire is to help Bevin in his great difficulties. 'Fortunately', he says, 'Winston is away.' I get the impression that the Tory Party are much embarrassed by Winston's presence. They cannot edge him aside; they can only throw him out; and that they do not wish to do. How I hope and pray that Winston in his old age does not dim all his own magnificence and glory. He might so easily become an embittered, truculent and unwise old man.

Anthony was looking amazingly well. Red in the face and younger by many years.

DIARY

4th June, 1946

I go to lunch in Lord North Street with the Walter Elliots. The other guests are Peter Thorneycroft and Jan Christiaan Smuts. Smuts is in terrific form. He is more genial than I remember him, and immensely friendly. He chatters all the time. He is less subtle (or should I say less sly?) than I remember him, and conveys the impression of a philosopher-king—very old, very wise, very convinced that in the end it is conduct and principle which decide events, not ingenuity. His face has shrunk and become smaller. The cords in his neck have become aged and haggard; but his eyes are as bright blue as ever with a dancing light in them.

He had just returned from a visit to Germany. He says that there are no signs of 'repentance'. He says that the Germans are submissive, obedient and resigned, but that they still believe in their hearts that we started the war, and that the stories about atrocities are pure propaganda. He had addressed the Senate at Hamburg. He had told them that Germany must repent. But she must do more than that; she must build again by her own efforts. All this searching for scapegoats was of no value: Germany must save herself. 'I also', he had said, 'have belonged to a defeated nation. I have looked round and seen the ruins of my country. I also have felt in moments of despair that no future was ever possible, that no human energy could suffice to rebuild such ruins. But that was only a mood. We turned and worked. We ceased to think in terms of the past. We made friends with our enemies. And now, look at South Africa—a great nation, almost a Great Power.' The Senators were so impressed that they almost wept.

He then spoke of Nuremberg. Jodl yesterday had stated that Germany had lost the war because she had been obliged to divert divisions to meet the British landing in Greece. That meant that she lost six weeks. She lost *time*—and with time she lost Moscow, Stalingrad and the war. Smuts recalled the decision which Winston, he and Wavell had made at the time. 'We had just won a victory. We knew that if we withdrew divisions from Libya, that victory would be reversed. We knew that only defeat faced us in Greece. But we made our decision, not on military principles, but on moral principles. Now we are proved right by the Director of Operations of the German Army.[1] This shows once again that to do the right thing is generally the right thing to do. It also shows, incidentally, the value of Nuremberg. Had we shot Jodl at sight, that precious piece of evidence would never have been obtained. A controversy would have rumbled down the corridors of time.'

He goes back to the time factor. He says that those who contend that time is an atmosphere and not a creative factor are denying all experience. There are situations in which time is the only solvent. Insoluble situations such as the present deadlock between the Soviets and the Western Powers. 'We should play for time—time at any cost, time in any form (it may take five years)—but if we can

[1] General Jodl was Chief of Operations Staff of the German High Command (O.K.W.), not merely of the German Army.

avoid committing ourselves to any serious violation of principle for those five years, then we shall once again have saved the world. My dread is that men will start attacking the Gurment'—he still pronounces 'Government' as 'Gurment'—'for not getting on with it. True statesmanship should see that in the present deadlock there is no solution except bad solutions. In five years, time may have loosened the deadlock.'

He talks about England. 'You are not an old country', he says. 'Believe me, my own country and certainly Canada and the United States are older than you. There is no touch of age about England. And why? Because you allow new ideas to enter your blood-stream. Your arteries remain elastic. Never in your history have you had so many young men of energy and intelligence. Never! I have seen them. They are superb.'

Peter Thorneycroft intervenes to say that he feels this in the present House, even in the Conservative Party. 'Our Party', he says, 'is far more able as well as more compact than it was in the last Parliament.' 'The Conservative Party', says Smuts, 'will again come to power. But it must find a faith and a policy. And to do that it must rid itself of its older men, perhaps even some of its older leaders, perhaps even of the greatest leader himself.'

They all feel that. They all feel that Winston must go. This saddens me. But he is not elastic in domestic affairs. He cramps their thought, and renders it pugnacious when it should be conciliatory.

Then he leaves us, the taut, nervous, inspired old man. It has done me good to see him again. I walk with Peter as far as the House.

DIARY   *14th July, 1946*

In the evening we discuss the rumour that I am to succeed Duff [Cooper] as Ambassador in Paris. Viti says that any such idea would be quite intolerable. Ben says that it would be convenient to stay at the Embassy. Nigel is all in favour of it. He says that he does not want to see me end my life on a flat note; that I should be good at the job; that I should be mad to refuse. I am amused by all this, especially as the issue will never arise.

At the end of July Harold Nicolson went to Paris to broadcast for the B.B.C. about the Peace Conference, and remained there until mid-

October, when the Conference ended. William Haley, the Director General, had suggested it himself, now that Harold Nicolson was once more made available for broadcasting by the end of his five-year term as a Governor. He was particularly well suited to the task. He found that he was almost the only survivor in Paris of the Peace Conference of 1919, and many of his talks contrasted the methods and leading figures of each occasion. He was on terms of friendship with many of the diplomatic participants and their expert staffs. He raised the art of political broadcasting to a new and highly individual level, combining direct reporting of the atmosphere of the Conference with far-ranging speculation on its significance. He spoke and wrote English and French with equal facility. He was doing what he did best and enjoyed most, turning new ideas round and round on the needle-point of his intelligence. The broadcasts were extremely successful. The B.B.C. had never, and has never since, commissioned so prolonged a series of talks on a complicated international conference, and they were listened to avidly.

Each week he broadcast two 15-minute talks live from Paris on the Home Service, which were simultaneously relayed to the Commonwealth, and another in French on the General Overseas Service. He broadcast either from a temporary studio set up in the Hotel Scribe or direct from Luxembourg Palace where the Conference was held. He lived for the first fortnight at the Ritz, until he discovered that the bill for his room alone came to more than his weekly salary of £50 from the B.B.C., and then he moved to the more modest Grand Hotel in the Boulevard des Capucines. He was extremely busy, since not only was he writing three articles a week (for the 'Spectator', the Paris 'Figaro' and a book-review for the 'Observer') in addition to his broadcasts, but he spent long hours at the Conference and engaged in a social life as active as that which he normally enjoyed in London. Separation from Sissinghurst was what irked him most. He exchanged daily letters with V. Sackville-West, who was also his most devoted listener. On one day, 11th August, they were able to hear each other, when she broadcast from Wales and he from Paris, and for a single weekend in September she joined him there.

The Paris Conference was a conference of 21 powers whose purpose was to draw up the draft texts of peace-treaties with Italy, Rumania, Hungary, Bulgaria and Finland. The major problems of

Germany and Austria were not even touched upon. None of the Treaties was actually signed in Paris, since the Great Powers reserved for themselves the right to amend the texts at a subsequent meeting of the Council of Foreign Ministers. The Conference met in an atmosphere of mounting antagonism between Russia and the United States. 'Instead of open covenants openly arrived at', said Harold Nicolson in one of his broadcasts, 'we have open insults openly hurled.' It was not so much a conference to decide the post-war fate of Italy and Hitler's allies in Eastern Europe as a struggle for power between the victorious nations of East and West. The immediate issues which dominated discussion were subjects like the international control of Trieste and the Danube, the question of the Italo-Yugoslav border and the distribution of Italian reparations. But behind it all was the larger question of Soviet influence in Eastern Europe and the degree of America's commitment to the defence of the West. In the end Russia secured almost all she wanted behind her iron curtain, but at the cost of creating what she most feared, an anti-Soviet alliance headed by the United States.

DIARY

26th July, 1946
Ritz Hotel, Paris

My impressions from this evening's conversation are that Gibson Parker[1] and Hall[2] will be the best of all adjutants. Parker is intelligent, active and speaks perfect French. Hall was Private Secretary to Dick Law at the F.O. and is in close touch with the Embassy. I believe that if we are very industrious and united, we can make the B.B.C. reports from Paris as useful and influential as our reports during the war. The newspapers after the first few days will become bored with the Conference. It will be our business to keep public interest alive. I see no reason why, if the thing is carefully done, we should not teach the British public that foreign affairs can be as interesting and as comprehensible as a test match. I am slightly startled by the size of my audience. Not only have I got two talks on the Home Service, but my talks overseas are to be relayed in every language, and my French talks are to be given live to Canada and South America. I shall probably be speaking to 20 million people.

[1] The head of the B.B.C.'s team in Paris, which also included Thomas Barman and Thomas Cadett.

[2] Donald Hall, head of the European Service of the B.B.C.

DIARY   *27th July, 1946*
                                                         Paris

I foresee that I shall have great difficulties with this job. The Conference will be dull and rather perfunctory. And I cannot tell the
truth without enraging the Russians. Moreover I do not yet feel
that I have got my 'sense of audience'. To whom am I talking? The
very fact that my talks are to be relayed all over the world means
that the audience becomes so composite as to have no personality at
all. And since the whole secret of broadcasting is to address oneself
to a *personal* audience, this impersonality will fuss and worry me. I
shall have to invent an audience, some imaginary person, sympathetic
and yet ignorant, interested but uninformed, and to that imaginary
disciple I shall address my talk. I shall invent a woman of 35 who
has experienced great unhappiness in life.

DIARY   *28th July, 1946*
                                                         Paris

I dash to the Gare du Nord to meet Elizabeth Bowen.[1] There are
large crowds at the station and cordons of gendarmes. '*Les délégations
arrivent.*' There is a special diplomatic train and a vast jam of police
and luggage. I see a haggard travel-stained face which I recognise
as that of Osbert Lancaster. Then Mackenzie King[2] arrives surrounded by police and bowing right and left to the photographers. Then
Léon Blum[3] walks along surrounded by adherents and unapplauded.
Finally I discover Elizabeth waiting dejectedly on the *perron* with
her luggage.

In all the rush and flurry of these battered people, I suddenly
perceive a clear clean figure, cool and clean as a cucumber, but
carrying sturdily a large suitcase. It is Shirley Morgan.[4] She looked
as if she had just come out of a cold bath. Everybody else looked as
if they had only just succeeded in escaping from a gas chamber.

I sit for a while on the terrace of the Café de la Paix having a beer.
These Parisian terraces always seem to retain their special atmos-

[1] The novelist.   [2] Prime Minister of Canada since 1935.
[3] Former Prime Minister of France, 1936–37 and in 1938, who was again to become
Prime Minister in December 1946.
[4] She was accompanying the British delegation as Private Secretary to Sir Gladwyn
Jebb, then Assistant Under Secretary of State at the Foreign Office.

phere, linking them with Manet and Toulouse-Lautrec. I think this special quality is due to (a) the presence of a large capital, the sense of many houses stretching all around, and the surge of people passing up and down on the pavement; (b) the extremely bright lights and awnings by which they are lit and protected; (c) but above all, perhaps, the relation between the space set apart for tables, the width of pavement and the large trees. In fact a special proportion.

I come home amused, and sleep.

DIARY   *29th July, 1946*
Paris

I go across to the Luxembourg for the opening of the Conference. The great theatre of the Senate is lit partly by sunlight and partly by spotlights. The delegations sit in the red plush stalls with little black book-rests in front of them. It is all like a first night at Her Majesty's or Covent Garden, except for the absence of women in the stalls. The minor delegates and experts enter first, meeting all their friends from San Francisco,[1] making polite handshakes and bows. Then at 4 pm. precisely the main delegates emerge from the back of the stage and walk across it, down the steps to the proscenium and then up among the stalls. Molotov and Vyshinsky stride across the stage with all the consciousness of power; Byrnes[2] and his delegation walk slowly and sedately with all the consciousness of great virtue; and then in trips little Attlee, hesitates on finding himself on the stage, tries to dart back again into the door through which he has come, and is then rescued by an official who leads him across the stage with a hand upon his elbow. A lamentable entry. In fact our delegation does not look impressive. Attlee, so small, so *chétif*; A. V. Alexander, sturdy but scrubby; Hector McNeil, Scotch and dour; Glenvil Hall,[3] a secondary school-teacher. How insignificant they look there in their red plush stalls! How different from Lloyd George and Balfour, how terribly different from Winston!

They all take their seats and the hum subsides. The *huissier* then

---

[1] The first meeting of the United Nations had been held at San Francisco, April–June, 1945.

[2] James E. Byrnes, Secretary of State to the United States, and the leading American delegate.

[3] William Glenvil Hall, Financial Secretary to the Treasury since 1945.

shouts, '*Monsieur le Président*', and Bidault[1] walks in with neat little feet. Any dignity which the meeting might have had is marred by the photographers and cinema-men. There are huge punch-and-judy boxes erected to the right and left of Bidault's chair, from which protrude the flashing eyes of cinematographs. And all the time American photographers creep about, now on the stage, now off the stage, flashing their cameras. It might be Hollywood itself. In a somewhat rasping voice Bidault opens the proceedings, making a short but conventional speech. '*Messieurs*', he concludes, dropping his manuscript on the desk, '*je déclare ouverte la Conférence de Paris.*'

(*To V.S-W., same date*).[2] Looking down upon Gladwyn [Jebb] sitting as a delegate in a plush armchair did give me a slight twinge; but not of envy; merely the 'elderly failure' twinge. But, as a matter of fact, I am glad to be free of responsibility, and these slight twinges of being out of official life are as nothing to the great tugs of misery which I feel when I go to my beloved but unwanting House of Commons.

DIARY   *4th August, 1946*
                                                                Paris

An unexpected and most undesired fame has descended upon me. I am Rip van Winkle, the veteran of 1919, the only man in Paris who remembers the last Conference. It would seem in fact that except for a dotard in the Brazilian delegation whose memory is unreliable, I am the only survivor of the former peacemaking. *Cela n'est pas rajeunissant.* The correspondent of the *New York Times* who came to interview me asked if I would tell him the differences etc. 'Of course', he says, 'there is a difference in personalities: they were giants in those days.' 'Nonsense', I say, 'don't you believe it. Mr Byrnes to my mind is more effective than President Wilson; Bevin is certainly a stronger and finer character than Lloyd George; old Orlando cannot be compared for force and capacity to Molotov; and in the circumstances Bidault is a far more suitable person than Clemenceau could ever have been.' He is distressed by this remark.

[1] Georges Bidault, the French Prime Minister and Foreign Minister.
[2] Throughout the Paris Conference, he sent carbon-copies of his diary to V.S-W., adding on any blank space a personal note of his own.

DIARY
5th August, 1946
Paris

I cannot adapt myself to this sort of Conference. It is a public performance, not a serious discussion. Yet this new method may achieve
something different in a different way. It becomes more and more
interesting the more I consider it. But I can only make it interesting
to the public by saying things that would cause trouble. For instance,
Russia is trying to make quite certain of her two-thirds veto[1] by
getting the Abyssinian vote in return for promising to back Abyssinia's claim to Eritrea. That shows how fantastic is this system of
voting. It means that Abyssinia is as important as the U.S.A. No
conference can be a serious conference in which such disproportions
of reality are permitted.

V.S-W. TO H.N.
8th August, 1946
Sissinghurst

I find that I have to have a new passport [to join H.N. in Paris] and
have been filling in the forms. This, as always, has flung me into a
rage.[2] You know I love you more than anybody has ever loved
anybody else, but I really do resent being treated as if I were your
dog. The whole thing is an insult to human dignity, and ought to be
revised. One is allowed no separate existence at all, but merely as a
dependent upon whomever one marries. Why not get me a collar
with your name and address engraved upon it?

DIARY
9th August, 1946
Paris

A. V. Alexander is enraged by the fact that the *Daily Worker* published my talk about Russia, in which I said that she was not wholly
in the wrong. I said, 'But of course I was right to be as forgiving
and understanding as possible'. He shrugged his shoulders, as if to
say, 'It is no use talking to such a man'. But A. V. imagines that he is
debating in the House of Commons and that Molotov is the Leader

[1] Much of the early debating had been about procedure. It had been agreed that
decisions should be of two kinds, those carried by simple majorities and those
carried by two-thirds. Russia had only seven dependable votes out of 21, and
needed one more.
[2] Because she was obliged to give her name as 'Mrs Harold Nicolson'.

of the Opposition. He tries to score off him the whole time. I am afraid that the feeling of our Labour Party towards the Russians is one of very deep suspicion and resentment.

I lunch with Gladwyn [Jebb], Oliver Harvey[1] and Hector McNeil. They also are a little distressed by my talk. I am annoyed by this. I say to them, 'Would you like me to submit my talks to you before delivery?' They are horrified by this idea, not wishing to assume responsibility. I say that then I must be allowed to develop my theme in my own way. Unless I take the line of trying to understand the Russian point of view, I shall only offend the Russians bitterly and do no good to anyone. There is much to be said for the Russian point of view (hoots from Hector McNeil), and we shall achieve nothing by ignoring it. 'You people', I say to them, 'start from the idea that Russia is the opponent who has to be scored off by every trick and device. I do not agree with you. Russia may be the enemy. But she is not the enemy yet, and it is our job to be patient and wise and sensible.' They do not like this one little bit. But it was a nice luncheon and I enjoyed it.

I go to the Luxembourg to do my talk. I am caught by Madame Tabouis.[2] Oh my God, what a fiend that woman is! She hates de Gaulle so much that at the mention of his name some faint tinge of colour (no, it is just the poison circulating) comes into her ivory face.

DIARY   11th August, 1946
                                                              Paris

I go across to the Scribe and do my 6.15 talk. Then to the recording room in order to hear Viti.[3] But I cannot get the machine to work. There are all sorts of flexes and plugs lying about the floor but I am too terrified to fix them, dreading short-circuits or electrocutions. Luckily Stannard, the engineer, comes to my rescue and we are just in time to hear Vita announced as Miss Victoria S-W. I expect a row, but she does her piece with swanlike calm. Only at the end, when she has to give her name and address, does she fling into the

[1] Then an Assistant Under Secretary of State at the Foreign Office. He succeeded Duff Cooper as Ambassador in Paris in 1947.

[2] Geneviève Tabouis, the diplomatic correspondent of l'Oeuvre, and one of the most feared journalists of her time.

[3] She was broadcasting from North Wales an appeal for the National Trust.

initial 'V' all the loathing which she has of her full name, or of my name, or of any name except V.S-W.

V.S-W. TO H.N.   *12th August, 1946*
                                            Bodnant, Tal-Y-Cafn, Wales

The Aberconways[1] are not wireless fans. They don't even know how to turn on their own set, which at best is only a loud-speaker relayed from the servants' hall, and they don't know the difference between the Home Service and the Welsh Regional. But I was having no nonsense, and finally we all successfully listened to you. I don't think that either Harry or Christabel [Aberconway] realised that one could enjoy a talk on the wireless, because they were quite *émerveillés*. It *was* a good talk, and I felt proud of you.

Then I myself went off to Bangor to appeal for the Trust. Having done my little piece, I was very energetic. I crossed the Menai Bridge and went to Plas Newydd[2] to see the Rex Whistler room. Charlie Anglesey received me with the utmost kindness; he *is* such a distinguished-looking man, with white hair now, and such charm of manner. The room is really lovely, and the view from Plas Newydd over the water and mountains is very beautiful indeed.

DIARY   *17th August, 1946*
                                                          Paris

I lunch at the Ritz with Carandini [the Italian Ambassador in London]. He realises that Italy cannot expect to obtain much from this conference. He hopes to widen the Trieste area, but he knows he will not succeed. He says that people when they are condemned to death always hope for a reprieve. It occupies their minds while they are awaiting execution. He says that de Gasperi [Italian Foreign Minister] has gone to see Molotov. The latter had received him quite jovially. De Gasperi had asked why it was that he had attacked Italy so bitterly from the tribune of the Conference. Molotov had smiled blandly and replied, 'Oh, you mustn't take that seriously.

[1] The second Lord Aberconway, President of the Royal Horticultural Society, and Chairman of John Brown.
[2] The great house of the Marquess of Anglesey overlooking the Menai Straits towards Snowdonia. Rex Whistler painted a huge fresco in the dining-room between 1936 and 1940.

That was just polemics.' I am quite sure that part of the misunderstanding of the Russians is due to the fact that they are not trained in
the courtesies of international intercourse. They are so accustomed
to using a highly coloured and highly charged language, that they
do not for one moment realise the impression which they are
creating. We take as deliberate insults remarks which are merely
stock-in-trade remarks and part of the current terms of Russian
propaganda.

DIARY   *18th August, 1946*
                                                            Paris

I dine with the Rumanian Ambassador and some of his delegation.
The man who interests me most is the Minister of Education
[Lucretin Patrascanu] who is a communist. I ask him whether
Russia is frightened. He says, 'No. She is not frightened at all. Why
should she be? She only wants to cash in on her great victory
(*encaisser sa victoire immense*).' What she cannot forgive is our attempt
to get out of the Potsdam Agreement. That agreement gave Russia
all that she could have hoped for and more than she expected. It may
have been wrong of us to sign such an agreement. But having done
so, we ought to stick to it, and our attempts to wriggle out of it
suggest weakness and deprive us of that moral authority which we
might possess and ought to possess. I agree with him absolutely. We
are not being honourable at this Conference; and if we cease to be
honourable, we cease to be anything at all.

DIARY   *22nd August, 1946*
                                                            Paris

I dine with V. V. Tilea[1] and the Opposition Rumanians. Gafencu
was there. He says that he is convinced that the Russians wish to
dominate the world, if possible without war but if necessary in spite
of war. For this they can rely heavily on their immense force at this
moment, partly because they have installed in the several surrounding countries minority Governments which depend on Russia for
their lives, and partly because of their fifth column in every country.
They believe that if they can keep the world in a state of anxiety for
several years, people will say in the end, 'Anything for peace', and
[1] Founder of the wartime Free Rumanian Movement in London.

74

will accept the Pax Scythica or Communistica. Now the only way in which the West can counter this is to pool their philosophy of liberalism, put up a united front, and above all offer the world an alternative to the Scythian peace, namely a peace of the United Nations. Otherwise Europe is doomed.

I walk back late down the Champs Elysées, watching the Sacré Coeur glowing benignly in its flood-lighting, and thinking how sad it is that I shall see a third world war in my lifetime.

DIARY   *6th September, 1946*
                                                                        Paris

I go to see Bevin in the morning. I find him installed at a Louis XV table in an ivory-coloured room at the George V. He is most welcoming and genial. He begins by saying polite things about my broadcasts. I say that it is difficult for me to put the Russian problem in its right perspective. He says that he has only just begun to understand how little we know of the Russians, and how much our gaps in interpretation are due to the actual misemployment of words. For instance, when he first met Molotov, he said to him, 'Let us assume that as a basis of discussion.' It was only later that he discovered that Molotov had interpreted the word 'basis' as implying a fundamental agreement. Bevin now uses the words 'as a preliminary suggestion'. Molotov understands that. The word 'preliminary' has become for Bevin one of the very few words which he knows the Russians comprehend.

Unfortunately, however, Mr Byrnes (being a victim of his Press) has insisted on full publicity for the Conference proceedings. This means that one can never think aloud without being overheard, and that all real negotiation is impossible. I say, 'But what about the Big Four meetings?' He chuckles at that. He says that the first one went splendidly, since he had prepared it in advance. But the second one was an absolute flop. 'I have my instructions', began Vyshinsky. 'Well', Bevin answered, 'I have no instructions other than those which I give to myself. Clearly, therefore, we are not discussing on the same level, and I had better turn you over to my deputy.' Vyshinsky blinked at that, but he could go no further. Therefore the meeting broke up pending Molotov's return.

Bevin thinks that the Russians are bitterly enraged with the

75

Americans for having forced a show-down over Yugoslavia. He thinks the insane Russian proposal to transfer the United Nations to Paris or Geneva was just a lunge-back at the United States. He agrees with me that all this scoring of points is lamentable. He had a talk with Skobolev (Trygve Lie's Number Two) whom he described as a 'reasonable man'. He had asked him what was at the back of Russia's incomprehensible conduct. Skobolev had answered, 'The atomic bomb, Mr Bevin.'

I ask him about the Danube. He says the United States are tiresome on the subject. The actual control of the river should obviously be in the hands of the riparian powers. All we ought to ask for is free access to ocean-going ships. The Americans were in a weak position owing to the Panama analogy. 'Believe me, 'arold, our trouble is that the Russians are frightened and the Yanks bomb-minded.' I ask him about the Dardanelles. He winks a genial wink. 'The Russians won't dare to go too far.'

In fact, he is on the whole optimistic. He says this: 'Now look 'ere, 'arold, when I took this job on I knew it wouldn't be a daisy. In fact, no Foreign Secretary has had to keep so many plates in the air at the same time. But what I said to my colleagues at the time was this: "I'll take on the job. But don't expect results before three years." Now it's patience you want in this sort of thing. I am not going to throw my weight about 'ere in Paris. I am just going to sit sturdy 'ere and 'elp.'

My God! How I like that man!

DIARY   *10th September, 1946*
Paris

In the evening we motor out to Versailles for the reception given by Georges Bidault as President of the Provisional Government. The big courtyard is lined by mounted Gardes Républicains and by Goums and Spahis in their scarlet cloaks. On the staircase there are men dressed in the liveries of the eighteenth century with wigs. Bidault receives us in the *antichambre du roi*, and we pass through the Oeil de Boeuf into the Galerie des Glaces. It is a lovely evening, and the sun is pouring in. An absolutely superb Savonnerie carpet is on the floor and there are two vast buffets. I have short talks with many old friends. I meet Yvon Delbos, and Emerald Cunard, and the Duff

Coopers, and Smuts and Marthe Bibesco and De Lattre de Tassigny.

I stand at the window where I stood twenty-seven years ago after the signing of the Treaty of Versailles, and look out on the ponds and canals turning green and purple in the sunset. In the Salon de la Paix there is a small orchestra playing minuets. When they stop playing, I can hear the fountains plashing. When the darkness falls they turn on the floodlighting. The fountains become cascades of silver. It is a scene of amazing magnificence and beauty. But the people look foul.

I bump into Molotov and shake hands with him. I have a talk with Karl Gruber [Foreign Minister of Austria]. I am introduced to Duclos, the communist leader. He is an unbelievably repulsive man. Tiny, grinning with gold teeth, slimy with cleverness.

H.N. TO V.S-W.   *30th September, 1946*
                                                  Grand Hotel, Paris

Tomorrow we shall have been married 33 years. I shall send you a telegram. If I put 'loving thoughts', the French telegraphists will get it wrong; but if I put *'tendres amitiés'*, they will get muddled at Cranbrook. So I shall put it in Aramaic. Oh my dearest Viti, what a long life we have had together, and what a happy, busy, profitable, useful one! I know that our love for each other is as enduring as life. We may die, we may go off our heads, we may take to drugs, we may be put in prison, we may grow the most dreadful carbuncles— but we shall love each other absolutely until d.d.u.p. ('death do us part' that abbreviation is supposed to be).

DIARY   *1st October, 1946*
                                                  Paris

We put on the recordings of the Nuremberg verdicts which were flown to Paris this evening. Obviously there was some hitch at the start, and we can hear a voice saying, 'The circuit is not working'. Apparently Goering came in, put on his head-phones and then made signs to show that he could not get the current. Eventually it was put right, and we could heard Lord Lawrence say, 'Can you hear me now?' 'Yes', said Goering. Then Lawrence said, 'The defendant, Hermann Goering, having been found guilty on all indictments, is condemned by the International Military Tribunal to death by

77

hanging.' Then comes Hess, who gets life imprisonment. Then Ribbentrop. 'The defendant (hesitation on Lawrence's part), Joachim von Ribbentrop, . . . is condemned to death by hanging.' I cannot bear it. To sit there in that familiar room at the Scribe and to hear these men being bumped off one by one. I take off my earphones and rise to go. I see the glistening surface of the disk revolving pitilessly, ticking off the lives of other men.

DIARY   *2nd October, 1946*
                                                            Paris

Alan Moorehead [the author] comes to see me. He says that the British public only interpret the Conference through my talks. He says that I can have no conception of the influence they have had. I am not sure that I like that. I never feel that being able to broadcast is a respectable gift. He says that I should feel more proud of my own responsibility. I am not proud; only anxious. What a nice man he is!

DIARY   *8th October, 1946*
                                                            Paris

I go to the Luxembourg. The séance has not yet begun and I wait patiently. Then suddenly Molotov appears and takes the chair. He rings his bell and calls on Bevin. There is applause as the old boy climbs the stairs to the tribune, very slowly and heavily. Molotov joins in the applause, clapping little white hands. Bevin stands there like an elephant and begins reading his speech. It would not have been a good speech in any case, but it is rendered worse by his delivery. He just reads it in an almost inaudible voice, and one feels he is thinking, 'Can I get through this?' There is no attempt at all to address, still less to convince, his audience. He is just reading a script. It is a lamentable performance and must convince everyone that he is far more ill than he seems. We all gaze at each other in dismay.

In the Scribe bar I find Frederick Voigt[1] and a *Manchester Guardian* chap. They agree that on the whole the Conference has done good. I wonder. I think it has. But it has all been so farcical in so many ways. And there has been no principle at all.

[1] Author, and Editor of *The Nineteenth Century and After*, 1938–46.

11th October, 1946
                                                                   Paris

Molotov slowly walks to the rostrum. He speaks in a quiet voice
with small gestures of his little hands: very feline it all is. He has a
slight stutter but masters it. From time to time he will emphasise
a point by jabbing downwards with a short finger. His speech was
really dreadful. He said that our desire to enter the Danube basin
was a hidden desire to encompass the economic servitude of Europe;
he said that America had made money out of the war and now
wanted to make even more money by penetrating into the Danube
basin; but Russia would protect these countries against enslavement
and the wiles of dollar diplomacy. Not a single argument of any
sense at all; just the old utterly meaningless slogans trotted out again.
It is very depressing.

DIARY   *16th October, 1946*
                                                                   Paris

Well, that is the end of the Paris Peace Conference. Byrnes' attempt
to impress Russia with the force of world opinion has only led
Russia to believe that he sought to gang up the small States against
her. It has convinced me that we cannot persuade Russia by argument, and that all we can do is to behave as well as possible and
convince her by example. But much bitterness and much distrust
has been created.

DIARY   *22nd October, 1946*
                                                                  London

I go to see Rab Butler, who is to lead for the Opposition in the
Foreign Office debate this afternoon. He has obtained from Bevin
the text of his opening speech. We go through it together. I give him
a few suggestions. He is very sensible and moderate, and agrees that
in Foreign Affairs one cannot make a party speech. But he is dreading
what Winston will say tomorrow. He says that Winston is 'a
magnificent animal' who has really no spiritual side at all. He is
gloomy, grouchy, sullen in his retirement, bursting with vigour
and vengeance. He says he fears he is going to trot out the bolshevik
bogey tomorrow and do much harm. Rab says that my broadcasts
from Paris have had 'an immense effect'. He thinks that for the first

time they have induced the ordinary public to take an interest in foreign affairs.

DIARY   *21st November, 1946*

I reach the age of sixty.

I talk at Chatham House on 'Peacemaking, 1919 and 1946'. It goes very well. There are many questions—all sensible. I then return to the Travellers and have a drink with Victor Cunard[1] and Moley Sargent.[2] I come back with Victor, who has taken a house immediately opposite this bloody tenement.[3]

I return across the road, conscious of my sixty years. Until about five years ago I detected no decline at all in physical vigour and felt as young as I did at thirty. In the last five years, however, I am conscious that my physical powers are on the decline. I am getting slightly deaf. Intellectually I observe no decline: I can write with the same facility, which is perhaps a fault. I do not notice that my curiosity, my interests or my powers of enjoyment and amusement have declined at all. What is sad about becoming sixty is that one loses all sense of adventure. It is unlikely now that the impossible will happen. I am very well aware, moreover, that I have not achieved either in the literary or the political world that status which my talents and hard work might seem to justify. In literature, the explanation is simple: although hard-working, I am not intelligent enough to write better than I do. In politics, it has been due partly to lack of push and even of courage, and partly to a combination of unfortunate events (Mosley, National Labour, my being identified with the Ministry of Information at a bad time, and so on). There was a moment in 1938 when it looked as if I had a political future, but that moment passed. I failed to seize it.

Now how much do I mind all this? I have no desire for office or power in any sense. I know quite honestly that if I were offered the Embassy in Paris or Rome, I should hesitate to accept, not only because Viti would hate it, but because I have no wish to be prominent and grand. But of course I am disappointed by my literary ill-

[1] Formerly *The Times* correspondent in Rome. He settled in Venice for most of his life.
[2] Sir Orme Sargent, Permanent Under Secretary for Foreign Affairs since 1945.
[3] 10 Neville Terrace, South Kensington.

success. Nor do I quite relish the idea that my reputation rests not so much upon my political or literary work, as upon my journalistic and broadcasting work. I regret all this quite faintly. I see, on the other hand, a long life behind me, dashed with sunshine and gay with every colour. And to have three people in my life such as Viti and Ben and Nigel is something greater than all material success. For if happiness is in fact the aim of life, then assuredly I have had forty years of happiness, from the day when as a little boy I walked down to the station at Wellington College with a surge of freedom in my heart. Since that hour of liberation I have had a wonderful succession of delights and interests. For which I thank my destiny.

DIARY   *6th December, 1946*

My book on *The English Sense of Humour* arrives from the Dropmore Press. It is very excellently produced. Ben remarks with some astringency that the exterior is superior to the interior.

I return to Neville Terrace to await my lecture.[1] Elvira[2] (who is acute as cute can be) realises that I am nervous. 'I have never seen you nervous before', she says. She is quite right. The reasons are (a) that I do not like lecturing on subjects on which I am not an expert; (b) that I dread letting Ben down in front of his colleagues; (c) that I am uneasy about the presence of Queen Mary.

V. and I drive to Burlington House. Queen Mary arrives on the tick accompanied by the Princess Royal. I give my lecture and it goes very well. I finish and step down from the platform. Queen Mary says, 'Your lecture was too short'. (It was 55 minutes.) 'No lecture', I reply, 'can be too short.' 'Yours was', she says. We then return to the Secretary's room and the Queen says that she wants to see the pictures again and compare them to what I had said. We go from picture to picture and the Queen nods her head. She is specially interested in Lawrence's treatment of Alexander I's red face. The Princess Royal, who used to be so stiff and difficult, is quite easy.

[1] H.N. was lecturing at Burlington House on the portraits painted by Sir Thomas Lawrence at the Congress of Vienna, which now hang in the Waterloo Chamber in Windsor Castle. They had been lent to the exhibition of pictures from the Royal Collection, which Ben had organised at Burlington House with Sir Anthony Blunt, the Surveyor of the King's pictures.
[2] Elvira Niggeman, H.N.'s secretary from 1938 to 1965.

Viti and I then motor home in the little car. We get to Sissinghurst at about 8.15 on a moonlit night. Vass [the head-gardener] has put in masses of wall-flowers which we can see by the light of the moon.

DIARY   9th December, 1946

It is now Monday, and since I came down on Friday night I have (a) finished my article for *Contact*; (b) done my Marginal Comment; (c) done my talk for the Overseas Service; (d) done an article for the B.B.C. Yearbook; (e) done another talk for the European Service; (f) done my article for the *Figaro*; (g) done two reviews. In fact, eight articles of sorts. That is too much. I have also read two books. The bad weather has some advantages.

DIARY   10th December, 1946

Ben tells me that the Palace have agreed to his becoming Editor of the *Burlington*. He takes over on 1st April.[1]

DIARY   12th December, 1946

Jack Churchill[2] tells me that somebody had asked Winston why Attlee did not go out to Moscow to get in touch with Stalin. 'He is too wise for that', replied Winston. 'He dare not absent himself from his Cabinet at home. He knows full well that when the mouse is away the cats will play.'

DIARY   29th December, 1946

In the afternoon I moon about with Vita trying to convince her that planning is an element in gardening. I want to show her that the top of the moat-walk bank must be planted with forethought and design. She wishes just to jab in the things which she has left over. The tragedy of the romantic temperament is that it dislikes form so much that it ignores the effect of masses. She wants to put in stuff which 'will give a lovely red colour in the autumn'. I wish to put in

[1] The Editorship of *The Burlington Magazine*, which he still (1968) retains, was to be the major interest of Ben's career. It is the leading journal of the history of the fine arts. At the end of 1946 he published short studies on Vermeer and Cézanne. On taking up the editorial chair of the *Burlington*, he resigned from the Deputy Surveyorship of the King's Pictures.

[2] Winston Churchill's younger brother.

stuff which will furnish shape to the perspective. In the end we part, not as friends.

What a lovely Christmas holiday I have had! So quiet, so busy, so useful. Ben and Niggs[1] take an amused view of our domestic affections, but are, I think, grateful for a comfortable home, admiring parents and an opportunity to work without interruption. Viti and I are equally amused by them, and so fond.

It has not been a very special year. I enjoyed Paris. But I shall not be really happy until I get back into Parliament.

[1] Family name for Nigel.

1947

Threat of world communism – fuel crisis – H.N. joins the Labour Party – the news breaks – his motives questioned by himself and others – meeting a French farmer – Cyril Joad and Thomas Mann – the Duke and Duchess of Windsor – André Gide – India gains her independence – the old and the new diplomacy – H.N. receives the Legion of Honour – dinner with Hugh Dalton – a motoring tour through southern England – 'Benjamin Constant' – V.S-W.'s feeling for Knole – 'dropping out of public life' – a talk with Bevin at Buckingham Palace – V.S-W. becomes a Companion of Honour – H.N. invited to stand as Labour candidate at North Croydon – he is adopted for the bye-election

The winter of 1947 was one of the severest ever known, and it coincided with a shortage of coal that obliged Emmanuel Shinwell, Minister of Fuel and Power, to impose strict rationing on electricity and gas. The whole nation suffered acutely. Kent was among the places worst hit. Sissinghurst was cut off for days by snow-drifts, and V. Sackville-West, now beginning to write 'Daughter of France', shivered in her tower. Harold Nicolson and his two sons managed somehow to go there each weekend. He was writing no new book, and the pattern of his life was now re-established around his articles, lectures, broadcasts (he became a frequent member of the Brains Trust), lunches, dinners and, whenever possible, gardening. Ben was about to take up the editorship of the 'Burlington Magazine'. I joined the staff of George Weidenfeld's Contact Publications on 1st January, having been demobilised on the completion of my official war-history of the Grenadier Guards, and made frequent visits to Leicester as the Conservative candidate.

It was at this moment, on 28th February, that Harold Nicolson joined the Labour Party. His motives are explained in the extracts which follow, but there was an uncharacteristic opportunism about his decision, a certain clumsiness about his timing and method, which denied him its expected fruits. He conceived it as the beginning of a new political career in the Commons or the Lords. In fact, it proved to be his political undoing, for it confused people's minds, including his own, about the roots of his political beliefs and judgement. The public attitude was one of amused indifference, except in Leicester, where his former supporters (now his son's) were horrified. V. Sackville-West's reaction was surprisingly mild.

DIARY   *2nd January, 1947*

I address the Council of Education in World Citizenship[1] upon the lessons of the Paris Peace Conference. There are present in Central Hall, Westminster, some 3,000 boys and girls between 16 and 18.

[1] An organ of the United Nations Association.

It is a pleasure to gaze upon such a sea of young faces. Individually they are as ugly as hell, but in the mass they have a youthful beauty. They suggest something *lampros* ['shining']. I gather that I was succeeded by J. B. Priestley who gave an address on Russia, America and ourselves. His line was that we should refuse to be drawn into a war between America and Russia. This was rapturously applauded. We always go through these stages of being beastly to our friends because we are frightened of our enemies. It is this that has earned us the reputation of *perfide Albion*.

DIARY   *5th January, 1947*

Raymond [Mortimer] reads my essay on the English sense of humour and lays it down without a word and picks up another book. When pressed, he says that it is very bad and sham philosophy, and that I ought not to try my hand at that sort of thing. I like that about Raymond. He never for one moment says what he doesn't think merely out of affection or a desire to please.

V.S-W. TO H.N.   *8th January, 1947*
                                                                Sissinghurst

I want to start on the Big Miss.[1] She isn't *quite* my sort of thing, but there are some aspects of the story which I find interesting. But *Le Grand Siècle* is not quite me somehow. Her own description of herself is fascinating as a psychological document. It is a study in self-delusion by a most sincere person. It is on these lines that I shall try to base my portrait of her. You see, she persuaded herself that she had no worldly ambition, yet spent half her time trying to marry Kings or Emperors, and it was only when she fell in love with Lauzun that she came round to her own conception of herself as a person without ambition. A very interesting character.

DIARY   *9th January, 1947*

I dine with General Jacob.[2] We discuss the international situation. I

[1] La Grande Mademoiselle, Duchesse de Montpensier, 1627–93. V.S-W. laid this book aside for some years for other work, and it was not published until 1959.
[2] General Sir Ian Jacob, Military Assistant Secretary to the War Cabinet, 1939–46.

say that in five years from now we may find that France, Spain, Italy, Greece and Germany have all gone communist. The smaller western powers will be like rabbits in the python's cage. The whole of India will be under communist direction and we shall have troubles in all our colonies and dependencies. At the same time there will have occurred in this country a split between the present Labour leaders (who take a patriotic or nationalist point of view) and their left wing (who take the international or Red Flag point of view). The latter will, owing to the acute poverty of the country, gain ground among the working classes. Thus, if a conflict comes between the U.S.A. and the U.S.S.R., we shall have a very active fifth column in this country. The great bourgeois mass, terrified as they will be by the prospect of atomic war, will wish only to appease Russia. The minority who see that we must side with America will be called war-mongers. And we shall thus lose our independence and our Commonwealth. I say that this is what will *probably* happen. To ignore this probability is to be both cowardly and blind. To be frightened of it is to deny one's own soul. Because nothing really happens which is as bad as the imagination forecasts. Time brings unexpected alterations. The danger may pass.

Jacob agrees with all this. He says that even if there is no chance of winning, we must always assume that we shall win. This leads him to talk about his experiences as assistant to Pug Ismay in the War Cabinet. He says that in 1940 our General Staff were convinced that the German drive across France was a carefully prepared plan culminating in the invasion of this country. He says that Montgomery was assuredly a very great general. Not for certain as great as Wellington, since he never had to cope with the same shortages of supply and support from home. But nonetheless a very great general, 'who could always impose his own battle on the enemy'. He told me that our inability to land behind the enemy in Italy was due entirely to the American refusal to give us enough landing craft. Thus, in a way, the Italian campaign was the worst we waged.

H.N. TO V.S-W.   *28th January, 1947*
                                                  10 Neville Terrace, S.W.7

Such a characteristic story for you. Ben had been asked to do an obituary on Bonnard[1] for the *New Statesman*. He did it and sent it along. Thereafter he thought he could give more polish to the thing by adding a neat epigram. So he telephoned to Pritchett[2] asking him to add the words, '*Le peintre est mort: vive le peintre*'. Pritchett seemed to be hesitant about the need for this epigram, but in the end agreed. Then Niggs dined with Ben at Brooks'. Ben told him of his epigram. Niggs said it was a very bad epigram and he must have it cancelled at once. So when I got back from dining with James [Pope-Hennessy], they both came into my room. 'Now Ben, ask Daddy what he thinks.' I was told the epigram. I said it was foolish and meaningless, and above all a very stale cliché. He must take it out at once. Niggs yelled with joy. Ben was half amused and half *penaud* ['crestfallen'].

DIARY   13th February, 1947

The coal crisis is really disastrous. The electricity is cut off between 9 and 12 and 2 and 4. The blackout is to be imposed. Our industry is at a standstill and it will take us months and months to recover from this disaster. There is a demand for vigorous leadership and of course all sorts of rumours. The most prevalent is that Attlee is going to retire in Bevin's favour. But I fear that Bevin is seriously ill with angina. He goes to Moscow with a doctor and a nurse.

I go down home. I am met by Viti as Copper [the chauffeur] has 'flu. There is ice on the roads and it is difficult to drive. We creep home. My God! What the poor people of this country have had to suffer in the last seven years!

DIARY   28th February, 1947

I write the attached letter[3] to the secretary of the Kensington Labour Party. I am glad to have taken this decision after all these months of

[1] Pierre Bonnard (1867–1947), the French Impressionist painter.
[2] V. S. Pritchett, Literary Editor of the *New Statesman*.
[3] '*Dear Sir, I am anxious to enrol myself as a member of the Labour Party and am not sure what is the proper procedure. I should not wish to undertake active political work in this area, but desire only to become a subscribing member of the Party. Could you let me know what I should do?*' The letter was answered on 3rd March, enclosing an enrolment form, but in such a manner that it was quite clear that the local Secretary did not realise who 'H. Nicolson' was. Transport House remained unaware of their new recruit until the news broke on 11th March.

worry and uncertainty.[1] It will lead to a row at home. But this is the best moment, when the Labour Party are being banged on the head, to make my act of faith. It is *not* an impulsive act.

This decision will expose me to much obloquy, misinterpretation, ridicule and attribution of false motive. People will say that I did this because I wanted to get a peerage. If I scrape my conscience I must admit that there is some truth in that accusation. I hate being out of Parliament. I do not want to fight an election. I should be at ease in the Upper House and able to do some good. If there were no prospect of my getting a peerage within a reasonable time, would I fight an election as a Socialist? I might. What I will not do is to abuse my former friends. I cannot get up and speak ill of Winston or Eden. Anyhow, one thing is certain. I could never have become a Tory. It would be madness to become a Liberal. Therefore becoming Labour is the only alternative to dropping out. That is not a noble motive. But what people will not know is that I am now convinced that the only angle from which to fight communism is the Labour angle. The only thing that worries me is that my integrity is my most valued possession. Will this make people doubt my integrity? I do not think so. Because God knows that my integrity is a solid thing within me. I am unambitious and devoted. I really am.

When I read the above again, I say to myself, 'You are making excuses, and very lame excuses, for yourself. That means that you are not spiritually at ease'. No, not exactly that. It is the rows I dread; how it will hurt Vita and Mummy; the publicity that may follow. I wish I were more tough.

DIARY   *2nd March, 1947*

Niggs has been preparing his address to the Leicester Conservatives. I did not know that this was impending. I trust that my joining the Labour Party will not be announced at the same time. I join them at this moment because they are in a bad way. Bertie Jarvis [chairman of West Leicester Conservative Association] launches his appeal at the same moment for the same reason. But if my joining the Labour Party comes out at the same moment, it will diminish the effect of

[1] This remark may suggest that the diary and letters had been full of speculation on his political future. But this is not so. There is no mention of this crucial decision until the moment when it was taken.

Niggs' appeal. I feel guilty about this. I feel even more guilty because I have not dared tell any of them that I wrote that letter on 28th February.

Life, unquestionably, is a highly complicated matter.

N.N.'s DIARY   5th March, 1947

Office all day. Nothing much. The shock comes in the evening. I had come back early, and was working in Daddy's room. Ben returns, and shortly afterwards, D. himself. He says, 'Now I'm going to tell you the awful thing I've done. Have a glass of sherry first, each of you.' So we took our medicine and waited. 'I've just joined the Labour Party', he said. I was struck dumb. Although I had known of this possibility for the past year, he had gone off and made his decision without telling us. He had rung up Transport House and asked for the address of the South Kensington representative, to whom he had then sent £1 and signed a form saying that he believed in the principles of the Labour Party. 'But do you really believe in them all?' I asked. 'Well, yes, on the whole', he said. 'There is nothing in the official policy that I object to. My only fear is of the extreme left wing, which may gain control. Then I should have to leave.' 'But what do you mean to do about it?' 'Well, I made it quite clear that I wouldn't take an active part because I don't want to attack old friends like Dick Law and Harold Macmillan. Of course everyone will say that I did it in order to get a peerage, and when I examine myself I realise that there is something in that. I would like a peerage. It would be much the best solution.'

I feel admiration for his resilience—that someone of his age and distinction should have taken such a step at a time when everyone imagined that he had retired from active politics and when the Labour Party was in disgrace. I can't say that I approve or like it. I would have wished to see him an Independent Member for one of the Universities. This decision will make me look a bit silly in Leicester—the father joins the young revolutionary party, the son the staid and stolid party. It is as if we appeared side by side, he dressed in running shorts, and I in a top-hat and tails. A Mr Bultitude act.

H.N. TO V.S-W.   *6th March, 1947*
                                    10 Neville Terrace, S.W.7

I must break to you the fact that I have joined the Labour Party. I have done this because in the end it was inevitable, and I had better do it when the night of misery is upon them rather than when they are basking in the sun of popular acclaim. I shall get a real scolding when I come down on Saturday. But I know I was right.

V.S-W. TO H.N.   *7th March, 1947*
                                    Sissinghurst

I am very glad about the National Trust.[1] Not so sure about the Labour Party, though not wholly hostile, especially if it leads eventually to Lord Cranfield.[2] Of course I don't really like you being associated with those people. I like Ernest Bevin and Philip Noel-Baker. I have a contemptuous tolerance of Attlee, but I *loathe* Aneurin Bevan, and Shinwell is just a public menace. I do not like people who cannot speak the King's English. The sort of people I like are Winston and Sir John Anderson.

DIARY   *9th March, 1947*

Viti's birthday.[3] My joining the Labour Party is taken quite calmly. I have not been scolded as I expected.

DIARY   *11th March, 1947*

All the newspapers have been ringing up. It appears that when Nigel got to Leicester yesterday, he discovered that Bertie Jarvis had told the Leicester papers that I had joined the Labour Party. Nigel then brought the whole thing into his speech, and did it very tactfully.[4]

[1] H.N. had just been appointed Vice-Chairman.
[2] See p. 44, note 1.   [3] She was 55.
[4] I said: 'In taking this step, he has not gone back on anything he has ever said. He never called himself a Conservative. His chief interest has always been in foreign affairs, and with the main lines of Mr Bevin's foreign policy he finds himself in complete agreement. As he feels that he cannot indefinitely remain an Independent, he has adhered to Mr Bevin's party, instead of standing outside the ring. I must add that I respect him for his decision. Naturally I cannot agree with it, for if I did, I would be a Socialist myself. I will be no less staunch a Conservative because of his attitude, and he, needless to say, will not be affected by mine.'

This was picked up by the Press Association who relayed it to London.

DIARY   *12th March, 1947*

The papers carry my betrayal of the nation quite calmly. There are no rude remarks.[1]

DIARY   *13th March, 1947*

I go to see Mummy. She takes my having joined the Labour Party as a cruel blow. She says, 'I never thought that I should see the day when one of my own sons betrayed his country.' Freddy [2nd Lord Carnock] is equally indignant. 'I suppose', he says, 'you will now resign from all your clubs.'

H.N. TO V.S-W.   *26th March, 1947*
                                            10 Neville Terrace, S.W.7

I met a Tory friend of mine yesterday who said, 'Our affection for you is not altered, but our trust in your judgement is'. I said, 'Well, that is all right provided that you do not accuse me of moral turpitude.' 'Of course we shan't do that, Harold, unless you get an Embassy or take a peerage.' So that if I get a peerage, it will be said that I joined the Labour Party in order to become Lord Bowlingreen. I don't see it like that inside myself, but viewed from the outside it is exactly like that. So that if I get it, instead of being an honour and the crown of my career, it will be a crown of thorns and a badge of shame. I do hope that I have not hurt Niggs' prospects by 'changing sides in order to be made a Lord'. I think he is perfectly able to stand on his own feet. But my tradition, which might have been an asset to him, has become a liability. Not being a party-man myself, I underestimate the amount of bitterness and passion which party polemics engender.

[1] They came in the *Sunday Express*: ' "Your choice is now between a Government led by Winston Churchill and Eden, and a Government led by Attlee. I prefer Churchill." Who said this? Mr Harold Nicolson in his Election Address in July 1945. He has changed his mind, just as he did when he left Mosley's New Party.'

H.N. TO V.S-W.   *2nd April, 1947*
                                        10 Neville Terrace, S.W.7

I met Emerald[1] who told me that last night she had been abusing
me for joining the Labour Party ('There's that horrid Harold. . . .'),
when Anthony Eden jumped on her. 'No', he said, 'he was quite
right. He is a person apart and has every right to his own decisions.
He will do a world of good in the Labour Party.' Emerald, who in
her funny way is a loyal soul, was much impressed by this.

DIARY   *4th April, 1947*

Vass [the head-gardener at Sissinghurst] has got over the Normandy
farmer, Monsieur Renoult, who sheltered him near Lisieux when he
baled out. We are introduced to him in the greenhouse. When told
by Viti that I must come to speak to this man, I feel an extraordinary
repugnance. I cannot explain it to myself. I know that I am embarrassed at having to talk to uneducated people, especially in French.
I know that the relations between myself and Vass, which are so
carefully balanced between employer and employed, may be a little
disturbed by this hero-host-gratitude business. I know that I hate
hanging about making conversation when I want to read or work.
But my repugnance is something more than my usual disinclination
for this sort of thing. I think it derives from two inhibitions. First,
my shyness at meeting people who have behaved heroically.
Secondly, my acute distaste at having to speak to French people
about conditions here, conditions there, and our joint relations to
the United States and Russia. These things fill me with such anxious
perplexity in any case that I am inhibited from stating them in terms
which simple people can understand. That provokes sadness. And
my hatred of sad situations is perhaps the worst of all the tangled
weeds in my system.

Anyhow, Monsieur Renoult is a splendid man with clear eyes and
a fine Norman accent. He tells us stories of his combats with the S.S.
and Gestapo. He is so pessimistic about the future of France that he
wishes to migrate to England. That also saddens me. The boys are
so exuberant, and Viti so understanding, that my frayed nerves are
again encased in comfort.

[1] Lady Cunard.

95

DIARY   *25th April, 1947*

I go with Charles Fletcher-Cooke[1] and Noel Annan[2] to a dinner of
the Haldane Society. It was my first Labour gathering. I loathed it.
After all, I was with two charming people of my own sort and the
audience was mainly composed of young lawyers and their girl-
friends. But the atmosphere of comradely fifth-rateness upset me.
Vegetable soup we had, and liver and onions and beer. There were
speeches by the Lord Chancellor, by Stafford Cripps, by [Sir Frank]
Soskice. They spoke about Law Reform. In the end we all sang the
Red Flag.

I always knew that I was a theoretical Socialist. I do feel profoundly that we can only avoid totalitarianism or tyranny by a
planned social economy. I believe we can achieve it in this country
without destroying the freedom of the individual. It is for this that
I am prepared to work. But the sham matiness and the *Red Flag*
business are to me abhorrent.

DIARY   *27th April, 1947*

Niggs has been up in Leicester to hear Lord Woolton.[3] He feels that
my joining the Labour Party has done much harm. They think I
told them lies. In Leicester, I have certainly sacrificed my reputation
for integrity. And for what? Not an agreeable thought.

*Joining the Labour Party made little immediate difference to Harold
Nicolson's life. He was rarely invited to address any political meetings,
and he neither resigned from his clubs nor gave up his weekly article
for the Conservative 'Spectator'. He filled every moment of his time in
the sort of way indicated by his diary-entry for 3rd June, included here
not for its intrinsic importance, but as typical of his life and diary at
this period. He had written an Introduction to a new edition of Benjamin Constant's 'Adolphe', and was so captivated by the character of
its author that he began to write a full-length biography of him.*

[1] He was then Labour candidate for East Dorset, but resigned from the Labour
Party shortly afterwards, and became Conservative Member for Darwen in
1951.
[2] Fellow of King's College, Cambridge, of which he became Provost in 1956.
[3] Chairman of the Conservative Party, 1946–55.

DIARY   *28th April, 1947*

I do my wireless talk and my article for the *Figaro*. In the afternoon I weed in the spring-garden. It is a cold but beautiful day, but I am unhappy and distressed. I find myself having *Angst* about the future of the world and my own country. Subversive movements seem to be gaining a hold in industry; there is a succession of unnecessary strikes; the food and export position is deplorable; and the energy that should be shown is not shown. When one adds to this the eternal disquiet caused by Russia, the dislocating tactics which they pursue, the lack of general confidence—all this inspires gloom. And my own immediate present fills me with apprehension. My Socialist convictions are purely academic and even negative. I hope by Socialism to preserve our essential personal liberties. But I feel I am being dragged into the wake of the future; not that I am in the van. The awful thought gnaws like a rat at my conscience that I should have accepted being out of public life and done nothing at all. I feel a decline in energy and faith. I am in a bad mood.

I read Charles du Bos on Benjamin Constant. When he was young, he suffered, or thought he suffered, tortures of unhappiness and self-dispraisal. Now, I, when young, was as happy and irresponsible as a lark. It is in my late age that happiness has become clouded. But if unhappiness comes to the young, it gives them depth. Coming at my age it confirms my superficiality. I am haunted by mental decay such as I saw creeping over Ramsay MacDonald. A gradual dimming of the lights.

DIARY   *9th May, 1947*

Sissinghurst is lovely. The spring-garden has lost its early bloom. The Forsythia is gone, and the primroses are looking a trifle tired. On the other hand, I have never seen the flowering trees so marvellous. The orchard is alive with blossom.

Viti had had Cyril Joad[1] to luncheon. He poured out to her his unhappiness and disappointments. He has lost his faith in agnosticism and has not found a compensating faith in God. He has lost his faith in Socialism and not found any faith to supplement it. Under-

---

[1] Head of the Department of Philosophy at Birkbeck College, University of London, since 1930, and the leading spirit in the B.B.C.'s Brains Trust, on which H.N. was a frequent participant. He was then aged 55.

neath, I suppose, he must feel that he is in a false position. He has acquired notoriety instead of fame; he knows that he is a popular, and as such a slightly comic, figure. He wishes he had acquired either the cloistered dignity of a scholar and philosopher, or the arena victories of the politician. He has no domestic background. He has quarrelled with his son; his daughters have married; his wife has left him. He is famous and alone.

DIARY   22nd May, 1947

I dine with Denis Saurat[1] and his wife to meet Thomas Mann.[2] It is rather a grim party with lager and uneatable food. I am the only other guest. Mann really believes that the English are the hope of the world. He feels that America is going fascist. That worries him. 'I do not wish to be a martyr to liberty a second time.' So he keeps very silent while in the U.S.A. He believes, however, that our great prestige and experience can save the world. Only we can establish 'humanistic socialism'. And we can only do so under the Labour Party. I like him so much. He is so easy and simple.

DIARY   28th May, 1947

I go to see Sibyl [Colefax]. When I come into the room, I find Osbert Lancaster there, and a young man with his back to the window. He says, 'Not recognise an old friend?' It is the Duke of Windsor. He is thin but more healthy-looking than when I last saw him. He has lost that fried-egg look around the eyes. He is very affable and chatty. I notice that he has stopped calling his wife 'Her Royal Highness'. He calls her 'the Duchess'. I notice also that people do not bow as they used to, and treat him less as a royalty than they did when he had recently been King. He takes all this quite for granted. I have an impression that he is happier.

The Duchess of Windsor then comes in. She also is much improved. That taut, predatory look has gone; she has softened. I have a talk with her alone. She says that they do not know where to live. They would like to live in England, but that is difficult. He retains his old love for Fort Belvedere. 'We are tired of wandering',

[1] Professor of French Literature at the University of London since 1926.
[2] The German author of *Death in Venice*, *The Magic Mountain* etc. He left Germany in protest against the Nazis in 1933, and had been living in the U.S.A. since 1938.

she says. 'We are not as young as we were. We want to settle down
and grow our own trees. He likes gardening, but it is no fun gardening in other people's gardens.' Where can they live? They are sick
of islands,[1] otherwise they might go to the Channel Islands. They
are sick of France. He likes America, but that can never be a home.
He wants a job to do. 'You see', she says, 'he was born to be a sales-
man. He would be an admirable representative of Rolls Royce.
But an ex-King cannot start selling motor-cars.' I feel really sorry
for them. She was so simple and sincere.

DIARY   *3rd June, 1947*

Up to London. I see from the evening papers that it is the hottest day
recorded in London for eighty years. I can well believe it. Elvira
[Niggeman] is working with Bobbety,[2] and I therefore do most of
my letters myself.

I lunch at the French Embassy. The party consists of English
littérateurs—namely, Cyril Connolly, Raymond [Mortimer], John
Lehmann, Peter Quennell and so on. It is held in honour of André
Gide.[3] The latter is being given an LL.D at Oxford. He is as pleased
as Punch. He asks me whether the undergraduates will demonstrate
for political or 'moral' reasons. I say that he need not worry. There
may be a few cries of 'Corydon!',[4] but they will be well meant. 'Ah,
Corydon, Corydon', he murmurs, but does not add *quae te dementia
cepit?*[5] He has a little Virgil in his pocket which he reads in buses.
He says he can read that, but no other form of Latin. I am wearing
a tropical form of trousers. '*Tiens!*' says Gide, '*vous avez mis votre
complet Viet Nam!*' He is boyishly demure, demurely boyish. And
he is almost eighty years of age!

I go to the Flower Show in Vincent Square. It is very poor—
exhausted, doubtless, by the heat and the efforts of the Chelsea

[1] He had been Governor of the Bahamas from 1940 until 1945.
[2] Lord Salisbury, for whom Miss Niggeman was working half-time. His father,
the fourth Marquess of Salisbury, had died on 4th April.
[3] The French essayist, critic, novelist and dramatist (1869–1951). In this year he
was awarded the Nobel Prize for literature.
[4] Gide's *Corydon* (1924) consisted in Socratic discussions on the theme of homo-
sexuality.
[5] Virgil, *Eclogue* II, 69: 'Ah Corydon, Corydon, what madness has gripped you?'
Corydon was a Greek shepherd who fell in love with the boy Alexis.

Show. The flowers are actually panting with fatigue. I see little that we have not got better at home.

At 3.30 today Attlee in the House announced the terms of the Indian settlement. There is to be partition between Pakistan and Hindustan. He pays a great tribute to Dickie Mountbatten. Winston replies and has nice things to say. I am sure that Dickie has done marvellously. But it is curious that we should regard as a hero the man who liquidates the Empire which other heroes such as Clive, Warren Hastings and Napier won for us. Very odd indeed.

DIARY   *10th June, 1947*

The Chinese Ambassador comes up to me and says nice things about my books. He asks me whether we in England were surprised at the long resistance put up by China. I say we were, as we had always supposed that the Chinese regarded war as an uncivilised practice, and soldiers as among the most despicable of mankind. He said that this was true, but they were fighting for their lives. 'We have', he said, 'a problem—I mean a proverb—in our country, which says, "Better to be a tile intact than a broken piece of jade." ' 'That is a very good proverb', I say. 'I shall take a note of it.' And I write it down in my notebook. 'I wonder', I say, 'whether Your Excellency could repeat that proverb in Chinese?' He then screws up his face and begins with closed eyes: '*Chiao young ui handj. . . .*' Then he stops. 'No', he says, 'I was mistaken in the problem. It is as follows: "Better to be a broken piece of jade than a tile intact." ' 'That also', I say, 'is an excellent proverb.' And I scratch out the first version and insert the second.

We get back from the party at 4.30, and I am given a lift, first by the Buccleuchs as far as the House of Lords, and thereafter by young Anglesey[1] who is just back from France. He is a charming boy and no fool at all.

DIARY   *1st July, 1947*

Gladwyn [Jebb] tells me that he doesn't know what is happening in Paris, but he doubts whether the thing can possibly succeed.[2]

[1] The seventh Marquess of Anglesey. He had succeeded his father in February, 1947, and was then aged 24. He married Shirley Morgan in 1948.

[2] The Council of Foreign Ministers had failed to reach any agreement on the future of Germany and Austria.

Molotov is trying to engineer a breakdown in such a manner as will appeal best to his own public, and will offer some chance to the French communists to make capital out of the event. He wants to weaken and discredit Bevin. But he is so ignorant of western ways, so ignorant of the sort of way in which an educated and enlightened public react, that he will only weaken the opponents of Bidault and Bevin.

This is one of the things which mark the difference between the old and the new diplomacy. The old boys, whether Louis XIV or even Napoleon, really did know more or less how their actions would affect public opinion abroad. Frederick the Great, for instance, was his own propaganda agent and a very skilled one. But Hitler and Stalin, with their utter ignorance of mentalities different from their own, always miscalculated the effect of their own actions in other countries. Now, this is dangerous. It tempts them to believe that they can go further than they can really go; and since they are unable to lose face by retreating, situations may be created out of that ignorance which are situations leading to war.

DIARY   *8th July, 1947*

I lunch at the French Embassy, where Cyril Connolly and I are invested with the Legion of Honour. Massigli asks us to stand side-by-side. He then stands opposite us and makes an allocution.[1] He does it very well, but I am overwhelmed by embarrassment. I feel angry with myself at getting so shy about so simple an occasion. Then he motions to his staff and they advance with little medallions on a tray. He pins them on to us and gives the accolade—cheek against cheek. I hate it. Then champagne is produced and we have a *vin d'honneur*, and then we lunch.

DIARY   *10th July, 1947*

At lunch at the Beefsteak we have an amusing talk about clique accents. There was the intonation of the Devonshire House circle, the nasal drawl of the ultras, the 1890 voice, the Bright People voice, the Bloomsbury voice and now the Bowra[2] voice.

[1] H.N. was described as: '*Ecrivain, diplomate et homme politique de renommé mondiale, qui n'a pas cessé un instant de croire en la France et en sa destineé. La France possède en lui un magnifique champion de sa cause.*'

[2] C. M. Bowra, Warden of Wadham College, Oxford, since 1938.

Then I go to Buckingham Palace for the garden party. It is raining slightly, but I wear my top-hat. I go to have some chocolate cake in the marquee with Alan Pryce-Jones and then I walk out again. Everybody is straining to see the bridal pair[1]—irreverently and shamelessly straining.

DIARY   *24th July, 1947*

I dine with the [Hugh] Daltons at No 11 Downing Street. They have a flat on the top floor. That domed dining-room where Neville Chamberlain expounded Munich to me is now a place for typists.

The other guests are Kenneth Younger, the Member for Grimsby, and his wife. He is a clever Wykehamist with freckles. He is P.P.S. to Philip Noel-Baker. He thinks that the Government ought to issue a statement explaining exactly to the country the nature of the danger threatening us and the inevitability of sacrifice. He thinks it a mistake for members of the Cabinet each to sing a different tune —now little trilolos of comfort, now deep dirges of despair. Dalton is not quite so sure whether he agrees with this. Even when the dollar-loan runs out, there are 'reserves'. We could live on these reserves for quite a bit. Younger seems to feel that it would be right for the Government to go to the country and ask for a fresh mandate when the cuts become necessary. Dalton says that it would be better to carry on till 1949 at least, 'so as to allow the new machines which we have created to run themselves in'.

Dalton told me, incidentally, that the Government propose to abolish University seats. There goes my chance of representing Oxford. He advises me to see the people at Transport House and get a constituency. He thinks I should be put on a list called List B.

DIARY   *2nd August, 1947*

It is difficult to view the future without despair. Winston at Woodstock today spoke of 'the inevitable genius of the British people'. But was it the British people? Was it not only the élite?

For ten days at the beginning of August, Harold Nicolson, V. Sackville-West and James Lees-Milne, the historian of architecture, went

---

[1] The engagement of Princess Elizabeth to Philip Mountbatten had been announced that morning.

on a motoring tour through the south of England as far west as Corn-wall. Their main purpose was to visit National Trust properties, but they took their work with them. Harold Nicolson wrote his weekly articles en route and V. Sackville-West her 'In Your Garden' column for the 'Observer'. In all they visited forty houses (not all of them owned by the National Trust), as well as several cathedrals and ancient monuments. Among the houses were West Wycombe, Littlecote, Ramsbury, Wilton, Stourhead, Montacute, Barrington Court, Killerton, Cotehele, Lacock Abbey, Corsham, Dyrham, Berkeley Castle, Nether Lypiatt, Charlecote, Packwood and Warwick Castle.

DIARY   *5th August, 1947*
                                                              Newbury

The first house we visit is West Wycombe.[1] The view from the top of the hill is most curious. On the right one sees West Wycombe park and house looking exactly like a Rex Whistler painting. And, in front, the long line of the London road which is almost wholly industrialised. On the one side lawns and trees and Palladian archi-tecture; on the other, iron and smoke. We go round the house. A charming tapestry room; a good dining-room and hall; a splendid mahogany staircase with inlaid treads; upstairs a well-proportioned gallery and a fine library without cases or books. The whole place is terribly dilapidated: the paper peeling off, the carpets with holes in them, the stuffing showing in the chairs. All that is perhaps inevitable. There are no servants at all.

DIARY   *6th August, 1947*
                                                        Long Crichel, Dorset

We go on to Ramsbury.[2] We drive in quite boldly and draw up in front of the house. Jim [Lees-Milne] had warned us that the owner, Sir Francis Burdett, was an old, fashionable gentleman who did not like tourists staring at his front door. While we are thus engaged, the door opens and out comes a stout old man with huge moustaches and a blue coat with brass buttons. Our first idea is to bolt, and in

[1] In Buckinghamshire. The house was rebuilt in about 1765 in the Adam manner, and was given to the National Trust in 1943 by Sir John Dashwood.
[2] Ramsbury Manor, Wiltshire, built for the Earl of Pembroke by John Webb in the 1660's. The owner, Sir Francis Burdett, was born in 1869 and died in 1951.

103

fact we do retreat a yard or two when the old man starts to run after us. We then stop, and he asks us angrily what we are doing. Viti says: 'We have made a mistake. We want to go to Littlecote.' It is quite clear that he does not believe us. An embarrassment occurs. Off we go at last, feeling uneasy and cross. The incident combined four things I most dislike: intruding upon the privacy of others; telling lies; being scolded; being made to look foolish. Silently we drive on to Avebury.

On to Wilton, having had a view of the spire of Salisbury Cathedral. We cross the courtyard and go to David Herbert's[1] little house. It is a charming folly contrived with really exquisite ingenuity and taste. David is dressed in *lederhosen* and a maroon shirt. He looks young and charming. We sit in his tiny little garden which he has designed so well, listen to his parrot squawking and have a cocktail. Then off we go again, reaching Long Crichel at 7.30 to be very warmly welcomed by Eddy [Sackville West].

DIARY   *8th August, 1947*
                                                                        Yeovil, Somerset

We go to Montacute.[2] First we go round the garden, where Viti gives some excellent advice on replanting. The whole thing is well kept up and a credit to the Trust. I go up to one of the deserted upstairs rooms and type a 'Marginal Comment', while Jim and Viti explore Somersetshire. It is a lovely day with soft clouds drifting across warm blue.

DIARY   *10th August, 1947*
                                                                        Burrator, Devon

We go to Bradley Manor,[3] which is a lovely little fifteenth-century house owned by the Trust. It is still lived in by the Woolners, who are poor, have many children and can't afford to keep the place in proper order. This is the ever recurrent National Trust problem—

[1] A younger son of the Earl of Pembroke. His cottage stood in the garden of the great house which had been partly reconstructed with the advice of Inigo Jones.
[2] In Somerset. One of the finest surviving Elizabethan houses in the country, given to the National Trust in 1931.
[3] Near Newton Abbot, Devon. It was given to the Trust in 1938 by Mrs A. H. Woolner.

we save a house from destruction, but have not sufficient income to keep it tidily.

We drive to Burrator. Eric[1] is in wonderful form. He has not got a single grey hair. We have lovely baths in the soft peat water.

DIARY   *11th August, 1947*
Wells

We cross Dartmoor by Two Bridges. The police are out at all the crossroads, since three convicts have escaped from Princeton. Our sympathies are entirely on the side of the convicts. It is a marvellous morning, and never have I seen the moor looking more lovely. There is a heavy heat-haze over the hills, but this does not obscure their outlines; merely dims and enlarges them. It is a most enjoyable drive.

DIARY   *12th August, 1947*
Bath

We go to Corsham,[2] where we have tea with Lady Methuen. Part of the house is a naval college, part is kept as staterooms, and part the Methuens live in. Outside in the lovely park spread huge elms. At the entrance there are the finest piers and stone balls that I have ever seen. There are magnificent family portraits—Gainsboroughs, Reynoldses, Romneys. A very fine Reynolds of the two Methuen children—the little girl wearing her brother's hat. We then go into the staterooms. The picture gallery is grand and high but too pompous for my taste. There are however superb pictures. A Filippo Lippi, a Holbein, a very fine Rubens, several Guido Renis and so on. It is too much to take in at one gasp. I am particularly struck by a series of super-Adam mirrors. The furniture also, being entirely Chippendale, is magnificent. I had never known that Corsham was so superb.

---

[1] H.N.'s older brother, who became the third Lord Carnock in 1952. He was then 63.
[2] Near Chippenham, Wiltshire. An Elizabethan and Georgian house belonging to Lord Methuen.

DIARY

13th August, 1947
Gloucester

We visit Nether Lypiatt,[1] but we miss the way, get lost in lanes and do not get there till 8 p.m. It is still light, and perhaps the place is actually improved by the soft twilight glow. The gardens, which were laid out by Lord Barrington, are very well designed, with vast quiet yews. I am entranced by the house, which is the only one which we have seen that I really covet. The music-room there seems to me the nicest room I have seen.

DIARY

14th August, 1947
Stratford-on-Avon

The harvest is in full swing in these wonderful Cotswold uplands, and a hot summer sun pours down upon troops of German prisoners slouching in twos and threes, but more often sullenly along the road alone. We have no right to use this slave labour and I feel ashamed.

We lunch at Chipping Campden. The inns and hotels in this hot weather stick to their prescribed menus and we have hot thick soup and stewed steak and kidneys. The soup tastes of cardboard with some pepper in it; the steak is uneatable; and then we have the inevitable apple and custard. Jim feels that all this proves that the English are lazy, lethargic, immensely stupid and in fact a detestable race.

We go on to Stratford-on-Avon and go straight to the theatre, where they are giving *The Merchant of Venice*. It is badly acted, badly produced and badly cast. But the audience is packed and they seem to love it. They even laugh at Gobbo. But the cast is really too bad for words. They have no standards, only a dramatic manner. It is really ghastly.

The remainder of the summer was spent mainly at Sissinghurst, with a week's visit in September to Switzerland in search of Benjamin Constant. It is a good example of Harold Nicolson's method of assembling material for a biography. The diary-entry for 10th November indicates how fully, but, to him, how unsatisfactorily, his time was now occupied—a quarter in politics, three-quarters outside, writing

[1] Near Stroud, Gloucestershire, the property of Mr. F. Nettlefold.

*at least ten thousand words a week, but all too few of them of any
lasting value.*

H.N. TO V.S-W.   *6th September, 1947*
                                              Hotel Richmond, Geneva

Yesterday I went to Lausanne, to visit existing, or now removed,
Constant sites. It is difficult to understand this sort of life towards
the end of the eighteenth century. Every member of the Constant
family seems to have possessed at least two country houses outside
the city as well as apartments both in Lausanne and Geneva. I
suppose there were vineyards attached. Some of them are nice little
villas with green shutters and dormer windows and terraces giving
on the lake. But it is difficult to recapture the *train de vie*. Were there
cooks in each of them, and butlers and *femmes de ménage*? Or did they
shut them up one at a time and transport the household? I don't
know. In each there is a fountain somewhere, or a spurt of cold clear
water from a pipe into a large stone trough. Each of these falls of
water has a different note, and speaks, now sturdy, now mincing,
in the voice that it spoke to Benjamin all those long years ago. But
they can tell me nothing about how many cooks they had or
gardeners.

V.S-W. TO H.N. (*in Geneva*)   *6th September, 1947*
                                                      Sissinghurst

I have decided what I shall write next. You will be horrified; you
won't see the point; you will say, 'Oh but that isn't your sort of
thing at all!' Nancy Astor will say, 'There, you see, Harold, what
did I tell you?'[1] But all the same, I see a good book in it, which will
give me scope to say a lot of things I want to say, related to the
present age and its troubles. Moreover there is no existent book (so
far as I can make out) on the subject, which is very odd indeed. And
as you know, I was repelled by the gross materialism of the age of
Louis XIV, though I could probably have made quite a readable
book out of La Grande Mademoiselle. Perhaps some day I shall do
her after all. But meanwhile I am going to write the Life of Cardinal
Newman.[2]

[1] Lady Astor thought that V.S-W. was about to become a Roman Catholic.
[2] She later abandoned this idea on hearing that Robert Sencourt was about to
publish a book on the same subject.

8th September, 1947
Geneva

I visit Coppet.[1] One walks down from the station past the wall of
the park. The wall is only five feet high, and in the middle it is
pierced by a grille. Just an ordinary iron railing it is, straight spikes
alternating with wobbly ones. I expect that it was through this
railing that Benjamin Constant and Charlotte[2] had their clandestine
interview.

From outside, the château is both elegant and imposing. Brown
tiles and woodwork of faded jade green. There is a fine forecourt
with a cobbled approach. We find the ladies of the house sitting in
the garden under an immense cedar. They are old Madame de
Marois, not so old Mlle Haussonville, and younger Madame
d'Andelot. They are typical *gratins* ['upper-crust society'], and speak
with the accents of the Rue de Varenne. The Swiss Minister to
Brussels arrives and we go in to tea. There is a fine stone staircase
to the first floor. A small anteroom, and then the big *salon*, with
tapestries and fine chairs dating from the time of Necker. Next to
it is the smaller room where we have tea. It is lined with de Staël
portraits, and the Gérard portrait of Madame de Staël. The Vigée-
Lebrun portrait is also there. But I knew all these. What interested
me more was a drawing of Madame de Staël at the age of 14. There
she sits very upright in her chair with her hands on her lap. Her hair
is done very elaborately and powdered. One can see the ugliness of
her mouth, the chubby cheeks, the pert and brilliant eyes.

We have an excellent tea with coffee cakes, and then Madame de
Marois conducts me downstairs. There is the library on the ground
floor where they used to act their plays. The refreshments were
handed in through the windows. Next to this huge room is what is
called Madame de Staël's bedroom, and beyond it what is called
Madame Récamier's[3] bedroom. The latter has a lovely Chinese

---

[1] Madame de Staël's house on the lake of Geneva. It was bought by her father,
Jacques Necker, in 1784, and it became her headquarters after her exile from
France in 1803. It was a centre of European cultural life, and Benjamin Constant,
also exiled by Napoleon for his political activities, was her constant companion.

[2] Charlotte de Hardenberg, whom Constant married secretly in 1808.

[3] Madame de Staël's closest woman friend, who was worshipped in vain by
Constant.

wall-paper; the former a heavy pompous bed. There is a show-case cluttered with Mme. de S.'s turbans and shawls. They are red silk and yellow silk and some cashmere. I forgot to say that the china at tea was blue china with an S and a baronial crown on it.

DIARY   *22nd September, 1947*
                                                              Sissinghurst

Bunny[1] comes to dinner. We discuss the economic situation arising out of the signature in Paris today of the document composed by the twenty-two nations in reply to the Marshall proposals.[2] I try to explain to them that the economic problem by which the world is faced is not communism versus capitalism but the machine versus man. In Russia the proportion between those who produce food and those who produce boots is a manageable proportion. In Great Britain it is wholly unmanageable. In the United States the propor-tion may become dangerous once there are factories that will produce more boots in a week than there are feet in America. It is no longer a problem of how much X can make by selling, but how many Ys and Zs there are to buy.

I do not believe that this problem can be solved except by world government. I do not believe that world government can be achieved except under the rule of a single Power. And I do not believe that such rule will be exercised except as the result of a final and devasting war between Russia and the United States. That is a nice thought to have to go to bed on. But although it may be the end of all things, there is no reason why one should cease to believe and hope in all things. I shall go on believing and hoping until I gutter out like a night-light.

At the United Nations today Vyshinsky compared Churchill to Hitler. Hector McNeil replied that in 1940 Winston would walk about under the bombs dropped by the Germans and perhaps served by Russian oil. Poor mankind—so much ingenuity and so little wisdom!

[1] Mrs Lindsay Drummond, a close friend and neighbour of the Nicolsons. Her mother-in-law, Mrs Laurence Drummond, had died on 9th September, and her husband, Lindsay Drummond, the publisher, inherited Sissinghurst Place.
[2] General Marshall had offered American economic aid to friendly countries on 5th June. The Paris conference presented an overall plan to the U.S.A.

V.S-W. TO H.N.   *24th September, 1947*
                                                           Sissinghurst

I've done my proofs of the little guide-book I wrote for the National
Trust on Knole.[1] They bit. I am always fascinated, as you are, by
the strange movements of the human heart. You see, I can write
quite coldly and unmovedly a guide-book about Knole, and can
also re-read it in proof, and then suddenly it will bite, like rodent
teeth closing on one's wrist, and I wake to the truth, 'This is *my*
Knole, which I love more than anything in the world except
Hadji', and then I can't bear to go on reading my own short little
bare guide-book about my Knole which has been given over to
someone else, not us.

Oh, Hadji, it's silly to mind, I know, but I do mind. I do mind. I
can't quite understand why I should care so dreadfully about Knole,
but I do. I can't get it out of my system. Why should stones and
rooms and shapes of courtyards matter so poignantly? I wish you
were here. I know you would understand. But nobody really feels
Knole as I do. Nobody really does.

H.N. TO V.S-W.   *25th September, 1947*
                                                 10 Neville Terrace, S.W.7

I think I really do understand about Knole. It is not merely a deep
love of certain rooms and courts and lights and shadows and smells.
It is not only a natural nostalgia for your own childhood. Nor is it
only the feeling that Knole symbolises for you a great personal
injustice.[2] It is the aching feeling that you alone really know and
understand, and that you alone are kept apart from it. I have always
felt that Knole was far more a person than a house. I do not think
that your sense of a personal identity is at all exaggerated or mystic.
I think it exists. I am sure that Knole 'knows' that you are different
from all other people. I mean, it is as if one had had only one deep
love in one's life and she had married someone else. And then the

[1] Knole had passed into the ownership of the National Trust earlier in the year.
[2] In the sense that although she was her father's only child, as a girl she could not
inherit Knole. She was very fond of her uncle Charles, who had succeeded her
father as Lord Sackville in 1928. She was not so fond of his American wife,
Anne, who did not really appreciate Knole. V.S-W. only once visited the house
between 1928 and Anne's death in 1961.

successful rival had not appreciated the woman, saying, 'Geraldine is so tiresome. She expects so much of one'. And you feel that nothing Geraldine could ever expect you to give could exceed your passion for giving her all she needs. Poor Mar![1] All this from a little brochure.

DIARY   *2nd October, 1947*

To the offices of *Time*. They had, as I had asked them, consulted Winston about my doing the introductory article to his book.[2] I had told them that I should not consent to do it unless Winston raised no objection. When my name was mentioned, he apparently went into a dirge about my having joined the Socialists. But he had no objection to me doing the article. 'Tell him', he said, 'that I shall sue him in every court for any libel.' So that is all right. I am to do 5–6,000 words by 1st December and they will pay me £400.

DIARY   *8th October, 1947*

I talk to Leo Amery.[3] He thinks there will be a conflict between Cripps[4] and Dalton. The former will wish to tell the public the harsh truth; the latter will wish to soap them over with half-lies. It is extraordinary how much respect Cripps arouses. He is really the leading figure in the country today.

DIARY   *29th October, 1947*

Dine with Enid Jones.[5] Sit next to Violet Bonham Carter. She abuses the Government for abandoning all moral principle. Until now she had believed that the Liberal Party were closer to the Socialists than to any other party. Now she doubts it. The Government not only lack ability and courage but also integrity. Take their retention of the German prisoners—slave labour. Take their refusal to allow in foreign workers — blind cowardice. No, she feels

---

[1] Her mother's name for V.S-W., which H.N. adopted early in their married life.
[2] In *Life* magazine, where Churchill's war-history was to be serialised.
[3] The former Secretary of State for the Dominions etc. He was then aged 73.
[4] Sir Stafford Cripps was then Minister of Economic Affairs, and succeeded Hugh Dalton as Chancellor of the Exchequer on 13th November, 1947.
[5] Enid Bagnold, the novelist and playwright, wife of Sir Roderick Jones, Chairman of Reuters.

closer to the left-wing Tories today. All of which suggests that the Liberal Party are about to create a common anti-communist front.

We talk about Winston, of whom she has been seeing much, since they are on the United Europe Committee together. She says that he is enormously influenced by words. A thing pungently expressed seems to him truer than wisdom dully produced. I think that this is true.

Afterwards we discuss with Desmond MacCarthy the question of day-dreams. We agree that we all have day-dreams, and usually dreams representing our own power and success wishes. Desmond says that the Victorians would suppress day-dreams in themselves and would never have admitted them to others. This rigidity of standards, this synthesis, did on the whole, he thinks, make for greater human happiness.

V.S-W. TO H.N.   *30th October, 1947*
                                                        Sissinghurst

Do you remember that we were saying about Shakespeare, how wise he was, even in little-known passages? I fell on this:

> '*O! it is excellent*
> *To have a giant's strength, but it is tyrannous*
> *To use it like a giant.*'[1]

Russia?

DIARY   *2nd November, 1947*

The Conservatives have gained 643 seats in the municipal elections and the Labour people lose 695. This is a real swing to the right. Very strange indeed. It is due partly, I think, to discomforts and lack of confidence, but also to the growing dislike of Russia and the extreme left. In Leicester the Tories have gained six seats. In West Leicester the vote has swung so much to the right that Niggs will win the seat if this holds. I am curiously divided. Partly I am pleased for Niggs' sake; partly I am pleased because it will snub the extremists in my own party; and partly I am pleased because it shows the strength of the middle bloc in this country. But I ought not, I suppose, to have been pleased at all if I were a real Socialist and a

[1] *Measure for Measure*, II ii 107.

true party man. I am an intellectual Socialist and in no sense extreme. The Liberals are the people I ought to have joined.

Shirley [Morgan] is staying here.[1] She is very sweet and nice, and both Vita and I like her enormously.

DIARY   9th November, 1947

Read Arthur Bryant on Pepys.[2] It is odd how the English love a man who is not a humbug like themselves. To my mind Pepys was a mean little man. Salacious in a grubby way; even in his peculations there was no magnificence. But he did stick in his office during the Plague, which was more than most men did. It is some relief to reflect that to be a good diarist one must have a little snouty sneaky mind.

DIARY   10th November, 1947

After dinner we listen to a broadcast of Attlee's speech at the Mansion House. It is very thin and frail. Attlee is a charming and intelligent man, but as a public speaker he is, compared to Winston, like a village fiddler after Paganini. It is all rather sad. I return to my room with the sense that we have become so much smaller. The old sweep and adventure have gone, and our old pipes are now of scrannel straw.

I discussed with Vita today the problem of my allocation of time. Now that I have dropped out of public life, I do nothing of any real importance. I do my 'Marginal Comment' once a week; my *Daily Telegraph* reviews once a week; my *Figaro* once every other week; and my many broadcasts. I also, when in London, have a succession of Boards and Committees.[3] I find that I seem to have less time for my own work than when I was a Member of Parliament. It is not lack of application on my part nor lack of orderly arrangement. It is just that these small diverse occupations interfere with my time-table. I should not engage in them, of course, were it not that they

[1] It was only possible for a rare visitor to stay at Sissinghurst if Ben slept on the sofa downstairs, and the visitor took his bedroom.
[2] Sir Arthur Bryant wrote three books on Pepys: *The Man in the Making* (1933), *The Years of Peril* (1935) and *The Saviour of the Navy* (1938).
[3] Among them were the National Trust, the National Portrait Gallery, the London Library, War Memorials and the Royal Literary Fund.

are my means of living. I get £15 a week from the *Spectator* and £20 a week from the *Daily Telegraph*. This enables me to be self-supporting.[1] But when Viti says that I am 'cheapening myself' by all these tittle-bat or stickleback activities, I feel she is right. But I have dropped out of the main stream, and all I can do is to paddle in the backwaters. I have not the strength of will, the *os*, to pull or push myself back into the stream. I knew at one moment the tide in the affairs of men, but I did not take it at the flow—I took it at the ebb. This does not mean bitterness or disappointment or even self-reproach. God knows that I am interested and happy enough. It just means a small degree of perplexity why I should not be wanted, and why, not being wanted, I have so little time for Benjamin Constant. Why, being so hard-working, have I so little free time? Well, well, 'It sinks, and I am ready to depart'.[2] No! Hell! It is *not* sinking, and I am not in the very least ready to depart—not for one moment. But I know that I am dropping out.

DIARY   *11th November, 1947*

I lecture to the Royal College of Physicians on 'The Health of Authors'. Lord Moran[3] takes the chair. I ask him how Winston is. He says that he is not well at all, and that it was madness for him with such a bad cold to go down to the House today. 'Nothing will persuade him to take care of his health. I told him that in his present condition he would make the worst speech of his life.' That evening I see a chap from the Commons who tells me that Winston has made one of the most brilliant and powerful speeches he has ever made. It was about the House of Lords. What vitality that blessed man has got!

---

[1] But V.S-W. had a considerable fortune of her own, and H.N. had no financial responsibility at all for Sissinghurst.
[2] '*I warmed both hands before the fire of life;*
    It sinks, and I am ready to depart.'
                                        Walter Savage Landor.
[3] President of the Royal College of Physicians, and Winston Churchill's doctor.

H.N. TO V.S-W.   *25th November, 1947*
                                               10 Neville Terrace, S.W.7

I had Nigel Clive[1] to dinner. He is such a clever and attractive man.
He loves the Greeks with that affectionate passion which all resident
Englishmen acquire. But he is pessimistic about it all. God how I
loathe these communists! My hatred for Mussolini was just a passing
dislike, my fear of Hitler but a momentary apprehension, compared
to my deep and burning detestation of the Marxists.

DIARY   *3rd December, 1947*

We got to a party at Buckingham Palace for the Foreign Ministers
Conference. As we enter the picture gallery, the delegations are
grouped on the right and the non-delegations on the left. Tommy
[Sir Alan] Lascelles comes up and says that Attlee wants to be introduced to Vita. I perform that ceremony. He is as gay and agreeable
as ever. We then file into the Blue Room where the King and Queen
and Queen Mary receive us. The King is in a good temper and grins
in a friendly way. We then pass on into the White Drawing Room
where there is a buffet. We lean against the buffet, have champagne
cocktails and watch Molotov talking to the Queen. Winston appears
in an old frock-coat which must have belonged to his father. His
eyes have taken on an empty stare with a glaze such as only occurs
in the eyes of much older people. He has long talks with [Georges]
Bidault and Molotov. I ask him whether he wants to see in advance
my article about him for *Life*. He says, 'No, do not bother. You are
always very kind to me.'

I have a talk with Bidault. He had just flown over from Paris. He
says the crisis is over; the communists have done themselves in; the
sabotage yesterday of a train near Arras has turned opinion, even
working-class opinion, against them. '*Ce monsieur là*', he says,
indicating Molotov, '*n'est pas intelligent. C'est un rond-de-cuir.*'[2]

The King and Queen then bow and leave us. I am taken under the
arm by Bevin and dragged to a seat. He is tired, having had to stand
up for two long hours. He has a drink. He tells me that yesterday he
had had a real heart-to-heart talk with Molotov in his (Bevin's) flat.

[1] He was Second Secretary in the British Embassy at Athens and was about to be
transferred to Jerusalem.
[2] 'A quill-driver', 'a bureaucrat'.

He spoke as follows: 'Now, Mr Molotov, what is it that you want? What are you after? Do you want to get Austria behind your Iron Curtain? You can't do that. Do you want Turkey and the Straits? You can't have them. Do you want Korea? You can't have that. You are putting your neck out too far, and one day you will have it chopped off. We know much more about you than you imagine. We know that you cannot stand a war. But you are behaving in such a way that one day there will be a showdown. And you will have to give way in the end and lose your credit with your own people. You cannot look on me as an enemy of Russia. Why, when our Government was trying to stamp out your Revolution, who was it that stopped it? It was I, Ernest Bevin. I called out the transport workers and they refused to load the ships. I wanted you to have your Revolution in your own way and without interference. Now again I am speaking as a friend. You are playing a very dangerous game. And I can't make out why. You don't really believe that any American wants to go to war with you—or, at least, no responsible American. We most certainly do not want to. But you are playing with fire, Mr Molotov, and one day you will be badly burnt. And I don't see the object of it all. If war comes between you and America in the East, then we may be able to remain neutral. But if war comes between you and America in the West, then we shall be on America's side. Make no mistake about that. That would be the end of Russia and of your Revolution. So please stop sticking out your neck in this way and tell me what you are after. What do you want?'

'I want a unified Germany', said Molotov.

'Why do you want that? Do you really believe that a unified Germany would go communist? They might pretend to. They would say all the right things and repeat all the correct formulas. But in their hearts they would be longing for the day when they could revenge their defeat at Stalingrad. You know that as well as I do.'

'Yes', said Molotov, 'I know that. But I want a unified Germany.' And that is all that he could get out of him.

DIARY   *4th December, 1947*

I read Evelyn Waugh's new novel [*The Loved One*], which is very bad indeed. Ben tells me that Jasper Ridley[1] wants me to become Master of Balliol. That would be an odd end to my varied life.

DIARY   *5th December, 1947*

Viti shows me a letter from the Prime Minister, saying that she has got the C.H.[2] I am overjoyed, but she takes it quite calmly. She says that it is my Civil Service mind which attaches importance to these things. But somewhere inside herself she is pleased, I think.

DIARY   *9th December, 1947*

Williams[3] rings me up from Transport House and asks whether I would take on the bye-election at North Croydon. I say I must have time to think it over.

This was an important development. Harold Nicolson and North Croydon approached each other with acute misgivings, but he was accepted by the local Labour Executive as their candidate. The bye-election was caused by the retirement of Henry Willink, Minister of Health, 1943-45. He had been the Conservative Member since 1940, and now left politics to become Master of Magdalene College, Cambridge. His majority in the 1945 Election had been 607 over the Labour candidate.

DIARY   *11th December, 1947*

I am really perplexed to know what to do about this North Croydon business. I gathered from Frank Pakenham[4] the other day that 'all difficulties' (which means Lord Addison's dislike of intellectuals) had been surmounted. He had expected my name to be on the list of those to be given a peerage in the New Year's Honours. Mr Hend-

[1] Chairman of Coutts Bank and Chairman of the Trustees of the Tate Gallery.
[2] The Companion of Honour. H.N. later learnt that Clement Attlee himself had proposed her name to the King. The Prime Minister was a great admirer of *The Land*.
[3] A. L. Williams, then Assistant National Agent of the Labour Party.
[4] Lord Pakenham (later Earl of Longford), then Chancellor of the Duchy of Lancaster.

ricks, Elvira [Niggeman's] friend at the House of Lords, who is
secretary to Addison, was also of the same opinion. He said to her,
'Well, we shall be seeing you here again soon.' She asked why.
'Well, your boss, you know. . . .' Evidently I have been taken off
the list at the last moment. Why? Is it because of Viti's C.H.? Or is
it because Transport House said that I was the chap to fight Croydon
for them?

My perplexity takes two forms. One is practical. If I refuse to
fight this seat, then they will feel that I am not a good member of
the party and I shall not be rewarded. If I fight the seat and lose
honourably, then all will be well. If I fight and win (which seems
impossible), then it will be a tremendous triumph. But If I fight and
lose badly—say drop 20,000 of the former Labour vote—then I
shall have missed both the lower and the upper House. But the main
perplexity is a moral one. If I refuse to do what they ask, I shall make
it clear to my own conscience that I joined the Labour Party in
order to get a peerage; and this will cause me such remorse that if
offered a peerage I shall decline to accept it. I absolutely loathe
fighting a bye-election in circumstances of great publicity. I may
make a muck of the whole thing. But the horror with which
the prospect fills me is in itself an indication that I should undertake this horrible task. I am worried also by its effect on Nigel's
prospects. I have not been able to consult him, as he has been in
Leicester.

I consult *sortes Biblicas*. My Bible opens at Ezekiel XL 22:
'And their windows, and their arches, and their palm-trees, were
after the measure of the gate that looketh towards the east; and
they went up unto it by seven steps; and the arches thereof were
before them.'
Evidently this message was intended to convey that I should be able
to fight Russia better from the Labour Party. But the bit I dislike is
the bit about 'seven steps'. Does that mean seven bye-elections? By
that time I would be 92.

(*Later*) I see Williams at Transport House. He begins by saying that
the party has a great favour to ask of me. 'You can help us in a way
that no other man can help us.' They do not expect to win the seat,
but they fear that it may show a terrible drop in figures since the '45
Election. I say that I will consent to meet the local Committee on

Thursday. I practically commit myself to fighting the seat if the local Committee adopts me.

I tell Niggs about it. He says, 'You are absolutely right to accept. Right morally, and right from the practical point of view.'

DIARY   *12th December, 1947*

National Trust all day. In the interval I lunch with Sibyl [Colefax]. The French Ambassador and his wife, James [Pope-Hennessy], Noel Coward and Sacheverell Sitwell. I sit next to Madame Massigli. She says that our habit of staying behind after dinner when the ladies go upstairs is quite intolerable. The other day, when Winston was dining, the men did not come upstairs until a quarter to one. But the Ambassador likes the system. He says it is the only way to get Englishmen to talk.

DIARY   *14th December, 1947*

Lord Baldwin has died. Poor old Baldwin. He was a man of little imagination and less vision, but he certainly had a gift for dealing with awkward situations. Generally his method was to evade them. But when he was forced to tackle them, as at the Abdication crisis, he did it very well. He was an agreeable, companionable man. He was really more simple than he seemed. Or rather his simplicity appeared so naïve that many thought it was put on for effect. I did not think so. He enjoyed life and had certain excellent principles.

DIARY   *17th December, 1947*

In the evening I go down to Croydon. On the platform at Victoria I meet Williams of Transport House and Frank Shepherd, their Southern Regional Organiser. They are evidently old cronies, but they have to be polite to me. The contrast between the ease and intimacy of their own relations and their joint uneasiness with me increases the sense of unreality. I feel like a cow being led garlanded to the altar, and they probably regard me as a very doubtful old horse.

We go to Cypress Road, South Norwood Hill. It is a small villa belonging to the Secretary of the local Labour Party, Mr Nicols. The Chairman arrives. A silent man. Others drop in and sit stiffly on chairs round the room. Then a blind woman led by a dog enters.

The dog crouches under her chair and whimpers slightly. When ten people have come in, the meeting starts. Williams explains briskly that a bye-election is not like a General Election. In the latter event local organisations can choose their own candidates. In bye-elections Transport House has a right to recommend. He does it quite tactfully, but a woman objects. She says they were promised that they would be given a list of candidates, and that they could choose the one they wanted. Now there is only one candidate. The Chairman ignores this interruption and calls on me to speak.

I make a short statement outlining all my disadvantages—Tom Mosley, National Labour, Churchill, my Election Address of 1945,[1] my inability to be violent or denunciatory, my belonging to the upper class, Vita, Nigel. I have the impression that they regard these things as very grave disadvantages, but are too frightened to say so. But there is one young man who has the courage to speak up. He says I am not the type they want. I am too right-wing. Would I swallow the whole of the Socialist programme? Would I agree to the nationalisation of land? I say that I would in such matters do what Cripps and Attlee decided on. If they felt it was wise to go as far as that, I should accept their decision. But I would not take an independent line and urge it against them or upon them. A vote is then taken. The woman who was angry with the Chairman, and the young man, vote against me. The others vote in favour. Result: 8 to 2. We then break up and walk back to the station.

I have a feeling that Williams and Shepherd feel it did not go too well. The differences between me and them were all too apparent. The similarities between us were not very wide or deep or strong. We come back by train. They get out at London Bridge. I say goodnight to them with forced geniality. I do not feel that I have been a comrade.

[1] See p. 94, note 1.

1948

The North Croydon bye-election – advice from Herbert Morrison – V.S-W. in North Africa – horrors of electioneering – defeated by 12,000 – 'Marginal Comment' on the election – a neighbour's house burnt down – H.N. invited to write the official biography of King George V – the advantages and disadvantages of acceptance – he accepts – Bevin's lack of social graces – 'Benjamin Constant' finished – murder of Count Bernadotte – H.N. visits Berlin during the blockade – Sir Brian Robertson and General Clay – a visit to Dublin – President Truman re-elected – the problem of the atomic bomb – planning 'King George V' – 'I have been a failure'

The bye-election campaign in North Croydon opened on 23rd February and Polling Day was on 11th March. There were three candidates: Harold Nicolson representing Labour; F. W. Harris, a local business man, the Conservatives; and for the Liberals, Air Vice-Marshal Donald Bennett, who had won great fame during the war as 'Pathfinder Bennett', commanding the Pathfinder Force of Bomber Command. The election aroused very wide public interest. In 1931 and 1935 the Conservative majorities had been huge. But in 1945 the result had been: Conservative 23,417, Labour 22,810, Liberal 10,714. Labour had a chance to overturn this slender majority of 607 and prove that the decline in their national popularity had been arrested; the Conservatives were equally determined to retain the seat. Bennett was the dark-horse: as a war-hero he might capture a large floating vote from both the other parties. Since the bye-election was of such importance, and Croydon so accessible from central London, scores of M.P.s came down to support their candidates, including Winston Churchill himself and several members of the Labour Government.

At the start of the campaign Harold Nicolson was miserable. He was living in acute discomfort in a local hotel and politically felt himself to be in a false position. Later his spirits rose, owing to the excitement of the battle and his discovery that he had no need to act out of character. His health and good temper stood the strain well. He made virtues of his disadvantages. He refused to attack his former Conservative friends, even when they spoke in Croydon against him, and played down purely party animosities. Typical of his manner was his reply to a heckler: 'No, I do not think that it is quite fair to say that the British businessman has trampled on the faces of the poor. But he has sometimes not been very careful where he put his feet.' He felt that he would not win, and in his heart he had no particular desire to win. To him it was a matter of putting up a sufficiently good perform-ance to satisfy himself and to earn him a seat in the House of Lords. His luke-warm attitude did not pass unnoticed by his supporters.

123

The problem of V. Sackville-West's non-appearance at his side was happily solved by the chance that she had long before accepted an invitation to lecture for the British Council in Morocco, Algeria and Tunisia. She was away throughout the election, from 14th February to 20th March, and the letters which he wrote to her also served (in carbon copies) as his diary. But his family was involved in other ways. In an unguarded moment he told a reporter that his mother, Lady Carnock, looked upon her son's candidature as 'a betrayal of the nation'; and I was obliged to dissociate myself from his politics by a public statement in Leicester. Mutual sympathy flowed by letter between us, but I could not visit him without prejudicing his chances as well as my own. Instead, we sent comforts to Croydon. 'It is like having a father on Devil's Island', I wrote to my mother in Casablanca: 'one does what one can through the Red Cross.'

DIARY   *7th January, 1948*

I gather that my name was on the list of peerages in the New Year honours. They then discovered that Vita's name was also on,[1] and they therefore took me off. I am glad in a way, as I should have felt remorse and conscience if I had got it without an effort. Now that I have the Croydon crucifixion to go through, I shall feel in the end that I have done something to deserve it. But if Viti finds out she will be enraged.

DIARY   *15th January, 1948*

I go to see Herbert Morrison [Deputy Prime Minister] at 11 Downing Street. He advises me not to stand on the defensive, but to compare what happened after the last war with what is happening now. Demobilisation, employment, prices, etc. He really is rather helpful and gives me many ideas. He is genial in every way. 'Well, Harold, if you win this seat, you will be given the V.C.'

---

[1] She received the C.H. from King George VI on 12th February. 'He had asked her about Knole. She said that it had gone to the National Trust. He raised his hands in despair. "Everything is going nowadays. Before long, I shall also have to go." '

30th January, 1948
Paris

I go round to the British Embassy. I wanted to talk to Oliver Harvey alone. But I find that he is giving a cocktail party for half his staff. I gatecrash and they are delighted to see me. I meet young Millard,[1] who used to be one of Anthony Eden's secretaries. A nice young man. He says to me, 'Well, you have now got an election on your shoulders.' I answer, 'Not yet, as far as I can see. Willink will probably not resign till March.' 'But haven't you seen—in the papers this morning—he *has* resigned, and Harris is the Conservative candidate.' How odd to hear of this decisive event in my life in Paris with all the typists around! But Millard is a clever man, and I am glad to have had the first news from him. That means, thank God, that my election will take place while Viti is away.

H.N. TO V.S-W. (*in Marrakesh, Morocco*)   *24th February, 1948*
Upper Norwood,
Croydon

You are lecturing tonight in Marrakesh and I am starting my campaign with an address to the Croydon Chamber of Commerce. You will be surrounded by mimosa and the smell of garlic, and I am surrounded by snow roofs and cold pavements.

Soon after I arrived, I went round to my Committee Rooms in Thornton Heath. It is a disused and requisitioned building. Most of the windows have holes in them, the doors won't shut, and it is very cold and draughty. I have to sit in my greatcoat all day with a muffler. Great icicles drip from my window-ledge. Huge posters of myself decorate the walls. No, I do not like it one little bit. The staff are charming and gay and efficient, and that makes a great difference. But the hours are ungainly. I mean, I don't know when I am supposed to get my meals. There is a tiny little restaurant near here where one can get fish and chips and coffee. But somehow that is not a diet to which I am accustomed.

I first met my opponents at the joint meeting at the Chamber of Commerce. Harris is stout, naïve, young—rather attractive, I thought. Bennett is young-looking, smart, determined, speaks with a faint Australian accent, very composed.

[1] Guy Millard, who served in the British Embassy in Paris from 1945 to 1949.

H.N. TO V.S-W. (*in Casablanca*)   *25th February, 1948*
Upper Norwood,
Croydon

I am feeling cold and lonely. There was a slight thaw yesterday, but the cold has returned. My bedroom is under the leads and the leads are under snow. My bedroom is therefore icy and they have no other. One gets back here at 10.30 after a series of meetings and I can get nothing to eat. So I sit hungry in front of the gas-fire. It has got a ring beside it, which when lit has a small coronal of blue flame. So I have bought a kettle and a tin of Ovaltine and give myself a mugful in my silver po. I have asked Mrs Staples [the cook at Sissinghurst] to send me a cake.

Yesterday I had a horrible day. I had to go round with the *Daily Herald* photographer for feature pictures. They are bringing out a special number for this election, and it is to contain pictures of me doing things. Well, the first thing they wanted me to do was to visit an old Trades Unionist of some 89 years of age. We drove up to his horrid little house. The old man was very ill in bed. He insisted upon getting up. He sat on the bed while the photographer dressed him. He panted terribly and I thought he was going to die. Then we sat him down in the armchair and I posed beside him. Suddenly he remembered that he had not brushed his hair and up he struggled again and poured a little oil into a tin and then dabbed a brush in it. Thereafter the photograph was taken.

Then I was taken into a grocer's shop. A woman customer was dragged in to give more life to the group. I told her who I was. 'Oh yes, I have often listened to you on the wireless. I should have voted for you had it not been for the Air Vice-Marshal. Such a raw deal that man has had—and a hero too.' So you see, I was right. Bennett will take from the floating vote. I may even get in. Off I went again to a housing estate. The photographer in the excitement of the chase made me climb up a ladder of an unfinished house and interview the workmen doing the roof. I had to make explanatory gestures to them. Not my sort of thing at all, and how wet one got walking across the *pays dévasté*.[1]

---

[1] These two photographs are reproduced facing p. 128.

H.N. TO V.S-W. (*in Fez, Morocco*)   *26th February, 1948*
Croydon

After a meeting last night, a man entered into conversation with me. 'By the way', he said, 'do your family object to you standing Labour?' 'Well, my mother said I had betrayed my country.' He was a Press Association man, and all the papers this morning have been ringing Mummy up. Oh my God!

H.N. TO N.N. (*in Leicester*)   *27th February, 1948*
Croydon

I am sorry to cancel your visit. But it is very thin-ice about my not being a good Socialist and having connections in the other camp. The lamentable reference, in a private conversation, to my poor old mother, has led to exploitation by the Tory Press—to throw doubt on the foreground of a man who has such a background. Your presence here, after people know about you, would only lead to further insinuations. They (the Tory Press) are hot on the scent. I have no *lebensraum* of authenticity to spare; and therefore my people here think it wiser if you did not come. In an odd way I derive some solace from your not coming down, because I am getting used to my loneliness, and it would revive it all if you appeared. Like going on an exeat when one is unhappy at school. I count the days till it will be over. I really do not think I have a chance. The tory vote is pretty solid and the floating vote (on which I had relied) will float to Pathfinder Bennett. Bless you, my dear Niggs, and do not waste too much sympathy on me. It is very good for one to have to lead this sort of life. It enhances the pleasures of privacy and the delights of ease.

The report of your Leicester speech was much liked by my people.[1]

N.N. TO H.N.   *28th February, 1948*
10 Neville Terrace, S.W.7

Leicester were in a fine state of excitement. They said how terrible it must be for me. 'Terrible?' I replied. 'Not at all. For the first time

[1] I had said: 'My father and I are no nearer to quarrelling than if we disagreed with each other about vivisection or in our taste for Turkish or Virginian cigarettes.' This was not liked in Leicester.

in my life I can enter a hall unaccompanied by my father's shadow, and it had woken people up to the idea that politics is more than just cups of tea and platitudinous speeches.' On the other hand, there are a lot of people who think that I am 'likely to go the same way'. But really I emerge as a better, because more independent, candidate than before. So don't think you have embarrassed me.

I shall probably not be going away next weekend, so if you feel that we could meet in a wood on Norwood Common or in the lavatories of Croydon Public Baths without attracting public attention, let me know and I will come flying down.

God, how I hope you get in. If anyone asks me, I shall say that I would be both pleased and sorry whichever candidate is successful. But to you I can say that there is absolutely no conflict of loyalties in my mind: I want you, unreservedly, unashamedly, to bring off this triumph.

H.N. TO V.S-W. (*in Fez, Morocco*)　　　　*29th February, 1948*
Croydon

I actually enjoy canvassing, and it does good. That is one of the advantages of being Labour. I have no hesitation about penetrating into working-class homes, and they are so grateful and loyal. It really moves me. I am so glad I belong to the Party now. I really feel much more comfortable as a Labour man than I ever did as a hybrid. There is a quality of mutual confidence which is moving and rare. It was a lovely warm day at last, and the whole thing seemed brighter and happier.

I was to have had a meeting at 7 but they came in at 6 to say that everyone had gone to a football match and the meeting was cancelled. I was overjoyed. But then the idea of coming back to this incredibly grim hotel filled me with despair. I suddenly realised that it would be quite simple to go and dine in London. So I took the train and went to the Travellers. There I had a stroke of luck. Roger Senhouse[1] was giving a dinner party and asked me to join them. It consisted of Leigh Ashton[2] and Bob Boothby.[3] We were very gay.

[1] The publisher and translator.
[2] Director of the Victoria and Albert Museum since 1945.
[3] (Sir) Robert Boothby had been Conservative M.P. for East Aberdeenshire since 1924.

Canvassing in North Croydon, February 1948 (see page 126)

V. Sackville-West in the library at Sissinghurst, 1949

Bob was most amusing and I laughed till my sides ached. How good for me! Leigh Ashton, when I described my hotel life and the publicity, said, 'But, my dear Harold, why on earth did you let yourself in for such a thing?' 'Well', I said, 'the chain of circumstance.' 'Chain of circumstance be damned', said Bob; 'change of life, you mean.'

H.N. TO V.S-W. (*in Algiers*)   *2nd March, 1948*
                                                                  Croydon

The B.B.C. wanted me to do a feature on the election for the Overseas Service. So their van accompanied me while I went canvassing. We had to make sure at the first house that the occupant was in. She was not very bright and did not understand what it was all about. But I was firm with her. I pushed her inside again and told her to open the front-door when I knocked. Then the B.B.C. man advanced with the microphone and telephoned to his colleague in the van. 'We shall start recording in ten seconds from . . . NOW.' On the tenth second I knocked on the door. He put the mike quite close to my knock so that it would be heard. Mrs Briggs opened the door, giggling sheepishly. I assumed a voice of delighted surprise: 'Mrs Briggs, I believe? I am Harold Nicolson, Labour candidate for this division. Now, Mrs Briggs, I want you to tell me all your troubles.' 'No', said Mrs Briggs, still giggling. 'No, I won't vote Labour, I won't. Me 'usband's a builder, 'e is.' (How terrible, I thought, that all this will reach the listening millions in Australia, the United States, the Union of South Africa and Singapore.) 'Now, surely, Mrs Briggs . . .', and I began to expound the benefits which had accrued to her from a Labour Government. To my surprise, she was quite genuinely shaken. 'Yes, I admit that, Mr Nicholls, I do truly.' In the end she said, 'Well, if you wish it, I will vote Labour, and get my man to do the same.' Now nobody, not even the B.B.C. young man, will believe that this was not a put-up job. But it wasn't. It was a marvellous recording. The B.B.C. man was delighted. 'What it is', he said, 'to have a practised broadcaster!'

This evening I have had four meetings. One of them was a huge meeting addressed by Dick Crossman [Labour M.P. for Coventry East since 1945]. He really is a wonderful speaker and must have got me votes.

H.N.D.   129   I.

Only eight more days of campaigning and one of polling. Then freedom.

H.N. TO V.S-W. (*in Tunis*)   *4th March, 1948*
                                              Croydon

Herbert Morrison telephoned and asked me to lunch with him in London. He gave me an excellent luncheon, the first really square meal I have had for weeks. We were alone. He quite sees that I have a poor chance and does not expect a victory. But he thinks that any other candidate would have lost many thousand Labour votes. He says that I am so right not to pretend not to be an aristocrat. 'Men of your class who join the movement make fools of themselves by trying to put on proletarian airs. We do not like it. What I like about you is that you never pretend to be anything but yourself. And if you will allow me to say so, Harold, a very good self it is.'

You know, this election will have done me a lot of good. It has given me self-confidence as a platform speaker and a queller of hecklers. It has improved my health, as it has forced me to give up smoking cigarettes. And, above all, it has brought me into intimate relations with the Labour movement, and made me feel at ease with them. That sense of wearing a new stiff jacket has quite gone. It is now as comfortable as an old tweed coat. They are such nice, decent people, they really are. It is a joy for me to be on their side.

I had two meetings this evening in the very heart of the Tory suburbs. They heckled me frightfully. But in the end I quietened them and the meeting ended in the highest good humour. I had a stroke of luck at the second meeting. A woman handed up a note to me on the platform: 'I have just left the Gallacher[1] meeting where Mr G. is recommending the communists to support you, for though (he says) you are a "sap", the workers will be able to use the Labour Party for the "progressive elements" of Asia.' I read this out and then made a passionate denunciation of communism. 'I do not want their beastly votes. I want British votes, not Russian votes.' The Tories were so moved by this that they burst into applause.

---

[1] William Gallacher, the communist M.P. for West Fife since 1935, and the only communist in the House of Commons.

H.N. TO V.S-W. *(in Tunis)*   *5th March, 1948*
Croydon

How often must you be asking yourself, 'I wonder what Hadji really wants?' Now, that is an interesting question, as I say to hecklers. I can analyse my feelings fairly clearly if I divide them into immediate and ultimate. Momentarily, I long to win this election. It would be a tremendous triumph; it would be a delight to my staff, whom I really love; it would give great encouragement to Socialism everywhere; it would be a smack for the Tories; and it would be a supreme justification of all the work and worry and self-denial I have put in here. But ultimately, I do not think I should enjoy the present House of Commons anything like as much as I enjoyed the last one. I should be kept too busy to do my books. I should cease to have any private life at all. And I should in the end be happier to get my peerage and have the ideal mixture between public and private life. Now *you* realise that in all this there does not enter at all the desire for fame or power. I have no urge for either. But I know that I have done well here, and that I have shown vigour and decency combined. I should like that to be proved and demonstrated by winning. But if it is not, then I shall feel quite happy only a few hours after my defeat.

This evening I had Hector McNeil to speak for me. He was splendid. He had dug out the speech I made in Manchester at the time of Munich.[1] It made a great effect. 'No man's record', shouted Hector, 'is as impeccable as that of the candidate whom you will have the honour to elect.' Great applause. I spoke after him. It was the best meeting we have had, beginning with wild Tory heckling and ending in calm and good temper all round. What is amusing is that some of my friends turn up suddenly. Guy Burgess came down as Hector's secretary.

H.N. TO V.S-W. *(in Tunis)*   *9th March, 1948*
Croydon

Even at this late stage, we do not know what the result is likely to be. I would like to lose by a very narrow majority. But I fear this is impossible. What I hope you will understand, darling, is that I

[1] See vol. 1 of these Diaries, pp. 373-4.

shall be so delighted to get the whole ordeal over that I shall not really mind what happens.

V.S-W. TO H.N. (*telegram*)   *10th March, 1948*
Tunis

Je pense à toi

H.N. TO V.S-W. (*telegram to Tunis*)   *12th March, 1948*
Croydon

Beaten by twelve thousand. Oh my. Hadji

V.S-W. TO H.N. (*telegram*)   *12th March, 1948*
Tunis

Heard wireless. You did very well. Am not disappointed. Hope you are not either. Much love

H.N. TO V.S-W. (*in Tunis*)   *12th March, 1948*
10 Neville Terrace, S.W.7

Yesterday was a heavenly day from dawn to dusk. Everybody turned out. It was an enormous poll. I spent the day going from committee room to committee room and polling station to polling station. Then at 7 I went up to London and dined with Ben and Niggs. I got back to the Town Hall at 10.30. The count had begun at 9. It was clear from the very start that Harris had a large majority. It was painful to stand there watching those bloody pencilled crosses always against the same name. As the night wore on (it was like Monte Carlo and rather amusing), Harris suddenly forged ahead. My worry, and Alan Herbert's [H.N.'s election agent] worry, was that I should have dropped the Labour vote below the 1945 figure. Then at the eleventh hour an urn was opened which was all for me. My vote jumped up suddenly. I had not merely kept the Labour vote solid, but increased it by 2,000.[1] Herbert and I shook hands silently and in relief.

[1] The result was:

Harris (Conservative)	36,200
Nicolson (Labour)	24,536
Bennett (Liberal)	6,321
Conservative majority	11,664

Winston Churchill telegraphed to Frederic Harris (who still, in 1968, remains

132

It was by then almost finished, and as I glanced back on the hall, the tellers, who until then had been so active and busy, were resting idle like croupiers when the game is over. The Mayor then climbed on the dais and announced the result. Then the photographers rushed in and we were made to clasp hands in a most shaming manner. Then, after speeches on the balcony, back to my hotel and that little odd room which had become so intimate to me and which I shall never see again.

No, my dearest, I do not mind. I did well on the whole, as you said in your telegram, bless you. And I should not like to represent Croydon, which is a bloody place. Nor should I like to be in the present House. All has turned out for the best, and what is more, it is OVER, and without disgrace.

V.S-W. TO H.N.   *12th March, 1948*
                                                       Tunis

Well, I wonder what you feel about it. Personally I know what I feel. I am *delighted* you got so many votes, and I know you will feel that you have done well, but I am frankly relieved (taking the long view) that you can now go to the Other Place with an absolutely free conscience. My only worry is that they will let you down over this.

I went round to the Consulate and heard the result at 9 a.m. on the Overseas Service. They gave all details and ended up by saying, 'Two of the candidates are well-known', which was a nasty one for Harris. Do you know, it was so odd—when I walked back from the Consulate, I found I was shaking all over!

'Marginal Comment' (Spectator)[1]   *19th March, 1948*
After three weeks of a bye-election it is agreeable to return to the

---

the Member for the Division): 'You have achieved a momentous victory.' His majority was over 11,000 more than Willink's in 1945, but H.N. had increased the Labour vote from 22,810 to 24,536. The real loser was Air Vice-Marshal Bennett, who dropped 4,000 Liberal votes and forfeited his deposit.

[1] This article is here reprinted (by permission of the Editor of the *Spectator*) for two reasons. First to give an example of H.N.'s journalistic style under stress; and, secondly, because it lost him any remaining chance of a Labour peerage. It infuriated his supporters.

amenities of private life. An experience such as that which I have recently undergone teaches one that it is sweet and decorous to pass unnoticed along the pavements or to sit unrecognised with other fellow-citizens upon an omnibus. The publicity of the last few days has much enhanced my sympathy for public men. How terrible it must be never for one instant to escape recognition and that self-consciousness which comes from being observed! How ghastly to realise that until that last long privacy in Westminster Abbey one will always (even if one grows or shaves off a beard) be spotted by the populace, and that for the rest of one's life people will push for autographs or stare at one while one sips one's soup or eats a banana! Pleasant indeed are the comforts of obscurity. All elections have about them an atmosphere of unreality, but the attention aroused by a bye-election renders even the most sedate candidate a motley to the view. The muscles of the cheek which operate the smile of comradeship, the smile of delighted recognition, the smile of glad benevolence, become strained and aching; one comes to realise what is meant by such expressions as tennis elbow or writer's cramp. The wave of the hand and arm, which Kings and Queens manage with such dignity, is irksome to a shy person; nor can any man accustomed to self-analysis and self-criticism feel happy when he observes himself flinging friendliness like confetti in the air, selling cheap what is most dear, and making public display of something so intimate and cherished. I have always disliked amateur theatricals; my songs become sadly out of tune once I sing them in another key; I was certainly not intended by nature or by training for one of the central figures in a harlequinade.

However determined one may be to utter no word, to make no gesture, which is misleading or insincere, the circumstances of an election, the fact that one is undeniably soliciting votes, do create around one an aura of falsity. It is this, I think, which renders any election odious to a person of sensibility. One does not mind the meetings; it is quite amusing to play variations upon one's central theme and message; and I am one of those strange people who really do enjoy being heckled. But what makes the whole procedure loathsome is that within a narrow space of time one seeks, and is bound to seek, to convey one's personality to an amorphous mass of people whom one has never met before and whom, in all likelihood, one will never meet again. Personality resembles the Mona Lisa of Pater; it is the deposit, little cell by cell, of strange thoughts and fantastic reveries and exquisite passions. It is ungainly to make such a private thing as one's own personality hop three paces in the public streets of Upper Norwood. I much dislike trying to produce within nineteen days a synthetic version of myself which, in effect if not in intention, must inevitably be a distorted version. At North Croydon this problem was enhanced by the fact that the division is a locality rather than a place. It possesses for the stranger no identity, no personality, no pulse even, of its own; it is a line drawn round an arbitrary number of streets and houses; there is but little local patriotism or character; there is no village pump. The denizens of this dormitory do not regard themselves as citizens of Norwood, Norbury or Thornton Heath. Thus the unreality of the external candidate is increased by the unreality of the place to which he brings his carpet-bag. It is not possible, within nineteen days, for two such people to get to know each other. Their initial intercourse at least is bound to be artificial and embarrassed.

How curious, moreover, in an election of this intensity, are the relations between the candidate and his staff! The candidate, arriving lonely in an unknown land, suddenly finds himself surrounded by a staff of ardent technicians. They treat him with that watchful solicitude which a Newmarket trainer lavishes upon his horse. When he arrives in the morning they cast a quick glance at him to see whether he is showing any signs of weariness; they are careful of him at street-crossings and will help him gingerly to descend from a tram; with but slight encouragement they would rub him with linseed or camphorated oil when he retires to bed. As the first week of testing merges on leaden feet into the second week of open combat, the staff acquire feelings of affection towards their horse, and feed the animal with crumpets, cake and constant cups of tea. He is not supposed to know anything or care anything about their organisation or the plans which they discuss. It is only from the street hoardings that he learns the dates of his meetings and the names of those who have been invited down from London to support him on the platform. As he wends his weary way he will be startled to be confronted by an enormous and unflattering portrait of himself bearing in huge letters words of exhortation and hope. From time to time, when canvassing, he will find neat leaflets issued in his name in which stirring messages are conveyed to the electorate in a voice and language far different from his own. Only those of the staff who are specially concerned with meetings and publicity will have time to attend his rallies or to listen to his inspiring speeches. The next morning the others will replace the telephone receiver for an instant and enquire perfunctorily, 'How did the meeting go last night?' But they will not listen for the answer, but will continue with admirable application to organise. All this, I am sure, is perfectly correct; after all, a horse on its way to Epsom is not expected to ask questions regarding the length of the course.

Instructive also is the procedure which is known as canvassing. I recommend it to all those who suffer from inhibitions or feelings of inferiority. Preceded by a loud-speaker van, decked like some prize steer with a huge rosette, the candidate is made to descend at the end of a street and to walk up the middle exuding charm. The canvassers will deploy to right and left, and the sound of door-knockers rapping mingles with the sound of the loud-speaker announcing that the candidate, in glorious person, is there for all to see. So soon as the canvassers find some housewife or tenant willing to shake hands with the candidate or to ask him questions, he is beckoned to the door. With modest courtesy he will approach this would-be constituent, raise his hat in adulation, and introduce himself in a few well-chosen words. Meanwhile the loud-speaker up the street is continuing its brazen appeal, interspersed with the more favourable items of the candidate's biography and the more popular passages of his speeches and election address. I discovered, to my surprise, that as a canvasser I was very bad indeed. It was not only that a certain native pride deters me from overt solicitation; it was not merely that I am averse from argument for argumentation's sake; it was also that I became so interested in the human problems confided to me that I would pause in my progress and lean against the doorway listening to the human tales. I would be recalled to my duties by a sudden change of tone on the loud-speaker; the flow of adulation would cease suddenly and a voice would proclaim, 'Please hurry up, Mr Nicolson, we haven't got all night before us.' Back I would go to the centre of the street, smiling the smile of elderly benevolence.

The worst of being old is that one is apt to see the other person's point of view. A good candidate should be convinced that he is more intelligent, far more honourable and infinitely more valuable to his country than any of his opponents. I have never been adept at that sort of thing. However convinced I may be of the rightness and inevitability of a given political doctrine, I am temperamentally unable to give even a faint breath of fanaticism to my conviction. 'This election', a hardened journalist remarked to me last week, 'stinks of kid gloves.' I admit that there was a certain sobriety in our methods. Perhaps a degree of passion is necessary if one is to arouse the emotions of the elector. Yet my main regret for not being different is that I may have been a disappointment to my trainer and the stable-hands.

H.N. TO V.S-W. (*in Marseilles*)   *18th March, 1948*
Sissinghurst

This is the last letter I shall write you during your absence. The day after tomorrow we shall be together again. Oh my dearest Viti, how I have missed you! I am a bivalve, and don't function properly when I am forced to be unicellular.

There was no peerage for Harold Nicolson in the Birthday Honours, but he waited in confident anticipation for the New Year list. He slipped back without pause into his former routine in London and at Sissinghurst, continuing his weekly articles and his research on Benjamin Constant.

DIARY   *21st March, 1948*

I observe that I have not really recovered from my election. Physically I am well enough, and not in the least tired. But psychologically I have had a shock. I notice that I am over-sensitive. For instance, this morning, when I opened the *Observer*, I said to Niggs, 'What a joy it is to open the newspaper without feeling that there will be something about oneself'. But there was. There was an article by Ivor Brown headed *A Bad Candidate?*, all about me. It was meant to be kindly and to suggest that a good Member could not be a good candidate. But I minded it much. In fact, it hung like an albatross on my heart all day, and blurred the pleasure of the return of Viti

137

and the return of the spring. Why should I, who am so easily wounded, continually expose myself to wounds? Nigel says it is because I have no powers of calculation and never foresee where my actions will land me. He may be right.

DIARY   *5th April, 1948*

I go with Violet [Bonham Carter] to a reception at the United States Embassy for Mrs Roosevelt. It is a grand party and most people are in white ties and decorations. I meet many friends—Aneurin Bevan, George Hall, Christopher Mayhew, Camrose, Woolton etc. The Prime Minister is there. He is very nice to me about North Croydon. 'You did well', he says. 'Now mind, Harold, don't you say you will abandon politics and return to your writing. We have other things we want of you.' I interpret that as the House of Lords.

DIARY   *10th April, 1948*

Martha[1] has two heart-attacks. She collapses panting on the lawn and Vita collapses beside her. Mac[2] arrives and takes Martha away. I find Viti pacing beside the moat in an agony of tears. It is strange how much I feel torn (as by pincers inside) when I see Viti miserable.

Shirley [Morgan] comes down with Niggs. She is a delightful person to have about. So composed and friendly and pretty.

DIARY   *25th April, 1948*

If any person in after-years reads this diary, he will think that I was preoccupied only with the garden, the friends who come over, the books I read. He will think that I was unaware of the cataclysm which may overwhelm us. That would not be true. Behind all my thoughts and all this sunshine is the dark cloud [of the Russian menace].

H.N. TO V.S-W.   *7th May, 1948*
                                                                              10 Neville Terrace, S.W.7

I went to look at the Roosevelt memorial.[3] The statue itself is a

[1] An Alsatian bitch which V.S-W. had had for thirteen years.

[2] Miss Macmillan, V.S-W.'s secretary.

[3] In Grosvenor Square. The memorial (by Sir William Reid Dick) had been unveiled by the King in April.

nightmare, but the surrounding, with its two pools and little fountains, is quite successful. But how difficult the proletariat are! In
principle I like to see such gardens thrown open to them. But they
destroy the grass, and there were little ragamuffins sailing cigarette-
cartons on the two pools. Yes, I fear my Socialism is purely cerebral;
I do not like the masses in the flesh.

DIARY   *9th May, 1948*

I read [Don Salvador de] Madariaga on *Hamlet*. His contention is
that we sentimentalise Hamlet and try to make him out a prince
of chivalry: in fact he was a Renaissance *condottiere* who believed in
virtù. His unhappiness arose from the fact that he was never able to
find self-expression. It is an ingenious theme, but too hard-driven.
Madariaga (although he mentions it) does not attribute sufficient
importance to Shakespeare's indifference to his audience.

DIARY   *15th May, 1948*

The end of the Palestinian Mandate and the birthday of the independent State of Israel. All the pleasure I might have felt at this
realisation of the hopes of Zionism is clouded by the fear of war and
the humiliation we have suffered.

DIARY   *22nd May, 1948*

I am sleeping soundly at 2.30 am. when Viti comes in and rouses me.
Bunny [Drummond] had telephoned from London to say that
Sissinghurst Place[1] was on fire and could we do anything? Viti had
gone to her window and seen a great orange blaze behind the trees.
We dress hurriedly and drive to the Place. By the time we get there
it is a blazing furnace and there is no hope of saving anything more
than was got out at the first moment. The butler, his wife and baby
had escaped in their night-clothes. With the help of some boys they
had been able to get out the tallboys and some cabinets and pictures.
But most of that careful collection has gone for ever. We go to the
Bull [Inn] and telephone to Bunny. A further fire-brigade arrives
and is very efficient. We stand helplessly on the lawn and watch the
azaleas and rhododendrons white and scarlet in the flickering glare.

[1] The mid-nineteenth-century house, less than a mile from the Castle, which
Lindsay Drummond had inherited from his mother six months before.

A huge round moon adds to the weirdness of the scene. From time to time a window will crash down or tiles come rattling. They manage to save the kitchen wing, but the main house which we knew so well is just a hollow shell. It was such a dignified, cultured house—so elegant in its simplicity—and we see it all disintegrate before our eyes.[1]

We come back at 5.30 while the dawn is creeping over the woods. It is very cold. I go to bed, but Viti stays up and gardens. She then goes to meet Bunny and Lindsay by the train at 8 am. and takes them to the ruin of their home. They behave admirably.

The Arab Legion (which is financed and officered by us) have almost captured Jerusalem. I do not know how the Government can justify this attack on the Holy City under our auspices. It will make a terrible effect abroad. We seem to be behaving badly and malevolently all round. I am losing faith in Bevin. He ought to have foreseen these things and prevented us from getting into so utterly false a position. I am deeply depressed.

DIARY   *25th May, 1948*

I talk to Esmond Rothermere at the Beefsteak. He tells me that he had great difficulty in getting his *Daily Mail* people to write an article in support of the Jews, or rather in criticism of our backing of the Arabs. They say that any such line would harm the paper, because of the strength of anti-semitism in the country.

DIARY   *27th May, 1948*

I go to Claridges to see Alan Moorehead. He had crossed the Atlantic with a young American writer of the name of Truman Capote who had scored a great success with his first book.[2] He is a nervous, sensitive young man with a pasty face. But I liked him. He said that Evelyn Waugh's *The Loved One* was not as good as it seemed since it lacked all tenderness. This was said so simply that I found it attractive.

DIARY   *28th May, 1948*

I had been expecting to be offered in the Birthday Honours the peer-

[1] This fire inspired the closing scene in V.S-W.'s novel *The Easter Party* (1953).
[2] *Other Voices, Other Rooms*. He was then aged 23.

age which I nearly got in the New Year. But I have not had a word from Attlee, and this means either that they are giving no peerages this birthday, or that my name is not among them. I am rather relieved really, as I have *Benjamin Constant* to finish in the later part of this year, and if they reform the House of Lords, they are certain to make me a life-peer. I should prefer that in many ways. But I am amused to find in myself a fat grub of snobbishness. I have always hated the name 'Nicolson' as being a common plebeian name. I don't mind it for myself, since 'Harold Nicolson' is familiar and all right. But I hate it for Viti. Thus if I were made a real peer, I could change it to 'Cranfield'. But if a life-peer, I could not change my name, and 'Lord Nicolson', and even more so, 'Lady Nicolson', would sound absurd. Now, really, at my age I ought not to mind such things. And yet I am conscious of that little grub or slug inside me. How little one knows oneself, even when one probes and pokes and is amused!

DIARY   *3rd June, 1948*

I get a letter from Tommy [Sir Alan] Lascelles saying he has a 'proposition' to make to me. What can it be? The *Life* of King George V? Or to come to Australia?[1]

Harold Nicolson's first guess was correct. He was invited to write the official biography of King George V. This book, which was to become the central interest of his life until its publication in 1952, was the most important book of his career and the keystone of his reputation as an historian. His diary records carefully his attitude to the most difficult of the problems connected with it, that of reticence and discretion. He began immediately to talk to people who had known King George, but before embarking intensively on the research, he had first to finish his book on Benjamin Constant, which he wrote in two months, between June and August. His secretary was justified in her comment that in 'King George V' he had found an anchor for his later middle age. He was gradually reconciled to the impossibility of returning to the House

---

[1] It had been announced in March that the King and Queen, with Princess Margaret, were to visit Australia and New Zealand in the spring of 1949. But the King developed arteriosclerosis in his right leg, and the tour was cancelled in November.

*of Commons, and as a peerage became increasingly unlikely, he desired
it correspondingly less.*

*This was the period of the Russian blockade of Berlin and the airlift.
Harold Nicolson was asked by the Foreign Office to fly to Berlin and
give four lectures as a demonstration of British solidarity with the
Berliners.*

H.N. TO V.S-W.   *8th June, 1948*
                                                         10 Neville Terrace, S.W.7

After Sibyl [Colefax's] luncheon yesterday I walked across the park
to Buckingham Palace and entered by the side-door. I was taken at
once into Tommy [Lascelles'] room. I sat down, and he started off
at once. He said that the King had often spoken to him during the
war about the need to have an official life of George V. They had
put it off from year to year. Then a few months ago, the King
had returned to the subject and said how important it was that
this life should be written before Tommy and Owen Morshead[1]
died. Tommy had therefore taken the opinion of five distinguished
figures (he did not say who they were, but I suppose people like
Halifax and Bobbety [Salisbury]), and three of these five had
suggested me. He therefore told the King, and the King said, 'What
do you feel yourself, Tommy?' Tommy, of course, had said that he
would not have wished to put forward the name of an old personal
friend, but that he agreed with the three elder statesmen. Then the
Queen also agreed, and Tommy was delegated to approach me.

At that stage I asked whether Queen Mary had given her assent.
He said that she had not been consulted. I said that I could not even
consider the proposal unless she gave her consent. He said, 'Very
well, we will ask her. If she objects, we shall have to persuade
her.'

I then said that in principle I did not like writing biographies when
I could not tell the whole truth. Tommy said (well, I thought), 'But
it is not meant to be an ordinary biography. It is something quite
different. You will be writing a book about a very ancient national
institution, and you need not descend to personalities.' He said that
I should not be expected to write one word that was not true. I
should not be expected to praise or exaggerate. But I must omit

[1] Sir Owen Morshead, the Librarian at Windsor Castle, 1926-58.

142

things and incidents which were discreditable. I could say this in the preface if it would ease my mind.

The idea is that I shall be shown every scrap of paper that exists. I would have a table of my own in the library at Windsor and go down there three days a week. Owen Morshead would help me. There was no hurry about the book. I could have four years if I liked.

I said that I could not give an answer at the moment. I should have to consult you. But I could tell him at the outset that I should not be free until next year as I must finish off Constant. He said that did not matter at all.

I asked, 'What about finances?' He said that the King would not pay me anything at all, even for secretarial expenses. All he would give me was a table to work at, a cupboard to keep my papers in, and a free run of his archives. It was for me to make such arrangements as I could with my publishers.

Well, that is the proposition. I have not got clear in my head what I really feel about it. I see the balance-sheet as follows:

Advantages: A definite task, taking me three years at least and bringing a large financial reward. Access to papers of deep interest and importance. Close collaboration with charming people such as Tommy and Morshead. The opportunity of writing the history of my own times. Added to all of which, I suppose, is the compliment of having been chosen.

Disadvantages: To have to write an 'official' biography. The lack of charm in the King with whom I am dealing. My inability (indeed my unwillingness) to make jokes about the monarchy. My not being allowed to mention discreditable or foolish things. My having to avoid personalities.

Now what do you think? As a writer you will see the fascination of the challenge. Is it possible to write the life in a way that will be really interesting, really true, while keeping to the convention of royal portraits?

I told Elvira [Niggeman], as she knew I had an appointment with Tommy. She was delighted, and as usual most intelligent. She said, 'But it is just what you need—an anchor. It will keep you busy for three years and prevent you doing silly things like Croydon. People say that young men need anchors. That may be true, but people

in later middle age need anchors far more.' All of which, in a way,
is true.

V.S-W. TO H.N.   *8th June, 1948*[1]
                                                        Sissinghurst

I am divided in my mind about George V. I do see that he would be
a good solid peg on which to hang a very interesting study of the
period. Very interesting indeed, if you were allowed a free hand.
But would the King want you to concentrate principally on his
father? Or would he allow you excursions all round? Tommy L.,
of course, would understand exactly how you wanted to write it,
but Tommy's employer probably has a Divine Right attitude, and
might not understand. Anyhow, it was a great compliment, and I
expect Queen Mary was the originator.

It was so like you to telephone. I had been wondering all day what
Tommy wanted of you. You are really an angel of consideration.
There is nobody like you. How glad I am that we sat on Angie
Manners' hat-box in the attic at Hatfield and agreed to share our
lives.[2]

H.N. TO V.S-W.   *9th June, 1948*
                                                  10 Neville Terrace, S.W.7

I had a note from Tommy this morning saying that Queen Mary
had approved the suggestion and thought I would be the best person.
So that is the last obstacle removed or line of retreat taken away. It
would be difficult to refuse now, even if I wanted to. But I do not
want to, and I can see that you approach it from almost exactly the
same angle. The preparation will be fascinating and the execution
difficult. I had already raised with Tommy the point you made in
your letter—is it to be the portrait of a dull individual or the picture
of a reign? He said the latter was the main purpose. I can see George
V getting more and more symbolic and less real.

[1] H.N. had telephoned the news to V.S-W. When she wrote this letter, she had
not received his.
[2] This is the only reference in the diaries, books or correspondence to the circumstances of their engagement in 1911. Angela Manners was one of the twin
daughters of the 3rd Lord Manners, and later married Colonel Malise Hore-
Ruthven.

But you will realise (and not be at all depressed by such realisation) that it means my saying goodbye for ever to active politics. By the time I have finished I shall be nearly 65, too old for the rough and tumble.

So I wrote to Tommy today and said Yes. I shall not regret it.

DIARY   *12th June, 1948*
Niggs says that my highbrow friends will think it wrong of me to write a book on a subject when I have to indulge in suppressions of the truth. What will interest people is to know exactly how far the King exercised his authority. If I hedge over that, the book will be valueless. If I tell what may be the truth, then what I say will be used against the monarchy by left-wing agitators. In fact I get discouragement from my family all round.

What a beautiful rose-scented day it is, all the same!

DIARY   *17th June, 1948*
I dine at the Persian Embassy. It is a big dinner for Bevin. He is in good form—noisy and vulgar. When the women go out, he forces me to sit in the chair next to him which the Ambassador should have occupied. Bevin is so optimistic that he is unconvincing. The trouble in Burma is nothing; the Palestine question is settling itself; the Sudan need not give us a moment's worry; and so on. He says that he pays no attention at all to the attacks of the American press. What do they matter? After all, it is the principle that counts, and nobody is going to tell him that in principle it does not pay better to remain friends with 200 million Moslems than with 200 thousand Jews, 'to say nothing of the oil'. Not a discreet way to talk.

One cannot help liking Bevin, but I fear I am conventional about diplomatic life, or rather my old inhibitions linger. Bevin addressed not a word to the Ambassador or the Persians, and confined his remarks to me and Lord Stansgate.[1] Moreover, he talked about things such as old Trades Union disputes which could not be understood by foreigners. He spoke very bitterly about the *New Statesman*. He also said how much he regretted that Dick Crossman with all his ability didn't possess a more stable character.

[1] Formerly William Wedgwood Benn, and Secretary of State for Air, 1945-46.

DIARY   *20th June, 1948*

I start writing *Benjamin Constant*. I am in a bad mood and it goes poorly.

H.N. TO V.S-W.   *28th June, 1948*
                                                      10 Neville Terrace, S.W.7

I got many congratulations on Georges Cinq. But why should they say it is 'a high honour'? It never struck me as that exactly. But I know that they consulted George Trevelyan[1] and he recommended me. That *is* a high honour.

DIARY   *16th July, 1948*

Two distressing things have happened. The Americans are sending squadrons of Flying Fortresses to land in East Anglia. And the Russians have stated that they will be carrying out the training of their fighter aeroplanes across our corridors to Berlin[2]. This is very dangerous, since it increases the prestige battle and may lead to accidents. The City is getting panicky. Yet I cannot seriously believe that war is possible. It is so different from previous wars and rumours of wars. It seems to be the final conflict for the mastery of the world. The prizes are so enormous; the losses so terrible. It is so easy to criticise; to blame Winston and Roosevelt for Yalta; to blame Bevin for having allowed this untenable Berlin position to consolidate itself. But as always, these things are governed, not by mistakes or intentions, but by the dreadful chain of circumstance.

The Barbarians are at the gate.

DIARY   *21st July, 1948*

I am reading Geoffrey Gorer's book *The Americans*, which I find excellent. He makes a great and valuable point about the American hatred of authority, with its implications of disrespect. He makes another good point about the difference in the American mind between relations to persons and relations to things: the former are

[1] The historian. Master of Trinity College, Cambridge, since 1940.
[2] Following a dispute over currency reform, the Russians blockaded the western sectors of Berlin, cutting off Germans and Allies alike from supplies of food light and fuel. The Allies thereupon undertook to supply West Berlin entirely by air, and did so until May 1949.

envisaged as feminine, the latter as masculine. A very intelligent book.

At dinner I sit next to Cromer.[1] He makes interesting points about George V. (1) He believed that princes ought to be brought up in fear of their father: 'I was always frightened of my father; they must be frightened of me.' (2) He had more than a sense of fun, even a sense of humour. He could say very acute and amusing things. (3) When he saw Ministers, he would never allow them to talk. He had mugged up the papers very conscientiously and would then give them his own ideas. (4) Queen Mary was much in awe of him. All suggestions that it was she who managed him are false. She would get Cromer and others to put to him the things she wanted. She would never put them to him herself.

DIARY   22nd July, 1948

I go to Buckingham Palace for the Garden Party. I have a talk with Anthony Eden. He tells me that in his long experience he has never known such enthusiasm as he had during his visit to Berlin. There were crowds when he came out of the lecture-hall, and they yelled and cheered. He was embarrassed, first because he does not like Germans, and secondly because he realised that it was an anti-Russian demonstration.

Nancy Astor is there and says at me loudly, 'The man who sold his soul'. I ask why. She says because I joined the Labour Party in order to get the Embassy in Paris. I say (a) I hate Embassies and left the Foreign Service in order to avoid one; (b) Vita would never have enjoyed an Embassy, and this in itself would have made it impossible. She says, 'Yes, you are right. I never thought of that.' Then the other side of her comes out, and she is charming. I really love that woman and admire her—but what enemies she must make among people who only see her silly sallies!

DIARY   12th August, 1948

I re-do chapter XI [of *Benjamin Constant*] and finish it. I then clear up my notes etc. I start dividing the primroses in the spring-garden. What a valuable and happy fortnight this has been! I have never written more easily or quickly. Perhaps too easily? Perhaps too quickly?

[1] 2nd Earl of Cromer, Permanent Lord-in-Waiting to the King since 1938.

DIARY   *26th August, 1948*

I finish the Bibliography and do my Introductory Note. I then think I have finished. But that is not true. I find I have inserted in my Bibliography Guy de Pourtalès' book *De Hamlet à Swann* (1924), which contains a chapter on Constant. I have not actually read this book, so I sit down and do it as an *acquit de conscience*. It contains a reprint of the *Débats* account of Constant's funeral. It does not accord with my account. So I rewrite the last page. Having done that I have really finished.

I then start on John Gore's book on George V.[1]

H.N. TO V.S-W.   *9th September, 1948*
                                              10 Neville Terrace, S.W.7

This afternoon poor old Benjamin [Constant] goes off to Constable. I feel quite sorry to say goodbye to him and to replace that gay companionship by the King. It will be fun being 'in search of George' but it will be hell writing the thing. I quite see that the Royal Family feel their myth is a piece of gossamer and must not be blown upon. What is a relief to me is that I shall not have to do much portraiture. I shall be able to leave all that to John Gore, who has already done it very well indeed.

DIARY   *17th September, 1948*

The nine o'clock News tells us of the murder of Count Bernadotte in Jerusalem by the Stern gang.[2] We are horrified. I have not felt such a shock for a long time, and the disgust at this outrage pierces my hardened nerves. The whole world will feel, as we feel, that here was a truly good man butchered by this age of violence. I suppose that it has always happened that when a new doctrine comes to supplant the old, the eternal principles of human justice also become out of date for a while. But it is not fair on our generation, who possess all the susceptibilities created by the old order, to have to face the atrocities of the new.

[1] *King George V. A Personal Memoir* (John Murray, 1941). This book described the King's private life – his homes, tastes and friendships – but not his reign.
[2] Count Folke Bernadotte of Sweden had recently been appointed United Nations Mediator in Palestine. He was assassinated by the extreme group of Jewish terrorists.

Viti and I walk out afterwards. There is an almost full moon and a windless, cloudless sky. The tower stands there delicate and solemn. We walk down to the moat. The poplars and the statue of Dionysus are reflected in the water. Rollo [an Alsatian puppy] slopes down to drink and makes silver circles. It is all so beautiful, so sedate, so gentle. And things like this can happen in the glare of a Palestine afternoon. What harm all this will do to UNO and the cause of Zionism. Poor Weizmann—his life's work sullied by these ghetto thugs. Will this event mean as much to ordinary men and women in Europe and the United States as it means to me? To me it is a symbol of reason being killed by murder. Such a good man, such a good man. . . . I wince at the very thought of what it means.

DIARY   23rd September, 1948

Frank Pakenham tells me that I was on the list for peerages last December, but then the P.M. found that Viti was getting the C.H. and this was awkward. At the King's birthday I might have come up again had it not been for the recency of Croydon. Do I really care? Yes, I do. I want to be back in public life in an easy indolent way. That is not disreputable. George V must claim my inner energy.

V.S-W. TO H.N.   26th September, 1948
                                                 Sissinghurst

It was such a relief to get that telephone message to say that you had arrived safely in Berlin.[1] It was just like you to have taken the trouble to get it sent, but really you would have been rewarded for your trouble if you could have known the relief it gave me. I slept soundly all night, whereas I hadn't slept much the night before. It is a perfect day here. Hot, like summer, and you among the ruins. You will hate all that; I know how much you will mind it. Oh Hadji, how much I wish you were here instead of in Berlin! With the world in such a mess, I cling more and more to the serenity and happiness of Sissinghurst and our life—our way of life, as we have made it.

---

[1] He had flown there via Hamburg, since all other forms of transport were cut off by the Russian blockade of West Berlin.

This is tormentingly interesting but more horrible than anything you can conceive. A deep unhappy helplessness seems to brood over these ruins. My main impression so far is one of utter bewilderment. I have never felt quite so *stupid* in my life. Everything contributes to this. My cold (which is pursuing a normal course), the fact that I have forgotten my German, the fact that Hitler changed the monuments from one place to another, so that my sense of direction is completely misled, the fact that every now and then I recognise things for a second and then they fade into oblivion.

I got here yesterday afternoon and went to have tea with the Director of Information in the Kurfürstendamm. At the end of the street loomed the ruined and blackened spire of the Gedächtnis-kirche, like the stump of a dirty old cigar. I drove to Brückenallee.[1] My house was just one pile of rubble. It is a nightmare fusion between the recognisable and the changed, as if you were to find Knole in Salisbury Plain.

They drove me to a large villa in the Grünewald where there is a Press club. It is pretty bleak, I assure you. Only one bulb in a chandelier, and of course no heating. The food was all British rations, not badly cooked. There is a sense of living in a dugout. It is far, far worse than I expected. One seems to be in a moon landscape across which figures flit. What a deeply unsettling experience it is. How deeply compassionate I feel for these people. Real aching sympathy.

So strange and quiet it all is. Not a sound among the ruins. Only very rarely does a military car pass along and one can hear it from a great distance. Beyond that and a few rare trams, there is no traffic. The few passers-by slouch miserably.

I went to see Sir Cecil Weir[2] who is head of the economic section. He is a bright little, neat little, old Scotsman—very tingling and alert. He is very optimistic. He says that the Western Zone is recover-

[1] Where he lived between 1927 and 1929, while Counsellor at the British Embassy.
[2] President of the Economic Sub-Commission of the Control Commission for Germany.

ing rapidly and that something like prosperity will come to it in two years. He says that we can manage to keep up the air-lift during the winter. He thinks that the Russians will stop short of provoking a war. Even if there is a war, the Russians will not be able to hold down Europe. Their satellites are resentful and seething. Well, well—I am not so sure.

H.N. TO V.S-W.   *28th September, 1948*
Berlin

I went round to our Control Headquarters in a huge Nazi building. Brian Robertson[1] is young, alert, strong, and, I should think, sensible. But very much the professional soldier with the soldier's suspicion of politico-intellectuals. He was wary with me, hiding himself behind a mask of politeness. From there I went to the American Headquarters. Very smart, like all American military and naval installations. Nothing shoddy about them. I was taken to see General Clay.[2] He is a formidable man—Napoleonic. Very piercing eyes and a delightful manner, perhaps owing to the fact that he had read and liked my books. How odd they are! He was seated in some state in a large room at a huge desk. Outside sat two aides-de-camp with aiguillettes on their uniforms. I enjoyed talking to him. He says that the chances of war are only one in ten. 'The Russians know they would be licked. If they cut our air-route, they know it is an act of war. They won't cut our air-route.'

All night the aeroplanes roared overhead bringing food to Berlin.

DIARY   *14th October, 1948*
London

I address the Foreign Press Association on Open and Secret Diplomacy. I then come in at the tail-end of one of Sibyl's Ordinaries.[3] I take Gladwyn [Jebb] to Pratt's. He is in despair about UNO. He says that the whole thing is just being turned into a farce; that the

[1] British Commander-in-Chief and Military Governor, Control Commission for Germany.
[2] General Lucius D. Clay, Commander-in-Chief European Command and Military Governor of the United States Zone of Germany.
[3] Lady Colefax had continued her wartime practice of giving a series of dinner-parties at the Dorchester, for which the guests paid.

Russians use it as a sounding-board for propaganda; that nobody discusses the matter at issue and nobody listens to anybody else's speeches. The whole organisation has been turned into nonsense.

H.N. TO V.S-W.   26th October, 1948
                                   10 Neville Terrace, S.W.7

I am worried about your eye.[1] I have got Elvira [Niggeman] to telephone my Dublin address to Mac so that she will be able to give me the latest bulletin. 'The life of V.S-W. is passing peacefully to its close.' That will throw me out of my stride when addressing Trinity College Philosophical Society.

How cold and lovely it was this morning. I walked about the platform of Staplehurst station (since my train was late owing to coast-fog) and watched the leaves turning. I thought how much nature had meant to me in life. I do derive intense pleasure from the loveliness of my whole world of Kent, and above all of Sissinghurst. I am sure we are right about that. Sissinghurst has a quality of mellowness, of retirement, of unflaunting dignity, which is just what we wanted to achieve and which in some ways we have achieved by chance. I think it is mainly due to the succession of privacies: the forecourt, the first arch, the main court, the tower arch, the lawn, the orchard. All a series of escapes from the world, giving the impression of cumulative escape.

DIARY   29th October, 1948
                                            Dublin

Walter Elliot[2] says that the British are about to enter a new phase of getting tough. They are tired of being banged about by Jews, Arabs and Malays; they will stand no nonsense from Eire.[3] When De

[1] She had a stye, but it had no permanent effect on her eyesight.
[2] Conservative M.P. for the Scottish Universities and former Minister of Health, 1938-40.
[3] In February De Valera's administration had been succeeded by a Coalition Government headed by John Costello, who on 7th September, in the course of a visit to the United States and Canada, announced his intention of repealing the External Relations Act of 1936, thereby severing the last link between Southern Ireland and the British Crown. The Dail passed the necessary legislation on 27th November, and the Republic of Ireland was formally proclaimed on Easter Monday, 1949.

Valera makes speeches threatening force against Ulster he adds two thousand votes to the Tories every time. What Eire does not realise is that she has lost the sympathy of the United States. In the present Presidential campaign not one word has been said on either side about Ireland. 'The Irish', Rugby[1] says rather grimly, 'would not put it like that. They would say that it was Ireland who has lost confidence in the United States.'

We lunch at the Kildare Street Club. Walter Elliot, myself, Rugby, Costello and MacBride.[2] It is a strange Victorian relic with carved capitals, a tessellated pavement and huge caribous upon the wall. Through this ghastly architecture pass broken-down peers and landlords dressed in tweeds.

Costello and MacBride have never entered the club before. Nor would anyone but Rugby have dared to bring them. I had the distinct impression that they were uneasy about the effect of their intention to repeal the External Relations Act. They were delighted by Winston having said that he longed for a United Ireland. 'Make no mistake about it', said Walter, 'what Winston meant was an Ireland united under the crown.' He says that if they cross the border, English opinion will force the Government to send two divisions to Ulster. 'And they will shoot, mark you. The English are a lazy but ruthless race. I know it well. We Scots have fought the English for generations and have learnt to respect them.' They pretend that the threat of force was one of the gravest errors that De Valera ever committed. I do not think we leave them happy.

I go to Shanganagh.[3] It is now a girls' school. Outside there is a man digging the lawn. I ask if we may go in. He is very courteous. We discover he is the teacher of Irish. He tells us with pride that all lessons are taught in that insufferable tongue. This must render the education of Irish youth ten times more difficult and slow than ours. I tell him that my grandmother lived there. He remembers her legend. He asks my name. 'Not the *famous* Harold Nicolson?', he

---

[1] The first Lord Rugby (Sir John Maffey), U.K. Representative to Eire since 1939, and formerly Governor General of the Sudan.

[2] Sean MacBride, Minister for External Affairs, Eire, 1948–51.

[3] Shanganagh Castle, which had belonged to H.N.'s grandfather, Archibald Rowan Hamilton (1817–60), and where he had spent some of his school holidays. His grandmother, Catherine Rowan Hamilton, died in 1919 in her 99th year.

asks. My word, what broadcasting does to one! They have ruined the ballroom by building out a sort of cement lounge, but the rest of the house is intact. Odd memories stir within me like slowly shifting toads. We walk down to the sea. As we come back, the sea-dusk is closing on the Wicklow mountains. A light goes up in one of the Shanganagh towers and then another. Childhood *Angst* grips me again. I am glad to escape hurriedly.

DIARY   3rd November, 1948

Truman has won! A singlehanded fight against the sneers of his enemies and the lack-lustre resignation of his friends. I have no idea at all how or why he brought it off. It will be a bitter blow for Dewey[1] and John Foster Dulles and Dr Gallup[2] and all those Republicans who were counting on jobs. There is a nasty streak in human nature which gives one a mean sense of *Schadenfreude* [pleasure at other people's discomfiture] when such confidence, such actual hubris, is punished by the Gods.

DIARY   4th November, 1948

I dine with Cyril Joad. I meet there Victor Gollancz, Kenneth Clark and Somerset Maugham. We talk about George V. Kenneth says he never saw an adult man write so slowly; he would form his letters with the patient caution of a schoolboy. We pass on to literary reputation and wonder whether Shaw will recover from his present decline. Gollancz says that Wells is not even mentioned today in book circles. The present Henry James boom is, Willy [Maugham] thinks, 'artificial'. Willy says that the two English writers most read in France today are himself and Charles Morgan. We pass on to the future of the publishing trade, and Gollancz says that unless we can print on cheaper paper and have yellow covers like the French, the publishing trade is doomed: expenses are far higher than profits. Willy says that France is dead. She may revive, but today she is dead. She has lost *'la fierté qui faisait croire à son génie'*.

---

[1] Thomas E. Dewey, the Republican candidate, who was defeated by over two million votes.
[2] The Gallup Poll had forecast a Dewey victory.

DIARY   *7th November, 1948*

I do my review. I then try, much to my fury, to find quotations in my own books for Doubleday Doran's *Dictionary of Quotations*. It just doesn't work. I am not given to apophthegms. My gift is to explain things at length and convey atmosphere.

DIARY   *29th November, 1948*

I spend the day inserting into my notebook all the public events in the reign of George V. It is laborious, but useful and restful. I then read Sidney Lee's biography of Edward VII, about which there hangs an aroma of feline skill.

Viti and I discuss after dinner whether Bertie Russell was right in stating that we should make war on Russia while we have the atomic bomb and they have not.[1] It is a difficult problem. I think it is probably true that Russia is preparing for the final battle for world mastery and that once she has enough bombs she will destroy Western Europe, occupy Asia and have a final death struggle with the Americas. If that happens and we are wiped out over here, the survivors in New Zealand may say that we were mad not to have prevented this while there was still time. Yet, if the decision rested with me, I think I should argue as follows: 'It may be true that we shall be wiped out, and that we could prevent this by provoking a war with Russia at this stage. It may be true that such a war would be successful and that we should then establish some centuries of Pax Americana—an admirable thing to establish. But there remains a doubt about all this. There is a chance that the danger may pass and peace can be secured by peace. I admit it is a frail chance—not one in ninety. To make war in defiance of that one chance is to commit a crime. Better to be wiped out by the crime of others than to preserve ourselves by committing a deliberate crime of our own. A preventive war is always evil. Let us rather die.'

And the New Zealander would say, 'The man was mad'—or cowardly, or stupid, or just weak.

---

[1] Bertrand Russell published a letter in *The Times* next day saying that he was not urging a preventive war, but that we should force a settlement on Russia by the threat of war.

DIARY   *5th December, 1948*

I have been thinking about the planning of my George V book. I realise that if I try to write all the notes in advance as I usually do, I shall forget the beginning by the time I reach the end. My first idea, therefore, was to do his early life and actually write the chapters on that period, at least in their first draft. But on second thoughts, I think I should be wiser to concentrate upon those episodes of which there are witnesses still alive. I should be furious if I devoted six months to the cruise of the *Bacchante*[1] only to learn that Queen Mary had died. Perhaps the crucial problem is his handling of the crisis of August 1931. Many people believe that he exercised undue pressure on Ramsay MacDonald to induce him to accept a National Government. On this point Wigram and Herbert Samuel, who were protagonists, are still alive. I must therefore concentrate on that issue and obtain their evidence while they are still available and in their right minds.

V.S-W. TO H.N.   *9th December, 1948*
                                                          Sissinghurst

I got home to find that the stag-hounds had been round here with their beastly barking and trumpets. They drove the stag into our lake. It was pursued by the hounds who started tearing at it. A hunt-servant went out in our boat to rescue it, and eventually it was brought to land and *carried* away, so injured and exhausted was it. Oh, what horrible people, and *what* a row I am going to make! Oh, if only I had been here! Incidentally, they have sunk our boat: it capsized, bless it, and tipped the hunt-servant into the water. Vass [the head-gardener] says that he would have let him drown, and only wishes that he had had a machine-gun to turn on him. You know how much I have always liked Vass. Now I like him 100 per cent more.

H.N. TO V.S-W.   *16th December, 1948*
                                                          10 Neville Terrace, S.W.7

There were immense crowds yesterday at the Palace to watch people

[1] Young Prince George (later George V) spent three years (1879–82) as a midshipman on H.M.S. *Bacchante*.

156

arriving for the christening.[1] It is the identification of natural human experience with this strange royal world that causes these emotions; one's own life enlarged into a fairy story.

DIARY   *31st December, 1948*

For me it has in some ways been a bad year. My Croydon venture was a misfortune. It shocked my Tory friends and it left upon the Labour people the impression that my heart was not in it. I hated it so much that I showed it, and they felt that I was not putting myself into the thing at all. The peerage which I so nearly got last year has now, it seems, eluded me. Nor am I feeling any younger. I feel that my political career (which was never very brilliant, in any case) is now closed for ever. I am glad that I was offered the life of George V. It was a compliment in itself, will provide interesting work, and gives me the excuse for doing nothing else. This great wet windy world (I am writing this on the morning of January 1) seems full of sorrow. But I have got the remains of 'flu on me and am not in a fit state to judge my own past, present or future. I know that I should thank Heaven for all the blessings that have been showered upon me. But it is now evident that I have not been a successful man but a failure; and this owing to lack of courage.

---

[1] Of Prince Charles. He was born on 14th November.

1949

---

*Start on the royal documents at Windsor – attempt to make
Attlee a popular personality – H.N. begins to review for
the Observer – Churchill and his war-history –Morrison on
the 1931 crisis – V.S-W. in Spain – interview with Queen
Mary – a lecture in the East End – the Brains Trust – making
the white garden at Sissinghurst – Bernard Berenson – the
peerage vanishes – research on King George – the Russians
get the bomb – the reputation of French and English writers –
'I do not like the Labour Party'*

Throughout the year Harold Nicolson worked on 'King George V'. Twice a week he travelled down to Windsor to study the royal archives in the Round Tower, where he was allotted a room of his own, and in London he interviewed most of the important surviving figures of the reign, including Queen Mary. He first wrote chapters xxvi and xxvii, on the 1931 crisis, and then returned to the King's early years. At the same time he continued to write for the 'Spectator', but gave up his articles for the Paris 'Figaro' and left the 'Daily Telegraph' for the 'Observer', for which he reviewed a book a week for the next fourteen years.

V. Sackville-West emerged from her seclusion at Sissinghurst to become a Justice of the Peace on the Cranbrook Bench, and sat on the National Trust's Gardens Committee as well as the Executive of the Society for the Preservation of Rural Kent. In March she undertook a lecture-tour of Spain ('my half-native land') for the British Council, visiting for the first time sites connected with St Teresa and her grandmother Pepita, of both of whom she had written biographies. In Granada she developed 'flu, but managed to conceal the fact from Harold Nicolson until her premature return to England.

DIARY   6th January, 1949

I go down to Windsor to inspect my future material. I first go to Owen Morshead's room and he shows me the George V diaries. They are bound in ordinary cloth and written neatly in that schoolboy writing. He says that there is nothing in them which shows anything of his personality. The actual act of writing was a labour to him. In the same cupboard are the diaries of Queen Victoria as transcribed by Princess Beatrice. The latter felt it was her duty in life to edit her mother's diary. She worked on it for twenty years. Every evening she would sit there copying out her mother's entries and each evening when she had finished, she tore out the sheets which she had edited and cast them into the fire. We shall never know what the old lady really confided to her diary.

Morshead says he does not think I shall have much trouble with the present King and Queen so long as I do not make mock of the principle of monarchy. Queen Mary will not mind a few jocular references. He thinks one of my difficulties will be King George's treatment of his children.

He then conducts me across to the Round Tower and I climb up the staircase to be greeted at the top by Miss Mackenzie.[1] I had asked her to produce some 'specimens' of the archives, and had suggested as a simple subject the appointment of Baldwin as Prime Minister. The file contains many very important memoranda from Stamfordham,[2] letters from Balfour and from Salisbury, and, to my amusement, my own letters about the incident when I was writing my Curzon book. Now these papers are most encouraging, and I suspect the others are as good. They really do contain ideas and facts which have not hitherto been seen.

DIARY   *14th January, 1949*

I attend a dinner of the Society of Socialist Journalists. The chief guests are the Prime Minister and Mrs Attlee as well as Hector McNeil. I have a talk before dinner with the P.M. He is very well now, and seems to have gained nervous energy since I last saw him. I ask him about the King. He says that the Dutch Prime Minister had told him that they have to walk out backwards after an audience. He feels that if our Court had insisted on that, there would be a Republic here already.

Attlee makes a usual sort of speech, and then there is a discussion. Journalists are very insensitive and cruel people. The discussion reminds me of doctors discussing a case with medical students around the patient's bed, indifferent to his feelings. Thus they all discuss how to make Attlee a popular figure. Obviously he lacks glamour and is bad at self-dramatisation, but couldn't we build him up as 'the simple man'? What the public wanted was the human touch. But Press Officers do not understand the Press. For example, one man, wishing to write an article about the nationalisa-

---

[1] Miss Mary Mackenzie, Registrar of the King's Archives.
[2] Lord Stamfordham, previously Sir Arthur Bigge. From 1895 to 1901 he was Principal Private Secretary to Queen Victoria, and Private Secretary to King George V, both as Duke of York and (until 1931) as King.

tion of steel, had asked Philip Jordan, as Attlee's Press Officer, to describe what the P.M. had had for breakfast that morning. Jordan had refused. ('And quite right too', shouted Philip, who was sitting next to me.) How was it that they had managed to make Baldwin a popular figure? Couldn't something of the sort be done even in a weak situation such as that of Attlee?

The nice little man took all this quite humbly. But I was glad that when he got up he hit back at them. 'Public Relations Officers', he said, 'do not exist in order to build up the personalities of Ministers. They exist in order to explain Government policy.' He says that Jordan was quite right not to disclose family and domestic details. Even a Prime Minister must have some right to privacy. Besides, that sort of thing is dangerous. He instances the dreadful fiasco which occurred when Worthington Evans'[1] P.R.O. tried to get him across as a popular figure known to his friends and staff as 'Worthy'. 'Moreover', he says, 'I should be a sad subject for any publicity expert. I have none of the qualities which create publicity.' It made all the decent ones among us like him more than ever. But what percentage were we of the whole?

DIARY   20th January, 1949

Nigel has got his friend Jim Rose of the *Observer* to offer me a weekly article of 800 words on one book to be chosen by myself. This would mean leaving the *Telegraph*. I should gain in having to read only one book, instead of three, a week. Moreover it is quite evident that the *Daily Telegraph* public is not one worth writing literary articles for.

H.N. TO V.S-W.   26th January, 1949
                                                   10 Neville Terrace, S.W.7

Pug Ismay told me that Winston is in too much of a hurry over his book.[2] It may be full of inaccuracies. He has a sailor to do the naval

---

[1] Sir Laming Worthington Evans, Secretary of State for War in Baldwin's second Government of 1924.

[2] His history of the Second World War. The first volume had been published in 1948. The next four followed at yearly intervals, and the sixth was published in 1954. General Lord Ismay, who had been Churchill's military adviser during the war, gave him 'invaluable aid' in preparing his war memoirs.

part, and an airman to do the air part, and expects Pug to do the military part and young Deakin[1] to be a sort of general editor. But he expects them all to produce their stuff within twelve hours. Pug thinks it is because Winston is convinced that the Tories will get in at the next Election and he wants to finish his book before he is once again Prime Minister.

V.S-W. TO H.N.   *23rd February, 1949*
                                                      Sissinghurst

Darling, this is the sort of thing that amuses us. I was copying out the list of places where I was to lecture, and I found ' "Modern English Fiction", *Malaga*'. Now supposing Pepita, as a little *muchacha* in Malaga, could have had a glimpse into the future, and foreseen her granddaughter not as 'a bird in the air' but as a lecturer on a platform, wouldn't she have been incredulous and surprised?

How Virginia [Woolf] would have appreciated this!

H.N. TO V.S-W. (*in Seville*)   *3rd March, 1949*
                                                 10 Neville Terrace, S.W.7

I went and worked all day at Windsor. It was a terribly cold day with a real north-easter howling round the great tower. But the view from my room was as lovely as ever. The towers below me, then the bend of the river, and, beyond, the hills above Marlow and Henley. I read all the Duke of Clarence's[2] letters to King George. Just a silly young army officer he was. I also read King George's letters to Queen Alexandra.[3] He simply worshipped her. They are much the best in the collection, since in them he really speaks his mind. His letters to his father are so stilted and conventional that they are no good at all.

H.N. TO V.S-W. (*in Granada*)   *4th March, 1949*
                                                 10 Neville Terrace, S.W.7

I had Herbert Morrison to lunch at the Club. He had just been on a Privy Council delegation to congratulate the King on the birth of a

[1] Colonel F. W. Deakin, of Wadham College, Oxford, who had also helped Churchill with *Marlborough. His Life and Times.*
[2] King George's elder brother, who died of pneumonia in 1892 at the age of 28.
[3] His mother (1844-1925), the daughter of King Christian IX of Denmark.

grandson. He said the King looked as fit as anything and was bursting with conversation. 'I am a monarchist', said Morrison. 'Your old boy was a good King, and so is this one. We may consider ourselves damned lucky.' I had a nice luncheon and pumped him hard. He had taken the trouble to write out a note of his reminiscences of 1931[1] and to consult other surviving colleagues. So it was a really valuable conversation and well worth the money the lunch cost me. Herbert is not ascetic. He enjoys his food and wine. He likes a cigar. But he is an alert, intelligent man and very fair-minded.

Think of wet pavements here, and cold dark wet slate roofs, and enjoy the *odeur pénétrante des buis* in the Generalife.[2] I do so hate not being in my own dear home. All that George V felt about Sandringham I feel about Sissinghurst.

V.S-W. TO H.N.   *10th March, 1949*
                                         Parador de San Francisco,
                                         Alhambra, Granada, Spain

Here I am in my *parador*. I found your letter of 4th March and the profile of you. It is good, I think. Is it by Bruce Lockhart?[3]

I have had an odd experience today. I have been to the street where Pepita was born in Malaga. Oh such a slum it is—very narrow. You could almost shake hands from one little balcony to the other opposite, crowded with people and children. But there can be no doubt at all that it was exactly the same when Pepita played there as a little girl.

Then we came to Granada by a fine mountain road with wide views, and there was the Sierra Nevada at the end of it, very thickly white, and the Alhambra hanging on to the hillside. I have no lecture here as the University has gone on strike![4]

---

[1] Herbert Morrison had been Minister of Transport in Ramsay MacDonald's Cabinet, and although one of the most junior Ministers, was the first to protest that he could not follow MacDonald into a Coalition Government.

[2] The 13th-century villa and garden attached to the Alhambra, Granada.

[3] H.N. had sent her a copy of the profile of him published in the *Observer* on 6th March, without telling her that it was written by his younger son.

[4] This was not the real reason. When she wrote this letter she had a temperature of 104.

DIARY   *15th March, 1949*
I am alarmed to find a telegram waiting for me on the breakfast
table: 'Lectures Barcelona cancelled. Arrive Dover 4.20 Thursday.
Please inform Sissinghurst. All well. Love Vita'. Now I do not
believe all is well. I fear the strain has been too much for her and
that she has broken down. I am worried but can only wait till
Thursday.
   I go to the Army & Navy Stores to get them to make me a suit
from the tweed Nigel gave me. I say I want it double-breasted. The
man is deeply shocked. 'Surely not, sir; not in the country.' I say
I don't care a hoot and it must be double-breasted. 'It will give you
that Continental look, sir.' 'That is what I require. I have always
wanted to be mistaken for an Austrian count.'
   I go to the Opera with the [Sir John] Andersons. It is very convenient going to the royal box, as one has dinner in the anteroom
during the intervals. There is *Lac des Cygnes* with Robert Helpmann
and Margot Fonteyn. I enjoy it very much indeed. Our party consists
of Nancy Rodd [Mitford] in a magnificent Paris frock, [Lady]
Pamela Berry and R. A. Butler. The latter in the intervals is interesting. He says that the Government have done very well so far, and
are certain to win the next Election. Cripps, especially, has been
superb. But when the lean days come, they will not be so good. He
feels that Cripps is bound to 'damp off'. He told him so to his face.
Cripps was amused. 'You do not realise how adaptable I am. I
could become the champion of luxury and private enterprise
overnight.'

DIARY   *21st March, 1949*
I go to see Queen Mary in Marlborough House. She seems smaller
than I expected. She asked me whether I wished to put any questions
to her. I said that in the course of my reading there would evidently
be many things that puzzled me, but that for the moment there were
very few things about which I was uncertain. For one thing, I
found that I had taken likes and dislikes, as always happened when
one steeped oneself in the life of an individual. I had acquired a great
liking for Queen Olga of Greece.[1] 'Quite right too', she said. 'The
Queen was a second mother to him.' Similarly I had taken a great
[1] The King's aunt.

dislike to Canon Dalton.[1] She was surprised by this at first. 'The King was very fond of him', she said ruminatively. I said I did not like the way he had written letters complaining of the naval officers and had not allowed the Princes to consort with their fellow-midshipmen. She said she had never heard of his sneaking about the naval officers, which was wrong. The segregation of the Princes was even more wrong. But what she had against Dalton was that he never tried really to educate the Princes. It was disgraceful that 'the King' had not been taught more. I asked her whether he could speak French really well. She did not quite like that question. 'No', she said, rather stiffly. She said that the King was by nature an immensely loyal man. He loved his old friends and servants. He was also extra-ordinarily truthful. He never liked 'going round and round', and at this she made a circular movement with her fingers.

I asked her who 'The Brat' was, who appears so often in the earlier diaries. She said (after some moments of thought) that she was the eldest daughter of the Crown Princess Frederick, who married a Saxe-Meiningen.

She then turned to the question of his relation with his sons. She said that the real difficulty had been with the Duke of Windsor and never with 'the present King', who always got on well with his father. I said that I had heard that he was good to the children when they were young, and good to them once they married; but that when they were young bachelors, he was so terrified that they might fall into bad company, that he nagged at them. She said this was true. She added that 'the present King' had been appalled when he succeeded. 'He was devoted to his brother, and the whole abdication crisis made him miserable. He sobbed on my shoulder for a whole hour—there, upon that sofa. But he has made good. Even his stam-mer has been corrected. And now he is so ill, poor boy, so ill.' This in such a sad voice.

She then asked me about Mummy [Lady Carnock] and Vita. I told her that the latter had been ill in Granada, and that I had had a sort of feeling about it. 'I believe in telepathy', she said. 'It was like

[1] Canon John Dalton, the father of Hugh Dalton, was appointed tutor to Prince George and Prince Eddy in 1871, and remained with one or other of the Princes for the next fourteen years. He died in 1931 at the age of 91.

that between the King and me. We knew what was happening to each other, even when separated.'

She then showed me some of her treasures, and we parted. It was a useful conversation. She is not reserved in the least. I shall find her a great help. She made me feel the meaning of the phrase *grande dame*.

DIARY   1st April, 1949

I lunch at the Beefsteak and have an amusing conversation with Oliver Esher,[1] Andrew McLaren[2] and Clive Bell[3] on survival after death. Clive is an agnostic; I a disbeliever; Andie a believer. I say that evolution is my theory. I want to give expression to such faculties as I possess even as a sweet-pea strives to be a better sweet-pea than other sweet-peas.

DIARY   10th April, 1949

I do not think that Viti is tired in the evenings. But she makes such an effort to hide anything which might worry me. I had forgotten to pick the flowers for London, and went out by moonlight into the orchard. Rollo galloped round in wide circles of delight snapping daffodils. I pick the ones he has snapped and also some of the forsythia sprigs on the edge of the moat. It is so calm and lovely, and the wind has dropped. From the end of the silent moat I can see the light in Viti's room.

DIARY   17th April, 1949

After tea, a great event happens. I actually begin writing *George V*. I am starting on the chapter dealing with the 1931 crisis, as I want to have that chapter checked by people while still in possession of their faculties. I do not get very far, but at least I have made a start.

After sunset I climb up the tower to pull down the flag. There is a great red glow in the west and the whole of Kent lies below me bathed in golden light. The garden looks so rich from that eminence —masses of blossom and daffodils among the dark of the yews. It truly is a most beautiful garden—so varied, so calm, so enclosed. It is a garden which I should envy much if it belonged to someone else.

[1] The 3rd Viscount Esher, Chairman of the National Trust.
[2] Labour M.P. for the Burslem division of Stoke-on-Trent, 1924-31 and 1935-45.
[3] The art-critic.

And all this calm reflects my deep *soulagement* at Vita's improvement in health. I have been so deeply worried since she returned from Spain.

H.N. TO V.S-W.   25th April, 1949
                                         10 Neville Terrace, S.W.7

Oh dear, it was a hard thing to leave my lovely home on such a Sunday afternoon in spring. But I am glad I did it. One ought sometimes to do these things—being really and truly unselfish. I mean, no possible profit of any sort could accrue to me by lecturing to Jimmy Mallon's Citizens Council in Whitechapel.[1] But Jimmy devotes his life to these people and just makes one feel ashamed of one's own self-indulgent existence. So that I should have harboured guilt (even as the box-edgings harbour slugs) had I not gone. As it is, I harbour virtue.

I dined with him first at the Reform Club, and then we took a taxi to the East End. My audience, I regret to say, consists very largely of West Indian negroes, who, it seems, have flooded into London in the hope of high wages. All they get are rude remarks, the denial of white women and a sense that they are shunned. The communists get hold of them and assure them that they are being 'exploited'. They thus constitute a serious social problem.

I do not think that many of the Jamaicans, Haitians and Trinidadians who were present quite understood my elaborate explanation of tolerance and the democratic State. But it was a good speech as speeches go, only it did not go properly. But Jimmy and Charles Tennyson liked it. The latter is the great-grandson of the huge bearded poet (he truly was a poet, darling, and I wish I had realised that more deeply when I wrote that slight book about him[2]), and has a swarthy Tennysonian look and is interested in community centres. A man after Jimmy's own heart.

When I got out, the pavements were wet and the red traffic-lights shone in them repeatedly. I hoped it was raining on my *Omphaloides* and on the lilac and on the paeonies. How lovely were the pictures that this list of words conjured up!

[1] James Mallon, Warden of Toynbee Hall. He was a Governor of the B.B.C. during the same period as H.N., 1941–46.
[2] *Tennyson*. Constable, 1923.

169

DIARY   *27th April, 1949*

The Prime Ministers of the Dominions plus Attlee plus Nehru go
to see the King this afternoon and inform him that India wishes to
be both a Republic and a Member of the Commonwealth. They
have drawn up a formula in which, with a smile of bland self-
satisfaction, they make a wholly illogical, meaningless, self-contra-
dictory but admirable statement. India refuses to recognise the King
in so far as India is concerned, but does recognise him as Head of the
Commonwealth and 'symbol of the free association of its independent member States'. Of course all this makes utter nonsense and will
make the French smile. Of course it will arouse in the British that
particularly irritating form of self-applause: 'Only we could be
quite so illogical as that.' But in fact it is a fine piece of good sense,
and will enhance Attlee's already growing prestige. People are
ceasing to think of him as a 'dear little man'. They realise that he has
vision and courage and integrity so compelling that it is a force in
itself.

DIARY   *24th May, 1949*

I take part in the Brains Trust. Gilbert Harding is the question-
master, and the team consists in Violet Bonham Carter, Beverley
Baxter,[1] Julian Huxley and Frank O'Connor.[2] The questions are:
'Is knowledge better than wisdom?'; 'Ought girls to do national
service as well as boys?'; 'Is the English sense of humour cynical?';
'What existing legislation should be repealed?' (I say that covering
sex offences); 'Is the telephone a boon or a bane?'; 'Is taste heredi-
tary?'; 'Do beer and beef form national character?'; 'What event in
history would you most like to have witnessed?' They are silly
about the last. Of course what we should have wanted to see is the
Crucifixion. But they say silly things like the first night of *Tristan
and Isolde*.

V.S-W. TO H.N.   *8th June, 1949*
                                                       Sissinghurst

Benjamin Constant is a very good book, Hadji. It makes me proud

[1] Editor of the *Daily Express* 1929-33, author, and Conservative M.P. since 1935.
[2] The pseudonym of the writer and journalist, whose real name was Michael
   O'Donovan.

of you all over again. It is a beautifully built-up book—you know, the way in which the characters emerge and solidify, and then put on their colours—a work of conscious art. I am glad Tray [Raymond Mortimer] appreciated it, because he has the highest standards and never says anything he doesn't mean.

DIARY   10th June, 1949

National Trust all day. We are getting more and more evidence that the present Government (or rather their supporters) do not like the Trust because it is managed by aristocrats working on a voluntary basis. One of the things I do not like about Socialists is their distrust of gratuitous public service. A man like Esher, for instance, devotes his whole life to the furtherance and protection of the arts. But as he gives his services free, he is regarded with some suspicion by the doctrinaires.

H.N. TO V.S-W.   15th June, 1949
                                                        10 Neville Terrace, S.W.7

I do hope you will keep to the original idea of making the delphinium beds into grey and white, and not be diverted into too much blue.[1] Moreover, it should be a July garden to carry on after the roses have declined in beauty. I think of it as *cineraria* in masses, Rabbit's Ears in masses, Lad's Love a good deal, some *Santolina*—the whole background being predominantly grey. Then out of this jungle growth I wish regale to rise. I know it means keeping regale seeds every year and having them brought on in pans. But that is not too much trouble, and once we get the succession going regularly, it does not matter how many of the old bulbs die off. So although I would welcome a fid or two of *Anchusa* or something else blue among these white and silver objects, I hope you will keep the main colour scheme firm. Otherwise it may all just look like a flower-border anywhere.

DIARY   26th June, 1949

I do my review of Bernard Berenson's *Sketch for a Self-Portrait*. I sense the conflict between sincerity and good feeling. He asks him-

[1] This was the origin of the White Garden, which has become the best-known of all the separate gardens at Sissinghurst.

self why he has not been able to inspire in others the confidence and affection he feels for them. Of course the answer is that he debauched his talent to make money and that he was harsh and selfish to his contemporaries. But he was good to young people—Kenneth Clark and Geoffrey Scott,[1] Ben and Nigel—and he did teach them all his zest for beauty. How can I insult a man of 85? Yet by writing an adulatory review of his book, I suppose I am sinning against pure integrity. Raymond [Mortimer], in such a quandary, would not review the book at all. But under my dreadful time-pressure I cannot afford not to review a book which I have read with care.

A dreadful woman bursts in upon us and wants to photograph us for a feature article in *Picture Post*. I am very firm, but Viti with her warm-heartedness is weak. She calls it 'being polite'. Anyhow I refuse to be photographed, and go off and weed. I am weeding away, grunting under a forsythia, when I realise she is behind me with her camera. All she can have photographed was a large grey-flannel bottom.[2]

DIARY   *7th July, 1949*

Rab Butler told Nigel that it had been suggested that I should be given a peerage in 1945, but Winston had said, 'Better wait a bit'. Supposing Winston had agreed, what a difference it would have made to my life! No Labour Party, no North Croydon, and probably no George V. But I should have minded missing the latter. It was not that I joined the Labour Party in order to get a peerage; it was rather that I had been told for certain that I was going to be on Attlee's list and thought it more decent, if I meant to accept (as I then did), to join the Party in advance. I simply loathe the status of an Independent and my political sympathies are closer to the Labour Party than anything else. So far, I feel I acted decently and perhaps wisely. But when nothing happened about the peerage, I was fixed in the Labour Party and Croydon. The realities, and above all the personalities, of Labour politics really revolted me. Thus I am left in a terribly false position which with great foresight and wisdom I might have avoided. Were I to be offered a peerage today, my

[1] Author of *Portrait of Zélide* etc. A great friend of V.S-W., he died in 1929.

[2] The resulting photograph, and one of V.S-W. taken on the same occasion, are reproduced facing p. 176.

inclination would be to refuse. I am getting too old to be an active force in politics, and I do not just want to be a Lord with no work to do.

H.N. TO V.S-W.   *12th July, 1949*
                                                     10 Neville Terrace, S.W.7

Raymond [Mortimer] was at the Committee of the London Library, and I walked away with him. What a dear friend he is—always so affectionate and gay and wise. I suppose I am fonder of him fundamentally than of any of my other friends. He is so *good* underneath, isn't he? I mean, all his little affectations are just surface things to a deeply dutiful and decent character. I like people to be *good*.

DIARY   *17th July, 1949*

I start writing Chapter I of my book on George V. I begin: 'Prince George was born at Marlborough House, London, at 1.30 a.m. on the morning of June 3, 1865.' I gaze at the sentence in wonder, realising what a long journey I have to go before I reach his death. It is like starting in a taxi on the way to Vladivostok.

DIARY   *25th July, 1949*

I lunch with Niggs and George Weidenfeld at the Travellers.[1] The latter has been asked by [Chaim] Weizmann to become his personal assistant. The problem is whether he should become an Israeli and get a definite job in the Israeli civil service. Or whether he shall remain a British subject, go on with *Contact*, and merely attach himself to Weizmann for short periods. It seems that as yet there is no constitutional provision for the powers which the President of Israel is to exercise. He may become as important as the President of the U.S.A. He may be relegated to obscurity like the President of Eire. Probably Weizmann himself will always enjoy special influence and prestige, but they will not want to bind themselves by written constitutional provisions to transfer any real power to future Presidents. At present, Weizmann is ignored when things are

[1] The publishing firm of Weidenfeld & Nicolson Ltd was about to emerge from their first venture, *Contact*. The new firm was launched on 10th November, 1949.

going well, and only appealed to when there are international difficulties.

I advise George to accept Weizmann's offer temporarily.

DIARY   *8th August, 1949*

I finish Chapter III [of *King George V*]. It will be difficult to prevent these early chapters being too bitty. I shall have to slide from my early chirrupy overture into a wider and more solemn note.

H.N. TO V.S-W.   *17th August, 1949*
                                                    10 Neville Terrace, S.W.7

I fear that I am getting a down on George V just now. He is all right as a gay young midshipman. He may be all right as a wise old King. But the intervening period when he was Duke of York, just shooting at Sandringham, is hard to manage or swallow. For seventeen years he did nothing at all but kill animals and stick in stamps.[1]

DIARY   *28th August, 1949*

I review Joad's book on Shaw. In the afternoon I plant some white *Muscari* and some Anemone 'Creagh Castle'. I talk to Moura[2] until she goes by the evening train. It is a joy to have her here. She really is one of the most delightful people I have ever known.

DIARY   *7th September, 1949*

T. S. Eliot is so modest and charming. He is off to lecture in Germany. He asked me whether they would expect a 'message'. I said the only thing to do was to treat them as ordinary members of

[1] In the book H.N. got round the difficulty as follows: 'These years . . . succeeded each other with placid similitude. Apart from occasional public functions and a few official journeys, he lived the life of a private country gentleman, unostentatious, comparatively retired, almost obscure. . . . Had it not been for his frequent and intimate conversations with his father, for his occasional meetings with leading politicians, his knowledge of public affairs would have been neither wider nor deeper than that acquired by any other landowner or sportsman from a daily perusal of *The Times*.'

[2] Baroness Budberg, who was born in Russia and by her first marriage was Moura Benckendorff.

cultured society, much as one would treat a dipsomaniac. 'Thank you', he says, 'I shall do that.'

I go to the British Museum, where they had ready for me the novel *Wrong on Both Sides*,[1] which made King George cry so frequently. It has no literary merit whatever, being written in the *Little Lord Fauntleroy* style. The theme is that of a proud and harsh old Earl who snubs and bullies the beautiful young Viscount, his son, but loves him deeply underneath. Interesting psychologically.

I dine with the Hamish Hamiltons to meet Judge Learned Hand.[2] The Judge, who is a dear, denies that there are any absolutes in life. I say that untruthfulness and cruelty are always wrong anywhere and in any circumstances. He shakes his fine head.

DIARY   *14th September, 1949*

I work the whole time on Chapter VI and finish with the death of King Edward VII just before dinner. But in my bath I decide that I must make two chapters of it. This is depressing, but right. One simply must be firm with oneself about getting the architecture of books right.

DIARY   *24th September, 1949*

We are all feeling depressed about the Russian atomic bomb.[3] We were told that they would not have one for five years, and they have got it in four. Does this really make so much difference? It may encourage the satellites to be more overweening, but it may also encourage Russia to be a little less nervous.

DIARY   *4th October, 1949*

I spend the morning visiting York Cottage,[4] the nest, the dairy, the gardens and the big house. There is nothing to differentiate the cottage from any of the villas at Surbiton. How right the Duke of

---

[1] By Vin Vincent, 1885.

[2] One of the judges of the United States Circuit Court, 1924-53.

[3] The news of the Russian mastery of the atomic secret had been announced from Downing Street and the White House on the previous day.

[4] At Sandringham. 'This most undesirable residence', wrote H.N. in *King George V*, 'remained his favourite home for thirty-three years. It was here that five of his six children were born.'

Windsor was to say to me, 'Until you have seen York Cottage you will never understand my father'. It is almost incredible that the heir to so vast a heritage lived in this horrible little house. It is now partly an estate office and partly flats. But it is still untenanted in the upper floors and we went all over it. The King's and Queen's baths had lids that shut down so that when not in use they could be used as tables. His study was a monstrous little cold room with a north window shrouded by shrubberies, and the walls are covered in red cloth which he had been given while on a visit to Paris. It is the cloth from which the trousers of the French private soldiers used to be made. On the walls he had some reproductions of Royal Academy pictures. The servants' rooms are mere attics with skylights. There is no garden.

The 'nest', built as a surprise for Queen Alexandra by old Probyn,[1] is a tiny sentry-box with tiles and inscriptions inside. One of the inscriptions is, 'Sunset and evening star, and one clear call for me'.[2] We then go to the main house. It reminds me of Clandeboye.[3] The hall, dining-room and drawing-room have been redecorated by the present Queen and are in good modern taste. There are Goya tapestries in the dining-room which are very gay. The corridors are full of bronze racehorses and regimental emblems and tusks.

DIARY   *20th November, 1949*

I talk to Viti about Knole, telling her that [Lord] Willingdon is resigning from the Trust and Niggs and Lionel[4] are taking over. She is pleased by this, but breaks down afterwards. Poor darling, she hides in the dark of my book-room and sobs and sobs into the corner. No person has ever loved anything as Viti has loved Knole.

DIARY   *19th December, 1949*

I go to Pratts, meeting Edward Boyle[5] on the way, and taking him

---

[1] Sir Dighton Probyn, Comptroller of Queen Alexandra's Household.

[2] From Tennyson's *Crossing the Bar*.

[3] Lord Dufferin's house in Northern Ireland, where H.N. spent some of his school-holidays.

[4] Lionel Sackville-West, now (1968) sixth Baron Sackville. The Trust was that of the Sackville Settled Estates, not of Knole itself.

[5] Sir Edward Boyle, the future Minister of Education, was then aged 26. H.N. had first met him when he was President of the Oxford Union in 1948.

Harold Nicolson and
(below) *V. Sackville-West in
the garden at Sissinghurst
June 1949 (see page 172)*

Bertrand Russell, Harold Nicolson and Lord Samuel at the B.B.C. before their discussion, 'Why defend Liberty?' on 24 January 1951 (see page 202)

with me. He is now a Tory candidate and assistant-editor of the *National Review*. He says that in the modern world, the age of the amateur statesman is over. We must now specialise, concentrate, limit ourselves. I fear that this is true.

DIARY   29th December, 1949

I lunch with Antoine Bibesco[1] at the Savoy. The others there are Ethel Sands[2] and Desmond MacCarthy.[3] I ask Antoine whether his friends realised how really ill Proust was. He said that they had come to take it all for granted, and that they were all startled when he died.[4] He said that Proust fully realised after 1914 that he would live as a great writer. Antoine, who had always predicted his genius, was delighted when his prophecy was justified. But others were a little annoyed that *le petit Marcel* should have achieved immortality.

We discuss why it is that people in England should admire French writers who are not admired in France and vice versa. For instance, Anatole France, who is not regarded today even as a good stylist. That brings us to Charles Morgan. Desmond as usual is generous about him. 'A most competent writer', he says, 'and one whom we should be mistaken to dismiss. His *Portrait in a Mirror* was a good book. The *Fountain* was popular in France because it describes noble adultery. The English are bored by noble adultery. The hedonists are irritated when adultery implies any moral scruples. The puritans are annoyed when any moral scruples are brought into relation with adultery. But to the French noble adultery is quite a new idea. They find it powerful.'

We also discuss the higher estimation of Maurice Baring in France. Desmond says, 'The English do not appreciate subtlety unless it is underlined. Maurice wrote so smoothly that the English swallowed him like junket, not realising how much flavour there really was. The French do not bolt things as we do; they keep the junket in their mouths for a while, and thus appreciate the flavour.'

[1] Prince Antoine Bibesco had been in the Rumanian Foreign Service before the second war, and married Lady Elizabeth Asquith in 1919.

[2] A painter and an old literary friend of H.N., who lived mostly in Normandy.

[3] Previously Editor of *Life and Letters*, Literary Editor of the *New Statesman*, and the leading literary critic on the *Sunday Times* for many years.

[4] Marcel Proust had suffered from asthma since he was a boy, and died in Paris in 1922.

31st December, 1949

Just before midnight I go out and walk in the spring-garden. There
is a bright moon. I hear the clock strike midnight and say 'rabbits'
between the sixth and seventh stroke. When it is finished, there is
a hush over the world, and only a light in my own sitting-room.
Then the bells of Frittenden ring out over the moon-drenched land.
I walk in again. I close the door and go to bed. That is the end of
1949.

It is not a year on which I shall look back with any special delight.
It was darkened for me by Vita getting so ill in Spain. She seems to
have recovered completely and her back is certainly much better.
But I do not think her nerves are in a good state, poor darling. She
gets easily flurried and falls into moods of confusion and inattention.
She forgets things badly, and is not able to concentrate on her work.
This makes her restless and at times unhappy.

For me it has been an uneventful year. My whole life, really, has
been taken up with George V—a book which I foresee will take me
much longer than I supposed. I find it a fascinating pursuit and I
enjoy my work. I am conscious also that it furnishes me with an
excuse for doing nothing else. Were it not for this constant and quite
reputable employment, I should at least have to pretend to indulge in
politics. Yet in my heart I know that for me politics are over for
ever. I have no longer that energy or zest which enabled me once to
overcome my distaste for the public platform or my fastidiousness
about political affiliations. I do believe, as I have always believed,
that Social Democracy is the only possible antidote to communism.
But I do not like the Labour Party. I am a mixture of an aristocrat
and a Bohemian. The bedintness[1] of the Labour people is as repug-
nant to me as is their gentility. I feel ill at ease, self-conscious,
insincere, unauthentic, in their presence. I have none of the histrionic
capacity of Hugh Dalton and William Jowitt. I cannot act parts. I
am glad therefore to have an excellent excuse to withdraw into my
Round Tower.

I am conscious also that during this year I have become much
older. I do not think that my deafness has seriously increased, nor
are my limbs much less supple than they were in 1948. But I have

[1] A Sackville expression, denoting the attitudes and manners of the lower-middle
class.

put on weight and lost many teeth and much hair, and perhaps vigour. I am not really conscious of a decline in my mental energy. But I have intimations that my thoughts move in the old grooves and do not push out into new grooves, and that my ways of expression are becoming stereotyped. It is not a good period of history into which to grow old. Money difficulties arise. I have to go on slogging away at articles and broadcasts in order to maintain my income. I cannot save; and when my mind decays, how shall I live? How? How? How? I do not want to become an *achthos aroures*[1] or a burden upon my sons. Nor am I temperamentally suited to old age. I have no liking for dignity, sobriety, repute and authority. I do not want to be reverenced. I suffer from the sad defects of every epicurean. But I have at least the honesty to remain convinced that the epicurean is the only philosophy, if rightly understood as the art of life. Which implies a certain degree of virtue.

Anyhow, goodbye to 1949, and thank you for not having been worse.

---

[1] 'A burden on the earth'. Homer's *Iliad*, xviii 104.

1950

The conscience of a biographer – General Election – small Labour majority – a glittering occasion at the French Embassy – Nigel in Cornwall – outbreak of the Korean war – progress of 'King George V' – visit to Bernard Berenson in Florence – death of Sibyl Colefax – the new House of Commons – Bernard Shaw's house – 'The year closes in a mist of anxiety'

Like 1949, 1950 was almost wholly taken up by 'King George V', with a break in September, when Harold Nicolson and V. Sackville-West motored to Florence. Over none of his other books did he spend more time or take greater care. There were not only the files to be read at Windsor, St James's Palace and Buckingham Palace, but all the printed documents and memoirs of the reign. The material was enormous. He decided to write the book in four parts: Part I from the King's birth in 1865 until his accession in 1910; Part II to the end of the First World War; Part III to 1924; Part IV to the King's death in 1936. As each part was finished, it was set up in a bound proof for submission to George VI and Queen Mary. The Royal Family requested very few changes. By the end of the year the biography had been completed as far as 1921, or about two-thirds of the whole.

Harold Nicolson took no part in the General Election of February, which resulted in a Labour victory by a narrow majority. I fought his old seat (now converted by boundary changes from West Leicester to North West Leicester) against his former opponent, Barnett Janner, but lost it by 7,600 votes. Soon afterwards I was adopted as Conservative candidate for the Labour seat of Falmouth and Camborne. In the world at large, the most important event was the outbreak of the Korean war in June, but Harold Nicolson, deeply engaged in his book, was taking a diminishing interest in foreign affairs.

V.S-W. TO H.N.   *3rd January, 1950*
                                                                      Sissinghurst

It drizzles. How fortunate we both are to have both indoor and outdoor occupations. If we can't garden, we can write. At least you can write: I can't. I am really rather depressed by my inability to write the simplest thing.[1] No, let me be truthful, I am not 'rather

[1] This was rather a blank period in V.S-W.'s literary output. In 1946 she had published her long poem, *The Garden*, and in 1947 *Nursery Rhymes*. Then there was no new book until her novel *The Easter Party*, which she began to write at

183

depressed', but mortally depressed. I am like a motor-car that has been standing in a cold garage and refuses to give out even one little *pétard* of a firing-spark. I daresay it will warm up again some day, but meanwhile it is as cold as a frog. I envy the vitality of Jane Carlyle.[1] I re-read Virginia [Woolf's] essay in *The Common Reader* 'Geraldine and Jane', and discovered with amusement that Geraldine [Jewsbury] had spent the last years of her life at Sevenoaks. I wonder where? In which house? Did she wander round the park at Knole?

DIARY   17th January, 1950

Down to Windsor. I lunch with Owen Morshead. I suggested that there might come a moment when my conscience as a biographer became strained. What would happen if I found something which was really damaging to the King—for instance, a threat to abdicate if the Home Rule Bill were passed? My duty to the student would be to publish this. But what if they asked me to cut it out? Could I resign my task? I fear I have no mystic feeling about the Monarchy. I regard it merely as a useful institution.

H.N. TO V.S-W.   25th January, 1950
                                                      10 Neville Terrace, S.W.7

I dined with Guy Burgess.[2] Oh my dear, what a sad, sad thing this constant drinking is! Guy used to have one of the most rapid and acute minds I knew. Now he is just an imitation (and a pretty bad one) of what he once was. Not that he was actually drunk yesterday. He was just soaked and silly. I felt angry about it.

---

the end of 1950 and published in 1953. But from May 1946 until January 1950 she wrote occasional articles for the *Observer* on gardening. In the latter year they became regular weekly articles entitled 'In Your Garden', which she continued to write for the next eleven years.

[1] Jane Welsh Carlyle (1801–66), the wife of Thomas Carlyle. Geraldine Jewsbury (1812–80) was the novelist, author of *Zoe, Right or Wrong* etc.

[2] He was then working in the Far Eastern Department of the Foreign Office, and was to join the staff of the Washington Embassy later in the year. He was recalled from Washington because he behaved too badly, and defected to Russia in May 1951.

DIARY   *2nd February, 1950*

Nigel goes up to Leicester to start his Election campaign. He has his adoption meeting tonight.

I drop Chapter VIII[1] at Buckingham Palace, as I want Tommy [Lascelles] to see it before anyone else. It is too delicate a subject to be trusted to clumsy hands. If I say that the King has no power at all, he may be hurt and say that he is a mere cypher. But if I indicate that in certain circumstances he can dissent from the advice of Ministers, then assuredly the Radical Press would claim that the Crown is too powerful.

V.S-W. TO N.N. (*in Leicester*)   *6th February, 1950*

Now listen, you must tell me if there is anything I could usefully send you to eat. I have sent some honey for your breakfast, and a cake, and some ginger biscuits. It is your supper which worries me, so I am also sending a tin of turkey, which you can keep to fall back on if you feel specially hungry one evening and can't get anything to eat at the hotel. But once you have opened it, you must turn it out of its tin on to a plate and *not keep it in the tin*. And put the plate somewhere cool, e.g., on a window-sill, *not* on top of a radiator. I have sent a tin-opener with it. A little butter for breakfast; and will send some more later in the week. Some chocolate and some cheese.[2]

They told me something at the B.B.C. which will interest you. If ever there is any attack on Winston in the political broadcasts, people start ringing up by the hundred. It is what provokes more telephone calls than anything.

The moat is overflowing. The ducks are blissful. They sail triumphantly over what ought to be, and once was, a bed of irises. Their world has returned to what they think the whole world ought to be: water. They got dreadfully puzzled when it became ice.

Now I take my leave of you, my precious, oh so precious, Niggs. But I never really take my leave, because you are in my heart and my thoughts all the time. Remember that I would come up at any moment if you wanted me to. If I could be of any use.

[1] The chapter was entitled 'The Monarchy', and it dealt with the whole subject of the royal prerogative.
[2] There was still food-rationing in Britain.

DIARY   *13th February, 1950*

Philip Jordan[1] tells me that Attlee says the enthusiasm of his meetings today far exceeds that of 1945. I think this is because Attlee himself has increased so much in repute and popularity. He says that Attlee expects to get back with a majority of 60. The Labour Whips say, 'If we have a majority of 80, we shall sleep comfortably; if we have a majority of 60, we shall have to take sleeping-draughts; if we have a majority of 40, we shall all be dead in two years.'

Philip Jordan also told me that he had asked Herbert Morrison why on earth I had not been sent to the Upper House. Herbert had replied, 'The boys wouldn't like it. They can't forgive him for North Croydon.' All of which means that Transport House were irritated by the flippant article I wrote in the *Spectator*.[2]

H.N. TO V.S-W.   *16th February, 1950*
                                                        10 Neville Terrace, S.W.7

The River Thames has risen just to the lip of the bank, and one feels that another cupful would send the playing fields of Eton aswim. The wind howled through my high gothic window and I had to draw the curtains and work by electric light crouched over the fire. If four days elapse without my being in the room, the cold of 1077 settles round it.

I do not think that Winston was right in raising the atom bomb question in that way at this moment. What I mean is, that to suggest talks with Stalin on the highest level inevitably makes people think, 'Winston could talk to Stalin on more or less the same level. But if Attlee goes, it would be like a mouse addressing a tiger. Therefore vote for Winston.' No—I agree with Bevin, it was a stunt, and unworthy of him.

[1] Public Relations Adviser to the Prime Minister since 1947. He died in June 1951.
[2] See pp. 133-7.

24th February, 1950

One of the most exciting days I have ever had.[1] In the morning it looks as if the Labour lead of sixty seats above all other parties will be maintained. I listen to the wireless at home for a bit, and then go down to the Dorchester where the Rothermeres have flung a party. There is food and champagne. From time to time the loudspeaker calls, 'Attention! Attention!', and then gives the state of the parties. I was on edge rather, expecting Nigel's result to come over at any moment. I then discover that they only announce the state of the parties every quarter of an hour and that the actual seats are put up on a rack at the end of the other room. I go to the rack and there I see: '*Leicester N.W.* Janner, B. (Lab.) 23,505; Nicolson, N. (C.) 15,912; Burrows, R. A. (L.) 5,036. Labour majority, 7,593.' I feel sick for a moment, but not really shattered. Poor Niggs. I see that in Leicester N.E. and S.W. the Tories have also been defeated and by larger majorities.

Having had this blow, I return to my champagne. At about 1 pm. the gap between Labour and Conservative begins suddenly to narrow. Excitement rises. People do not behave well. They boo a Labour victory and hoot with joy at a Conservative victory. They roar with laughter when a Liberal forfeits his deposit. This sickens me, and I leave.

When I get back, the wireless tells me that the gap has narrowed to 1. I then go to the B.B.C. I find them in a state. All their programmes have been dislocated by the Election results, and nobody wants to go on the air while the result is still so unpredictable. I do my 'World Affairs' talk on the assumption that it will be a close thing. Then I am dragged in to do two improvised commentaries, one at 7.45 and one at 9.30. By the latter time it is clear that the Labour Party has a majority of 24 over the Tories and of 17 over all parties. But even as I am spouting away at the microphone, a card is handed to me saying that the gap has been further reduced.

I come back rather bewildered and rather sad. Sad because of Niggs

[1] Polling had taken place on the previous day, but in a great many constituencies the votes were not counted until the morning of the 24th. For a period of about ten minutes the Labour-held seats were equalled by the other two parties combined. The final result was: Labour, 315; Conservatives, 298; Liberal, 9; Irish Nationalists, 2; Speaker, 1. None of the 100 Communist candidates was returned, and of the 476 Liberal candidates, over 300 lost their deposits.

mainly, but also because this dead-heat means a deadlock and there is little prospect of any firm Government being established without a second Election. Labour cannot carry on with a Socialist policy when it is now clear that the country dislikes it.

The bright spots are the high percentage of 85 per cent who went to the polls; the sobriety of the Election—no stunts, no emotionalism, just sober political thought; and the elimination of the communists and fellow-travellers. I am sorry, of course, for the Liberals, but they asked for it.

H.N. TO V.S-W.

9th March, 1950
10 Neville Terrace, S.W.7

I went to the French Embassy for the reception for Vincent Auriol.[1] James [Pope-Hennessy] and I and Clive [Bell] stood at the back and watched while the King and Queen came round and did *cercle*. Then they retired to their own supper-room and we all started talking to our friends. While thus engaged a *maître de cérémonie* came up and said that the President wanted to talk to me. *Grand ami de la France.* So I was dragged through the two crowded salons into the ultimate Royal (so Royal) supper-room and presented to Auriol. He is a dear, and speaks with a strong accent—not exactly meridional but regional. He said how sorry he was that I no longer wrote for the *Figaro*. But I evaded that subject, as I do not really want to start writing for it again. Well, after an exchange of civilities, I shook hands and was about to join the common herd, when I heard a voice say, 'Just the man I want to see'. It was the King. He talked to me for about twenty minutes about the book. From time to time René Massigli came up to interrupt, but the King ignored him. In the end he said, 'I seem to be neglecting my duties. I should like to talk for hours about this. You must come and stay at Windsor.' I had been so interested in our conversation that I had not noticed that there were only about twelve people in the room—the Kings and Queens and Presidents and so on. So I bowed my bow and then talked to the Queen (she did not ask, thank God, whether you were there) and to Princess Elizabeth, and then rejoined the proletariat.

[1] The President of the French Republic, M. Vincent Auriol, was on a State visit to Britain.

But no—I was seized by the arm and this was Winston. 'So you did not stand for your party', he said. 'Cowardice or conversion?' I said that I had not stood because Niggs was standing as a Conservative. 'Oh yes', he said, 'Birmingham, wasn't it?' I said, 'Leicester.' He said, 'Well, I knew it was a hopeless seat—beastly place, Leicester.'[1] He then asked what the King had been talking to me about for all that time. I said it was the book. He said, 'Oh yes, I remember. I want to talk to you about that. I have much information, very much information. Clemmie, remember to ask Harold to lunch one day.' At that moment Attlee passed. 'Well, Attlee', Winston said, 'if we have many more parties like this, we shall be in a coalition together without noticing it at all.'

Then I went away. But doesn't it all sound like something one has made up in one's bath? Anyhow, you must get an evening dress.[2] Even off the peg.

DIARY   13th March, 1950

I go to Hampstead to see Cyril Joad who is ill in bed. He has thrombosis and is not well at all. We discuss old age. He says that he minds losing his sexual powers, but that he finds the tenderness of women appeals to him more than ever before. I say that although my physical powers have declined, my imaginative powers are more alive than ever. *Je connais l'art d'évoquer les choses.* He says this is because I have never been a wholly adult person.

DIARY   31st March, 1950

Léon Blum[3] is dead, and this means that I must scrap the 'Marginal Comment' I wrote yesterday and do something about that clever charming man. I also decide that Paléologue's[4] book is too bad to review. So much of my work this week is wasted. Considering that every hour is packed tight with George V, these wastages distress

[1] Winston Churchill stood unsuccessfully as Liberal candidate for Leicester in 1923.
[2] V.S-W.'s last evening dress was bought in 1927. She had been asked to the party, but refused, with the excuse that she had nothing suitable to wear.
[3] Prime Minister of France in March-April, 1938, and again in 1946.
[4] Maurice Georges Paléologue, the French diplomatist and writer. The book under review was his life of the Empress of Austria.

me. But they ought not to do so unduly. After all, there is no real time-pressure about George V, and the book must be allowed to write itself.

DIARY   28th May, 1950

I am becoming fatter and developing a paunch. I notice that it affects the way I walk. I move more slowly, and with a swinging movement like an elephant. It is dreadful when one notices in one-self the movements and gait of an old man.

H.N. TO V.S-W.   7th June, 1950
                                                              10 Neville Terrace, S.W.7

Nigel went down to Cornwall to open a fête.[1] There was a competition to judge the weight of a pig. Niggs refused to take part in this competition since he had not the slightest idea whether a pig ought to weigh 10 stone or 3 stone. But they crowded round him and insisted. He was in an agony, since his utter ignorance might be exposed and the story would fly from one end of Cornwall to the other. But fortunately the man who was pushing him onwards to the abyss got so excited that he forgot to hide the paper on which he had recorded the guesses of others. Out of the corner of his eye our sly-boot son saw figures written—'62 lbs', '58 lbs', '49 lbs', and so on. With a display of willing surrender he said, 'Very well, I will enter the competition after all'. He walked round and round the pig, gazing at it with an expert eye. Then he stepped back and thought deeply. The crowd which had collected waited in suspense. 'Fifty-seven pounds!' said Niggs loudly and with decision. 'My God!' the man yelled. 'You've won it!' So Niggs goes down in Cornish history as the candidate who won a pig at his first fête.

DIARY   15th June, 1950

I am horrified by the Labour manifesto.[2] It will do immense harm

[1] I had been adopted as Conservative Candidate for Falmouth and Camborne on 13th May.

[2] On 13th June the Labour Party had issued a statement opposing the Schuman Plan for surrendering some sovereign powers to a supra-national Coal and Steel Authority. This was the beginning of Britain's exclusion from the Continental six.

abroad and shake any authority which we have left. It is a truly deplorable document. It means that Dalton, who sponsored it, cannot possibly succeed Bevin. I am deeply distressed by it. How I wish I had not been such an impulsive fool as to join the Labour Party. It was certainly the cardinal error of my life. But I cannot redeem it now.

DIARY   *28th June, 1950*

Rab [Butler], whom I meet at dinner, is worried about the Korean situation and feels that the Americans have rather rushed UNO.[1] It certainly looks as if they had acted first and then obtained the consent of the Security Council afterwards. We discuss the political situation and Rab says that he thinks the Election will come in July.[2] He says that Winston gives fortnightly luncheons at the Savoy to his Shadow Cabinet. At luncheon yesterday he said, 'The old man is very good to me. I could not have managed this [Korean] situation had I been in Attlee's place. I should have been called a war-monger.' 'What old man?' asked David Maxwell Fyfe innocently. 'God, Sir Donald,' replied Winston. It seems he always calls David 'Sir Donald'.

V.S-W. TO H.N.   *24th July, 1950*
                                                        Sissinghurst

Darling, I do think you are doing your book so well. You see, parts of it are *forcément* not my sort of thing, yet your exposition is so lucid that I get interested and want to go on reading. Of course I pounce with delight on the Hadji-bits[3] and wish there were more of them. Not that I want you to make it flippant, as you said, but there is only one Hadji and hundreds of historians. You have a touch like nobody else, and I think you are suppressing it a little too much. For

---

[1] On 25th June North Korean forces invaded the Southern Korean Republic. Two days later President Truman promised military support to South Korea, and Attlee pledged British support for the American Resolution calling on all members of the United Nations to resist communist aggression.

[2] The next General Election did not come until October 1951.

[3] She meant phrases and passages in his own very individual style, compared to narrative in his 'police-court manner' which he adopted for the greater part of *King George V*.

instance, it would not be detracting from the seriousness of the book to put in a few words of description or comment on people like Mr Balfour, Lloyd George or Mr Asquith. I think the austerity which you have imposed on yourself is slightly overdone. Is this tiresome of me? No, I do not think so; for it does not affect what you call the canvas, but means only a few bright flowers stitched in here and there.

H.N. TO V.S-W.   *25th July, 1950*
                                        10 Neville Terrace, S.W.7

I know you are right in thinking that I should make my book less documentary and more alive. I shall certainly try at later stages to introduce more vivid pictures of people and places. It may be that I have been so preoccupied with rendering the style and tone an equable surface (like linen) that I have refrained too austerely from any brocade. But I am sure that in a book of this length it would be a mistake to try to be 'bright'. One has just got to be intelligent. I am enjoying the book, with a purely personal enjoyment. I like the treasure-hunt element in delving into papers. But I do sometimes realise that it will take me four years of my life, and that when at last I have finished it, I shall be left with *picciol verso or è*.[1]

DIARY   *28th July, 1950*

The state of public opinion after Winston's grim speech regarding the armed might of Russia is that of paralysed shock. The dreadful thing is that we can do nothing and that we know nothing. Nobody has any idea what is in the heads of those twelve men in the Kremlin. We are in a condition of blind and dumb dread.

DIARY   *9th August, 1950*

I am cutting my diary down during this period, as most of it is just work, work, work on King George V.

---

[1] *Ahi, fu una nota del poema eterno*
Quel ch'io sentiva e picciol verso or è. Carducci.
'Ah, it was an idea for a great poem that I had in mind, and all I have produced is a little ditty.'

Harold Nicolson and V. Sackville-West with Rollo on the steps of the Tower at Sissinghurst

DIARY   *17th August, 1950*

Paddy Leigh Fermor[1] tells me two Winston stories, each of which he guarantees. Somebody said, 'One never hears of Baldwin nowadays —he might as well be dead.' 'No', said Winston, 'not dead. But the candle in that great turnip has gone out.' The other story was that when Winston was at the Admiralty, the Board objected to some suggestion of his on the grounds that it would not be in accord with naval tradition. 'Naval tradition? Naval tradition?' said Winston. 'Monstrous. Nothing but rum, sodomy, prayers and the lash.'

H.N. TO V.S-W.   *6th September, 1950*
                                             10 Neville Terrace, S.W.7

I go on with my chapters. It is funny how everything depends on habit. I mean, I am used to 'Marginal Comment' and my reviews and broadcasts. They go quite quickly. But when I start writing *George V* again after a long interval,[2] my mind seems encased in mud and furnished with boots of lead.

DIARY   *23rd September, 1950*
                                                            Florence

A glorious hot day. We drive to Vallombrosa,[3] where we stay the night. We are received by Nicky[4] and walk out to see the sunset where we find B.B. and Luisa.[5] They tell us that they have received a telegram saying that Sibyl [Colefax] died in her sleep yesterday at 6.30 in the morning. We are shocked. At dinner B.B. is the gracious host. He talks well. He tells us about Rilke. 'He must have been a very small man', said Vita. 'Small?' said B.B. 'Not in the least. He was my size. But I suppose you would call me small.' B.B. is neat and tidy, but only about 5 ft. 3. He does not care for the moderns. He deplores Ben wasting his energies on the *Burlington*. He says that all the pioneer-work in art-criticism was done long ago, and only

[1] The traveller, phil-Hellene and author of *Mani* etc.
[2] After a long pause for research, he now embarked on the chapters dealing with the First World War.
[3] The village in the mountains above Florence, where Bernard Berenson had a country house.
[4] Nicky Mariano, Berenson's secretary and constant companion.
[5] Luisa Vertova, Berenson's assistant librarian, whom Ben married in 1955

finicky subjects remain. He says that there are so few English art-historians that Ben is obliged to fall back on foreigners, whose style is heavy and dull. He has a great belief in Ben. 'There is', he says, 'something very important at the bottom of that well.'

DIARY   6th October, 1950

I go to Lord North Street. Daker[1] tells me that on her last night Sibyl had the idea that Arthur[2] was waiting in the street below. She kept on asking the nurse to let him in. She suffered nothing and just died while still half asleep. On the table in the hall was her visitors' book with the last dinner she gave in it. All rather tragic. I shall miss her very much.

DIARY   26th October, 1950

I go down to Westminster early in the morning to attend the opening of the new House of Commons.[3] It is curious being back there again, and all the policemen and servants are as polite as ever. I go up to the new Strangers Gallery, where I meet several of my old colleagues of the wartime Parliament who are aged but amicable. The new House is not a pretty building, but I am sure it is infinitely more convenient in terms of air-conditioning and acoustics. But it is so obviously a compromise—a fake of a fake—that it lacks spirit; and the green they have chosen for the benches and the faint olive with which they have toned down the oak are dyspeptic colours.

It all goes as if it were an ordinary meeting. There are jokes as Members come in, and then the cry 'Speaker!' Then Don [Dean of Westminster] and the new Chaplain [Rev. Charles Smyth] come in and we have prayers. Very strange to be turning round again with my face to the wall and praying God to strengthen me to resist prejudices and partial affections. Then comes 'Order! Order!' quite startlingly through the microphones behind our heads. The Speaker makes an apt speech; the P.M. makes an apt speech; Winston makes a delightful speech—quite in his old form. Then Clem Davies and

[1] Lady Colefax's maid, at 19 Lord North Street.
[2] Sir Arthur Colefax, who died in 1936.
[3] The old Chamber of the House of Commons was destroyed by German bombs on 10th May, 1941. The new Chamber, which followed the neo-Gothic style of the old, was designed by Sir Giles Gilbert Scott.

[Earl] Winterton make speeches, and it is all over. The others go to Westminster Hall to meet the King, but I have to do a 'Marginal Comment' immediately, so I come back and type away. I am not sorry, as the House of Commons scene was so intimate and moving that I did not wish to blur my memory.

DIARY   *28th November, 1950*

Dine at the Beefsteak. The Lord Chancellor [Lord Jowitt] is there, and Clive [Bell] and Jo Grimond.[1] Everybody is terribly distressed by the Korean situation. Only a few days ago [General] MacArthur was saying, 'Home by Christmas', and now he is saying, 'This is a new war'. Evidently the Intelligence entirely misinterpreted the presence of the Chinese. Now a major offensive is being launched by 200,000 Chinese and our troops may be cut up. There seems no end to this tangle. But it was right, all the same, to do what was done.

I met Alan Pryce-Jones[2] at luncheon, he having arrived that morning from New York after six weeks in the U.S.A. He says they were in a panic on Sunday over Korea. The Americans are even more touchy than usual. He was reproved by a perfectly intelligent woman for saying that someone 'came out here during the war'. Apparently 'out' sounds back-of-beyond and is very wounding. One must say 'over' here.

V.S-W. TO H.N.   *7th December, 1950*
                                               Sissinghurst

Darling, I must write you another little note just to say how happy I am writing. It does make the whole difference in life. I just tell you this, because I like sharing things with you. I have been so miserable in the last two or three years, not being able to write; really worried I have been, thinking that it was gone from me for ever. I don't mean by this that I think my novel [*The Easter Party*] will be any good—you know that I am not a good novelist—but at any rate it is exciting just doing it. It keeps me alive, living in an imaginary

[1] He had become Liberal M.P. for Orkney and Shetland in the General Election earlier in the year, and was to become Leader of the Liberal Party in 1956 on Clement Davies' retirement from the leadership. He remained Leader till 1967.
[2] The Editor of the *Times Literary Supplement*, 1948–59.

world which seems more real than the ordinary world. Of course I would rather write poetry. Perhaps that will also return to me one day.

Oh Hadji, my Knole, my Knole! I have just been writing to Uncle Charlie [Lord Sackville] to ask him if he could supply me with a key to the garden-gate. I always had a master-key, but it got lost during the sale at Long Barn. It isn't that I would ever want to use it; it is only that I would like to have it by me, in case on some summer evening I wanted to go there, as I have often been tempted to do, letting myself into the garden secretly, and I couldn't bear the idea of being locked out. Oh God, I do wish that Knole hadn't got such a hold on my heart! If only I had been Dada's son, instead of his daughter! I hoped that I had damped down the fire into embers, but the embers blow up into a flame at one breath, so easily.

DIARY   *11th December, 1950*

I go down to Hertfordshire with Jim Lees-Milne and Jack Rathbone[1] to see Bernard Shaw's house which he left to the Trust. We first go into the garden. A sloping lawn and rough grass intersected by a few rose-beds. A bank, with a statue of St Joan. A hut in which he worked. Everything as he left it. Postcards, envelopes, a calendar marking the day of his death,[2] curiously enough a Bible and prayer-book and Crockford's Directory, a pair of mittens. The grass path and the bed around the statue of St Joan are still strewn with his ashes and those of Mrs Shaw. The Trustees and the doctor got both urns and put them on the dining-room table. They then emptied the one into the other and stirred them with a kitchen spoon. They went out into the garden and emptied spoonfuls of the mixture on to the flower beds and paths. All this some fifteen days ago, but the remains are still there. Just like the stuff Viti puts down for slugs.

We see the housekeeper, a nice Scotch body. She would like to stay on, but how can we afford her? Shaw has left us nothing at all.

---

[1] Secretary of the National Trust since 1949.

[2] George Bernard Shaw died on 2nd November, 1950. His wife Charlotte had died in 1943. He had presented his house, Shaw's Corner, near Ayot St Lawrence, to the National Trust in 1944, and lived there from 1906 until his death. A great part of his fortune was bequeathed to the propagation of a new English alphabet.

The house is dreadful and not really lettable. It will, moreover, be difficult to show to tourists as it is so small. It will be essential to keep the furniture exactly as it is. All his hats and coats and nailbrushes etc are here. His long woollen stockings and his thick underclothes. The pictures, apart from one of Samuel Butler and two of Stalin and one of Gandhi, are exclusively of himself. Even the door-knocker is an image of himself.

We decide that morally we must accept Shaw's house. I am not happy about it. I do not think that Shaw will be a great literary figure in 2000 A.D. He is an amazingly brilliant contemporary; but not in the Hardy class.

DIARY   *29th December, 1950*

I dine at the French Embassy. Only the Massiglis and Pierre Brisson[1] with Gérard André.[2] Brisson is very depressed about the state of the world. He seems to think war inevitable and dreads the effect in France. He contends that although in every war there has been a fifth column, the present situation is unique, since four million Frenchmen and 180 deputies openly avow that their only patriotism is to serve the interests of Russia.

DIARY   *31st December, 1950*

So ends a horrible year with worse to come. I fear that the dis-comfiture of UNO in Korea is a bad portent. It indicates that although these international organisations can cope with small opposition, they become hesitant when the opposition is serious. We are all oppressed by a terrible sense of weakness and foreboding. We cannot count for one moment on France, Italy or Germany, and even the United States is afflicted with cold feet, taking the form of Hoover isolationism. The year closes in a mist of anxiety. We shall be lucky if we get through 1951 without a war.

How futile all my heavy work on George V seems in comparison to these gigantic ordeals and menaces! More and more do I cling, in almost desperate affection, to Viti, Ben, Nigel and my work and garden.

[1] Editor of the Paris *Figaro*.
[2] First Secretary at the French Embassy in London.

1951

'The Easter Party' – B.B.C. discussion with Lords Russell and Samuel on liberty – King George and his children – death of Lady Carnock – MacArthur dismissed – the young generation and the old – Aneurin Bevan and Harold Wilson resign – the South Bank Exhibition – George III's ghost – Guy Burgess and Donald Maclean abscond to Russia – Herbert Morrison as Foreign Secretary – Olivier in 'Antony and Cleopatra' – 'King George V' finished – the 1951 General Election won by the Conservatives – meeting with Adenauer – Alexander the Great – Nigel adopted for Bournemouth East

'King George V' was finished on 19th September, 1951, just over three years after it was started. Harold Nicolson's diary suffered from his concentration on this single theme. It became scrappy compared to the diary of former years, but the proof that there had been no decline in his literary powers is to be found in 'King George V' itself and in the fifty-two 'Marginal Comments' of this year. George VI finished reading the last part of the biography of his father in spite of his growing infirmity from lung-cancer, and approved it warmly.

Lady Carnock, Harold Nicolson's mother, died on Good Friday, 23rd March, at the age of 90, and Lord Carnock, his eldest brother, took over Ben's rooms in Neville Terrace. Harold Nicolson became Chairman of the London Library and President of the Classical Association.

Polling Day in the 1951 General Election was on 25th October, and Winston Churchill again became Prime Minister when his Party gained a narrow victory. Apart from the defeat of the Labour Government, the main events at home were the resignation in April of Aneurin Bevan and Harold Wilson from the Cabinet, the defection to Russia of Burgess and Maclean, and the Festival of Britain in the summer. Abroad, President Truman dismissed General MacArthur from command of the United States forces in Korea for threatening to extend the war to China, and in June truce negotiations opened between the two sides.

H.N. TO V.S-W.   9th January, 1951
                                            10 Neville Terrace, S.W.7

What a lovely day today! I hope you had a nice quiet time with your real dog and your fictional dog,[1] and that nobody interrupted. I know that you will be able to avoid coyness or winsomeness in writing about a dog, but it is a difficult feat. But you never are silly

[1] Her real dog was her Alsatian, Rollo; her fictional dog was Svend, also an Alsatian, belonging to the hero of her novel, *The Easter Party*. The second, of course, was a portrait of the first.

201

with or about these animals, or indulge in baby-talk. I know you will write very seriously and solemnly and not try to be bright.

H.N. TO V.S-W.   *17th January, 1951*
                                              10 Neville Terrace, S.W.7

My mother is too pathetic for words. She just sits and cries. She is also rather irritable and suspicious. In fact, I fear her mind is giving way. People ought not to live over 85. I think it such a terrible thing that one should go on living and cease to be oneself—leaving a different picture of oneself behind. Life can be very hard and tragic.

I have no news. I went to Windsor yesterday. The Thames was very full and quick and angry. I am reading Roy Harrod's book on Keynes[1] which I find entrancing. Really that Cambridge set were more gifted than anything we have seen since. They make Balliol look like an old cart-horse.

DIARY   *22nd January, 1951*

I lunch with Bertie Russell and [Viscount] Samuel to discuss our talk for Wednesday. Russell is passionately anti-communist, which he regards as philosophically absurd and materially wicked. I ask him what he thought of Keynes. 'Obviously a nice man, but I did not enjoy his company. He made me feel a fool.'

DIARY   *24th January, 1951*

Dine at Broadcasting House with Russell and Samuel, and afterwards we broadcast a discussion on 'Why defend liberty?' Russell makes some good points. He says that the reason why communists are so zealous in pursuit of their own ideal is because they are a minority and because they are not quite positive that it is true. Russell himself came to the conclusion that Marx's theory of value was bunk as early as 1895. He cannot conceive how any intelligent young man can be taken in by it. As for zeal, nobody has any zeal about arithmetic. It is not the vaccinationists but the anti-vaccinationists who generate zeal. Zeal is a bad mark for a cause.

---

[1] *The Life of John Maynard Keynes,* 1951.

H.N. TO V.S-W.   *25th January, 1951*
10 Neville Terrace, S.W.7

I sent to Tommy Lascelles the piece I had done on the relations between King George and his children. I had put in everything I wanted to say, and expected him to cut something out. I did not want to submit to Queen Mary and the present King anything that would certainly be rejected, and thought that Tommy with his knowledge of the Royal mind could tell me what to modify and what would cause pain. But he telephoned to say that there was nothing that he thought I ought to alter. They may be stung by it, but that is just too bad. He also said that he had had a talk at Sandringham with Queen Mary, and that she had spoken very highly of my book. 'You may be sure', he said, 'that you have her solidly on your side.' Good. Tommy is really a great help. So quick in his replies, so certain, so humorous and so friendly.

H.N. TO V.S-W.   *7th February, 1951*
10 Neville Terrace, S.W.7

About the enclosed.[1] I want peace as much as anybody and I dread war as much as anybody. If it were our Government that was endangering peace, I should be all in favour of these manifestos and pronouncements. But the whole point is that it is not us but the Russians who are endangering the peace. Therefore all these matters should be approached from the point of view, 'What will be the effect of this on Russia?' Now, you cannot imagine for a moment that Russia will be impressed by a lot of writers sending letters to Nehru. The only thing that will impress her is the fact that we on the whole are more powerful than she is, and that if we are united and organise our power, she would be bound to lose a war. Therefore she will not start a war. But she may be misled by letters and movements such as this to think that there is a powerful movement among the intelligentzia aimed at deterring our Government from arming properly. Thus the letter would do far more harm than good. If I were you, I would reply in accordance with the enclosed draft.

[1] A round-robin letter which intellectuals were invited to sign. It was addressed to Pandit Nehru, and congratulated him on the neutral stance which the Indian Government had taken in the Cold War.

DIARY   *8th February, 1951*

Tommy [Lascelles] tells me that the present King never tells him exactly what happens at his interviews with Ministers. The late King always sent for Stamfordham after he had seen a Minister and told him exactly what had happened. Stamfordham then went off and wrote it down and sent his memorandum to the King for his approval. The present King just says to Tommy, 'Oh, he was optimistic as usual' or 'He was worried about the coal situation', and never goes into any detail.

DIARY   *12th March, 1951*

I go round to see Mummy. She is half-conscious, and only recognises me when I shout at her, 'I am Harold'. She smiles so affectionately and murmurs, 'My darling, darling Harold'.

DIARY   *23rd March, 1951*

Gwen [Lady St Levan] telephones at 7.50 am. to say that the nurse says that Mummy is dying and we had better get round there soon. We have a hurried breakfast and walk to Tedworth Square. When we get there we are told that she is just dead. She died at 8.10. I see the undertaker and make all the arrangements. They come and take her away at 6.30.

H.N. TO V.S-W.   *28th March, 1951*
                                                   10 Neville Terrace, S.W.7

Well, my dear old Mummy is no more than a handful of dust. I dislike having ceased suddenly to be anybody's son. It means that one is now definitely classed with the older generation and there is nobody older than oneself.

That angel Vi[1] telephoned to reassure me about your 'flu. What a saint she is! I could have kissed the telephone. I shall erect for her a Temple of Gratitude, composed entirely of topaz and porphyry, and put it at the end of the moat walk.

DIARY   *12th April, 1951*

In the morning I do my overseas talk, devoted entirely to the

[1] Mrs Alexander Pym, who lived near Charing, some ten miles from Sissinghurst. She had become, and remains, a very close friend of the Nicolsons.

dismissal of MacArthur. Of course the Republicans are going to exploit all this against Truman, and will say that MacArthur was dismissed owing to our representations. This will make us all the more suspicious of American leadership, when the fortunes of the world may be at the mercy of some senatorial lobby or some press stunt.

H.N. TO V.S-W.   *19th April, 1951*

I dined with Philip Toynbee[1] to meet his new wife. She has one of those wide American accents like very fat flat nibs. But affectionate and gentle. The only other guest was David Astor,[2] whom I find delightful in his shy way. Really a very charming man. They discussed the differences between their generation and mine. They decided that it was a difference between liberal individualism and marxism. They are all marxists in the sense that they believe that we are nothing more than flies on the wheel of destiny. Whereas I am a believer in the value of individual effort. I said that anyhow it was far more fun to be like me. They said it was a sham and a fraud. I said, 'Not at all.' They said that the whole world that I had been brought up in and inherited was a sham and a fraud also. I said, 'Nonsense, so there.' It was all very amicable, but I did feel a gap. I prefer our warmer blood.

Bless you, my own saint, whom I love deeply and think of all the day long. 'Is she walking in the orchards among the daffodils?' 'Is she being bothered by persons from Porlock?' 'Is she climbing up to the top of the tower?'

DIARY   *23rd April, 1951*

Harold Wilson resigns[3] and Bevan makes his resignation speech in the Commons. It was a dull speech for the House, but exceedingly able as a bid for future power. It will have shaken the Government badly. I do not see how they can hang on much longer.

---

[1] The author and literary critic, then aged 34. He had been a member of the *Observer's* editorial staff since 1950.
[2] Editor of the *Observer* since 1948. He was aged 39.
[3] He had been President of the Board of Trade since 1947, and resigned with Aneurin Bevan in protest against the imposition of charges on certain of the health services.

DIARY   *4th May, 1951*

Viti and I go to the South Bank Exhibition.[1] We are entranced from
the first moment. It is rather a nuisance that we keep on running into
the King and Queen, but nonetheless we enjoy it uproariously. It is
the most intelligent exhibition I have ever visited. I have never seen
people so cheered up or amused, in spite of a fine drizzle of rain.

DIARY   *10th May, 1951*

Owen Morshead tells me the story of George III's ghost. The King
had been shut up in the bachelor flat at Windsor which is now the
library. The only thing of which he was conscious (except Handel)
was the stamp of the guard on the terrace. He would always toddle
to the window, salute, and the ensign in charge of the guard would
cry, 'Eyes right!' A week after his death, there the King still was.
The ensign hesitated what to do, and then called 'Eyes right!' The
spectre saluted. Owen Morshead asked George V whether this was
correct. 'Perfectly', the King answered, 'I was told of it by the ensign
in question.' Now, this is not impossible. Supposing the ensign was
born in 1800, the episode took place in 1820, and the ensign could
have told the King in about 1884.[2]

DIARY   *7th June, 1951*

I come back to Neville Terrace and am horrified to read headlines
in the evening papers that Donald Maclean and Guy Burgess have
absconded.[3] If I thought that Guy was a brave man, I should imagine

---

[1] The exhibition, on the south bank of the river near Waterloo Station, was held
in commemoration of Prince Albert's Exhibition of 1851 and to demonstrate
Britain's economic recovery. It was the central feature of the nationwide
Festival of Britain, which the King had declared open on the previous day from
the steps of St Paul's.

[2] George III, who had been mad and blind since 1811, died in 1820. King George
V was born in 1865. The Ensign was Sir William Knollys, who died in 1883.

[3] Donald Maclean was head of the American department in the Foreign Office,
and Guy Burgess was a more junior official in the Far Eastern department. Both
had been communists at the University. Burgess later claimed that the idea of
defecting to Moscow was Maclean's, and that he (Burgess) went with him 'to
help him', and because he thought Maclean's criticisms of British foreign policy
were right. They went, like ordinary trippers, from Southampton to St Malo,
and thence by Berne and Prague to Moscow.

that he had gone to join the Communists. As I know him to be a coward, I suppose that he was suspected of passing things on to the Bolshies, and realising his guilt, did a bunk. Apparently he and Maclean went off by car to Southampton and took the night boat. I fear that all this will mean a witch-hunt.

DIARY   *8th June, 1951*

Everyone is discussing the Maclean-Burgess affair. I mind dreadfully (1) because it shames my dear old profession; (2) because it will enrage the Americans; (3) because it will make everyone suspicious of quite innocent people; (4) because I fear poor Guy will be rendered very unhappy in the end. If he has done a bunk to Russia, they will only use him for a month or so, and then shove him quietly into some salt-mine. During my dreams, his absurd face stares at me with drunken, unseeing eyes.

DIARY   *17th June, 1951*

After dinner V. and I listen to myself on the Third Programme doing my piece about Nature in Greek Poetry.[1] It really is a vigorous and interesting talk and I am pleased by it. A lovely moon at night.

H.N. TO V.S-W.   *3rd July, 1951*
                                                              10 Neville Terrace, S.W.7

It was not at all nice leaving our garden on so lovely a day, and when it is blazing in all its calm beauty. I agree with you that we have certainly created something of great loveliness, and that all the trouble you have taken has had its reward. We must go on and on. The garden today is a thing of exceptional merit; but we must make it one of the loveliest in all England. The bones are there and much of the flesh. Now we must attach rare cosmetics, lovely clothes and unusual jewellery. I never have any fear that you will commit an error of taste. I believe that you will be ruthless enough to remove anything that does not look well or do well (Paulownia? Catalpa?). In any case, it is a great work upon which we are engaged, and a solace for our senility.

[1] This was a shortened version of the lecture he had delivered on 4th April at Liverpool University as President of the Classical Association.

H.N. TO V.S-W.   *1st August, 1951*
                                                  10 Neville Terrace, S.W.7

I am worried about Morrison.[1] Dick Law[2] told me that his speech
on Foreign Affairs on Monday was absolutely deplorable. Everybody squirmed in agony. He pronounced the first syllable of 'Tigris'
to rhyme with 'pig', and called the Euphrates the 'You Frates', in
two separate words. Now, I do not mind people pronouncing
foreign names incorrectly, but to pronounce the Tigris and
Euphrates in that way indicates not only lack of education, but also
the fact that one has never heard the Middle East discussed by men
of experience. It is that which is so terrifying.

DIARY   *8th August, 1951*

Elvira [Niggeman] joins me at Windsor, and we finish off all the
documents at 2.40! I go up to the top of the Round Tower to
celebrate. I shall not again be coming to Windsor except to verify
references. The long slogging work of three years is finished.

DIARY   *29th August, 1951*

I go to the B.B.C. to listen to recordings of King George's broadcasts. His voice is so like the present King's. Very virile, rather
bronchial, very emphatic. I notice the closed 'o' as in 'those'; it is
what the B.B.C. would call 'off-white', meaning slightly cockney.
I then go to the London Library and look up the actual texts of
what I have just heard.

　　Viti and I go to a matinée to see Olivier and Vivien Leigh in
Antony and Cleopatra. The minor parts are very poorly played; the
production is excellent; Larry and Vivien good—she beautiful to
look at, but not grand enough for so superb a part.

DIARY   *6th September, 1951*

I go on with Chapter XXIX and reach sheet 17. But I realise that it
is out of scale and that I must do it all over again tomorrow. That
means that if I am to finish the chapter, I shall probably have to

---

[1] Herbert Morrison was Foreign Secretary from March to October, 1951.
[2] Conservative M.P. since 1931. Minister of Education, 1945. He was created
　Lord Coleraine in 1954.

run over into next week. But I am getting obsessed by my own time-table. What does it really matter if the book is finished on October 1 or October 14? What matters is that I should never rest content with what I know to be poor balance and composition.

DIARY *19th September, 1951*

This morning at 1.20 pm. I write the last words of Chapter XXX and thus of my life of King George V. I was first asked to do the book on 7th June, 1948, but at the time I was finishing *Benjamin Constant* and did not get down to it till September. Thus it has taken me roughly three years. I have enjoyed it immensely. It has been a most congenial task.

After tea I start on my 'Author's Note'. Then there are the genealogical trees to do, and the index and the illustrations and the proof revisions. But the main battle is over. I am satisfied. It was hard, hard work, but I think the result is pretty solid. I have a Gibbon feel.

After the news this evening, Clem Attlee, in a very short, sharp sentence delivered with great dignity, announced that Parliament would be dissolved on October 5 and Polling Day would be on October 25. My word!

DIARY *23rd September, 1951*

I do a rather bad review of Noel Annan's book.[1] I then revise the whole last section of *George V*. I weed a bit. Wilson Harris [Editor of the *Spectator*] rings up at 6.15 and asks whether I can do an obituary of the King.[2] This startles me rather. It seems that Harris had seen Lord Moran at the London Library yesterday, and that Moran had shaken his head gravely. In the evening we listen to the bulletin on the King. He was operated on the lung and his condition will continue to cause anxiety for some days.

[1] *Leslie Stephen: His thought and character in relation to his time.*
[2] King George VI was suffering from cancer of the lung, but this was not revealed publicly until after his death, and it is unlikely that he knew it himself. There was also a fear that the operation might weaken his heart.

DIARY   *27th September, 1951*

I rather diddle about in the morning. It is very odd not having a book to write. I must start on Friday on my new book.[1]

DIARY   *4th October, 1951*

I lunch with the *Spectator* staff and Wilson Harris. The outside guests are Norman Angell and . . . now, here I notice the decay of my mind: he is the coming man in the Tory Party, and I forget his name. 'Peter Ibbotson', I think it is, and yet I know it isn't; just a blank, without the faintest stirrings of association that one has.[2] Anyhow, he says that the only cure is to 'release the pound' and remove all exchange controls. That will teach people true economics. He thinks that patriotism will win this Election, and that the Abadan incident[3] has acted as a catharsis and precipitated floating feelings into a sediment of feeling that 'We cannot go on being pushed around by Persians and wops as we are now'. He does not want to stress the cost of living, because if the Tories get in, they will at first be able to do nothing about it. Nor does he want to say that Bevan is going to abolish the Free Society, since he feels that no British elector ever believes that any British subject would impose totalitarianism.

I come back and have a talk with Niggs. He is writing his Election speeches and takes the night train to Cornwall. We part with our usual reserve. 'Good luck, Niggs.' 'Goodbye, Daddy.' But I know that he realises how deep is my devotion for him; even as I realise that under all his reserve he is fond of me.

H.N. TO V.S-W.   *18th October, 1951*
                                        10 Neville Terrace, S.W.7

I don't want to lunch out on Sunday. I like being alone with my old Dutch and planting Dutch bulbs in the mud. I enjoy being left undisturbed in 'the curious and lovely place in which you live'.[4]

---

[1] But he did not start his next book, *Good Behaviour*, until October 1952.

[2] It was David Eccles.

[3] The Anglo-Iranian Oil Company had been nationalised by the Persian Prime Minister, Dr Mussadiq, and in October the whole Anglo-Iranian staff were expelled from Abadan.

[4] A phrase from a letter which V.S-W. had received from Jacquetta Hawkes (later Mrs J. B. Priestley), who had been visiting Sissinghurst.

Now that I have got as much soap as I need at home, I don't mind so much about the Election. But, darling, I DO DO DO DO DO DO mind. I am really unhappy deep inside about the condition of my beloved country. I do love it so, and its woods and its people. I fear I am just as bad as an old blimp colonel thinking it is going to the dogs. Yah Boo! Vote for Deedes indeed![1] Bloodsucker!

DIARY   *25th October, 1951*
Polling Day. We have a meeting of a sub-committee at the London Library to consider who is to be President in Ilchester's place. We decide to separate the posts of President and Chairman and to choose for the latter not a man of eminence, but a man who attends meetings. They therefore choose me.[2]

My thoughts have been all day with Nigel. I go to the B.B.C. at 10.30 tonight and do not leave until 5 am. on

26th October, 1951,
having given three commentaries to the Empire, at 11,1 and 4 am., and then a general discussion at 4.30. William Clark[3] and McKenzie[4] also commentate. Labour leads during the night, as always happens, since the industrial seats are counted first. But they are only 25 ahead by 4 am. I come back and go to bed, but I am not sleepy. I get up at the usual time and return to the B.B.C. at 10.30 am. We remain there until 4.30. As the day goes on, the Tories catch up and by about 12.45 it is clear that they will have a majority.[5] The Liberals tumble right and left. From time to time I go down from the chart-room to broadcast, and during one of my absences the news of Nigel's result comes in. I ring up Elvira [Niggeman], and she says sadly, 'Nigel not in'. 'GOT IN?' 'No—*not* in.' The figures

[1] H.N. voted Labour; V.S-W. voted for William Deedes, Conservative M.P. for Ashford.
[2] He remained Chairman till 1957; his President was T. S. Eliot.
[3] Then Diplomatic Correspondent of the *Observer*. Public Relations Adviser to the Prime Minister, 1955–56, and since 1960, Director of the Overseas Development Institute.
[4] Robert McKenzie, lecturer in politics at London University and author of *British Political Parties*.
[5] The final result was: Conservatives, 321; Labour, 295; Liberals, 6; Others, 3.

for Falmouth were: Hayman, 20,850; Nigel, 19,847; the Liberal, 4,343. I am sick at heart.

DIARY   *15th November, 1951*

In the evening I take the chair at a B.B.C. Forum on the theme 'Are cliques necessary?' I have Bob Boothby and Kingsley Martin, and we have a good discussion. I speak about the Souls, Kingsley about Bloomsbury and Bob about Cliveden and Sibyl [Colefax]. We say that the disappearance of Society means that young men have no opportunity of meeting the great men of their age.

Bob had been to see Winston this afternoon. He says he is getting 'very, very old; tragically old'. Winston wants him to lead the British Delegation to the discussions on United Europe. If he does well at this, he may get a job. 'I would have you know', said Winston, 'what a deep concern I take in your career.' Bob was pleased but not convinced.

H.N. TO V.S-W.   *5th December, 1951*
                                          10 Neville Terrace, S.W.7

I went to a party for Adenauer.[1] He is looking well and young. He said that I had given him *viele freudige Stunden* [many happy hours] by *Public Faces*. It is always a matter of sadness to me that the books I take long to write never seem to attract anyone, whereas the ones I write in ten days or so seem to acquire fame immortal.[2]

V.S-W. TO H.N.   *6th December, 1951*
                                                       Sissinghurst

You are a silly goose to mind people praising *Public Faces* and not paying attention to any of your other books! What about *Peacemaking* and *The Congress of Vienna* and your book about your father? I suppose every author is annoyed by the same sort of thing. I get furious inside when people drag up *The Edwardians*, and of course the *Observer*[3] is worst of all.

[1] Konrad Adenauer, the German Chancellor, was then aged 75.
[2] H.N. had written his novel *Public Faces* between 12th April and 19th July, 1932.
[3] Her gardening articles, which were attracting an enormous correspondence from readers of the *Observer*.

H.N. TO V.S-W.   *11th December, 1951*
                                                    10 Neville Terrace, S.W.7

Do you know how much *Life* offer me for my 5,000 word article on Alexander the Great? They offer me 2,000 dollars. Now, that is more than I shall probably make over *King George V.* Three years work compared to a fortnight's work. But I know that is not a logical point of view. I mean, it is rather like Whistler who, when asked whether he felt justified in charging 100 guineas for a sketch that had taken him two hours to make, replied, 'Not two hours—a lifetime'. Which is true in a way.

DIARY   *18th December, 1951*

Niggs has been placed on the short-list of candidates for the Bournemouth seat.[1] Would he come down on the 29th? Great excitement. Of course, if he were adopted, he would be in Parliament for the rest of his life and end up as Viscount Bournemouth. But he has little chance.

DIARY   *25th December, 1951*

A real spring day with birds singing and little noses pushing up from the soil. I avert my gaze from such unwise and unseasonable precocity. We give each other Christmas presents. I give Viti some bath-towels (which I like, but she doesn't), some sherry glasses (which she doesn't like either), a flag for the tower (which she would have had to get in any case) and a new edition of *Larousse* (which she hates). Not a successful Christmas-gift ceremony.

DIARY

I have my bath at 7.30 and am out of it by 7.50. Then I hear Viti running up the stairs and banging on the door. 'Nigel has been adopted!' she shouts. I open the door and she is all excited. He had just telephoned. How miraculous!

---

[1] A bye-election had been made necessary by the elevation to the peerage of Brendan Bracken, the sitting Member for Bournemouth East and Christchurch. He became Viscount Bracken of Christchurch.

DIARY   *30th December, 1951*

Nigel arrives, having motored from Bournemouth all along the coast. So far from being triumphant, he is almost depressed. We three, who had been in ecstasies, feel slightly chilled. He minds about Roy Harrod[1] being defeated, saying that it is pretty cheap for him to get in by charming the wives of bank managers, when a person of such real value is excluded. Roy had travelled overnight from Northern Ireland. He had finished his speech by the time Niggs arrived. Niggs then did his piece, and Quickswood[2] told him that he had been chosen. Afterwards Quickswood said that Roy had dished his chances by lecturing them about economics. I think it was this that had made Niggs feel a worm. Had he won their suffrages by being too amiable, flattering and conciliatory? If so, the honours went to Roy, who was too proud a man to conciliate the wives of drapers. But there are other things that worry him. He thinks Bournemouth one of the saddest places he has ever seen. He feels sore about his beloved Falmouth. He is a romantic. He is rather staggered by it all—by the astonishing fact that ten minutes can determine one's whole life. But underneath I think that he is more pleased than he lets on.

---

[1] Tutor in economics at Christ Church, Oxford, 1922–67. Joint Editor of the *Economic Journal*, 1945–61, member of Churchill's private statistical staff during the war and of various international economic commissions. Author of *The Life of John Maynard Keynes* etc.

[2] Lord Quickswood (Lord Hugh Cecil), President of the Bournemouth East Conservative Association. He had been Provost of Eton, 1936–44.

1952

Visit to Denmark – Nigel elected for Bournemouth on the day of King George VI's death – lecture in Rome – Keats' tomb – Athens and Olympia – Georges Simenon – R. A. Butler on the Conservative leadership – death of Lord Carnock – C.1 Albany – H.N. presents first copy of 'King George V' to Queen Mary – universal praise for his book – Bodnant – H.N. offered the K.C.V.O. – starts on 'Good Behaviour' – the Queen's radiance – Eisenhower President of the United States

'*King George V*' *was published on 14th August, and was widely praised for its historical scholarship and its style. It sold 10,000 copies within the first fortnight and earned Harold Nicolson £4,000 and a knighthood. The first was more welcome to him than the second. Towards the end of the year he started his research for '*Good Behaviour*', a study in changing social attitudes and etiquette, and he continued to write his weekly review for the '*Observer*'. But he wrote his last '*Marginal Comment*' for the '*Spectator*' in December, having maintained it weekly since the beginning of 1939, with a break of a year in 1940–1, when he was a junior Minister in Churchill's Government. He did not explain in his diary his reasons for abandoning it, but in his valedictory article he wrote: 'I may end by repeating, even imitating myself. I wish to postpone the date when my friends will whisper sadly among each other that I am becoming, have in fact become, a bore. . . . People should refrain from dancing once the joints begin to creak.'*

This was a year of much travel. He lectured in Denmark in January, in Rome and Athens in February and March, in Paris in May, in Germany in September, and in August he motored with V. Sackville-West through Wales to both parts of Ireland, taking her for the first time to the great houses where he had spent much of his childhood. They returned through the eastern counties of England to face the problem of the Queen's offer to him of the K.C.V.O.

There were three events of importance to him in his personal life. His brother, Frederick Nicolson, second Lord Carnock, who had been living with him in Kensington for the past year, died in distressing circumstances on 31st May. He then gave up his lease of 10 Neville Terrace and moved to C.1 Albany, Piccadilly, which was to remain his London home until his retirement in 1965. Thirdly, at the beginning of the year, on the day when King George VI died, his younger son was elected to Parliament as Conservative Member for Bournemouth East and Christchurch.

217

DIARY   *2nd January, 1952*

Horrible income tax demands and letters from my bank about overdrafts. I am going to get into debt and have nothing to fall back on. I simply cannot work any harder than I do, and it means that I shall have to cut down all my expenses. My financial position has always been precarious, mainly because I have no responsibilities other than for myself.

DIARY   *11th January, 1952*

I get a letter from Tommy [Lascelles] saying that the King has no comments to make on Part IV, so the thing goes off today to Constable's. FINISHED.

DIARY   *21st January, 1952*
                                                               Copenhagen

We lunch with Mr and Mrs Lundsgaard in a small house on the Roskilde Fjord. Nice simple people. There are no riches to be seen in this country and little poverty. Small houses, simple ways. Even the Roskilde cathedral is a small church. We admire the brickwork outside, but the inside, except for some fine iron railings, is cold and grim. The tombs[1] are vast marble sarcophagi or just coffins. Not a very entrancing sight.

DIARY   *22nd January, 1952*
                                                               Copenhagen

We go to Slot Rosenborg. A curious 17th-century castle in the middle of the town. There are masses of small rooms, and on the upper floor a long Knights' Hall with a throne at the end. In front of the throne are strewn all carelessly on the black and white floor three vast metal lions. The whole thing is interesting to me as showing how deep the Teutonic influence was in these areas. It has a German look—heavy, ugly, over-decorated, dark. There was a Garter robe belonging to one of the old kings—probably the oldest Garter robe in existence. It looked very miffy. I lunch with the Ambassador [Sir Alec Randall]. It is a fine day, and all the copper pinnacles and domes show light-green. This is a graceful city.

[1] Roskilde was the capital of Denmark until 1443. The Cathedral contains the tombs of most of the Danish kings from Harold I (987).

DIARY   *6th February, 1952*

Polling Day in Bournemouth. It is about 11.20 in the morning. We draw up at Nigel's Central Committee Room to find Cowley[1] waiting on the pavement with an expression of solemn anxiety. 'Something terrible has happened', he says. 'The King is dead.'[2] We are stunned, but almost at once we relate this national misfortune to the question of Polling Day at Bournemouth on this sixth of February 1952. Will the Conservative voters be too shocked to indulge in anything so mundane as voting? Will they jump to the conclusion that the Election is cancelled? How are we to let them know? Obviously all loudspeakers must be withdrawn from the streets. But the Labour people will have their voters gathered together in the workshops and they will vote in strength. Supposing no Tory voters come at all? Then Labour will win. In the shock of the moment these nightmares loom as large as the huge photographs of Nigel on the hoardings. He himself gets a little white. Viti suggests aptly that we should get on to the B.B.C. and persuade them to put out on the 1 o'clock news that the poll is still on.

I have to go back by the 12.40 train. Viti remains behind. I read Arrian on Alexander[3] all the way up, but am unable to concentrate. To the B.B.C. At 7 I go to the Travellers. By that time I am convinced that Nigel will lose the seat. I pace the corridors of the Travellers up and down, waiting for a telephone call. It comes at 7.30. Niggs' voice. 'It is not as bad as we feared. They started voting again after 3. About 60 per cent of those who voted last time.' I am much relieved.

Princess Elizabeth is flying back from Kenya. She became Queen while perched in a tree in Africa, watching the rhinoceros come down to the pool to drink.

DIARY   *7th February, 1952*

I feel calmer this morning when I get up. But as the day passes, my nerves begin to jangle again. To soothe myself I write a broadcast for tomorrow. I wait for the 1 pm. news. I turn it on at 12.55 and get the weather report. While I am listening, Elvira [Niggeman],

[1] Arthur Cowley, the Conservative Election Agent.
[2] He had died at Sandringham, quite unexpectedly, very early that morning.
[3] For his article on Alexander the Great for *Life* magazine.

arrayed in deep mourning, dashes in with a piece of paper in her hand. 'You have a son M.P.', she says, and puts the telephone through. It is Viti at the other end. The figures are: Niggs, 22,480; Labour, 8,498; Liberal, 3,673; Independent, 1,692. Both the latter forfeit their deposits. Majority, 13,982. I am wild with relief.

Oh I am so happy about Niggs; everything seems sunlit. I dash off from my luncheon and then attend a meeting at the National Portrait Gallery. George Trevelyan is there and G. M. Young and Don [the Dean of Westminster] and the rest. An easy meeting. I then go to the Travellers for some tea. On the tape is the result of the Bournemouth election and Niggs' little speech. He claims to be the first M.P. to be elected in the reign of Queen Elizabeth II. How furious the great Elizabeth would be to know that she had been succeeded by this sweet girl!

DIARY   *22nd February, 1952*
                                                                          Rome

Victor Mallet[1] picks me up and we go off on what poor Sibyl [Colefax] would have called 'a delicious round'. We go first to the Villa Papa Giulia, where we are received by John Ward-Perkins, the Director of the British School at Rome, who shows us the Etruscan treasures. I am so happy to be in that lovely villa again, but the absence of Vita tugs at my heart as it always does when I experience an aesthetic pleasure. I never miss her when I am talking politics. But when I see something that gives me intense pleasure, I turn round to share it with her and she is not there. She and I feel exactly the same about this sort of thing. We are shown the Apollo. It amuses me because of my interest in memory. I saw it last some twenty years ago and imagined that I remembered it perfectly. But in fact I had confused it with the old statues in the Acropolis museum, to which, of course, it bears no resemblance whatsoever. They are serene; it is fierce. It is one of the most fascinating and problematic statues in the world.

Then we go down to the Ara Pacis and the tomb of that beast Augustus, and the Campidoglio and the Piazza Navona, where we get out and walk up and down. How supremely Roman it is! Then

[1] British Ambassador in Rome, 1947-53.

we passed the Trevi fountain and the Quattro Fontane and get back to the Embassy.

I change, and prepare my lecture. It takes place at the Open Gate Club. It is a small exclusive club, and the gate is not open in the least. We hang about and a few people drift in and there is a small room and no lectern and many Ambassadors and a few men from the Italian Foreign Office and it goes none too well. How odd it is that at Copenhagen a few weeks ago I should have given that very lecture[1] amid universal applause. It wasn't a flop exactly, but it was not a success. They were not sure whether I was being flippant or serious.

DIARY   *23rd February, 1952*
                                                              Rome

I go to the Keats-Shelley house.[2] It is in excellent order. I gaze with respect at the little rosettes on the ceiling at which Keats must have stared in the agony of his last hours. We go to the cemetery. The tomb of what remained of Shelley is ruined by the fact that the beast [Edward] Trelawny is lying next to him. Pushing even after death. The Keats tomb is pathetic, away by the tomb of Cestus.

DIARY   *28th February, 1952*
                                                             Athens

Lady Peake[3] and I go to the Agora, where we are met by the Director, Professor Thompson,[4] and taken round stone by stone. We examine the Tholos and then the Temple of Apollo Patroos. The Stoa Basileios, where Socrates was tried, has had its end cut off by the railway, but one can imagine what he saw when he looked up at the Acropolis. What fascinated me most was the platform of the Eponymous Heroes, to which the 'tablets' were affixed. They were put up on a marble hoarding surmounted by these great

[1] It was on 'The Old Diplomacy and the New'.
[2] In the Piazza di Spagna, where John Keats had died exactly 131 years before, on 23rd February, 1821.
[3] The wife of Sir Charles Peake, British Ambassador in Athens, 1951–57.
[4] The excavation of the Agora in the centre of Athens was then being undertaken by the American School working under the direction of Professor Homer Thompson.

statues and protected from the rain by a moulded coping. On each side ran a rail or parapet on which those reading the tablets could lean. The rest is rather mucked up by Romans and Pergamites, but the whole site is sacred and to me full of memories. Three hours we were poking about there, and I was not bored for one instant.

The Prime Minister, General Plastiras, is at dinner. He looks magnificent from a distance with his white Kaiser moustache; but his wrists and hands are those of an old woman. We talk about Alexander the Great and avoid politics.

N.N. TO H.N. (*in Athens*)   *3rd March, 1952*
                                                           House of Commons

I have already witnessed many a stirring scene, the best of which was the Foreign Affairs debate last Wednesday. Herbert Morrison spoke for an hour so badly that people shuffled and groaned. It made a deplorable effect, and Winston's case was won before he got up. He started off pugnaciously and then pretended to go dull on us. 'I must ask for the patience of the House', he said, 'if I go back a bit to the record of the last Government.' Everybody relaxed, feeling that we knew all this past-history already and needn't listen. Then suddenly he lifted his head and brought out this story about Attlee having agreed to bomb the Chinese airfields.[1] There was pandemonium. I was sitting directly opposite Attlee. He was sitting hunched up like an elf just out of its chrysalis, and stared at Winston, turning slowly white. The Labour benches howled—anything to make a noise to cover up the moment of shock. Winston sat back beaming. Bevan—a most charming, dangerous man—did his best to launch a counter-attack, but it was too late. We had won. I was sitting in the smoking-room afterwards with Cranborne[2] when Winston came up to us, with a cigar and a glass of brandy. 'It was a great day', he said, 'a great triumph, and I am glad that you joined us in time to witness it.'

[1] The Labour Opposition were criticising Churchill for having agreed with the Americans that should the Chinese launch an offensive in Korea, the United Nations' forces would retaliate by bombing the Communist airfields in Manchuria. Churchill now revealed that the Labour Government had already agreed in principle to this same decision.
[2] Viscount Cranborne, son of Lord Salisbury, and M.P. for Bournemouth West, 1950–54.

How much better he is in the House than on a platform! How he loves it! He is looking white and fatty, a most unhealthy look, you would say, if he were anyone else, but somehow out of this sickly mountain comes a volcanic flash.

DIARY   *12th March, 1952*
                                                          Olympia, Greece

It is a gorgeous day, and Eremanthus is thick in snow and the sea blue. We arrive at Olympia at about 1 pm. It is a sea of anemone and iris. It is really rather an ugly place, as the columns are of stone and lie like black rhinoceros sleeping in the grass. We visit the museum and see the Apollo.[1] Surely one of the greatest statues in the world. We also see the Hermes dangling the baby Bacchus. The face of a mannequin set on the body of an androgyne.[2] I hate that statue and do not believe it is by Praxiteles. It is devoid of Greek grandeur.

We then come back [to Patras] and I give a lecture on the British Monarchy.

DIARY   *24th April, 1952*

In the afternoon I have a discussion on the wireless with Simenon.[3] His wife comes with him. She is like a Madonna in middle age and he clearly adores her. She manages all his business. He is a nervous excitable man, striding about the room puffing at his pipe. He does not speak English very well, but just well enough to get across to the Third Programme people. He tells me he has written three hundred books in his life, 148 of which are in his own name. He says he has decided to write one Maigret book a year and then leave time for straight fictional works. He says his method is to soak himself in the atmosphere of a place for three days; then to soak himself in his main character; thereafter the plot and the minor characters form themselves. His identification with his main character is so intense that if the man is old, he himself for three days adopts the movements

[1] The central figure from the pediment of the Temple of Zeus at Olympia.
[2] 'A male with female characteristics.' It has been called 'the one undisputed surviving work by Praxiteles', but other scholars have argued that it is a Roman copy.
[3] Georges Simenon, the French writer of detective fiction and the originator of Maigret.

of a dotard. If the main character is a drunkard, he himself will start drinking hard. Then he writes in a fever for ten days and the book is finished. He says that the necessity of soaking himself in atmosphere and then writing about it is why he always moves from place to place. He is now writing a novel about American life. He will one day, when he knows us better, write about London. He says his son, aged 13, has never read a single book he has written. I rather liked both him and his wife.

DIARY   *28th April, 1952*

I have a B.B.C. discussion with Monty Mackenzie[1] on getting old. He contends that there is no difference at all. I contend that it is the greatest of human tragedies. He contends that physically there are few disadvantages. What does it really matter if one walks two miles an hour instead of four miles an hour? He notices no difference in his memory, character or powers of invention. It was a good discussion.

DIARY   *22nd May, 1952*

Freddy[2] is very ill, I fear. His head makes that deep indentation in the pillow which is made by the very weak. He cannot move his legs in bed. It is pitiful to see him die.

Rab [Butler] drives me to the Albany. He is, as usual, very outspoken. He says that the difficulty is that Anthony [Eden] is assumed to be the heir apparent. He says that in any case Anthony has more appeal than he has, because Anthony has charm. I say I hope he will not seek to mimic charm, but remain reliable. He agrees. He says that Winston is so brave in war and so cowardly in peace; the Tory Government ought to convey the impression of people who are absolutely certain of themselves; as it is, they convey the impression of a wobble.

At the Albany I walk for the first time to C.1.[3]

---

[1] Sir Compton Mackenzie, then aged 69. H.N. was 65.
[2] Lord Carnock, H.N.'s elder brother.
[3] The decision to leave 10 Neville Terrace, a house which he had always hated, was taken when it became obvious that Lord Carnock could not live long. The lease of C.1 Albany fell vacant, and H.N. shared the flat with John Sparrow and myself.

DIARY   *31st May, 1952*

Viti wakes me at 7 am. to say that Freddy is dead. I go up to London
and on the way try to begin a Marginal Comment on Lady Desborough. I drive straight to Sister Agnes' Home for Officers. We
arrange that the cremation will take place on Thursday and the
funeral at Sissinghurst on Friday. I then go to see Freddy lying there.
He died in his sleep at 6.15 without any pain or struggle. Poor old
boy, it is such a wasted, lonely end.

I take the 4.38 home. It has rained today after a long drought, and
the garden is fresh and beautiful. The roses are about to come to
their best. I walk with Viti in the garden after dinner when all the
half-light plays on the flowers. It is peace unutterable, but in my heart
there is great sorrow for Freddy. There ought to be relief, I suppose,
that he is eased of all his loneliness and self-contempt, and that he
died without suffering. But there is just sorrow at the thought of so
wasted a life. I feel aching pity for him, and wish I were one of those
who felt that he had been united with Mummy in some happy state.
The mere fact that I want at this moment to find that sort of comfort
convinces me more than ever that the belief in life-after-death is a
human illusion. But why should I live in such beauty, and surrounded by so many affections and interests, when poor old Freddy
(who never thought an unkind thought about anyone) was condemned to a life so ineffective and miserable?[1]

DIARY   *9th June, 1952*

We were saddened this morning to hear on the wireless that
Desmond MacCarthy[2] had died at Cambridge, two days after
getting an honorary degree. His was assuredly one of the gentlest
minds of my generation.

---

[1] Lord Carnock was nearly four years older than H.N., and died at the age of 69.
He had had quite a distinguished military career as A.D.C. to the Viceroy and
in the 15th Hussars, but was retired as a Major in 1919. He was called to the Bar,
but had made little progress when he succeeded to the title in 1928. He was a
useful Chairman of House of Lords' Committees until the Second War, and then
lived with his mother in semi-retirement. He never married.

[2] Sir Desmond MacCarthy (he had been knighted in 1951) was 75.

DIARY   *17th July, 1952*

All day long people carry in furniture [to C.1 Albany], and I stand
there telling them what to do. It is very exhausting. Despair settles
down on us when we discover that the kitchen table refuses to go
down to the kitchen. But then suddenly we find that the big Dutch
table goes splendidly into the window and forms an ideal writing-
table *de parade*. All thereafter seems to settle in. Exhausted I go to the
Travellers and have a bottle of champagne. Then back to Albany.
Niggs gets back early from the House and we sit for the first time in
our room and find it very pleasant. We then scribble our names on
the top of the bathroom wall and I do a Marginal Comment on
changing houses.

DIARY   *29th July, 1952*

Constable send round three copies of the revised and improved
George V. It is excellently produced. I send a copy to the Queen and
to the Queen Mother. After lunch I go round to Marlborough
House and am received by Queen Mary. She is getting older and
toddles on her feet. But her mind is as clear as ever. She said two
things which touched me. I was speaking of the King's forth-
rightness, 'Yes', she says, 'he was sometimes too outspoken. We in
our position have often to avoid answering indiscreet questions. I
remember that I once had a Lady-in-Waiting who was a fool and
used to ask indiscreet questions of my husband in the motor-car. He
always answered exactly what he thought. I had to get rid of the
woman.' Then she said, when looking closely at the picture of
Prince George as a young man, 'How like he was to my poor silly
son!' She stroked the book affectionately, and kept on murmuring,
'Very well done. Very dignified.'

DIARY   *14th August, 1952*

King George V is published. There is a leader in *The Times* and in the
Manchester Guardian, and an excellent review by Duff Cooper in the
Daily Telegraph. All the other papers treat it as news. Seldom
have I seen such prominence given to a single book.

I go down to Oxford. I go to the Warden's house and find John[1]
and an undergraduate called Colin Fenton—a red-haired man with

[1] John Sparrow had been appointed Warden of All Souls in March.

falcon eyes and exquisite manners. Then we go to the Codrington Library where I give a lecture on 'The position of England in 1900 and 1952'. Although some forty people are turned away, the audience at the end of the room look like a confirmation class. Afterwards the Wheeler-Bennetts[1] drive me out to Garsington. It is a delightful house with most charming hosts.

DIARY   *17th August, 1952*
                                              Bodnant, North Wales

There is an excellent review of *George V* by Kingsley Martin in the *New Statesman*. Also a really good one by [Lord] Samuel in the *Sunday Times*. A rather cross one by Walter Elliot in the *Observer*. But the whole effect is one of wide and lengthy adulation. How much of this is due to the very real respect that people have for King George? Never have I witnessed such a chorus of praise. I suppose I ought to feel elated. But somehow I am rather indifferent and do not experience any inner feelings of self-satisfaction. Christabel [Aberconway] says this is due to my 'loss of vitality'. Yes, I am becoming an old man.

DIARY   *18th August, 1952*

At Bodnant. A happy day. It drizzles a bit, but Vita and I are conducted by Harry [Aberconway] round the garden. He devotes his whole day to us. In the morning we go round the dell, which is the most extensive, most varied and most tasteful piece of planting I have ever seen. We then go round the rest of the garden after luncheon. Then after tea we go through the nurseries and glass-houses. I have no doubt at all that this is the richest garden I have ever seen. Knowledge and taste are combined with enormous expenditure to render it one of the wonders of the world. Viti is wonderful at remembering the names of everything, and she is happy and looks so well and lovely when it is all over.

---

[1] Sir John Wheeler-Bennett, who within a few months was to be appointed official biographer to King George VI.

DIARY   *27th August, 1952*
                                          Houghton Hall, Norfolk

We drive down from Yorkshire and reach Houghton at 4.45.
Warmly greeted by Rock and Sybil.[1] We have tea, and are then
taken over the state-rooms. Everything is in superb condition, and
added to the treasures of the Walpoles and the Cholmondeleys are
Philip Sassoon's pictures and carpets. I have never seen a house so
perfect and self-contained.

I get a letter from Tommy [Lascelles] saying it will be difficult for
me to get out of the K.C.V.O. We have a nice dinner and go to
bed. Vita does not seem tired at all. The beauty of this house and
park gives her great serenity. But she does *not* want to be Lady
Nicolson.

DIARY   *28th August, 1952*
                                                     Houghton

We visit the garden and the long white room and the gymnasium
and the tennis-court. This house really is a manifestation of Kent's
genius. Every detail is a work of art—not a hinge scamped—even
the backs of things are as perfect as the side that shows. Sibyl has
beautiful objects of every sort that are displayed on the tables and
add luxury to this amazing setting. Certainly the loveliest 18th-
century house that I have ever seen. It is touching to notice how
Rock and Sibyl adore it. She is a wonderful guide, and shows one
the house in small doses at a time.

I have a talk to Viti about my K.C.V.O. She feels that, embarrassing as it is, it would be difficult to refuse. After all this ululation
about the book, a C.V.O. would give the impression that the
Sovereign was displeased. But how far rather I would be given a
dozen bottles of champagne or a travelling clock!

---

[1] The Marquess and Marchioness of Cholmondeley. Lady Cholmondeley was the
sister of Philip Sassoon, and Lord Cholmondeley was Lord Great Chamberlain.
Their splendid house, Houghton, was designed in the 1720's for the Prime
Minister, Sir Robert Walpole, by Colen Campbell. William Kent's hand is
seen in every part of the house, from the painted walls to the furniture.

H.N. TO SIR ALAN LASCELLES   *31st August, 1952*
                                               C.1 Albany, Piccadilly, W.1

I have received two letters from you which I must now answer.

In the first, that of 21st August, you were so good as to convey to me the congratulations of Her Majesty upon the excellent reception of my life of King George V. I am humbly grateful to the Queen for the interest she has taken in the book and for the appreciation which she has been gracious to express.

In the second—a private letter of 22nd August—you envisage the possibility of my being offered the K.C.V.O., and you ask me whether my previous disinclination remains obdurate. I do not think that literary people should be accorded knighthoods, although, if you asked me to state rational grounds for this objection, I should be unable to do so. For family reasons also, I do not want to change the shape of my own name or that of Vita. On the other hand, I quite see that, after the reception the book has had, the conferment of a C.V.O. might suggest to people that my biography had not been accorded full royal approval. To maintain my objections might be considered churlish and embarrassing.

I have discussed the matter with Vita, who is always so wise in such matters, and I now write to say that I should be honoured to accept a K.C.V.O. if it were offered.

DIARY   *15th October, 1952*

I start taking notes for my new book on Manners [*Good Behaviour*].

DIARY   *16th October, 1952*

I go to the Anglo-German dinner at the Piccadilly. I have William Clark as my guest, and also have Douglas Jay[1] and Hugh Fraser[2] at my table. Herbert Morrison is there and a distinguished company. Eden makes quite a good speech and Schlange-Schoeningen[3] an honourable one. I have to reply, and get through it all right, but I am not really good at after-dinner speeches. I cannot make or invent the sort of jokes they expect, and my sort of jokes are not laughed at. It is embarrassing in front of so distinguished an audience, and with

[1] Financial Secretary to the Treasury, 1950–51.
[2] Conservative M.P. for Stafford and Stone.
[3] Dr Hans Schlange-Schoeningen, German Chargé d'Affaires in London.

229

Eden and the German Chargé d'Affaires as the two main speakers, to have to get up at the end and say a few bright and witty words. I do not feel important enough on such occasions, and have the old, old dread that people will regard me as showing off. Deep, deep are the roots left by a public-school education. Anyhow, Eden in his speech was very polite about my *George V*, referring to it as 'this great book'. Clarissa[1] was there, looking as lovely as a peach.

DIARY   *20th October, 1952*

I read Vita's novel *The Easter Party*. It is beautifully constructed and well-written, and very moving.

DIARY   *4th November, 1952*

Gerry [Wellington] told me how struck he was by the Queen's astonishing radiance at the opening of Parliament this morning—her lovely teeth, hair and eyes, and that amazing quality of skin. Then add the wonderful voice and the romance, and you have a deeply moving effect.

DIARY   *5th November, 1952*

I turn on the wireless at 8 am. to hear Eisenhower's voice.[2] It comes through the atmospherics of the Atlantic and the wild yells of his supporters. He is President-Elect. No details yet, but it seems the Republicans captured two southern States.[3] Anyhow, thank God all that is over and that the U.S. can now become comparatively normal again.

We have a dinner at the House of Commons for the Brains Trust people. We discuss Eisenhower as President. Professor Goodhart[4] says he will be good for NATO which is the rock to which we cling now that UNO is dead and done for. But what can he do in Korea? The electors will expect him to end the war, but he cannot do that without either abandoning the prisoners or bringing in new

[1] Clarissa Churchill, who had married Anthony Eden earlier in the year.
[2] In the Presidential Campaign of 1952, General Eisenhower defeated his Democratic opponent, Adlai Stevenson, by 442 electoral votes to 89.
[3] Actually, four – Tennessee, Virginia, Florida and Texas.
[4] Master of University College, Oxford, 1951–63, and Professor of Jurisprudence at Oxford until 1951.

divisions from Formosa. In fact he is out on a limb. Goodhart says that he hopes Foster Dulles does not become Secretary of State, as he is deeply anti-British.

DIARY   *25th November, 1952*

To Oxford. I am met at the station by the Master of Balliol [Sir David Lindsay Keir] who drives me to the Master's Lodgings. Very warm and gay they are. We walk across to Hall. My speech goes well enough, but they do not laugh at my jokes. Anyhow, they applaud me well. I like the Master and feel that under him the dear place may revive.

DIARY   *30th December, 1952*

A charming letter from [Sir William] Haley, expressing his regret at my abandoning Marginal Comment.[1] Of course, now that I have decided to do so, all sorts of ideas come into my head, and I regret being unable to express them.

DIARY   *31st December, 1952*

This has been a good year. I minded Freddy's death more than I expected, more for the tragedy of such a failure than the actual loss. It was dreadful seeing a person whom I had known so gay and full of life just becoming a miserable hulk. Apart from that tragedy, everything has been bright. Niggs got into the House by a huge majority. Ben has been gaining in reputation as a scholar and writer. Vita has written her novel and has been far better in health. And *King George V* really had an immense success. The summer was lovely and the garden more beautiful than ever before. A year, moreover, in which I left Neville Terrace, haunted by atrocious memories of Freddy's last months, and came to the pleasant walks of Albany. In fact as good a year as can be, and no war yet.

[1] The last of his 670 articles was published on 26th December.

1953

H.N. knighted – the purpose of a diary – break-up of the British Empire – Hugh Gaitskell on political reputation – H.N. receives his knighthood from the Queen – death of Stalin and of Queen Mary – Nigel's engagement and marriage – speech at the Royal Academy Banquet – the Queen of Spain on her childhood – deputation to the Minister of Education – Coronation Day of Queen Elizabeth II – armistice in Korea – American idealisation of the common man – Adlai Stevenson – a motor-tour of Scotland – Hidcote – the nature of the Good Life – H.N. delivers the Chichele lecture in Oxford – Robert Schuman – Virginia Woolf's Diary – T. S. Eliot lectures on 'The Three Voices of Poetry' – Charlie Chaplin – Tennyson reciting his poems

Coronation year saw the end of the Korean fighting and the death of Stalin. For Harold Nicolson it was the year when he received his knighthood and his younger son was married. He was busy with his new book 'Good Behaviour' and with many lectures, of which the most important were the Chichele Lectures at Oxford on the Evolution of Diplomatic Method. He received honorary degrees at Newcastle and Dublin, and became (to his great pleasure) an Honorary Fellow of Balliol. There was only one holiday—in Scotland in August.

V. Sackville-West published 'The Easter Party' in January, probably the least successful of her novels, and resumed writing 'Daughter of France', a biography of La Grande Mademoiselle. A second collection of her 'Observer' gardening articles appeared in October under the title 'In Your Garden Again'. She began to keep a diary, but it was little more than a brief record of visitors to Sissinghurst, and she often missed a day completely. A few extracts from it will appear in the following pages until the year of her death.

DIARY   1st January, 1953

My K.C.V.O. is published in the Birthday Honours and I get masses of telegrams. One that pleases me is from Balliol.

DIARY   3rd January, 1953

We go to a party at Bunny [Drummond's]. Eustace[1] is there and he is amused that his peerage and my knighthood should have come in the same list, when forty-two years ago we figured on the same list in the diplomatic entrance exam. But as usual he is ahead of me. It is a nice party with all the neighbours. But why is it that I hate so much being congratulated on my K.C.V.O.? Partly natural shyness. Partly because it is embarrassing to express pleasure about something one loathes. And partly a conceited feeling that after all the work I

[1] Lord Eustace Percy, formerly in the Foreign Service, and President of the Board of Education, 1924–29. He had been Rector of King's College, Newcastle, since 1937, and was now created Lord Percy of Newcastle.

have done in life, a knighthood is a pitiful business, putting me in the third eleven. I know that the K.C.V.O. is not supposed to be an assessment of my contribution to life, but rather a present from the Queen for a service rendered to the Monarchy. But other people do not realise that, and I feel as if I had got a fourth prize in scripture when I should have liked the Newcastle. So one is really much more snobbish and vain than one imagines.

James [Pope-Hennessy] says that my diary is too boring for words and that there is no use going on with it. But it has become a habit, and it is useful for reference. He thinks that no diary is of any value unless it expresses personal opinions, feelings and gossip, and recounts all that is said. I must try to render it less of an engagement book, as otherwise I agree that it is not worth the trouble entailed. So henceforward my diary will be an expression of deep internal thoughts and emotions. But no gossip. I do not think it right to record day by day all the turpitude or sexual aberrations of my friends. I love them too dearly for that.

V.S-W.'S DIARY   17th January, 1953

I read Cecil Day Lewis's *Visit to Italy*, which H. has to review for the *Observer*. I read it at intervals throughout the night, which is perhaps the best way to read it—in bits and sections. The *Elegy at Settignano* seems to me a really beautiful poem—a real contribution to English literature. It moved and exhilarated me. It was a lovely experience to read it at 3 in the morning, all alone with no danger of interruption, only the darkness outside. So private.

DIARY   25th January, 1953

My poor Viti is hurt by a review of her new novel [*The Easter Party*] by Marghanita Laski, which is contemptuous and wounding. When such things occur to me, I become depressed and miserable. But Viti just gets angry, which I suppose is better. But it is agony for me to see her hurt, and it shows what pain can be given by an unfavourable review.

DIARY   12th February, 1953

Eden announced in the House today that we have signed an agreement with Neguib abandoning the Sudan. I know this was inevitable, but it is sad for me to see the fruit of that great work picked before it is even half ripe. The Labour people cheered vociferously. How difficult it is to make up one's mind about that! I see that true democratic principles render imperialism illogical; but nobody will persuade me that our work in the Sudan was anything but a real civilising and selfless mission.

DIARY   *18th February, 1953*

I discuss with Eustace Percy, [Lord] Simon and Hugh Gaitskell the question of political reputation. Eustace says it depends on 'the bulk of a man', instancing the extraordinary hold that Pitt had over his contemporaries. We compare the moral influence of Asquith and the human influence of Baldwin with the ingenuity of Lloyd George. The latter was in a sense the 'greatest' of all three, but he did not *leave* an impact, whereas they did.

DIARY   *26th February, 1953*

I go to Buckingham Palace for my investiture and audience. I am introduced as Mr Nicolson. The Queen is standing by the fireplace and I advance and bow. She says not one word, but motions me to a faldstool that is ostentatiously standing in the centre of the room. Beside it there is a table with a scabbard and a sword. I kneel down and the Queen lays the sword, gently but quite firmly, first on my left and then on my right shoulder. I then rise and she gives me her hand to kiss. She then gives me the box containing the star, and says with a pleasant smile, 'This is a personal present.' Then she motions me to a chair and we sit down.

DIARY   *4th March, 1953*

Niggs comes back holding out the *Evening Standard* with banner headlines, 'Stalin has had a stroke and is dying.' My God, what danger that means!

V.S-W.'S DIARY   *16th March, 1953*

I revive the idea of writing about La Grande Mademoiselle.

DIARY   *24th March, 1953*

Queen Mary dies at 10.20, and Winston announces it in sobs at 10.45.

DIARY   *30th March, 1953*

Niggs rings up and says that he is going to be married. I keep my
head, being determined that Viti shall be the first to hear. So I tell
him not to go out till 2.45, by which time she will have got back.
She does get back almost at that instant and she rings up Niggs at
Albany. He says that the girl is Miss Philippa Tennyson-d'Eyncourt,
that she is 24 years of age and that they are to be married in August.
I saw her a few days ago when she picked up Niggs at Albany. My
only impression was that she was exceedingly pretty. We are all
excited. I am so happy about it. A red-letter day.

DIARY   *31st March, 1953*

We go to Queen Mary's funeral at Windsor. We meet Shirley and
Henry [Anglesey] at Paddington, and they get into our carriage.
Shirley is as charming as ever and so pretty. Viti has borrowed a hat
from Bunny [Drummond], and a veil from Mrs Copper,[1] and is
wearing her beastly pony coat. On reaching Windsor we walk up
to St George's Chapel. There are crowds in the streets and flowers
spread everywhere on the lawns. We are in the side-aisle, but can
just see into the choir and the backs of people standing round the
coffin. We then come out into the spring sunshine and walk quietly
back to the train.

DIARY   *1st April, 1953*

There is a dinner at the House of Commons for the Old Brains
Trust team. We discuss Russia. Does the present change in tactics
mean a change of heart or merely a device to separate England and
America? The general opinion is that it certainly indicates internal
weakness and therefore an easing of the external menace. I think
there is a good chance now of ending this Korean war. But if Russia
wanted, she could create economic chaos in the West by offering
disarmament-terms such as few Governments could resist. What
people do not seem to realise is the incredible stupidity of Russian
policy since 1945. At that date they had a real opportunity of winning Europe for Communism, but their lies and cruelty have lost
them all sympathy and discredited the Communist cause.

[1] The wife of the chauffeur at Sissinghurst.

H.N. TO PHILIPPA TENNYSON-D'EYNCOURT   *1st April, 1953*
C.1 Albany, W.1

I am glad you are coming to Sissinghurst on Saturday, as it will give us time to get to know you and to break through the awful embarrassment inseparable from such introductions. You will find us shy, eccentric, untidy, but most benevolent. You will find Sissinghurst the strangest conglomeration of shapeless buildings that you ever saw, but it is an affectionate house and very mellow and English.

Viti says that she asked you to call her 'Vita', and you must call me 'Harold'. That is far simpler. I always called my own beloved father-in-law 'Lionel', and it seemed quite natural after the first ten years or so.

DIARY   *16th April, 1953*

I ask Malcolm Sargent[1] whether the musical profession is as mean and jealous as the acting profession. He says it is far worse. I really think that writers are the only people who do not wish to devour their competitors.

DIARY   *30th April, 1953*

The Royal Academy Banquet. Coming up in the train, I think out my speech, or rather I learn it by heart, as I had already written it out. It had poured with rain all day, and when I enter the yard of Burlington House, it is all umbrellas. There is a Guard of Honour for Winston formed by the Artists Rifles. They look more like rifles than artists.

I am placed at the top table between the French and Portuguese Ambassadors. I eat no dinner and sip no drink. I get Alan Herbert to come out with me before the speeches and we are caught in the lavatory when the band plays *God Save* for the Royal Toast. I creep back into my seat. Winston speaks first. Then [Field Marshal] Alexander, and then me. I repeat my piece all right, but it is *not* liked. Alan Herbert is far, far better, and the impression I give is one of nervous pomposity. Afterwards we disperse into the rooms and I meet many old friends. They do not congratulate me with

[1] Sir Malcolm Sargent was then Chief Conductor of the B.B.C. Symphony Orchestra.

either warmth or conviction. I return miserable and humiliated to Albany.

DIARY   *6th May, 1953*

I lunch at the Austrian Embassy to meet the Queen of Spain.[1] She is unlike other royalties since she really is interested in the past. She began by saying that Queen Mary had given her a copy of my book and had said to her, 'It is not only a true book, as you will see, Ena, but it is also beautiful'. She tells me that at the age of five she had acted as bridesmaid to George V. She remembers it perfectly, mainly because she got into trouble. She had been told that she must keep quite silent, since nobody ever spoke in church. Then, when she heard the Archbishop beginning to read the prayers, she piped up, 'But, Mummy, *that* man is talking'. Queen Victoria told her afterwards that she had been 'very pert'. She also remembers that after the service there was a buffet at St James's Palace and that the children were in the corridor. An old gentleman with an odd collar and fur said, 'I want to see the royal children play'. They did not know what he meant and hung shyly, but Princess Patricia said, 'He wants us to dance'. So they danced in front of him up and down the corridor and he beamed at them. She now realises that it was Mr Gladstone.

She said that Queen Victoria never understood children and asked them so many questions that they became confused. She had a horrible bag of gold and coral out of which she would take sovereigns and give them to them. When it was too snowy at Balmoral to go out to Crathie church, she would give them Bible talks in her room. That was a great ordeal, as she always lost her temper with their stupidity. She can still recall her lovely girlish voice and that silver laugh. But no liberties were permitted. The Battenberg children, being resident family, were always given dull nursery meals—beef, mutton and milk-puddings—but visiting children were allowed éclairs and ices. Once, Princess Ena, in indignation at this, said as her grace, 'Thank God for my dull dinner'. Queen Victoria was enraged at this and punished her.

[1] The daughter of Princess Beatrice (youngest daughter of Queen Victoria) and wife of King Alfonso XIII of Spain. Her father was Prince Henry of Battenberg. Her pet-name was Ena, but she was christened Victoria Eugenie. In 1953 she was aged 66.

I enjoyed my conversation and returned to Albany meaning to record it. Elvira [Niggeman] said, 'Honours heap upon you.' There was a letter from the Master of Balliol saying that I am to be elected an Honorary Fellow. Only Niggs, and perhaps Viti, know that of all honours this earth can give, that is the one I most desire.

DIARY   *28th May, 1953*

I go with Mrs G. D. H. Cole[1] to see Florence Horsbrugh, the Minister of Education. She has that sulky bewildered manner that I have noticed before in Fabians. Florence is ministerial and firm. We were asking that a licence be granted to rebuild Morley College.[2] She replies that she cannot allocate material and labour to Morley College without cutting down work on primary and secondary schools, and that they must have priority. Mrs Cole mumbles and grumbles that this is all nonsense—but how can she prove it in terms of steel and cement? I fear that I am always impressed when reasonable people meet my requests with reasonable denials. I have no fanatic gifts. I can see that Mrs Cole regards me as a weak and useless brother.

V.S-W.'S DIARY   *2nd June, 1953*

Mount Everest has been climbed by Edmund Hillary and Tensing. I am furious about this.[3]

DIARY   *2nd June, 1953*

Coronation Day. We are called at 6 and walk round to the Travellers. There is television in the dining-room and we see the whole service quite beautifully. I am much moved. Then we have an excellent luncheon and go to our places on the stand. After a short wait the troops appear. There is a long pause while the Guardsmen wait in front of us and the rain pours down on their bearskins. This

---

[1] Margaret Cole, the author and lecturer. She was the wife of G. D. H. Cole, the Professor of Political Theory at Oxford, and herself a notable writer and speaker on political subjects.

[2] The important adult-educational College in South London of which H.N. became President in 1953.

[3] This was so typical of her! She regretted that there was no longer any spot on earth inaccessible to man.

is due to the horse-artillery being unable to get their guns up the slippery slope of St James's Street. But off they move again and eventually comes Winston in his Garter robes waving his plumed hat and making the V sign, the Queen of Tonga immense and in an open carriage getting drenched, the Queen Mother and Princess Margaret, and finally the vast gold coach. The procession characteristically is ended by an ambulance for any horses that might get hurt.

DIARY   8th June, 1953

An agreement regarding the prisoners is signed at Panmunjom. It may be a prelude to an armistice in Korea. Syngman Rhee is being tiresome and wishes to continue the struggle. The Americans are not fortunate in their puppets.

DIARY   21st June, 1953

Ben today made a strange remark while we were discussing what effect a private school has on little boys, and how they separated their home from their school life. 'It is an effect', says Ben, 'which lasts all one's life. To this day I have a horror of rendering myself conspicuous.' Considering that his hair is like that of a gollywog and his clothes noticeable the other end of Trafalgar Square, this was an odd assertion. Yet it was made in absolute sincerity, and with that naïveté which is part of his compelling charm.

DIARY   29th June, 1953

I have a really full Sissinghurst day. I write my review of Samuel Butler. I then write an obituary of Winston for the *Observer*. I hope to God he isn't going to die. I then garden for a bit, and write my Overseas Talk for Tuesday. About 5,000 words in all.

DIARY   4th July, 1953
                                                   Newcastle-on-Tyne

We process in robes to the City Hall where there are many graduands. I am the only honorary doctor and I come first. I sit there in my robes and watch three hundred men and women receiving degrees—not one of them that is not a monster of ugliness. How strange that the human nose and chin should be subject to such ungainly variations!

DIARY   *14th July, 1953*

Dinner with the Literary Society at the Garrick. Peter Fleming and John Betjeman have each received a request to contribute to the American broadcast series on 'What I Believe'. Peter says that he believes in the Life Spirit. John says that he believes that Christ was God and that he died for the sins of the world. He believes in the after-life in which we shall meet all the people we loved but none of those we disliked. I say, 'But what happens to those people who rather like me whereas I hate them?' He says, 'That is what I *wish* to believe. I cannot face extinction.' He looks so sad, bless him.

DIARY   *16th July, 1953*

There is an American at the Beefsteak called Colonel Nicholas. I beg him that when he returns to New York he will not encourage the idea that England is deluged under a flood of anti-American hatred. It isn't that. It is that we are frightened that the destinies of the world should be in the hands of a giant with the limbs of an undergraduate, the emotions of a spinster and the brain of a pea-hen. He says, 'The difference is that we are a democracy and you are not.' What he really means is that they idolise the common man and woman and we only pay attention to the uncommon man. He is utterly unable to explain how McCarthy's witch-hunting and book-burning can be reconciled with democratic principles. In fact he is a foolish man who thinks only in terms of small-town politics.

DIARY   *21st July, 1953*

Walter Monckton tells me that Winston has had a stroke, as people suspected. His left eyelid has slipped and his left arm is not easy to use. He is ashamed to be seen in that condition, but is otherwise quite well.

DIARY   *29th July, 1953*

I go to a reception for Adlai Stevenson. It is packed. I am introduced to him, and he tells me that he has never forgotten how kind I was giving him luncheon and taking him into the House in 1939. I have no recollection at all of this incident. He is not like what I imagined him. A heavy man, with slim body, but heavy appearance, reddish face, alert eyes, a rather prancing manner—in fact a deception.

DIARY   *30th July, 1953*

Nigel's wedding-day. Red-letter or black-letter day? We go in a car to St Margaret's. There is an awning and a large crowd. Philippa arrives on the dot, and then the lovely ceremony begins. Afterwards we drive off to Fishmonger's Hall. Everything there is magnificent, and V. and I stand beside the Tennyson d'Eyncourts shaking hands with troops of people. Ben makes a sweet little speech, and then Niggs replies, referring to our happily married life and love for each other. This brings a lump to my throat and tears to V.'s eyes. Then off they go in their little car to Sissinghurst.

I feel crushed and exhausted and sad. I shall miss him dreadfully. But there must be no self-pity about all this. Philippa will be an addition, and there will be grandchildren, and I know that even from my own selfish point of view, this means an increase in happiness and not a decrease.

DIARY   *12th August, 1953*

I go to Lime Grove and dub my television obituary of Winston. It rather amuses me. We go through it five times before we get it right.[1]

V.S-W.'S DIARY   *23rd August, 1953*
                                                        Aviemore, Inverness

Go to Inverewe[2] early. Then we have the most beautiful drive we have yet had. We don't take the ordinary Inverness road, but go by the mountains and past Little Loch Broom. At one point, Gruinard, we see the Shiants,[3] a great thrill for me. After miles of enchanted desolation, we lunch at a wayside inn, the first human habitation for miles and miles, called Altguish; quite a good luncheon. Eventually a main road to Aviemore, and we leave all that beauty behind us. I finish my article on Walter de la Mare. An unforgettable day, and sunny.

---

[1] This recording was televised twelve years later, on Sir Winston's death in January 1965.
[2] The great garden created by Osgood Mackenzie in the north-west Highlands, now the property of the Scottish National Trust.
[3] The islands in the Outer Hebrides belonging to myself.

DIARY   *28th August, 1953*

We drive to Hidcote. We go over the garden. It is nonsense to say
that it is not as good as it was. It is still the loveliest small garden in
England. The wilderness, however, needs drastic clearing out. We
leave about 11 and drive to Stow-on-the-Wold, and then Burford
and Newbury, crossing the stripling Thames. At Newbury we have
a poor luncheon at the inn. They give us what they call *Tartelettes
de Fruit*—a crumbly piece of shortbread with two cherries and
artificial cream. I despair of English cooking. It is no good training
the producer; it is the consumer who must be taught to notice
when food is lazily cooked.

We get home at ten to 6. Telephone to Nigel and Philippa. They
got back from their honeymoon today. Niggs says he feels ten years
younger. It is time he had some gaiety in his life. Vita is wonderful
but not vivacious; I am sometimes amusing, but glum on the whole
rather than gay. Philippa provides that levity and simplicity that he
needed in his life.

The garden is looking well, and we prefer it to all those we have
seen, with the exception of Hidcote.

DIARY   *28th September, 1953*

The Americans, after three years of negotiation, have come to an
agreement with Franco whereby they obtain bases in Spain. They
are also obliging the Greeks to get rid of our naval mission and to
have an American one instead. Gradually they are ousting us out of
all world authority. I mind this, as I feel it is humiliating and
insidious. But I also mind it because it gives grounds for anti-
American feeling, which is, I am sure, a dangerous and quite useless
state of mind. They are decent folk in every way, but they tread on
traditions in a way that hurts.

DIARY   *30th September, 1953*

I dine at the Garrick with Fred Warner,[1] and listen with him to Alan Pryce-Jones giving the third of his series of talks on the Good Life. I am convinced that the good life is successful activity in congenial surroundings—or, in other words, the fullest expression of one's personality and the fullest exercise of those special gifts one happens to possess. Fred and I discuss this afterwards. I say that every individual knows what is his special line of self-expression, since when he extends that line he feels pleasure, and when he neglects or runs counter to it, he experiences pain. Fred says that the pain-pleasure principle of conscience is a subjective guide and unreliable. On the one hand it inclines people to approve those indulgences which suit their own temperament, and on the other hand it takes no account of such qualities as one may deliberately cultivate. For instance, a naturally unpunctual person can by taking trouble become punctual or a timid person can cultivate courage or at least audacity. They are going against their own original temperament; yet they were doing well and not badly. I reply feebly that in each of those instances the real temperament was punctual and brave, and that it was only superficially the reverse. Yes, yes—I know that a shallow philosophy is untenable when you examine it; but a deeper one leads to such deep depression and creates even less valuable results.

H.N. TO PHILIPPA NICOLSON   *13th October, 1953*
                                                  C.1 Albany, W.1

Nigel has told me the news.[2] I have seldom seen an adult human-being combine so much shyness, pride, affection and anxiety in a single sentence. He says that your mother doesn't believe it is true. But he says that the doctor, who knows even more about such matters than your mother, says that it is a fact—a curious little fact at present, and one that will make you feel a different person and so very odd, but nonetheless a fact. A tiny fact of immense importance. Now, horrible, sordid and ignorant as this remark may seem, the same experience has revealed itself to 240,000,003 women even

---

[1] The young Foreign Office official, who had recently returned from the Moscow Embassy, and became a close friend of H.N.
[2] She was expecting a baby.

during this present year. I know that this is not the same. Other babies are just population statistics, but this one is endowed with beauty, power, a lovely singing voice, profound domestic affections and a good eye for a horse. But although I know that your present experience is exceptional and unique, I may perhaps be allowed to murmur that the same thing *has* occurred before in the history of man. I know you will be careful No water-shoots in Battersea Park, no Grand National, not even a nice afternoon on roller-skates at Boscombe Hippodrome. Just a quiet Philippa, expectant but unruffled, amused and not fussy, and conscious of the devotion of her curious husband and the love that surrounds her right away from Hampshire to Kent.

V.S-W'S DIARY   *14th October, 1953*

Oh God, how I wish I could get Virginia back! Reading her diary[1] makes me regret her so poignantly, and also feeling that towards the end I might have done something to stop her from taking her life.

DIARY   *28th October, 1953*

I fiddle with my Chichele lectures and then go to lunch at the French Embassy, where there are Robert Schuman,[2] Layton, Pakenham, Woodrow Wyatt[3] and others. Bob Boothby says that Winston has let the world and his colleagues down by backing out of European Union once he achieved office. Schuman is amused—gently, paternally, amused—at this outburst on the part of a Conservative. In the evening I take the chair for him at Chatham House. He reads a long speech about Franco-German relations. It is a wise speech recognising that the old idea of *contrainte* is completely out of date. He speaks sadly to me afterwards about the disasters in Indo-China.[4]

[1] A selection from Virginia Woolf's Diaries was about to be published, and V.S-W. was reviewing the book for *Encounter*.

[2] The French Foreign Secretary, who had been Prime Minister of France, 1947-48, and Minister of Foreign Affairs in eight subsequent Governments.

[3] Labour M.P. for Aston, 1945-55, and Parliamentary Under Secretary of State for War in 1951.

[4] The French position in Indo-China was becoming politically and militarily untenable. If they were to leave the country without handing it over to the communists, they must first weaken the Vietminh by military means. Success eluded them, and the position was to deteriorate further in 1954.

He fears that all these years of fighting will have been in vain, since France will have to abandon that empire. He is depressed but resigned. A nice man with none of the usual perky sharpness of French politicians.

DIARY   *1st November, 1953*

I work at my fourth Chichele lecture all day, and then read Livy and Virginia Woolf. She rightly says that to a diary one entrusts a mood rather than an expression of continuous personality. There is nothing of her distinction, charm and occasional affection and kindness in her diary. She seems neurotic, vain and envious. But it is fascinating nonetheless.

I know the mood that is entrusted to my diary. It is the time-table mood.

DIARY   *2nd November, 1953*

I finish Chichele 4. I try to weed, but the soil is too sticky and my trowel becomes so greasy that I cannot operate it. I pick flowers for tomorrow instead[1]—the last of the dahlias and the artemisia. I finish Virginia's book with some sadness. Her melancholy was terrible, poor Virginia. Always there is in my mind the picture of that lovely body weighted down by stones in the mud and slime.

DIARY   *5th November, 1953*

I dine at the House for one of the Brains Trust dinners. We discuss the Press and Television. Gilbert Harding and Quintin Hogg[2] are really admirable. The general view is that the Press is all right but does not present its news in the right order. Television will abolish newspapers, cinemas, the stage and reading, and is the *deinotatos* ['most powerful'] force ever invented. It is all amusing and good talk. Old Lord Samuel is there and delightful.

DIARY   *19th November, 1953*

I read Winston's book[3] furiously all day and finish it. I then go to

[1] Every week throughout his life H.N. took a basket of flowers from the country for his rooms in London.
[2] He had succeeded his father as Viscount Hailsham in 1950.
[3] The last volume of his History of the Second World War, *Triumph and Tragedy*.

248

hear T. S. Eliot speak on 'The Three Voices of Poetry'. The lecture takes place in Central Hall, and I have never seen such a crowd for any literary lecture. They told me that there were more than 2,500 people there, and they remained silent throughout. I am on the platform and Norman Birkett takes the chair. Tom talks about his Three Voices—the voice of the poet talking to himself or nobody, the voice of a poet addressing an audience, the voice of a poet speaking through a dramatic character. He has much to say that is new. He says that for him inspiration is like matter that must be expelled, and ease only comes when it has been expelled in the form of a poem.

We go on afterwards and dine at the National Book League. It is a pleasant dinner and both Tom and Norman Birkett are in good form. I had to propose a vote of thanks this evening, but the audience were obviously so moved by Tom's lecture that I did it in ten words.

DIARY   *8th December, 1953*

I wake up at 6 to find that the plan of my book on Manners [*Good Behaviour*] has suddenly become quite clear during the night. This is unconscious cerebration. All yesterday I was feeling so stupid and inert.

I lunch with Irene Ravensdale.[1] What odd guests are there! Peggy Ashcroft,[2] the Eshers, the Austrian Ambassador, and Charles Chaplin and his wife. Charlie has become tubby and white and gap-toothed. I ask him whether he is recognised now in tubes and buses.[3] He says not if he wears glasses. But sometimes he forgets to put them on, and sees a startled look coming over the faces of people sitting opposite.

DIARY   *26th December, 1953*

After dinner we listen on the wireless to records of Tennyson reciting his poems. The old boy recites the *Charge of the Heavy Brigade*, ditto of the Light Brigade, *The Northern Farmer*, and the last two stanzas of *Maud*. The latter are by far the best, and something of the bitter

[1] Baroness Ravensdale, eldest daughter of Lord Curzon, who was a peeress in her own right, and was also created a Life Peeress in 1958.
[2] The actress, then appearing as Cleopatra in *Antony and Cleopatra*.
[3] See vol. I of these diaries, p. 93.

passion and resentment of the poem comes across. His voice is thinner, higher, than I expected—but that may have been because the records were played at the wrong speed. But the insistence on the metre, which Ellen Terry had told me about, is very apparent, and the broad Lincolnshire 'o' comes out as in 'roaed' for 'rode' It is most curious and strange and true.

H.N. TO PHILIPPA NICOLSON   *28th December, 1953*
                                                     Sissinghurst

By this morning's post I received your Christmas present—six handkerchiefs of white samite, mystic, wonderful,[1] which will be preserved for those great occasions when I dine with Emperors and Princes or Queen Mothers or Mr Henry Channon. When opened, these handkerchiefs have a silken and transparent quality that differentiates them from the dish-cloths I customarily use. And each time I pull out these handkerchiefs I shall reflect upon how nice it is to possess a daughter-in-law who gives one handkerchiefs that one can pull out.

We have had an agreeable Christmas. Vita and Ben and I were so happy here alone, working away and feeding the ducks and digging up weeds—and then we had to change and put on London clothes and go out to parties. Peace and goodwill are all very well, but too much goodwill destroys peace. There is one thing that I feel we lack as a family, and that is social gaiety. Vita is always thinking about Louis XIV, Ben is always thinking about Pollaiuolo, Nigel worries about coast erosion, and I am immersed in my reflections upon the nature of courtesy. The result is that we do not enjoy cocktail parties and make such an effort not to show our displeasure that we become taut, strained, dehydrated, absurd and unreal. Now the one thing we are not is unreal. So I hate Christmas, and I wish David's royal city were not celebrated in vermouth and gin.

Will you thank Nigel for his shaving-lotion? I see his point It is good for an old gentleman, lapped as I am in the roses of luxury, to have something really astringent to remind me of the asperities of life. Hitherto I have withstood the smarting with courage, coming to breakfast with a heavenly aroma of lilies-of-the-valley wafting around me, and tears of manly endurance making furrows down

[1] From Tennyson's *The Passing of Arthur*.

my cheeks. 'One, two, three!', I say, to ginger up my courage. I apply the shirt of Nessus to my shaven chin; I run up and down the room in agony while the pain lasts; and then off I go, proud, grateful, rejoicing in my own fortitude, and in the ambrosia that it spreads.

1954

Death of Duff Cooper – failure of Foreign Ministers' Conference in Berlin – the growing reputation of the garden at Sissinghurst – Anthony Eden on Persia and Egypt – Jean Cocteau – popularity of V.S-W.'s gardening articles in the 'Observer' – birth of Juliet Nicolson – H.N.'s dissatisfaction with 'Good Behaviour' – a happy holiday in the Dordogne –Montaigne – Alain-Fournier and George Sand – V.S-W. distressed by myxomatosis – Dame Edith Evans – Arnold Toynbee and 'A Study of History' – Robert Birley at Eton – V.S-W. refuses to give Sissinghurst to the National Trust – reads her poems to the Royal Literary Society – farewell to the Massiglis – 'Good Behaviour' finished

'Good Behaviour' was finished by the end of the year. It had taken Harold Nicolson unusually long to write. This was partly because it required research into periods and topics unfamiliar to him, such as the Middle Ages and the manners of the Far East; and partly because he was diverted from the book by other activities. It had long been his habit to spend the inside of every week in London, where he was separated from his works of reference and was exposed to constant interruptions. He was still a member of many Committees, and Chairman of some of them. He was still reviewing a book a week for the 'Observer'. He gave many lectures. He spoke regularly on Foreign Affairs for the B.B.C.'s overseas service. There were articles, forewords to other people's books, appeals from young authors for advice which he never refused, and a stream of visitors to Albany, which he was now sharing with John Sparrow and Colin Fenton.

His real work was done at Sissinghurst at weekends. Here he resented social interruptions almost as much as he welcomed them in London, and he was happiest when alone with V. Sackville-West and Ben. She struggled on with 'La Grande Mademoiselle', who had begun to dominate her life ('The Big Miss stands behind me with a whip'), and in spite of all her preoccupation with the garden, the estate and the local Bench, she made fairly good progress with the book during the year. In August she and Harold Nicolson motored together to the Dordogne in search of literary and historical sites and the Lascaux caves (what they called a 'randonnée spéléologique'). The other personal event of the year was the birth of their first grandchild, Juliet, on 9th June.

DIARY   1st January, 1954

The 9 o'clock news tells us that Duff [Cooper] has died on his way to the West Indies in a French liner. This is a shock. What mortality is all around us! Poor, poor Diana.

DIARY   *7th January, 1954*

I go to the memorial service for Duff Cooper at St Margaret's. Bobbety Salisbury reads the lessons and Bob Boothby makes an excellent address in a ringing voice. The church is packed, Winston and all the Cabinet being there. It is a distressing occasion, and the mixture of a society-gathering and a requiem is always disconcerting. I lunch with the Vansittarts. I then go to the *Observer* to collect a biography of that bore Addison. John [Sparrow] comes up for the opera and we have an easy happy chat. He is so excellent as a friend and so stimulating as a companion. I dine at the Beefsteak.

DIARY   *11th January, 1954*

I review as politely as I can Peter Smithers' book on Joseph Addison. I finish Jack Wheeler-Bennett's book *Nemesis of Power*.[1] It really is a magnificent work.

Lord Simon has died. He was almost 81. John Sparrow wrote his epitaph many years ago:

> This stone, with not unpardonable pride,
> Proves by its record what the world denied:
> Simon could do a natural thing—he died.

But then John Simon helped John Sparrow to become Warden of All Souls, and the latter came to regret his epigram. He became fond of him. Simon was a man who wished to be agreeable, but could never inspire confidence in his sincerity. Yet he was capable of great generosity.

DIARY   *17th January, 1954*

I read Paddy Leigh Fermor's essay on monasteries[2] which is impressive. He is becoming an important writer. Viti discovers that what I thought was a fine crop of myosotis is in fact salad. I weed it up sadly all afternoon. I read *Emma*.[3] A happy day together—one of those beads on the necklace of my life that not even death or illness or madness or drink can destroy.

[1] *Nemesis of Power: The German Army in Politics, 1918-45.*
[2] *A Time to Keep Silence*
[3] H.N. was rereading all Jane Austen's novels as background for his chapter on 'Respectability' in *Good Behaviour*.

DIARY   *14th February, 1954*

Sad, sad, that it looks as if the Berlin Conference were breaking down.[1] What turmoil I have lived in since 1914! I mind it all for our children's sake. I shall be dead, perhaps, before the catastrophe occurs. Anyhow it doesn't matter. I have had my life, and a lovely, wonderful life it has been.

H.N. TO V.S-W.   *9th March, 1954*
                                                          C.1 Albany, W.1

Did you feel very old when you got up this morning?[2] It is horrible this business about Time's Winged Chariot. It simply does not give us a chance at all. And I do want to get the spring-border really perfect before I die, and I want to write five more books, and I want to see Jemima and Jasper[3] grow up, and, oh dear, what a lot of things I want!

DIARY   *14th March, 1954*

I feel livery and empty of mind and soul. I write rottenly about Manners. It simply does not make sense and is just senile chatter. It is too cold even to feed the ducks in comfort, and I return to my warm room and read Julian Huxley's book on the Middle East [*From An Antique Land*]. It is odd that so clever a man can write so badly. My cold is better but my mind is a sponge filled with husks.

V.S-W. TO H.N.   *16th March, 1954*
                                                          Sissinghurst

The Editor of *Gardening Illustrated* wants to do an article about our garden. That is nice of him, and furthermore he wants to incorporate the article in a book he is doing for *Country Life*. It *is* funny, isn't it, that our own dear garden should be taking its place among the better known gardens of England? Oh, if only we could have the last twenty years all over again! We wouldn't make any change in

[1] The conference of Foreign Secretaries, meeting in Berlin to determine the future of Germany and Austria, ended on 19th February without agreement.
[2] She was 62.   [3] Imaginary names for his unborn grandchildren.

H.N.D.   257   R the design, but I should like to go back and make a great many changes in the planting. Beastly garden.[1]

H.N. TO V.S-W.   8th April, 1954
                                                      C.1 Albany, W.1

I dined with Anthony Eden at Carlton Gardens. It was a dinner of reconciliation with the Persian Ambassador. Woolton was there and Herbert Morrison and John Maud and the F.O. chaps. Anthony told me that the oil agreement was practically complete[2] and that it was hung up merely owing to some snag in American Company Law. He is very keen to get it, as he says that it is more important even than the Suez Canal. The latter problem, he fears, will hang on indefinitely, since it is impossible to make an agreement with these young and transitory majors in Cairo.[3]

V.S-W TO H.N.   13th April, 1954
                                                      Sissinghurst

This morning I got a parcel of books I had ordered from Paris. Amongst them the *Journal de Jean Héroard*, Louis XIII's doctor. I haven't yet looked at them properly, but opened Héroard *au hasard*, and fell on this: '*Il (Louis XIII) fait faire la cornemuse au chien Patout, dont il riait à l'outrance, lui qui n'était pas grand rieur.*'[4] I am *longing* to get at these books.

H.N. TO V.S-W.   12th May, 1954
                                                      C.1 Albany, W.1

I went to the English Speaking Union dinner last night for Lou Douglas.[5] My word, he made a good speech! A direct all-out

[1] This needs some explanation. She did not, of course, think the garden at Sissinghurst beastly. But she always noticed the gaps and the failures. As she went round it with H.N., she would point out these lapses, and say, 'Beastly garden!', as if it had let her down. The phrase became part of their vocabulary.
[2] The formation of a consortium to market Iranian oil, in return for which the Iranian Government agreed to pay £25 million compensation to the Anglo-Iranian Oil Company.
[3] This was the period of the struggle for power between Neguib and Nasser.
[4] 'He gets his dog Patout to howl like a bagpipe, which made him roar with laughter, although he was not a man much given to laughing.'
[5] Lewis W. Douglas, U.S. Ambassador in London, 1947-50.

attack on McCarthy. I enjoyed it, and you know that I do not enjoy public dinners.

DIARY   *18th May, 1954*
                                                                      Paris

Hugh Thomas[1] and I go to Véfour for lunch. They say there are no tables free, and I am about to leave when I am caught by Jean Cocteau who insists on our having a table next to him. He is amusing and interesting. He tells me that he knew Alain-Fournier[2] well, and in fact they lived together for a few months. He has a little brass plaque let into the back of the bench at Véfour saying, 'Here sat Jean Cocteau'. The next table has a similar plaque saying, 'Here died Fragonard',[3] and in fact he did die splosh into his plate.

V.S-W. TO H.N.   *2nd June, 1954*

Never again will I write in the *Observer* about being ill. Besides, I wasn't ill; it was simply that I couldn't think what to write about. It brought me so many deeply concerned letters of sympathy and enquiry. How false and fleeting is journalistic popularity! I often think how empty and lonely some people's lives must be, that they project themselves into the lives of unknown people. One can understand the glamour appeal of film-stars or Princess Margaret. But why us?

DIARY   *9th June, 1954*

At 8.40 a.m. Nigel telephones to say that Philippa had a daughter at 3.45 this morning [at Shirley House, Bransgore, Hampshire]. Oh dear, I am so delighted. I telephone to Viti who had already heard the news. I feel all different being a grandfather, and thirty years younger.

DIARY   *10th June, 1954*

I go with Ben to Westminster Abbey where we have the unveiling of the Keats-Shelley memorial. The Poet Laureate [John Masefield]

[1] Ex-President of the Cambridge Union, and author of *The Spanish Civil War* (1961).
[2] Author of *Le Grand Meaulnes*, who was killed in 1914 at the age of 28.
[3] Jean Honoré Fragonard (1732–1806), the painter of scenes of gallantry and romance.

makes a good speech, the American Ambassador says a few words, and Don the Dean reads a prayer by Donne the Dean.

DIARY   15th June, 1954

I see the flags at half-mast in Fleet Street and on the posters the news that Camrose has died. He was a staunch friend and wise counsellor. He showed that one could be a Press Lord and a gentleman. He was an example to the newspaper world, and I am wretched at his death.

I dine at the Literary Society. Halifax says that Chamberlain's great fault was that he sneered at people; he sneered at the Labour Members and they never forgave him. He agrees that he was a frightfully conceited man.

DIARY   27th June, 1954

I am depressed by my Manners book and wish I had never embarked upon it. In fact I am feeling old, deaf, stupid, with no new ideas. Nothing agreeable can happen in future and the disagreeable things are large and numerous. This is just a mood.

DIARY   11th July, 1954

I do my wireless talk on Modesty in Literature. I weed well, as the soil is in excellent condition. Giles [St Aubyn][1] works all day. He is perfectly charming, having retained all his boyish frankness, and added knowledge, wisdom, taste and a faculty for expressing himself well. He has developed into a remarkable young man.

H.N. TO JULIET NICOLSON (aged 7 weeks)[2]   31st July, 1954
                                                        Sissinghurst

Now that you have been admitted into the Church and had a paragraph all to yourself in the *Daily Telegraph*, you should be able, if not to read, then at least to take in, private letters.

I thought it noble of you to remain quiescent while your god-father and godmother promised such glum things on your behalf. But I did not think it noble of you to sneak when I gave you a

---

[1] H.N.'s nephew. He was now aged 29, and a master at Eton.
[2] She had been christened by the Bishop of Winchester in the chapel at Shirley House on 30th July.

silver spoon and you went and bashed your own eye and forehead with it. It is foolish, in any case, to bash oneself with spoons. But it is evil for a girl about to be blessed by a bishop to sneak about her grandfather. You did not see the look your mother gave me. You did not realise the deep suspicion with which your nurse thereafter regarded me. (What an ass that woman was, flattering you like that; and how weak of you to respond with a grin to her blandishments.)

Will you tell your father that were I a Conservative, I should blush at the way they have behaved over Cyprus. 'We cannot allow self-determination for Cyprus since it is a vital strategic base. We could not have remained in the Canal Zone, since, because it is a vital strategic base, it would have been bombed out of existence.' Nothing shows up the Tories so badly as situations which they know to be false. It emphasises the falsity both of the situations and of the 1922 Committee.

And will you tell your mother that I really believe that you will have large eyes as lovely as she has and a character as sweet as hers, and that I really will not spoil you when you reach the age of 2, since I detest spoiled children. And even if I do spoil you, I shall do so surreptitiously in order to avoid a look from her like the spoon-look.

DIARY   *17th August, 1954*
                                          Beynac, Dordogne, France

We enter the Lascaux woods[1] and go down to the cave. It has been done up with steps, lighting and handrails since Vita first saw it eight years ago by the light of Monsieur Laval's hurricane-lamp. The guide is Monsieur Ravidat, whose dog Robot first discovered the caves. He tells Viti that M. Laval was so entranced by the discovery that he took to drink and died. As always, the real thing is utterly different from what one imagined. I have gazed with attention at the many reproductions of the Lascaux paintings, but the reality was so distinct from them. The impression I got was one of effective

[1] The Lascaux cave, near Montignac, was discovered in September 1940. M. Ravidat was one of five boys exploring the hillside, when their dog disappeared down a hole. Following, they discovered the now famous cave-paintings, of which the oldest dates from about 30,000 B.C. M. Laval was the local school-master, whom the boys told of their discovery.

colour. The drawings I knew already, but what was startling was the actual variation of colour produced by so few different paints.

DIARY   *19th August, 1954*

We go to see the Château de Montaigne [1] One enters it by a short avenue of conifers. There is a vast modern castle built by some wealthy merchant of Bordeaux on the *emplacement* and according to the design of the original, which was burnt. But Montaigne himself lived in a little tower, no larger than an oast-house, detached from the main building. There is a chapel on the ground floor with a hole cut in the roof, by which he could hear prayers in his bedroom above without going down. The bedroom is small and low, with the remains of Italian painted decoration. There is a privy outside it, with a shoot down to the ground. Some of the steps of the stone staircase are worn by the little man's feet. Then comes his study. The beams in the roof are inscribed with mottoes in Greek and Latin, all of them bearing on the theme that worldly activity is the vanity of vanities, and the only possible life is one of seclusion and study. There are extracts from his writings referring to the room, 'where I can get away from the company of others and be King of my own'. It looks as if the poor old man, only just five foot in height and bowed at that, was bullied by his wife and family and enjoyed this distant refuge 'looking down on my garden and woods'. It is extremely moving, and V. and I are entranced.

DIARY   *25th August, 1954*
                                                    Nohant, Indre, France

We branch off the main road and go to Epineuil-le-Fleuriel, which is the place where Alain-Fournier lived as a child and the background of *Le Grand Meaulnes*. It is a small village spread along four crossroads with a small post-office and a church like the Weald. The postmistress tell us that many visitors come, mostly Belgians for some odd reason. She points to a larger house opposite with a small *tourelle* which she says is *la grande maison* in the *Grand Meaulnes*. I do not remember that and must look it up. We then go to the schoolhouse, which is tiny. A small courtyard with a tree in the middle no

[1] The château near Bordeaux where Michel de Montaigne, the essayist (1533–92), was born and died.

larger than the cottage-garden at home. A low schoolhouse with two small classrooms. We enter them, as they are empty. The benches and the master's desk must be exactly those that he sat at and where his father taught. It is astonishing that so restricted and meagre a site should have produced that great fountain of romanticism.

Then we go on to Nohant. The George Sand[1] house is outside the village. A small eighteenth-century house with a forecourt and a grille. The custodian takes us first to the family graveyard beside the cemetery but in the park. There are members of the family and a great black basalt tomb for Madame Sand. A very old and overgrown yew-tree overhangs the graves, and it is all very wet and dank. We then return to the house some hundred yards away. There is a huge kitchen-garden which must have contained roses and flowers, and a little *parc* with overgrown conifers and two cedars which Madame Sand planted to commemorate her children. The hall is simple and there is a country staircase. We are taken into the dining-room, where there is luncheon laid for some ten people. Madame Sand's grand-daughter, who lives in the house, likes to pretend that her grandmother is still entertaining. There are grapes and peaches in the fruit-dishes and wine in the little *flacons*. Against the glasses are propped the name-cards of the guests—Turgenev, Balzac, Flaubert, Jerome Bonaparte and the family. It is most strange. It is a nice dining-room with pretty country china, and we are struck by the absence of anything in 1860 bad taste. The floor is of uneven rustic tiles everywhere, even in Madame Sand's bedroom. We are taken there. It is the room where she died. A tiny bed with curtains of blue, and the same sort of *Toile de Jouy* on the walls. Next door is her writing-room. A small ugly little desk in the middle; a range of bookcases; a collection of quartz and shells. Outside the cedars darken the room. We then go to the drawing-room decorated with pictures of Maurice de Saxe[2] and paintings by her son. There is a harp and a tiny little piano at which Chopin improvised. We

---

[1] The novelist (1804-76) and friend f Chopin, whose real name was Baronne Dudevant, *née* Dupin. She was brought up in this house and lived there from 1848 onwards.

[2] Marshal Saxe (1696-1750), victor of Fontenoy, and an ancestor of George Sand.

then go downstairs again and through a dark and narrow passage to the theatre where she kept her marionettes.

V.S-W. TO H.N.   *31st August, 1954*
                                                        Sissinghurst

I miss you! It is dreadful, getting so used to your daily companion-ship, my most perfect companion, whether travelling or at home. But we *were* happy, weren't we?, and we can think back on that lovely country with the poplars and the green grass and the hanging woods and the quiet river and the strange caves and the patient pious oxen and the castles and the *manoirs*. I can't tell you how happy it makes me to think that you liked and understood the Dordogne in exactly the same way as I do. It is horrid to have to communicate with you by letter instead of just shouting 'Hadji!' whenever I want you. But as a result we have stored up a great cellar-full of vintage happiness and love—as we always do when we get away together alone.

H.N. TO V.S-W.   *2nd September, 1954*
                                                    C.1 Albany, W.1

I went up to Nottingham to declare open their Book Festival. We passed through Leicester, and I gazed out on that ugly and feature-less city, thinking how strange it was that I had for so long been identified with those brick houses with their ironwork railings and their clean little steps.

I read Montaigne all the way up and back, and the picture of that small tower and the mottoes on the beams remained with me, hanging there in the air. How glad I am we went. It is a pearl among pilgrimages. And to think of that fat silky river sliding past the hotel terrace at Beynac!

V.S-W. TO H.N.   *14th September, 1954*
                                                        Sissinghurst

I got into such a rage. I listened to a B.B.C. Home Service pro-gramme about myxomatosis, and it was all from the point of view of the farmer or the tame-rabbit breeder whose trade might be threatened. And *not one word* about what the rabbits might suffer—just profit, profit, profit, or loss of profit. That is all men think of—

just their purses—and I do think it is disgusting. It makes me sick with life. I know you will think me silly and sentimental, but I don't care if you do. I *know* there is something beyond material profit in this beastly utilitarian world. You can't deny this. It is the thing that makes me love you, and you love me. It is what takes the place of religion in people who are not that way inclined. It is all the same thing: all paths meet at the end of a long converging perspective—whether the end of it is what is called science, or God, or the Creator—that is what I profoundly believe.

Sorry, darling. I got carried away on a storm of temper, thinking of those wretched swollen rabbits I had seen in our lane. I think I had better stop now. You don't like it when I take up lost causes, although you can take them up with violence sometimes yourself. Only then it is something like Cyprus and ENOSIS, or the reconstruction of Germany—shaking hands with blood-stained murderers, who would start it all up again if they saw the chance.[1]

H.N. TO V.S-W.   *16th September, 1954*
                                                    C.1 Albany, W.1

I agree absolutely with you about cruelty to rabbits. I wish you would write a letter to *The Listener* about it. I do not share the view that rabbits are less sensitive than dogs. Supposing that someone took Mrs Price[2] away from me and injected her with some agonising disease? I agree with you wholly about this and do not think it sentimental at all. I wish you would write. Your name carries such weight.

I spent yesterday morning going through the letters from Winston to Eddie Marsh[3] which Christopher Hassall[4] left with me. They are interesting in a way. But one sees that, underneath, Eddie was silly about politics. I mean, Winston never consulted him about serious things. Nonetheless they reveal that Winston really had a deep affection for the little squeaky.

[1] This rapid switch from her revulsion from myxomatosis to her dislike of the Germans was most characteristic. She never forgave Germany.
[2] Not a rabbit, but one of the ducks on the moat at Sissinghurst.
[3] Sir Edward Marsh, the man-of-letters who first became secretary to Winston Churchill in 1905.
[4] His biography of Sir Edward Marsh was published in 1959.

Then Richard Ward[1] came and I took him along to Albemarle Street to see the Byron relics. Jock Murray, as always, was an angel and took so much trouble. He opened a drawer, saying to Richard Ward, 'It's Portugal, isn't it, that you go to next week?' 'Yes, Lisbon.' 'Well, this may interest you. . .', and at that he flung a huge tress of hair at Richard with a label on it in Byron's writing, 'Lisbon—March 12, 1811'. It was still quite fresh and brown. But what passes my understanding is how any woman could have allowed the English lord to take such a vast fid of hair away with him. It must have left the wench almost bald.

DIARY *22nd September, 1954*

Viti and I have supper with Rose Macaulay, and then we drive off to the Aldwych Theatre to see Edith Evans in Christopher Fry's *The Dark is Light Enough*. I can scarcely hear a word, which shows me how deaf I am becoming. But it seems a silly pretentious play to me, redeemed only by the excellence of Edith's acting. We come back and have supper with pink champagne. Edith Evans joins us and is charming. Like all the older generation, she regrets that younger people are not trained sufficiently. She says her own training was rigorous and at times almost unendurable. Unlike most actresses, she says nothing unkind about other actresses, speaking with real warmth of admiration about Peggy Ashcroft.

V.S-W. TO H.N. *29th September, 1954*
Sissinghurst

Oh Hadji! Shakespeare! Shakespeare! What a man! *What* a poet! I am writing untidily, because I have got this piece of paper propped on the *Concordance*, and it goes on a curve. But, oh Hadji, *what* a poet! Any line is stuffed with the real thing: it bursts through. I was trying to look up bits about Berkeley Castle,[2] but it is no good trying to look up special references in Shakespeare; one gets caught up in something else, and one goes on reading. See *Richard II*, Act III, Scene iii. Oh how exciting it is—and how dull Mr Foster Dulles appears in contrast!

[1] He was about to take up an appointment with the British Institute in Lisbon.
[2] V.S-W. had been invited to write the official guidebook to Berkeley Castle.

266

H.N. TO V.S-W.   *30th September, 1954*
                                                  C.1 Albany, W.1

Tomorrow is a fiesta day.[1] How little did I or you realise when we
said 'Till death do us part' on that October day at Knole that it
would be so absolutely true. But what should I do without you?
What should I do? I should be as lonely as a mouse in Santa Sophia.
Just vastness and emptiness all around me. But I think one is wise
not to brood on such disasters, and to live day by day grateful for
each evening when it arrives without misfortune, accumulating a
store of happiness on which to feed during the darkness and the
cold.

DIARY   *12th October, 1954*

I take the chair at a Press Conference given by Chatham House in
celebration of the completion of Arnold Toynbee's *A Study of
History*, the last two volumes of which come out on Thursday.[2] I
make a speech in which I welcome 'our more slender but no less
weighty Gibbon'. Not a smile does this quip evoke. I am hopeless at
making an amusing speech, since my jokes never seem to the British
public to be jokes at all. The only thing I am at all good at is making
funeral orations. Anyhow, Toynbee made a speech and then they
asked questions to which he replied with consummate charm and
brilliance. One journalist asked him what purpose had impelled
him to devote thirty-five years of his life to this single great work.
Toynbee rose politely in his seat and replied with the one word,
'Curiosity'. I like that sort of thing.

DIARY   *20th October, 1954*

I go down to Eton to lunch with Birley.[3] After lunch a boy of the
name of Shaw appears and does a recitation from Arketall.[4] He had
chosen the recitation for Speeches, and Birley, in his amused way,
had said, 'Well, I have the author coming here on Wednesday, and
if you come in after luncheon, he will show you exactly how Curzon

[1] Their wedding anniversary.
[2] Two further volumes were published later, vol. xi in 1958 and vol. xii in
1961.
[3] Robert Birley, Head Master of Eton, 1949–63.
[4] Curzon's valet, to whom a chapter is devoted in *Some People*.

talked'. I should have died of shame at his age, but Shaw took it
calmly. How wonderful Eton and Birley are at giving self-confidence
to a lad!

Birley tells me that the Council school boys sent to Eton get
on perfectly. One of them, whose father is still a house-painter,
is Captain of his House. The difficulty, of course, is in the
holidays.

V.S-W.'S DIARY   29th November, 1954

H. said that Nigel had sounded him on whether I would ever
consider giving Sissinghurst to the National Trust. I said, Never,
never, never! *Au grand jamais, jamais.* Never, never, never! Not that
hard little metal plate at my door! Nigel can do what he likes when
I am dead, but so long as I live, no National Trust or any other
foreign body shall have my darling. No, no. Over my corpse or my
ashes, not otherwise. No, no. I felt myself flush with rage. It is bad
enough to have lost my Knole, but they shan't take Sissinghurst
from me. That at least is my own. *Il y a des choses qu'on peut pas
supporter.* They shan't; they shan't; I won't. They can't make me. I
won't. They can't make me. I never would.[1]

DIARY   1st December, 1954

[Sir] Arthur Bryant tells me a nice story. His old housemaster at
Harrow, a Mr Mayo, told him that as a young master he had had to
cope with a most unruly class. In despair he had exclaimed, 'I don't
know what to do with you boys!', and a voice had answered him,
'Please, sir, teach us!' The voice came from a chubby imp with
carrot hair—Winston Churchill. Mayo never forgot it.

DIARY   16th December, 1954

Viti and I go to the Royal Literary Society where she reads her
poems to an appreciative audience. Cecil Day Lewis is in the chair
and is charming. Viti is asked for an encore and, rather bewildered,
begins with the opening of *The Land*. Then she suddenly realises
that the word 'Boeotian' is approaching, and she always forgets how

[1] There is no mention of this outburst in H.N.'s diary of the same day. It is
referred to in the Introduction to this volume, p. 24.

to pronounce it.[1] So when she reaches the word, she pauses and exclaims 'Harold!' in agony. So I say in a loud voice, 'Boeotian!' The audience were much amused, but some of them thought it must be a put-up job.

DIARY   *21st December, 1954*

Viti and I dine at the Arts Council where Kenneth and Jane Clark throw a huge party of sixty for the Massiglis.[2] We sit at different tables. I am between the new P.R.A., Professor Richardson, and Charles Morgan. The heads of all the professions are there. Tom Eliot for literature, the Oliviers for the theatre, Margot Fonteyn for the ballet, William Walton for music, Graham Sutherland for art, and Lord and Lady Waverley for the Port of London Authority. It is well done and a success.

DIARY   *28th December, 1954*

I work at Chapter I and finish it, and therefore my book on Manners.[3]

[1] The lines were: *The scythesmen swept, nor cared*
                        What crop had ripened, whether oats in Greece
                        Or oats in Kent; the shepherd on the ridge
                        Like his Boeotian forebear kept his flocks,
                        And still their outlines on our tenderer sky
                        Simple and classic rear their grave design
                        As once in Thebes, as once in Lombardy.

V.S-W. was always nervous of pronouncing 'Boeotian' as 'Boetian', as indeed she did in some gramophone recordings of *The Land* which she made in 1935.
[2] René Massigli was leaving the French Embassy in London, having been Ambassador since 1944. He was awarded the Companion of Honour. It was the first time that this decoration had ever been conferred on a foreigner. He became Secretary-General at the Quai d'Orsay in January 1955.
[3] He wrote the first chapter last, and did not choose the title, *Good Behaviour*, until he had finished the book.

1955

'*La Grande Mademoiselle*' – *H.N. lectures in Munich and Bonn* – *a luncheon for the Shah at Buckingham Palace* – *a visit to Portugal* – *H.N. develops acute sciatica* – *he has two strokes in March and May* – *V.S-W. also temporarily crippled* – *resignation of Winston Churchill* – *Anthony Eden becomes PrimeMinister* – *Ben's engagement to Luisa Vertova* – *H.N. begins his biography of Sainte-Beuve* – *Conservative victory in General Election* – *Ben's marriage in Florence* – *Winston Churchill in old age* – *Publication of* '*Good Behaviour*' – *motor-tour of Provence* – *Memoirs of Charles de Gaulle* – *the Duke of Windsor* – *V.S-W. awarded the Gold Medal of the Royal Horticultural Society* – *H.N. bored with Sainte-Beuve* – '*Richard III*' – *Gaitskell elected Leader of the Labour Party*

*T*his was the year when Churchill resigned and Anthony Eden became Prime Minister; when Attlee was made an Earl and Hugh Gaitskell succeeded him as Labour leader; when the General Election in May returned the Conservative Government with an increased majority. It was the year of the month-long newspaper strike followed by the railway strike, of the Cyprus crisis and the Summit Conference in Geneva. But for Harold Nicolson and V. Sackville-West it was a year in which personal problems dominated public events. Following visits to Germany in January and Portugal in February, he suffered two minor strokes, on the 11th March and 15th May. He was less immediately affected by them than by an acute attack of sciatica resulting from an injection too close to the sciatic nerve, but he was at first convinced that he had not long to live. However, after a prolonged rest at Sissinghurst, he resumed his ordinary life without any noticeable diminution in his physical and mental agility. There was no interruption to his weekly book-reviews. 'Good Behaviour' was published in September, and had an excellent reception; and he started work on his biography of Sainte-Beuve, the French nineteenth-century critic.

V. Sackville-West was also temporarily crippled. Following arthritis in her back and hand, she damaged a bone at the base of her spine, and could only walk with great difficulty. Their daughter-in-law, Philippa, was sent to bed for six months with tuberculosis. By the end of the year they had all more or less recovered from these misfortunes (the latter with the help of streptomycin), and other events helped to restore their spirits. In August Ben was married to Luisa Vertova in Florence. V. Sackville-West received the Veitch Gold Medal of the Royal Horticultural Society. I was re-elected to Parliament for Bournemouth East with an increased majority. And, most curative of all, Harold Nicolson and his wife went on another motoring holiday to France in October, this time continuing through the Dordogne into Provence.

V.S-W.'S DIARY   *8th January, 1955*

After dinner we listened to me broadcasting about Virginia [Woolf] and the writing of *Orlando*.[1] I finished writing a new brochure for Sackville College,[2] and also did an Introduction for Graham Thomas' book about Shrub roses. This is all very well, but what about *La Grande Mademoiselle?*

H.N. TO V.S-W.   *12th January, 1955*
                                                  C.1 Albany, W.1

I hated the idea of you sitting up there with Mademoiselle, and in pain with your back and hand. So I telephoned. You sounded sad at having lost your mobility and youth. It is horrible having this dragon eternally watching you, and beginning to nibble and chew at you when the weather gets too damp or you move books. Dragons ought to know that women-of-letters are apt to move books frequently and ought to show more consideration. But I hate to think of you in pain. I mind that even more than you mind me being in taxis or aeroplanes.

I had my London Library Committee. I am afraid that they mumble rather, and that my deafness becomes more and more apparent. I should hate to resign, but it is a bore for the members of a Committee if the Chairman is deaf. Oh dear! how age creeps up on one—slouch, slough, slop. Not like a winged chariot, but like an old pedlar in snow-boots which are too big for him.

DIARY   *25th January, 1955*
                                                  Rotterdam–Munich

It is cold and dark when the steamer reaches Rotterdam, and I walk through a grim customs house and passport-office staffed by Dutch in battledress. The Rheingold express is hot and comfortable. The cold dawn reflects patches of snow on the ugly Low Country plains. I have breakfast, and read Veronica Wedgwood's excellent first volume on Charles I [*The King's Peace*]. She makes him out obstinate, irresolute, unreliable, lazy, treacherous, confused and actually

---

[1] Her talk was reprinted in *The Listener* of 27th January. It was her first public avowal that she was the model for Orlando.

[2] A home for old people at East Grinstead.

274

stupid. But it is a clear, fluent book. We pass Cologne, but the Rhine is at its ugliest—yellow and angry, with low clouds over the top of the hills. We reach Munich at 6.30.

DIARY *26th January, 1955*
Hotel Vier Jahreszeiten, Munich

Kurt Wagenseil[1] comes and we go out together. It is a clear winter day. There are ruins on all sides—the Palace, the Opera, the theatre —great gaping façades. But they are rebuilding the place with speed, and their architecture, though austere and simple, is not repulsive. One misses the old gaiety of the baroque. We go to see my publishers. Then there is a luncheon given for me by the Bavarian Government—the Prime Minister (Dr Wilhelm Hoegner), the Deputy P.M. (Dr Baumgartner), and Staats Sekretär Dr Haas. Hoegner is an elderly amused man, only a year younger than myself. He says he does not agree with Adenauer's policy, much as he respects the man himself. Germany does not desire another war or another army. She would be defenceless in war, since the Russians are only a few hours from Frankfurt, and soldiers in Germany have always interfered with politics. I think many people feel this, and I do not blame them.

I then change and go to my lecture at the State Bank. The room, although large, is overcrowded, and many people are turned away. I speak on 'Statesmen I have known'. My talk goes well. At last we return to the hotel, and there is a sort of sit-down reception in the hall, and I get some beer and talk to the Editor of the *Münchener Merkur*. Bed at 11.30. Finish Miss Wedgwood, bless her.

DIARY *28th January, 1955*
Bonn

It is a lovely day and the Rhine sparkles below my window.[2] I see across to the Petersberg, where poor Neville Chamberlain spent that frightful night during the Godesberg conversations. I go downstairs, where there is a big official luncheon. The American High Com-

---

[1] A well-known translator of foreign books, including several by H. N.
[2] He was staying in the Residence of the British High Commissioner, Sir Frederick Hoyer Millar.

missioner, Conant of Harvard,[1] a nice dry man. Brentano,[2] who is the pet of Adenauer. James Midgely, the *Times* correspondent, who is first class. And Dr Erler,[3] who is an earnest and intelligent man. He says that if there were a free vote, 90 per cent of Germans would vote against rearmament. They feel that the Soviet offer of conversations ought to be considered and they are angered with Adenauer for turning them down so sharply.

DIARY   *6th February, 1955*

I work at my Duff article[4] and find it absurdly difficult. It is not my gift to compress into tiny spaces. In fact it gives me more trouble than five articles.

DIARY   *12th February, 1955*

I finish Duff, but have got eight pages instead of five. It is like writing a chapter of Ezekiel on a sixpence.

DIARY   *18th February, 1955*

Viti and I go to Buckingham Palace for a luncheon for the Shah.[5] In come Winston and Clemmie, looking grand. Then the Iranian Ambassador. Then the Queen Mother. Then the Queen and the Duke. And finally the Shah and his wife. Viti sits between Sir Ivone Kirkpatrick and Winston. The latter is in his best mood and talks gaily to her about history. On his other side is Madame Soheily [the Iranian Ambassadress] and he recites Omar Khayyam at her. He tells Viti that he is astonished to discover that we never had central heating in this country from the day the Romans left until the day the American heiresses arrived. After luncheon we stand around in groups and Winston is very nice to me. He says, 'It was sad you leaving the House. You were developing into a good

---

[1] James B. Conant, President of Harvard University, 1933–53, and American High Commissioner (after 1955, Ambassador) to the Federal Republic of Germany, 1953–57.

[2] Dr Heinrich von Brentano. Later in 1955 he became German Foreign Minister.

[3] Fritz Erler, a leading figure in the German Socialist party and their spokesman in the Bundestag on Defence. He died young in 1967.

[4] He was writing the article on Duff Cooper for the Dictionary of National Biography.

[5] The Shah of Persia and Queen Soraya were on a State visit to Britain.

debater.' He looks far, far better than when I last saw him. The children then come in and are very well-behaved and natural. Prince Charles crams his mouth with coffee-sugar; Princess Anne picks at it delicately.[1]

H.N. TO V.S-W.   24th February, 1955
                                             C.1 Albany, W.1

When I got back from having my hair cut, I found Philippa and Nigel there. They had been to see the specialist who had confirmed the dread verdict that she had contracted t.b. She is to go into hospital for four weeks and then go to bed (we hope at Shirley House) for four or five months longer. She gazed out of the window at the snow on the roof of the Rope Walk with dark eyes of despair. My heart ached for them.

H.N. TO V.S-W.   26th February, 1955
                                             British Embassy, Paris

Gladwyn [Jebb] is very hospitable, and the Embassy is very clean and grand. It is truly a superb house. I have a huge bedroom and bathroom looking out on the courtyard, which must be the same as I had as a child.[2] I can remember standing up on the window-sill and watching the carriages drive in for a party—two lamps shining for a moment under the arch.

After dinner I found your sweet dear letter in the grand hall, and went to bed all comfy and slept the sleep of men of good digestion who have eaten too much pâté de foie gras.

V.S-W. TO H.N. (in Lisbon)   26th February, 1955
                                             Sissinghurst

It is now 9 pm. I listened to the news (you see how I follow you hour by hour) in case there had been a railway accident on the Paris-Madrid line. Goodness, how I do worry about you. I pray to God, 'Please keep him safe and bring him back safe to me'. Why does one do this, when one does not really believe in prayer? One

[1] Prince Charles was then six and Princess Anne four.
[2] When H.N. was six, he stayed with his uncle, Lord Dufferin, then British Ambassador in Paris. The visit is described in his Helen's Tower (1937).

277

knows jolly well that it will make no difference at all. Yet one's instinct is to pray. Why?

H.N. TO V.S-W.   28th February, 1955
                                                           Lisbon

I had to change at Irun, and queue no less than six times—French customs, French passport, Spanish passport, Spanish customs (where in their dictator way they plunged black hands into my luggage), Spanish currency and then ticket supplements. I got into the wagon-lit and dined. I slept like one of those tops that don't hum at all but only emit what Colin [Fenton] calls 'heavy breathing' and I call snores. I woke up at Salamanca and experienced the lovely moment when one pulls up blinds and sees sun and *euphorbia*. Then I dressed, gazed with contempt at Ciudad Rodrigo (which is but a squalid dukedom) and crossed the Spanish frontier into Portugal. Suddenly there were vast bushes of mimosa and fruit-trees in full bud. I fear that Spain looked very poor and squalid, but I agree they are proud. Even the beggars shivering in their ponchos against the north-east wind seem to have been painted with Velazquez serenity. Portugal is feminine and self-satisfied and pink and white, but we were two hours late, so I arrived in almost dark.

H.N. TO V.S-W.   3rd March, 1955
                                                           Lisbon

An embarrassing thing happened at dinner with the Counsellor [of the British Embassy] last night. My nose started to bleed. I was taken to a little room and given cotton wool and Hydrogen Perox-ide. But it went on—drip, drip, drip. The Duke of Palmella, who was at the dinner-party, insisted on sending for his doctor. He put one of those lighted mirrors on his forehead, examined my poor nostril and shoved something suppository up it. By that time my shirt-front was messy and it was not possible to join the ladies in that condition. So the doctor took me back to the hotel in his car and ordered me an injection. A dear old lady arrived and shoved some sort of stuff into my bottom. Don't worry. This should reach you Saturday morning, and I should reach you Sunday night.

V.S-W.'S DIARY   *10th March, 1955*

H. came down at 7.30. He has sciatica, all due to that injection in
Lisbon. He thinks I don't sympathise, but I do. It is only that I have
been so much accustomed to pain for so many years, that perhaps I
am not sympathetic enough when pain takes him by surprise.
Sciatica can be agony.

V.S-W.'S DIARY   *11th March, 1955*

Oh dear, this has been a dreadful day, or, rather, evening. H. got up
at 7.30 pm. to have a bath while I made his bed, and came back
saying he had lost all power in his left hand and that his arm felt
numb. I looked at him and saw that his poor mouth was all twisted,
also his speech was so thick that I could only just understand what
he said. I feared that he had had a stroke, and rang up Dr Parish who
confirmed it. He was perfectly clear in his mind and insisted on going
on with the proofs of his Manners book, which he had been doing
all day. But he soon gave it up and said he would go to sleep.

I spent much of the night wondering how I could most tidily
dispose of myself if he died, as I should not care to go on living
without him. 'She for a little tried. . . .'[1] But I shouldn't even try.[2]

DIARY   *13th March, 1955*

Dr Parish comes. He finds my circulation good, my heart nothing
to worry about, and my blood-pressure normal. He clearly connects
the Lisbon bleedings with my black-out. He says I must take it easy
for the next fortnight. I should have to do that in any case if my
sciatica gets no better. I therefore chuck all my engagements. I also
refuse rather sadly an invitation to lecture this autumn at Harvard.
I should have liked that.

---

[1] *'He first deceased; she for a little tried*
   To live without him: liked it not, and died.
      Sir Henry Wotton (1568-1639). *Death of Sir Albert Moreton's Wife.*
[2] In H.N.'s diary, his first stroke is described as occurring on 12th March. V.S-W.
   is probably right in saying that it took place on the 11th, as he wrote up his
   diary several days later when he began to recover, and she wrote hers that night.

27th March, 1955
                                                                     Sissinghurst

Sissinghurst has become a cripples' home. On Thursday Vita was
going down her turret staircase when she lost her balance. Owing to
the weakness of her back muscles, which in turn is due to arthritis,
she could not recover herself, and to prevent herself falling downstairs, she sat down abruptly on the step. This gave her a frightful
bruise and terrific pain in getting up or sitting down. I was afraid
she had broken something. She refused to go to bed or see a doctor
(she always does), and she limped about all yesterday in real agony.
I, on the other hand, am perfectly all right if sitting up or lying
down, but if I walk from here to the dining-room, I suffer much
sciatic pain and have to sit down and pant. So the whole family is
in a state. Yesterday we had two neighbours to luncheon and we
both nearly screamed aloud in pain. But they insisted on staying to
watch the Boat Race (damn those filthy Cambridge people, they
always cheat) and then the Grand National. Vita and I felt inhos-
pitable. Ben lapsed into silence, thinking about the wall-paintings at
Schifanoia.

Then today Mrs Aldrich, the wife of the American Ambassador,
brought her sister to visit the cripples' home. Nice people they were,
but we were not in a receptive mood. Anyhow, I have done the
proofs of Juliet's book[1] and an article about Lady Astor, and now I
have to do a review and the index to Juliet's book and then some
broadcasts, and then I hope to have two legs that function.

I read an awful thing today in a book. It was about a man who
suffered from incurable sciatica. But he was a Cossack living in
Baku, and Soviet science is not all that good.

31st March, 1955

I do my third talk for the Third Programme and finish my index.
I start reading Chapman on the Dreyfus case.[2] None of the newspapers are being published except the *Manchester Guardian*. It is fine
but cold. Vita is still in pain. I find that my sciatica is improving in
the sense that I can now lie without suffering in any position in bed.

---

[1] *Good Behaviour* was dedicated 'To Juliet, aged one'.
[2] *The Dreyfus Case: A Reassessment*, by Professor G. P. Chapman.

DIARY   *5th April, 1955*

At 4.30 Winston handed in his resignation to the Queen, who was
graciously pleased to accept it. I suppose she will send for Anthony
[Eden] tomorrow.

DIARY   *6th April, 1955*

At 11.30 today Anthony drives to the Palace and kisses hands on his
appointment as Prime Minister. Winston goes off to Chartwell.
There are fine tributes to him in both Houses. Bless his heart.

DIARY   *13th April, 1955*

I am dictating to Elvira [Niggeman] when Vita rings up from
Sissinghurst. She had received a letter from Ben telling her that he is
engaged to Luisa.[1] Well I'm blowed! I telegraph to Ben and to
Luisa. I pray that it will work out all right. I think it will. Anyhow,
I am delighted.

H.N. TO PHILIPPA NICOLSON   *17th April, 1955*
                                                         Sissinghurst

Vita's back, so she says, is better, but I doubt it. The X-Ray makes it
clear that she has cracked a bone called the 'sacrum' (which is an
idiotic name for any bone to have), and she ought to remain motion-
less until the crack fills up. But will she do anything of the sort? Of
course not. She hates being fussed over, and I try to be tactful and
strew cushions in her path in the hope that she will lie upon them.
But not she. Poor darling, she can't sit or even lie with comfort, and
cannot do any writing at all. But the garden really is a sight for sore
eyes, as a woman remarked to me today. 'I am sorry', I said with
really exquisite courtesy, 'that your eyes should be sore.' 'I was only
talking in proverbs', she answered rather crossly.

DIARY   *28th April, 1955*

I have Nirad Chaudhuri to luncheon. I had forgotten that four years
ago I reviewed his book *The Autobiography of an Unknown Indian*. He
says that Nehru has got no successors, that in ten years the English

[1] Luisa Vertova, the daughter of Professor Giacomo Vertova, of Florence. She
   had been in charge of photographs and research in the Berenson Library for
   the past ten years.

language will have died out in India, that public life will become
corrupt, that all culture will perish, and that India will revert to an
inert and savage Hindu State.

H.N. TO V.S-W.   3rd May, 1955
                                                        C.1 Albany, W.1

Nigel's adoption meeting was a howling success. He had got Philippa
to record from her bed a message to the meeting. When he had
finished his speech, he said, 'I am afraid I have not been able to
bring my wife with me, but I have done the next best thing: I have
brought her voice to speak to you.' Then he turned on Philippa's
tape-recording. 'It is a great sorrow to me on this, the first Election
since my marriage, not to be able to help my husband. But I have
been ordered by my doctor to remain for four months in bed.' All
very carefully written out by Nigel and spoken in that clear young
voice. But the effect was not what Niggs expected. He thought they
would regard it as an ingenious compliment. But not at all. They all
pulled out their handkerchiefs and sobbed.

DIARY   15th May, 1955
                                                        Sissinghurst

I have had a second small stroke. I had a good breakfast, came over
to my room, and got up to take a book out of the shelf. I noticed
that the fingers in the right hand were too numb to type, so I started
rubbing them. I then thought that I would go out for a breath of air
and found that my right leg was wonky. It felt as if my foot or shoe
was encased in lead. I staggered up to my bedroom and rang my bell
for Mrs Staples[1] and she came. She summoned Viti who arrived
looking rather white, bless her, and sent for Dr Parish. He said it was
probably 'an arterial spasm', since it had passed off so quickly. But
he warned me that arterial spasms, if repeated, lead to clots, and clots
to real apoplectic strokes. I must in future take things more easily. I
realise that I shall become a semi-invalid. And I am not ready to
depart at all, although both hands have been warmed.[2]

[1] The cook at Sissinghurst, who remained with the Nicolsons from 1926 to 1968.
[2] See p. 114, note 2.

DIARY   *16th May, 1955*

Stay in bed all day. I do my review of Holstein,[1] finish reading
Trollope's autobiography and read Haller on Eulenburg,[2] Vol. II.
It is sad to see the blossom falling and to feel that I may never see it
again. But that is surely better than never having noticed or seen
blossom at all. I might be Lord Beaverbrook or live in Lapland
instead of Kent.

DIARY   *22nd May, 1955*

I start on my Eulenburg article for *History Today*. I decided that my
next book, once I have got Hotch Potch[3] into shape, will be on
Sainte-Beuve. It is just what I want—a long spell of leisurely reading
and not much travel or research, to which I am no longer up. So I
get Ben to help me take down all *Les Causeries du Lundi* from a top
shelf. I know that in all probability I shall not live to write such a
book. But I hate not having a book on the stocks, and it cheers Vita
up to see me having such confidence in my future. I don't think she
was quite taken in, but she was touched by the experiment.

DIARY   *27th May, 1955*

Nigel's Election result comes through. He increased his majority by
about 5,000 over the bye-election, and 1,000 over Brendan Bracken.
What a lovely result! The Tories will have a majority of between
60 and 70 in the new House.

DIARY   *8th June, 1955*

I lunch with Baba Metcalfe. The Halifaxes and Lou Douglas there.
Lou says that Foster Dulles suffers from an inferiority complex, and
therefore always tries to say the thing that will please his audience
without reflecting that by so doing he causes offence to other people
and destroys confidence in his own good faith.

---

[1] The memoirs of Friedrich von Holstein (1837–1909), the German diplomatist.
[2] The Prussian statesman.
[3] A collection of articles and speeches which he was publishing in book-form
under the title *The English Sense of Humour and Other Essays.*

H.N. TO V.S-W. *16th June, 1955*
C.1 Albany, W.1

This is a business letter. I have heard from the Income Tax people who want to know 'what proposals I can make for paying what I owe them in arrears' on *King George V*. I had put aside £1,500 for this, but they want £1,800 more. Now, can you lend me £1,000 from your capital? I would pay you 4 per cent interest. Oh dear, George V may have brought me fame, but he has also brought me ruin and that beastly K.C.V.O.

DIARY *19th June, 1955*

I wish I were able to have confidence in my own health. The bore of this apoplectic condition is that one never knows how bad one is. One feels perfectly well, and then the fear of a stroke comes down on one for no reason. I do not mind so much when I am here at home, but I should get terribly fussed and apprehensive were I among strangers. I do not notice that my mental or physical powers are in any way affected. I mean, I seem to read and write as well as I did before Portugal. But that may be an illusion. The fact remains that at any moment I may pass out and become paralytic.

Viti has bought her Jaguar,[1] which is an insane thing to have done, but wise.

DIARY *5th July, 1955*

I dine with Walter Elliot. Nancy Astor is there, and Henry Brooke[2] and Selwyn Lloyd.[3] Nancy really is a marvel—and looks still a girl. I do not think that she ever considers for a moment the things she says. She said to someone, 'Of course I suppose you leave such things to your homely little wife?'

V.S-W.'S DIARY *29th July, 1955*

The Americans are going to launch small satellites to revolve round the earth at 18,000 m.p.h. about 200 to 300 miles up.

[1] A second-hand Jaguar car in place of the Austin which they had for ten years.
[2] Financial Secretary to the Treasury, 1954-57, and later Home Secretary.
[3] Then Minister of Defence.

DIARY   *6th August, 1955*
                                              Florence

Ben's birthday. He is 41. Luisa and Ben go off to Florence and V. and I remain at I Tatti.[1] She writes an *Observer* article, and I read Proust on Sainte-Beuve, which is delightful. Although written in 1908, the style and method are already perfected. Afterwards we drive up to Vallombrosa, and are met by Nicky Mariano. Berenson comes in from the *petits appartements* and we have *cercle*. He looks smaller than he was, and is as frail as an egg-shell. His skull looks as if it would crack easily. He is seriously deaf, but though he complains of loss of memory, he appears to me as alert and waspish as ever.

DIARY   *8th August, 1955*
                                              Florence

At 5.30 we drive to the Palazzo Vecchio, and stand under the statue of David with his enormous hands and buttocks. Madame Vertova and Luisa arrive. It seems that Signor Vertova, who is nervous, has had a heart-attack and cannot come. We go up to the Sala di Matrimonio. It is a high room with early eighteenth-century tapestries. Red gilt and damask chairs, rather faded. There are some twenty close relations and friends present. The Councillor appears, an old gentleman with a tumbly beard, dressed in evening tails with a black tie, and round his middle a huge *écharpe* of the national colours. They sign registers and then the old boy starts an oration which goes on for 45 minutes. In the end they have to pull his coat to get him to stop. I cannot hear a word he says, but Viti hears him and is amused. He makes *punchinello* gestures, and evidently much enjoys such a speech. He warns Ben not to behave either like Hamlet or Othello, and that Italians are more *espansivi* than the English, and that he must kiss Luisa when he leaves the house and again on his return. The audience titter slightly at his jokes. He begins by calling Ben 'Benedict', but it soon becomes 'Benedetto'. Then he presents Luisa with a bouquet on behalf of the Commune and Ben with a book by Mazzini entitled *The Duty of Man*. Everyone seems to have forgotten about the ring, and Ben just shoves it on as an afterthought.

---

[1] Bernard Berenson's villa just outside Florence.

V.S-W.'S DIARY   *8th August, 1955*
                                                           Florence

What a day! But feeling so happy about Ben and Luisa. Not only is
she perfectly suited to him, but I like her being a Florentine, as
Florence has always meant so much in my life. The only thing that
I could have liked better was for Luisa to be a Spaniard: but that
would have made terrible complications with Hadji, who most
unaccountably and unreasonably doesn't like Spain.

DIARY   *10th August, 1955*

We get back to Sissinghurst at 7.20 in the evening. I am relieved to
have got through it all without exhaustion or a stroke. Signor
Vertova stood it far less well than I did, but I fear he has a greater
prospect of life than I have. To me the expression 'worse than death'
has always seemed meaningless. But now that death may swoop
down on me at any instant, I do not find it meaningless. There *are*
worse things. I should rather die than lose Viti, or than be exposed
to public obloquy and lose my repute and honour, or to suffer
through Nigel or Ben, or to end in agony or squalor. I am not
frightened at all of death: but it saddens me, as I do not wish to say
goodbye to all whom I love, or to leave this beautiful and varied
world. But an experience such as that of the last six days, when I
have been surrounded by so much beauty and pleasure, is a *chose
acquise*, that cannot be taken away.

DIARY   *28th August, 1955*

Dear Luisa, I fear she must find Sissinghurst rather grey and sad after
I Tatti and Vallombrosa. Viti and I are always so busy, and so is Ben.
She likes conversation, and we are unused to it. I suppose we are an
eccentric family, although benevolent in most ways. I remain
eternally grateful to destiny or God for having surrounded me with
such affection.

DIARY   *29th August, 1955*

V. drops Ben and Luisa at Sevenoaks station and then goes on to
Chartwell to pick up Juliet Duff. Winston, she finds, is very deaf,
very friendly, rather vague about his words, and is nice to Rollo,

which is appreciated. He shows her the portrait being done of him by a Dutch artist for the Chamber in Holland. Viti was pleased because he introduced her to the Dutch painter as 'Miss Sackville-West'. Juliet, who had been spending the whole weekend there, says that Winston hates being alone, is happy with his painting and his history of the English Speaking Peoples, awaits death with fortitude, loves his ducks, his budgerigars and his poodle Rufus, and is a resigned and happy man. He told her that at his last audience with the Queen she had said to him, 'Would you like a Dukedom or anything like that?'

V.S-W. TO H.N.   *30th August, 1955*
                                                            Sissinghurst

Darling, I do love that book of yours [*Good Behaviour*]. I hope it has the success it deserves. Nobody but you could have written it. You see, quite apart from your wide reading and knowledge and general attitude of humanism and civility towards life, which is all part of your own character, you do *write* so well. Better, I think, than you have ever before. The texture of your prose is now so tight, so economical, and yet at moments so lyrical. Where I think you have been so skilful is in putting all your facts and information into a chapter, or even into a section of a chapter, so that one feels convinced, and then ending up the chapter or the section with a few lines which are just pure Hadji, and sum up all that you have said before: 'Huge dark eyes . . .' 'Dear Horace . . .' I haven't got the book here, so I am just remembering a few phrases.

DIARY   *3rd September, 1955*

I get a letter from S.P.B. Mais[1] about *Good Behaviour*. He says it is by far and away my best book. What utter nonsense! My book on my father[2] is my best book, and after that *Some People*, and after that *King George V*. Anyhow, it was nice of him to write.

V.S-W. TO H.N.   *21st September, 1955*
                                                            Sissinghurst

How strange and curious, Hadji, is the pattern of life! A trite

[1] The novelist, traveller and critic.
[2] *Lord Carnock. A Study in the Old Diplomacy.* 1930.

reflection, but when one makes it in terms of one's own life, it doesn't seem trite at all but a new discovery. Tolstoy had this sense very deeply, and that is partly what makes him so supreme a novelist. I mean, how little you and I thought when Ben was born on that August day, or Nigel on that January day, or Luisa in Florence on that ? day, or Philippa in London on that December day, let alone you in Persia on a November day or me at Knole on a March day, that we should all knot up eventually in this cat's-cradle of a pattern that life imposes on us. And perhaps in the end, when you and I are just two little handfuls of dust, those descendants of ours will be living in the place we have made and loved.

DIARY   *2nd October, 1955*

In the evening we listen to Gilbert Murray, who is approaching 90, giving a wireless talk on peace efforts during the past forty years. It is a magnificent talk, factual, fair, balanced and well-composed. The person he most blames is President Wilson, and I fear that he is right. He ends up by saying that our one hope is that the two most powerful countries in the world should know that war would not be an adventure but a disaster. He is a great old man if ever there was one.

DIARY   *10th October, 1955*
                                              Cahors, Lot, France

We buy a flower-pot for some poplar cuttings. We have noticed that there are two kinds of poplar—the regular lombardy poplar which has not changed colour, and the other fluffy sort which is all loose and gold. We take some of these on the road to Eyzies, fill the pot with grit and sand and soil, water it from the tumbler in the luncheon basket, and ram firm. The country is incredibly beautiful with the changing autumn tints and the lawns and rocks. Oxen crawl along with carts loaded with huge casks of wine and grapes.

We leave the hotel at Cahors for a moment and see an English car with an inscription written in lipstick on the back-window: 'Just married. No hand signals!' We agree that this is about the most bedint[1] thing we have ever seen.

[1] See page 178, note 1.

DIARY   *13th October, 1955*
                                                 Aix-en-Provence

We do some sightseeing in Nîmes. The arena is opposite our hotel.
It is in a remarkable state of preservation and is still used for bullfights.
The upper edge still contains the small buttresses in which the masts
were fixed to carry the *velum*, which must indeed have been a
gigantic affair. Tragedy and fear and frightful atrocities on the
Teutones and Cimbri were inflicted in this round, or rather oval,
space. How can people of any imagination admire the Romans? We
then go on to the Maison Carrée, which is in a marvellous state of
preservation, although they have dished the inside by turning it into
a fourth-rate museum. But the porch is a worthy thing, and I feel
less furious with the Romans.

DIARY   *18th October, 1955*
                                                 Aix-en-Provence

I spend the morning reading de Gaulle.[1] I find it illuminating both as
regards events and his own character. He admits that he staged the
Saint Pierre and Miquelon episode to test the Americans.[2] What
depresses one in his book is his deep suspicion of ulterior motives.
But it is a moving book and does him credit.

We visit the Cézanne studio in the north of Aix. It is a little house
with a huge atelier and a north window. We are shown over by a
nice old lady. It contains many of Cézanne's brushes, his easel, his
coats, his hats, his walking-sticks and a still-life composed of real
vegetables representing his onion picture. There are photographs of
him as a cross old man. It is an interesting pilgrimage and in spite
of the fact that it is all far cleaner and tidier than anything that
Cézanne possessed, it does bring back the old man. For one thing, it
shows us that he was in fact extremely well off.

DIARY   *26th October, 1955*

Alan Moorehead lunches with me at the Travellers. He is working
on a book about Gallipoli, and wanted to talk about the Young
Turks. He agrees with me that if Roger Keyes had been in command
of the fleet and Montgomery of the army, we should have pushed

[1] General de Gaulle's first volume of memoirs, *The Call to Honour, 1940–1942*.
[2] The west-Atlantic islands which were seized by Admiral Muselier in 1942.

through to Constantinople, shortened the first war, and perhaps forced the Russian Revolution into different channels.

DIARY   *31st October, 1955*

Princess Margaret issues a statement that for religious reasons she has decided not to marry Group Captain Peter Townsend. This is a great act of self-sacrifice, and the country will admire and love her for it. I feel rather moved. It will be awkward meeting the Duke of Windsor at dinner after this.

DIARY   *9th November, 1955*

I dine with Baba [Metcalfe] to meet the Duke of Windsor. The American Ambassador and Mrs Aldrich are there. The Duke is looking far fitter than he seemed when I saw him last time. He chatters and chatters. He tells me that they have lost the telephone notes which I rescued from the Grand Cerf at Evreux, and that the Duchess is miserable because she wanted to reproduce them in her autobiography which she is now writing.[1] He pretends to be very busy and happy, but I feel this is false and that he is unoccupied and miserable. He has a vast cigar which he chews and wets but does not even light and then lays aside.

V.S-W.'S DIARY   *12th November, 1955*

I had a horrid night. I was worried about H. I am always afraid of finding him in the morning, having had another attack in his sleep. I dread the moment when I go down the staircase and call out to him, for fear that he may not answer, and then I should have to open his door and find—what? Oh dear, the approach of the end of life is sad.

DIARY   *17th November, 1955*

Viti has been awarded a Veitch Gold Medal by the Royal Horticultural Society, 'in recognition of her services to horticulture'. I am so pleased, and so is she.

Harold Macmillan[2] returns from Geneva after a complete failure

---

[1] *The Heart has its Reasons*, 1956. For the Evreux incident, see pp. 304–7 of vol. I of H.N.'s diaries.

[2] He was Foreign Secretary from April to December, 1955.

of the Foreign Minister's Conference. They have failed to agree about Germany: they have failed to induce Molotov to open even a chink in the iron curtain: and they have really made no progress on disarmament.

H.N. TO V.S-W.   *1st December, 1955*
                                                    C.1 Albany, W.1

I am discouraged about Sainte-Beuve. I find *Port-Royal* really dreadfully dull, since I am uninterested in sin and redemption, and don't care at all for the doctrine of Jansenism or la Mère Angélique. I have a naturally pagan soul—*anima naturaliter pagana*. It is not that I am wholly material or despise spiritual things. It is that I hate the idea that God enjoys people mortifying the flesh and being inelegant. And they were all such *bores*. I always said that it was a mistake to embark on the biography of a man whom one does not respect or like, but I thought the amusing side of S-B. would carry me along. But *Port-Royal* has got me bogged. I don't want to publish a bad book at the end of my life, and I may chuck the whole thing.

DIARY   *4th December, 1955*

Viti is writing a short story and is furious at having to come across to dinner. The difficulty with her is that if she is interrupted, she can never start again. So instead of going to her tower after dinner, she retires to bed at 9.15. I never know what to do about these things. She is upset by Cyril Connolly's review of Steegmuller's book.[1] He praises it, and she says that she will not go on with hers, thus wasting three years' work. It is no good at all saying that if she had not dawdled so frightfully, she would have got her book out six months before Mr Steegmuller's.

H.N. TO V.S-W.   *14th December, 1955*
                                                    C.1 Albany, W.1

I went with Baba [Metcalfe], the Douglas Fairbankses and the Walter Moncktons to the first night of Olivier's *Richard III*. The Queen was there, radiant in pink and diamonds. Oh, I did love the film so! They took John Gielgud by the heels and pushed him head-forward

[1] Francis Steegmuller, the American writer, had just published his book on La Grande Mademoiselle. This event caused V.S-W. great distress.

into a butt of Malvoisie; they cut off Hastings' head on a block; they strangled the young princes; and in the end off they went to Bosworth Field which, for film-purposes, was situated in the vicinity of Madrid with a distant line of Castilian mountains—not one little bit like Shropshire. But Olivier was superb, really superb, and in the end he is cut to pieces and thrown over the back of a packhorse and carried away a bleeding corpse quite dead. The crown is found under a bush and placed on the head of Henry Tudor. Oh my word, what a film! Then off we all went to supper with Douglas Fairbanks. Twenty-one people, including the Oliviers. I got back at 2 am. to find John [Sparrow] sitting up for me all anxious, thinking that I was dead too.

DIARY   *14th December, 1955*

Hugh Gaitskell has been elected leader of my Party by a huge majority. It would have been better had they chosen Nye Bevan.

DIARY   *29th December, 1955*

I lunched at the Beefsteak with James [Pope-Hennessy], and found Massigli there and William Jowitt. Massigli is over for only two days. He was warmly welcomed by all members of the club. Jowitt said to me that he is tired of party politics, and will henceforward adopt the role of elder statesman. I remarked, 'That will be a new experience for you', but he did not detect the irony.

The *Sunday Express* telephoned to ask me what was my main wish for 1956. I replied, 'Not to be telephoned to by the *Sunday Express* when I am busy.'

DIARY   *31st December, 1955*

This may be the last year of my life, but what a rich one it has been! Sunshine all the time, and long days with Viti in the garden, and the boys so happy and well, a grandchild growing, and another coming. If I die tonight, my only feeling, if the capacity for any feeling remains to me, will be immense gratitude.

1956

H.N. feels he is getting old – stands as candidate for the
Professorship of Poetry at Oxford against Wystan Auden –
defeated by narrow majority – Vivien Leigh on acting
Shakespeare – proposal to abolish capital punishment – the
Queen Mother at Aintree – visit to London of Bulganin
and Khrushchev – visit to Port Royal and Versailles with
Nancy Mitford – Gladwyn Jebb at the Paris Embassy – H.N.
anticipates his own death – the problem of Cyprus – Churchill
writes his 'History of the English-Speaking Peoples' –
Aneurin Bevan on Anthony Eden – the Suez crisis – birth
of Vanessa Nicolson –Menzies in Cairo – emergency session
of the House of Commons – mounting concern about the
possible use of force in Egypt – H.N. finishes 'Sainte-Beuve' –
a short holiday in Spain – the Russians quell the Budapest
rising – Israel's attack on Egypt and the Anglo-French
ultimatum – H.N.'s criticisms of Anthony Eden – Nigel
abstains in the vote of confidence – strong reaction against
him in Bournemouth – the impact of the Suez crisis on H.N.
– he receives a handsome seventieth birthday present – Alan
Moorehead's 'Gallipoli' – 'You are the only person I have
ever really loved'

Harold Nicolson had not quite recovered from his two strokes and became more careful in accepting invitations to lecture or to dinner-parties. But the habit of years and the pleasure which he took in his life and friends saved him from vegetating at Sissinghurst or becoming prematurely old. He even agreed to stand for the vacant Chair of Poetry at Oxford, but it was Wystan Auden who was elected.

Two political controversies dominated the first half of the year before the Suez crisis obliterated every other topic. The first was the civil war in Cyprus, on which Harold Nicolson took an increasingly pro-Hellenistic line. The second was the issue of capital punishment, which came to a head with the passage through the House of Commons of Sydney Silverman's Death Penalty Abolition Bill and its rejection by the Lords. It was this controversy which first estranged me from some of my Conservative electors in Bournemouth, for while they were strongly opposed to abolition, I was so much in favour of it that I seconded the Third Reading of the Silverman Bill.

H.N. TO V.S-W.   *19th January, 1956*
                                              C.1 Albany, W.1

I did my talk for Mau Mau.[1] Then I dined at the Pakistani Embassy. There was a fine Maharani there who was the daughter of Abdul Mejid, the last Sultan of Turkey. My word, her diamonds were large! I did not enjoy the dinner. There was the Foreign Secretary [Selwyn Lloyd], the Minister of Defence [Sir Walter Monckton], the Minister of Education [Sir David Eccles] and some little black secretaries. The dinner itself was good. But I get nervous now on these public occasions and was glad to get away. I shall not accept any further diplomatic invitations for dinner. I shall lunch only. I am getting old, Father William, the young man said.

[1] His usual method of describing the Overseas Service of the B.B.C.

H.N. TO V.S-W.   *25th January, 1956*
                                                    C.1 Albany, W.1

I have had an odd proposition made to me. Would I stand as candidate for the Professorship of Poetry at Oxford? It wasn't John [Sparrow's] idea—it emanated from some other quarter. It seems now that Cecil Day Lewis has completed his term of office, Enid Starkie[1] has put up W. H. Auden as candidate. This has enraged the older members, as Auden went to America during the war. They ask me to stand as his opponent. I understand that there are no other candidates as yet.[2] Now, of course, my first instinct was to say No. Partly because I am not a poet: partly because I do not like opposing Wystan Auden: and partly because of my health. But I am always carried away by the mention of Oxford even on a pot of marmalade, and it would be a great and glamorous honour. As for health, it means only one lecture a term, and that would not be a strain on me. The appointment lasts for five years and is purely honorific, although expenses are paid. So I said Yes, and now you will be cross with me. Anyhow, I expect they will choose Auden in the end and I rather hope they do. But, oh dear, I should like to be Professor of Poetry at Oxford!

V.S-W. TO H.N.   *26th January, 1956*
                                                    Sissinghurst

Oh dear, dear, FIDGET! Not content with being Chairman of the London Library, Vice-Chairman of the National Trust, Trustee of the National Portrait Gallery, D.Litt. of Grenoble University, President of the Anglo-Iranian Society, and God knows what besides, you must go and become Professor of Poetry at Oxford! Well, I do understand it, I really do. It is a great compliment to have been asked.

DIARY   *29th January, 1956*

There is a nasty paragraph in the *Sunday Times* about the Oxford Chair of Poetry. It says that Auden is the best poet of the last twenty-

---

[1] Fellow of Somerville College, Oxford, since 1934, and Reader in French Literature at the University of Oxford.
[2] A third candidate appeared later—Professor Wilson Knight, Professor of English Literature at Leeds University, 1956-62.

five years, and that the post needs a poet and not 'the urbane H.N.'. I wish to God I hadn't agreed to stand, as I hate this sort of controversy and rather agree that Auden would be better. It all comes, not exactly from my impulsiveness, but rather from a hatred of giving way to my old age and invalidism.

V.S-W.'S DIARY   29th January, 1956

I got *Mademoiselle* out, and tried to start on her again. It does not go well. She had gone stale on me, and then came the American, Mr Steegmuller, damn his guts! Poor man. He doesn't know what he has done to me.

H.N. TO V.S-W.   1st February, 1956
                                                 C.1 Albany, W.1

I dined with Baba Metcalfe. The Oliviers were there and the Douglas Fairbanks. Vivien Leigh says she misses Sibyl [Colefax] so much. She says that one of the things that we don't realise about Shakespeare is how wonderful he is to act. 'Shaw is like a train. One just speaks the words and sits in one's place. But Shakespeare is like bathing in the sea—one swims where one wants.' I thought that a good metaphor.

H.N. TO V.S-W.   7th February, 1956
                                                 C.1 Albany, W.1

There was a leading article in the *Manchester Guardian* about the Professorship, not rude to me, but representing my party as the reactionaries, the old school, the traditionalists, and so on. Auden is in New York, from where he has issued a statement that he has no statement to make. I do not mind if I am not elected in the very least. But I do not like being classed as 'right-wing' against the sweetness and light of Auden's left-wing. What a kettle-of-fish for me to have fallen into!

H.N. TO V.S-W.   8th February, 1956
                                                 C.1 Albany, W.1

Oh I had such fun just now! A woman telephoned asking whether I was Fergus & Fergus, and would I have her fiancé's kilt ready by the first of March without fail? I said that we were an old Scotch firm, perhaps a wee bit old-fashioned, but that we did not think that a young woman should mention her fiancé's kilt. She gasped in astonishment. I said, 'I am afraid that I cannot answer so delicate a question, and you must get your fiancé to write to us himself.' 'But he is in the Cameroons!' she wailed. 'Oh', I answered, 'I thought you said he was in the Black Watch.' By then she was getting suspicious, so I replaced the receiver.

DIARY   9th February, 1956
John Sparrow telephones from Oxford with the result. Auden, 216; myself, 192; Wilson Knight, 91. He says that all the women dons and most of the scientists voted against me. There was some excitement, and 'Vote Auden' was chalked up on the walls of New College. I was leading by two votes at midday, but then the women poured out and did me down. I am delighted by this result. What I dreaded was either that Wystan Auden would be beaten by me by a tiny majority, thus enraging the undergraduates, or else I should be beaten by a vast majority. As it is, my vote is most honourable and there is no humiliating defeat, and youth gets what it wanted. I am glad we did no canvassing on our side.

V.S-W.'S DIARY   17th February, 1956
The House of Commons rejected the Bill to abolish hanging for murder.[1] Nigel voted in favour of abolition. I disagree profoundly. I think there ought to be degrees of murder, and I think *hanging* ought to be abolished. The death penalty should be carried out more humanely by an injection or a sleeping draught from which the condemned man never awoke.

H.N. TO V.S-W.   1st March, 1956
                                                        C.1 Albany, W.1
I am worried by the agitation in Nigel's constituency. It is unfortunate that he always seems to espouse causes which are unpopular with his Party—Israel, abolition of the death penalty, Cyprus. He is too progressive for those old Bournemouth tabby-cats. I hate that type of person. He has had many letters referring him to the Old Testa-

[1] She got this wrong: it was not the Bill, but a general Motion on the subject: and it was not lost, but won by 293 to 262 on a free vote.

ment—'an eye for an eye', and that sort of thing. He can reply to them all by referring them to the Sermon on the Mount. I wish the Archbishops would make a statement. I mean, they are glib enough to give their views about disarmament or UNO or Mr Dulles, but here, where there is a direct moral issue on which Christians seek for guidance, they remain dumb.

DIARY   *2nd March, 1956*

The King of Jordan has summarily dismissed Glubb Pasha, which is an insult and a symptom. It looks as if we have lost the struggle in Asia and the Middle East. The whole Arab world against us, and Greece as well. It is evident that prestige is based on force alone. The moment wealth or power declines, the whole pack turns against us. All very sad. Evidently the Russians realise that the colonial front is the easiest on which to stir up unrest and cause dissension between us and the United States.

H.N. TO V.S-W.   *28th March, 1956*
                                                                            C.1 Albany, W.1

At luncheon yesterday I sat between Michael Adeane[1] and the young Duke of Devonshire. They had both been standing with the royal party at Aintree when Devon Loch collapsed.[2] They said it was a really horrible sight. The public and the people in the enclosure took it for granted that the horse had won and turned towards the royal box and made a demonstration, yelling and waving their hats. Then someone shouted out that there had been an accident, and the ovation stopped suddenly as if a light had been switched off. There was a complete hush. The Princess Royal panted, 'It can't be true! It can't be true!' The Queen Mother never turned a hair. 'I must go down', she said, 'and comfort those poor people.' So down she went, dried the jockey's tears, patted Peter Cazalet [the trainer] on the shoulder and insisted on seeing the stable-lads who were also in tears. 'I hope the Russians saw it', said Devonshire. 'It was the most perfect display of dignity that I have ever witnessed.' In fact Malenkov and his party were in a box nearby.

[1] Private Secretary to the Queen since 1953.
[2] The Queen Mother's horse, Devon Loch, was seized by an attack of cramp within a few paces of winning the Grand National.

H.N. TO V.S-W.   *24th April, 1956*
                                                       C.1 Albany, W.1

I am worried about the televising of Sissinghurst. It is so rare that we
differ on such things, that when we do, each leans over backwards
to please the other. But in this case I think your reasoning is better
than mine. I have a vague prejudice against (a) exposing my intimate
affections to the public gaze; (b) indulging in private theatricals.
But it is a garden matter, and in garden matters *voluntas deae suprema
lex*. So I withdraw my objections.[1]

H.N. TO   *25th April, 1956*
                                                       C.1 Albany, W.1

My Labour friends tell me that the dinner given by the Labour
Executive to Bulganin and Khrushchev was a ghastly failure.
Khrushchev made a speech saying that it was Russia alone who
defeated Germany. George Brown exclaimed, 'May God forgive
you!' Khrushchev broke off and asked the interpreter what he had
said. It was translated. Khrushchev then banged the table and said,
'What I say is true!' George Brown is not the mild type of Socialist.
He replied, 'We lost almost half a million men while you were
Hitler's allies!' *Silence pénible*. At the Speaker's luncheon yesterday
George Brown went up with outstretched hand to apologise, but
Khrushchev put his hand behind his back and said sharply, '*Niet!*'
My friend told me that in a long experience of unsuccessful banquets,
that will live in his memory as the most acid failure that he has ever
witnessed. Apparently the Russians are furious at the undergraduates
ragging them at Oxford, and have told *Pravda* to say that it was a
demonstration organised by fascist elements. Poor silly boys. I think
they were rude in a way, but fascist, no!

DIARY   *9th May, 1956*
                                                     British Embassy, Paris

I lunch at the Embassy with Cynthia [Jebb], Nancy Mitford and
Antonia Pakenham[2]. Then we get into the huge car and drive to

[1] The B.B.C. had asked to televise Sissinghurst. H.N. passed on the suggestion
to V.S-W. but expressed his own doubts. She wanted to accept, and he (in the
above letter) withdrew his objections. But then she changed her mind to please
him, and the garden was not televised.

[2] She married Hugh Fraser in September 1956.

Port Royal.[1] It is, as usual, a holiday, and the museum at Port Royal is closed. One should always visit these places, as no description suffices. The valley is sharper and steeper than I imagined, and the monastery more hidden in the depths. There are some remains of the chapel and a tomb-stone marking the place more or less where Racine was buried before being transferred. The line of the cloister is marked by a row of trees. The hill slopes up rapidly to Les Granges at the top. The nightingale sings. Antonia, being a Jansenist, is rather moved. So am I.

Then off we go to Versailles. We draw up in front of the château, but are not allowed in, as Tito is there. We then go round hoping to see the Trianon, but that also is barred by gendarmes. I ask Nancy to show us the Parc aux Cerfs.[2] Again a surprise. I had envisaged a pavilion somewhere attached to the park. But not at all. It was in the Rue St Médéric, in the middle of the town, a small eighteenth-century house in the street, which might have belonged to the local doctor. 'You admit,' says Nancy, 'that my King had simple tastes.' She says that often he was in such a hurry to get there, that he did not bother to change and arrived wearing the Order of the Saint-Esprit. They explained to the prostitutes in the Rue St Médéric that he was a Polish cousin of the Queen.

We drive back through the park at St Cloud which is looking superb with its clipped avenues and its vast chestnuts. The whole route through the Bois and up the Avenue Foch is stiff with police lining the pavements for Tito. But there is no crowd at all.

Gladwyn [Jebb] returns very late from a party at the Czech Embassy. We do not dine till 9, but Gladwyn gives me a bottle of Mouton Rothschild 1948 which is the best claret I have ever drunk. He tells me that the French communist party are in a fix about Stalin. They recently expelled one of their members for writing an article suggesting that Stalinism was not quite so wonderful as all that. If they are now to toe the Moscow line, they will prove to the

[1] Originally a Cistercian convent, it became the centre of Jansenist learning, associated with Racine, Pascal and Sainte-Beuve. In 1710, the buildings were razed to the ground by the Pope's orders.
[2] The rendezvous for some of Louis XV's degrading love-affairs. In 1953 Nancy Mitford had published her life of Madame de Pompadour, the King's mistress.

world that they are a satellite party. Gladwyn says that we are wrong
to think that France is a poor, distraught country. We never realise
that France may be badly governed but it is excellently adminis-
tered. Moreover, people are rich and prosperous. Wages and
employment are high. If they lose Algeria, it will be a severe blow
to them. They may then seek for a strong government in the person
of de Gaulle.

What an odd man Gladwyn is! Had I not known him so well for
so many years, I might think him rude and disagreeable. He gives
me the impression of intellectual strength.

H.N. TO V.S-W.   *29th May, 1956*
                                                 C.1 Albany, W.1

Alas, May is leaving us, and how superb it has been! I walked round
the garden last night between 7 and 7.25 absolutely drinking in the
beauty of the sunset and the soft lights playing across the Weald
towards the Downs. I felt that no garden has ever been so beautiful
as our garden, no May ever so beautiful as this May, no duck ever
possessed of such personality as Fanny, and nobody ever so showered
with love and happiness as I am. So I entered into a mood of universal gratitude, and then a little worm came and said that I was being
selfish about the Canaries.[1]

But, darling, it really is a combination of negatives, of which my
extreme prejudice against Franco is the easiest to abandon. We must
face the fact that it is probable that before long and at any time I shall
have a serious stroke. I have got so much out of life that the prospect
of death fills me with no apprehension. Of course I want to live to
see Carlo[2] become a person, Juliet a little girl, and our relations with
Greece placed upon a footing of amity. Of course I loathe the
prospect of being separated from you and all those very numerous
people whom I love. But I shan't be there to feel sorrow. Thus I
concentrate my worry upon the situation that I shall leave behind,
and dread a complicated death or extreme squalor at the end. That
is the worst of those like me who have no belief in the life hereafter:

[1] They were planning a winter cruise, and one suggestion from V.S-W. was that
they should go to the Canary Islands. H.N. had resisted this idea, because the
islands belonged to Spain.
[2] Luisa was expecting a baby.

they do not want to say goodbye ungainlily, since deathbed scenes and circumstances may leave sad memories, and I should wish to be remembered only as a person who was alive and happy. It is because of this that I fuss about crematoria, not wanting you to be faced by the problem of the disposal of the corpse. Thus if we went to some remote island in the Canaries, I should be worrying about this corpse business. Even in February I should prefer to remain at home where there are lovely quick crematoria waiting to receive me. So shall we go to Malaga in October, and abandon all ideas of the Amazon or the Canaries?

H.N. TO V.S-W.   *30th May, 1956*
                                                       C.1 Albany, W.1

You know that there is some idea that Mrs Clare Boothe Luce will succeed Aldrich as American Ambassador in London? Well, dear old Mrs Aldrich, bless her heart, meeting Mrs Luce's husband at a luncheon-party, exclaimed in a loud voice, 'I hear you are after my job!'

DIARY   *12th June, 1956*

I attend a meeting of the Cyprus Conciliation Committee in the House of Commons. Clem Davies is in the Chair. There are present, among others, Attlee, Bertie Russell, John Strachey, Tom Driberg, Listowel and so on. Sir John Harding [Governor of Cyprus] attends. He is a nice little officer with kind eyes and great patience. It must be maddening for him to be faced by all these doctrinaires, but his rage with us is nobly concealed. His theme is that Eoka[1] consists of some fifty wild-men, mostly financed from Greece, and that it is they who terrorise the community. He hopes to eliminate them by the end of the year, and then responsible people will emerge capable of reaching an agreement. Attlee says that he well remembers being told that Irish and Indian nationalism were artificial movements engineered by a handful of agitators. This might be the case in Cyprus, but he doubts it. Harding says that he is only expressing his personal opinion and he may be wrong, but he is convinced that once Eoka is suppressed, the moderates will have the courage to take some respon-

[1] The organisation of Greek Cypriots who were terrorising the island in their campaign for the union of Cyprus with Greece (Enosis).

sibility. Crossman points out that when he was in Cyprus two years ago, long before terrorism had started, the 'moderates' were refusing to co-operate. It seemed improbable to him that they would be more willing today to come out of hiding than they were before the troubles started. Harding is somewhat disconcerted by this, but repeats his formula about 'law and order'. Mrs Jeger[1] suggests that Makarios[2] should be brought to London, and to our surprise Harding does not reject that idea, but says that he can say nothing while the discussion with Alan Lennox-Boyd [the Colonial Secretary] continues, but there will be a statement soon.

DIARY   23rd June, 1956

I go on with Chapter IX [of Sainte-Beuve]. It does not go easily. I am not sure whether it is a temporary mind-block, whether I am just getting stale, or whether old age has really brought with it cerebral decay.

H.N. TO V.S-W.   4th July, 1956
                                                           C.1 Albany, W.1

I saw my old friend, Alan Hodge, who now edits History Today with Peter Quennell, and in the intervals helps Winston with his book.[3] It will go down as far as the death of Queen Victoria, and they have got as far as 1815. He told me that Winston now stays in bed all morning. He has a tame budgerigar whom he calls 'Toby'. It keeps fluttering about his bedroom. Winston is convinced that it talks. Everyone else thinks that it merely twitters and chatters, but he is positive that again and again it repeats the cheerful phrase, 'Sir Winston will be pleased'.

H.N. TO V.S-W.   12th July, 1956
                                                           C.1 Albany, W.1

Eric [Lord Carnock] came up yesterday to vote in favour of the abolition of hanging Bill. Charlie [Lord Sackville] and Sam [Lord St Levan] voted against. 'Three uncles', Nigel snorted, 'left the back-

---

[1] Mrs Lena Jeger, Labour M.P. for Holborn and St Pancras South.
[2] Archbishop Makarios had been deported to the Seychelles on 9th March.
[3] A History of the English Speaking Peoples (1956–58).

woods to vote, and only one of them voted the right way!' But he was pleased that all the bishops were on his side.[1]

H.N. TO V.S-W.   *26th July, 1956*
                                                  C.1 Albany, W.1

I went to a party given yesterday by Bob Boothby. Nye Bevan was there, and talked to me about the decay of the present government. He attributes it entirely to Eden, who, he says, is much disliked, weak and vacillating, and, in fact, hopeless. He was not talking as an Opposition leader, but as a student of politics. I heard the same thing today at the Club. They said that the character of a government is determined by the character of the Prime Minister. To choose Eden had been a mistake, since he was not a strong man. He interfered with his colleagues and did not control them, and gave the impression to the House that he did not know his own mind. Now when I hear a man abused like that, I immediately wish to take his side. But I fear that it is all too true.

The crisis which stemmed from Nasser's nationalisation of the Suez Canal, and ended in the abortive attempt by Britain and France to regain control of it by force, profoundly affected Harold Nicolson, as it did all his countrymen. For some years past his interest in foreign affairs, while always active, had grown steadily less articulate. It was only on the Overseas Service of the B.B.C. that he had been giving public expression to his views. Now once again he felt himself passionately involved. His first reaction was that Nasser should not be allowed to escape unpunished for his behaviour. But as Anthony Eden's intention to resort to force became increasingly evident, he feared the consequences which in fact occurred.

The story of Suez is so familiar that it need not be summarised in this introductory note, and the pages that follow retell enough of it to make unnecessary a chain of footnotes. The value of this record is that it gives the contemporary impressions of a man who, though not himself in Parliament, was in constant touch with leaders of opinion and

---

[1] Sydney Silverman's Bill, which had passed through the Commons, was rejected by the Lords, and in the autumn the Government brought in their compromise Homicide Bill, which confined the death penalty to the more heinous forms of murder.

had a son in the House of Commons. I figure largely in this narrative, not only as a source of information to my father, but because my opposition to the Suez policy caused a deep breach between myself and the Bournemouth East Conservative Association, and led eventually to the loss of my seat in Parliament. It was a shattering experience for all of us, but it left behind no shadow of remorse or self-pity. These pages are reproduced twelve years after the event, not in self-justification, but as an addition to the contemporary records of those days, and as an illustration of the tremendous impact of the Suez crisis upon many families like our own.

DIARY   *27th July, 1956*

The Egyptians under Nasser have nationalised the Suez Canal. That is a pretty resounding slap in our face.

DIARY   *31st July, 1956*

Nigel says that most of the Tories are breathing fire and slaughter against the Egyptians, but that he expects that in the end 'wiser counsels' will prevail. That means that under American pressure we shall enable Nasser to get away with it. I wish sometimes that we were less encumbered and more powerful.

Later Nigel tells me about the Foreign Affairs Committee yesterday. The Committee had asked the Prime Minister to speak, but this hurt Selwyn Lloyd's feelings, since it is the Foreign Secretary who should address them on such occasions. He therefore arrived determined to demonstrate that he was a strong and powerful Minister. He said that in some ways it was a good thing that matters had come to a show-down, since it was unthinkable that we should ever allow the Canal to fall into the hands of a single Power who could use its position to blackmail both East and West. The Government were going to insist that the Canal should for perpetuity be placed under international control. In order to strengthen their hand, they were going to summon a conference of all Canal users and present Egypt with a joint plan. Meanwhile they were taking 'certain measures' which would be announced shortly, some of which would be unpleasant. If we allowed Nasser to get away with it, the other Arab states would proceed to nationalise the pipe-lines crossing their territory and even the wells themselves.

This tough attitude was much appreciated by the Tories. Nigel got up to ask when the measures of compulsion would be applied. Would they be applied if Nasser refused any International Consortium, or would they be applied only if he closed the Canal, which he is most unlikely to do? This intervention was not liked by the Committee. Killearn[1] welcomed the tough line Lloyd had indicated, and especially his promise that 'immediate sanctions' would be applied. Selwyn Lloyd in his reply said that he had never said that any sanctions would be 'immediate'. He added that the nationalisation issue was not the central one and that it should be dismissed from our minds. What mattered was that 'the waterway should be kept open'. That means, in effect, that Nasser has won all along the line. Dulles is bound to say that the American public, in a Presidential Election year, will not stand for anything that might lead to war in order to defend British oil-interests and our lifeline with the Empire. Thus the business will not mean merely a frightful loss of prestige, but also increased tension in Anglo-American relations. Selwyn Lloyd will be much blamed by the 1922 Committee for having rattled his sabre and then laid it aside.

DIARY   *2nd August, 1956*

Talks continue all day between Pineau,[2] Dulles and Eden. It looks as if Dulles agrees with the idea of an international conference but disagrees with the use of force. The difficulty is that Nasser has not, as far as I can see, violated any International Treaty. What the treaties provide is that the Canal should be open in time of peace and war, not who should own the Canal. So we cannot persuade the Americans that the situation justifies the use of force, and I am not absolutely sure myself whether we should use it or threaten it. In fact the Government have shown their accustomed irresolution and confusion of purpose.

H.N. TO V.S-W.   *9th August, 1956*
                                                        C.1 Albany, W.1

In the midst of death we are in life. It was so absurd last night. We

[1] Lord Killearn, High Commissioner for Egypt and the Sudan, 1934-36, and British Ambassador to Egypt, 1936-46.
[2] Christian Pineau, French Foreign Minister, February, 1956—June, 1957.

had people coming here to listen to Eden's broadcast—James [Pope-Hennessy], Lucien Freud, Hugh Thomas and Niggs. We heard the broadcast and then went into the sitting-room to discuss it. I left them to go to bed, and had not taken off my clothes when Ben telephoned to say that it had begun.[1] Then I got rid of our guests and started to go to bed again, when Niggs came in in his pyjamas and said it was a girl.

What a relief! I was worried about Luisa, but it seems to have gone off in a flash, and here is Vanessa Pepita a citizen of the world. Ben was so relieved that there was not an inch left for regret that it was not a boy. I was disappointed. But I do not wish to be rude to Vanessa so soon after her arrival.

H.N. TO V.S-W.   *15th August, 1956*
                                                          C.1 Albany, W.1

I am sorry that Vanessa howled so loudly when introduced to her grandmother. But I do so love it when you come up to London and bless these rooms with your presence. I love seeing you in London. It is like a country-bred puppy on a lead, seeking to escape up some side-street from the crowds on the pavement and the fierce traffic in the street. Your hand was trembling with panic when we crossed Piccadilly. How one loves the odd corners of people whom one loves!

V.S-W. TO H.N.   *5th September, 1956*
                                                          Sissinghurst

I have been getting into such a rage over the form I have to fill up for my new passport, as I have to supply all sorts of information about your father. *Your* father, mark you, not mine. I do think it is time the Foreign Office changed its Victorian attitude towards women. It is like that label they tied on Vanessa at the hospital, saying FEMALE INFANT NICOLSON. Oh, that made me so cross!

---

[1] The birth of H.N.'s second grandchild, Vanessa Nicolson. She was born on the anniversary of her parents' wedding-day at the Princess Beatrice Hospital in Kensington.

DIARY   *6th September, 1956*

It looks as if the Menzies talks in Cairo have come to a deadlock.[1]
Meanwhile, the TUC have passed a resolution calling on the
Government not to use force against Egypt without the consent of
UNO. As UNO is divided on the subject, and in any case Russia
will impose a veto on sanctions, this is like telling Nasser that he
can go ahead.

DIARY   *12th September, 1956*

The House meets in an emergency session. I dine at the Beefsteak
where I find many peers back from the House of Lords debate. They
are a little shaken by the fact that Lord McNair[2] stated that we were
breaking the Charter of the United Nations by moving troops in
such a way as to constitute a threat of force. Shortly after I get home,
Nigel appears. He had returned from Oslo this morning and went
straight to the House from the station. He was in time to hear the
P.M.'s statement and Gaitskell's reply. Eden had brought out his
Users' Association proposal,[3] and had indicated that if Egypt refused
to co-operate, we and France, with the tacit approval of America,
would use force. This led to an outburst in the House, the Tories
cheering wildly and the Labour people shouting 'Resign!' and
'Warmongers!' Niggs himself is rather alarmed by this bellicose
attitude, which he regards as bluff. No government could drag the
country into war over the Suez Canal with the Opposition against
them.

DIARY   *13th September, 1956*

Nigel tells me that the 1922 Committee were not at all pleased with
the Government's attitude, apart from the blood-and-thunder boys.
They feel that the Government have been careless about putting us
in the right, and that to reject the suggestion that we should go to

---

[1] (Sir) Robert Menzies, Prime Minister of Australia, had taken to Cairo the proposals of the 18-Power London Conference to establish an international Board
to operate the Canal. It was turned down by Nasser.

[2] President of the International Court of Justice, 1952–55.

[3] This proposal, originating with Foster Dulles, was for co-operation between
Egypt and the main users of the Canal on pilotage, signalling, collection of tolls
etc.

the Security Council is a major error. They know that the Council will prove ineffective, but to say that they are useless in advance is to alienate opinion at home and abroad. Eden was impressed by this argument. Therefore, when the debate reached its climax and Gaitskell begged him to give a pledge that he will go to UNO before the guns begin, he said irritably, and, as it were, in an aside, 'Of course we shall go to UNO.' Now, if he had said that at the outset, no heat would have been generated, and perhaps there would have been no Division. But to put it in an irritated aside confirms the impression that he has lost his hold, and that although he plays the right cards, he plays them in the wrong order and in the wrong manner. The Labour Party were under the impression that it was Gaitskell who had wrung this concession from him, but it was really the 1922 Committee.

DIARY   *15th September, 1956*

I go on with *Sainte-Beuve* and finish him at 12.20 this morning. I do not have the usual feeling of elation, since I regard the book as bad, and as clear and overt evidence of my waning powers.

Nasser, as was expected, has refused the plan for a Users' Association. He describes the proposal as an act of war. The Russians have issued a threatening communiqué saying that they cannot remain indifferent to war in the Middle East.

From 30th September until 19th October Harold Nicolson went on holiday, motoring through France with V. Sackville-West and Philippa to Cadaques and Tossa in north-east Spain. I was in Strasbourg, attending a meeting of the Council of Europe as a member of the British delegation.

H.N. TO PHILIPPA NICOLSON   *22nd October, 1956*
                                                              Sissinghurst

That was a happy holiday, wasn't it? Your presence was a delight to us. You are so quick and competent. You do not fall into fountains, nor lose tickets, nor break wine-glasses in hotels. And it was a joy for Vita and me to have someone so gay and lovely with us to share this experience, as we share so much of life together.

There is an excellent report in *The Times*[1] today about Strasbourg.
It says what I feel, namely that the Council of Europe is meaningless
but valuable. It is a lot of eye-wash Optrex, it is. But it is valuable
in giving backbench M.P.s diplomatic experience.

DIARY   *24th October, 1956*

Nationalism has spread to Eastern Europe. The Polish demonstrations have died down and Gomulka asserts undying friendship for
Moscow. But he is a weak man, and sooner or later will be replaced.
In Hungary a more serious outbreak has occurred, and Russian
troops have had to be called in to restore order No news about any
Czech risings. But a certain disintegration is apparent It will die
down and emerge in stronger form. I hope to live to see the conclusion.

DIARY   *29th October, 1956*

Israel has launched against Egypt an attack that seems more serious
than a reprisal raid. In fact they seem to have penetrated to within
a few miles of the Canal. They claim that they are clearing up
fedayeen posts, but it looks as if they were starting a preventive war
by cutting Egypt off from Jordan and isolating Egyptian forces in
the Sinai peninsula. Very neatly timed, when Russia is busy in
Eastern Europe, we and the French are at daggers drawn with
Nasser, and the Americans within eight days of a Presidential
Election.[2] What happens now to the Tripartite Declaration of
1950?[3]

Eden and Selwyn Lloyd today made revoltingly unctuous statements in the House about Hungary. When people rise against
foreign oppression, they are hailed as patriots and heroes; but the
Greeks whom we are shooting and hanging in Cyprus are dismissed
as terrorists. What cant!

[1] By Frank Giles.
[2] The election in which General Eisenhower defeated Adlai Stevenson.
[3] By which Britain, France and the U.S. undertook to go to the help of any victim
of aggression in a conflict between Jew and Arab.

H.N. TO V.S-W.   *31st October, 1956*
                                            C.1 Albany, W.1

I lunched yesterday with the Rothschild firm in their City premises.
They were crushed and saddened by the woes of Israel and they sat
down and wept, hanging up their harps in the counting house.
Oliver Franks[1] was there. He is a wise man and he was deeply
worried by the situation. He would have been even more worried
had he known that the Government had addressed an ultimatum to
Egypt and Israel. That news only broke at 4 pm. How they can have
done such a thing with the whole of world opinion against us passes
my comprehension. We shall now be accused of exploiting the
crime of the Jews in invading Sinai in order to resume control of the
Canal. To do this we have sacrificed our principles and practically
destroyed UNO and the Charter. We are in danger of being
denounced as aggressors. Of course, if the occupation of Port Said,
Ismailia and Suez proceeds without a hitch or much loss of life, and
if we can maintain ourselves on the Canal against the united armies
of Arabia, then the Tories will acclaim it as an act of great resolution
and courage. But to risk a war with more than half the country
against you, with America and UNO opposed, and even the
Dominions voting against us, is an act of insane recklessness and an
example of lack of all principle.

Niggs, who has just appeared, is also in despair, and thinks of
resigning from the Party and of chucking up his whole Parliamentary career. I am allowing him to simmer down and am lunching
with him. I shall preach discretion and silence. But he says rightly
that if he does not speak out now, it will be thought later that he
waited to see how things turned out. He says that the mood of his
Party is like that at the outbreak of the Crimean or Boer wars.

H.N. TO V.S-W.   *1st November, 1956*
                                            C.1 Albany, W.1

What distresses Nigel is that even the sane members of his Party
appear delighted that we have banged Nasser on the head and told
Dulles not to interfere He felt that his was a very lone hand. I
begged him not to be too violent or impulsive.

[1] British Ambassador in Washington, 1948–52, and Chairman of Lloyds Bank,
1954–62.

What happens now if the Assembly by a two-thirds majority order us to withdraw our forces and indemnify Egypt for our attack? I suppose we withdraw from UNO. That means a breach with America, which we can ill afford. I have not met a single sensible person who defends what has been done, and Niggs says that opinion in the Party will swing right round if we do not have a quick and overwhelming success against Egypt. The slightest check will make the Tories feel that Eden was impulsive and ill-advised, and he will have to resign the leadership to Butler.

Oh my country! How I love my country!

V.S-W. TO H.N.   *1st November, 1956*
                                                  Sissinghurst

I am appalled by the situation. Granted that Anthony Eden may have lost his wits, surely his entire Cabinet can't have? He surely must have consulted them? I don't understand any of it.

DIARY   *1st November, 1956*

I go up to Oxford. By the time I reach Wadham, Maurice Bowra and David Cecil have gone into Hall. We then adjourn to the Common Room where there is port and fruit. The purpose of my visit was to discuss with Maurice and David the award of the Duff Cooper Memorial Prize. We decide, subject to Diana [Cooper's] approval, to give it to Alan Moorehead's *Gallipoli*, which is a book Duff would have liked.

Maurice talks about the exquisite manners of the undergraduate today. If he asks them to have a glass of sherry, they write him elegantly phrased letters of thanks. We discuss how the books which we admired in our youth survive into old age. The one who comes out worst of this discussion is Meredith, who must have meant to us the subtleties that Freud provided for our successors but which seem to us just crinkum-crankum.

It is pleasant to be in Oxford again, and I listen to the bells in the drizzly night before retiring to sleep.

DIARY   *2nd November, 1956*

There was such an uproar in the House last night that the Speaker had to suspend the sitting. The United Nations Assembly has voted

with but five exceptions[1] ordering a cease-fire Eden refused to tell
Gaitskell what we would do next. There is a suggestion put forward
by Canada that UNO should police the area, but it will take a
long time before the police-force can be assembled, and meanwhile
we and France will go ahead. We have practically destroyed the
Egyptian air-force, the Israelis have captured Gaza, El Arish and
100 tanks, and the Egyptian army in Sinai has been routed. Seeing
these things, the other Arab leaders have remained quiescent In fact
the whole Egyptian bluff has been called good and proper But that
makes no difference. Success does not render a dirty trick any less
dirty.

Nigel has had a telegram signed by most of the dons at Balliol
asking him to vote against the Government His line is that he cannot
help to destroy the Government at the outset of what may prove,
even now, to be a serious war. He suspects that behind it all there is
a very nasty plot on the part of the French They arranged that Israel
would invade Egypt and not Jordan, that we should intervene
simultaneously and destroy the Egyptian air-force, and that Iraq
would thereafter lead the Arab world, Nasser be eliminated, and
Iraq and Israel be paid for their participation in the conspiracy by
being allowed to partition Jordan. It looks as if something like that
has happened, since otherwise the gamble is inexplicable. It is truly
one of the most disgraceful transactions in the whole of our history.
It will take years for us to regain our moral authority in the world.

I take the 3.15 train home. We listen to the news on television.
There is a shocking picture of the captured Egyptian destroyer being
towed into Haifa, with the crowds on the jetties actually dancing
with derision. But these things do not excuse our crime.

DIARY   *3rd November, 1956*

We listen to the Prime Minister on television. It is a dishonest but
able performance. He says he is a man of peace and so on; that he
had felt bound to intervene when the Israelis 'went in'; that there
was 'no time' to consult our friends such as the U.S.A. and the
Dominions. Meanwhile, he says, the Israelis have 'captured' the
Egyptian army in Palestine and the Armistice Commission are
seeking to secure their return to Egypt without arms.

[1] Britain, France, Australia, New Zealand and Israel.

Dulles has taken this occasion to develop acute appendicitis and to retire to hospital. The Russians seem to be closing in on Budapest.

DIARY   *4th November, 1956*

Anthony Nutting[1] has resigned. This is extremely important, since it deprives backbench Members of the excuse, 'The Government must know best'. Nutting knew everything, and has yet decided that it is evil. The central fact remains that Eden has deliberately ignored a recommendation passed by the overwhelming majority of the United Nations Assembly. This is a breach of law. I am not surprised that the House, at their special meeting yesterday, should have burst into disorder.

I telephoned Nigel this morning. He says that, feeling as he does, he can scarcely vote for the Government. He was disgusted by the hypocrisy of Eden's broadcast He says that he thinks some twenty Tories will abstain, although this may mean the fall of the Government. But, thank God, he is not going to resign his seat or announce that he will not stand at the next Election.

The Russians have sent seven divisions into Hungary and are closing in on Budapest. But we have no right to speak a word of criticism.

N N.'S DIARY   *4th November, 1956*

At 6 pm., four hours before Gaitskell's broadcast, I went to see Major Grant,[2] and handed him a letter saying that I no longer felt able to support the Government's policy in Egypt. The letter gave my reasons, the chief of which was that I cannot believe that a policy which leads to the condemnation of Britain by almost the whole world can be expedient, just or necessary. Major Grant did not like this argument. He did not see that there was any moral issue involved at all, and has completely swallowed the P.M.'s specious argument that he has intervened solely to stop Jews killing Arabs. I told him that I was prepared to take the consequences of my action, but that I did not want to publish my letter until the crisis in Egypt had ended, as otherwise I might be accused of stabbing the troops in the back. All the same, there is a limit to anybody's capacity to

[1] Minister of State for Foreign Affairs since 1954.
[2] Major S. Grant, Chairman of the Bournemouth East Conservative Association.

pretend that he wholly approves of a policy which he utterly abhors.

I went back to Shirley House and heard Gaitskell's T.V. speech in answer to Eden. He put the case well, but unfortunately ended by appealing directly to the Tory M.P.s who were troubled in their consciences. I suppose he had an audience of 20 million, but his talk was really addressed to thirty people, of whom I was one. I told Philippa that I felt the moment had come for my big decision, and that she must be prepared for a storm to burst over our heads, and even for the loss of my seat. She immediately agreed that I was right to do this.

N.N.'S DIARY   5th November, 1956

The troops began landing at Port Said at dawn this morning. I went up to London. At the House I found about sixty letters about the crisis, the great majority of which begged me to come out into the open against the Government. I also found a message from Alec Spearman[1] who was holding a meeting at noon of the new Tory rebels. I was too late to attend, but I rang him up and he read out to me a letter which they had drafted to the P.M., calling on the Government to offer to place their troops in Suez under the immediate command of the United Nations. I signed this later in the morning.

I had lunch at the House with a group of Tory diehards. They began abusing those of us who feel that the country's name has been blemished, and I could not contain myself. I told them that perhaps the United Nations would score its first and greatest moral victory in this very House of Commons this very week. I left them buzzing. They had been back to their constituencies and gleefully reported that the working-classes are all behind the Government, and that the protests are confined to a few professional men. I know this to be untrue.

At 3.30 Selwyn Lloyd, looking a great deal cockier than in recent days, made a statement on Hungary which immediately aroused the Opposition into a furious comparison between Budapest and Suez. Anthony Wedgwood Benn read out a proclamation which had been broadcast this morning from Cyprus to the Egyptians, telling

[1] Sir Alexander Spearman, Conservative M.P. for Scarborough since 1941.

them that their villages would be destroyed because they had committed the sin of supporting Nasser. There was a moment of intense anger, which Eden interrupted by rising to read out a despatch he had just received from H.Q. Middle East, saying that Port Said had capitulated. The Tories rose as one man, as if they were acclaiming a new Battle of Britain. I hissed at my neighbour, 'Don't get up!', and I think we were the only two Tories not to cheer Eden. I was called out at that moment by Charles Judd.[1] I told him what I was thinking and that I felt the time had now come for me to make my protest public.

When the House rose at 5.30, I went along to Alec Spearman's flat at 32 Queen Anne's Gate. Upstairs I found the following: Walter Elliot, Bob Boothby, Lionel Heald,[2] John Foster,[3] Jakie Astor,[4] Philip Bell[5] and David Price.[6] We sat down to consider a new draft of the letter to the P.M. I said that I thought we should in some way indicate that we deeply regretted what had been done, and I wanted them to insert the words 'in order to restore Britain's credit in the eyes of the world', but they said that this letter, by the very fact that it came from a group such as ours, would indicate our strong disapproval of what had happened. I made it clear that if I signed the letter, I would hold myself free to make a public, and much stronger, protest later. I signed it.

I dined with Robin McDouall[7] at the Travellers. Like all decent people, he agreed that it would be quite outrageous if no single Tory on the back-benches associated himself with the storm of rage which our action has created throughout the country and the world. In bed at Albany, I drafted a new letter to Major Grant, saying that I could keep quiet no longer.

H.N. TO V.S-W.   *7th November, 1956*

Well! That really is a fiasco! I experienced shameful relief when I

[1] Director General of the United Nations Association.
[2] Sir Lionel Heald, Conservative M.P. for Chertsey, and Attorney-General, 1951-54.
[3] Conservative M.P. for Northwich and a Queen's Counsel.
[4] Conservative M.P. for the Sutton Division of Plymouth since 1951.
[5] Conservative M.P. for Bolton East, 1951-60.
[6] Conservative M.P. for Eastleigh since 1955.
[7] Secretary of the Travellers Club.

heard of the cease-fire, but I fear that we have not heard the end of the story by a long chalk (whatever that may be). Eden has failed all along the line. The Canal will now be blocked for weeks: Nasser is regarded as a hero and a martyr: our oil-supplies will be cut for two months at least: we have shown that we have not a friend in the world: our reputation is tarnished: and in the end, at the first serious threat from Bulganin, we have had to climb down. It is about the worst fiasco in history, and my deep prayer is that it will now cease and we shall be able to hide our shame in silence.

H.N. TO V.S-W.   *8th November, 1956*
                                                        C.1 Albany, W.1

At the club, Bobbety [Salisbury] sought to defend the policy of the Government, but Halifax, Waverley, Oliver Franks and other eminent men said that our action had been iniquitous from the start and a failure in the end. I agree, of course. Our smash-and-grab raid got stuck at the smash.

Nigel heard yesterday afternoon that there was a meeting in Bournemouth of the United Nations Association. He jumped into the train and went down there, taking Philippa with him. He spoke strongly against the policy of the Government, and said that he intended to abstain in the vote of confidence. Philippa, who was in the audience, said that there were murmurs of 'Traitor!' and 'Renegade!' Of course, he was terribly unwise. But there are times when wisdom becomes akin to caution, caution to expediency, and expediency to subordinating one's conscience to one's interest. I am entirely behind him in what he has done, and feel that he has timed things beautifully. Poor Philippa sat there with wide anxious eyes.

DIARY   *10th November, 1956*

The analogy with the Munich crisis is curiously close. Even as people then said, 'Chamberlain has saved us from war', now people say, 'Eden has saved us from war', forgetting that we have been humiliated in the face of the world and broken our word. The sad thing is that whereas at the time of Munich, we who opposed Chamberlain were proved right in six months, it will never become utterly apparent how bad Eden's action was.

I read the Lytton-Virginia[1] letters and am appalled by their silliness, dirtiness and cattishness.

H.N. TO V.S-W.   *15th November, 1956*
                                                  C.1 Albany, W.1

Nigel's Executive met last night and reprimanded him for his speech but did not ask him to resign. There will be a full meeting of the Association in three weeks' time which he will address. For the moment, all Tory opinion, bemused though it be, is in favour of Eden. Simple minds work simply. The ladies of Bournemouth do not like the Russians, the Americans or Nasser: Eden has dealt a blow to these three enemies: therefore Eden must be right. It is as simple as that. Nigel and I have always believed that there was some collusion between the French and the Israelis to which we were a consenting party. If the story gets out, I do not see how the Government can survive. It is an utterly disgraceful tale.

DIARY   *16th November, 1956*

I lunch at the Travellers. The Foreign Office are enraged. They were never consulted, nor were any of our representatives in the Middle East. The latter feel that they have been badly let down, and that all their patient work during the last years has been destroyed in a night. This view will drift back and cause anxiety.

Nasser has gone on sinking block-ships in the Canal, and it will take months and months to open the waterway. The UNO troops have begun to arrive at Ismailia.

                                                  20th November, 1956
Dear Harold,

Many of your friends wished to join in celebrating your seventieth birthday,[2] and various ways of doing this were suggested, among them a dinner and the giving of a picture or a piece of silver. After

---

[1] *The Letters of Virginia Woolf and Lytton Strachey*, edited by Leonard Woolf and James Strachey.
[2] His birthday fell on 21st November, and this letter was delivered on that day, enclosing a cheque for £1,370. With this money he went on his Journey to Java, and dedicated the ensuing book to the 255 friends who had subscribed towards the present.

discussion, nothing seemed so good as simply to give you a cheque, which you could spend on what pleased you best.

Some doubts were expressed: this raising of a subscription—was it not treating you like a public monument? What would happen if we all began giving each other presents at seventy? Would you not be very angry when you heard of it? Some even of your greatest admirers expressed such doubts as these. But all misgivings disappeared before the enthusiasm for the project displayed by your friends, young and old, and a suggestion that the scheme should be confined to the younger generation was indignantly over-ruled by their elders who refused to be left out.

So the invitation went out, or was meant to go, to all your friends. But it may be that owing to amateur organisation, and the need to keep the plan secret from yourself, a number of people were omitted.

The accompanying list contains the names of all the contributors. This letter is signed by the originators of the scheme, and it is on their heads that your wrath must fall if you disapprove of what has been done. But we hope that you will not disapprove, and will accept this cheque simply as a proof of the affection felt for you by your friends.

DIANA COOPER	ROSE MACAULAY
RUPERT HART-DAVIS	RAYMOND MORTIMER
A. P. HERBERT	ALAN PRYCE-JONES
GLADWYN JEBB	JOHN SPARROW
ENID BAGNOLD JONES	WELLINGTON
L. E. JONES	

ELVIRA NIGGEMAN TO V.S-W.   21st November, 1956
                                         C.1 Albany, W.1

Everything went according to plan today—not a hitch. The cheque was delivered by hand after I arrived, so that I was able to see Sir Harold's reaction, which was one of stunned amazement Then telegrams and presents flowed in. Then Philippa and Juliet arrived, and I went to his room and told him that there was a large parcel, and should I bring it in? He looked at me with that 'It is rather a nuisance to be interrupted' look, but said, 'Very well; bring it in', and in they went, which was a lovely surprise. Then he had to go out.

It was a moving moment when he had on his overcoat and was looking down at Juliet in her overcoat, both staring at each other unblinkingly and bridging that gulf between them that the old and the very young seem so often to do.

DIARY   *24th November, 1956*

I am an absurd person. Going through the list of subscribers to my present, I find names that I don't know, or people whom I have scarcely met. There are only three or four of them, but my embarrassment at their having been asked is so intense that it poisons my pleasure at all the rest.

DIARY   *27th November, 1956*

I dine at the 200th Dinner of the 63 Club which is held in the Royal College of Physicians. The health of the guests is proposed by Sir Russell Brain[1] and replied to by Douglas Woodruff.[2] The latter says that my real claim to immortality will not be my books, so much as my Diary. Poor chap! If he only realised what a pitiable little engagement book it is!

DIARY   *28th November, 1956*

I broadcast for Mau Mau. The B.B.C. are very fussy about not making any controversial remarks about Suez. I go on to Enid Jones' house in Hyde Park Gate where there is to be a presentation to Alan Moorehead of the Duff Cooper prize for his *Gallipoli*. We are greeted by Diana [Cooper] looking too beautiful, and I find all Duff's special friends there—all somewhat aged in appearance. Then Winston comes in with Clemmie. He is very tottery and is helped to a chair. I say a few introductory words, and then Winston reads from a piece of paper his bit about Duff. He hands the prize to Moorehead, who replies in excellent terms. Meanwhile Winston has drunk his glass of champagne and says to me, 'I think I should like to say a little more'. So up he gets and adds a few charming impromptu words. It is a moving occasion.

[1] President of the Royal College of Physicians.
[2] The author and Editor of *The Tablet*.

DIARY   *3rd December, 1956*

In the House today Selwyn Lloyd announced that we are clearing
out of the Canal forthwith. He claims that our action stopped a war
and brought in UNO. I suppose that some people will believe him.

V.S-W. TO H.N.   *4th December, 1956*
                                                        Sissinghurst

It is dark, and I am in my tower. I went to see Ozzie.[1] He looks
ghastly ill and has now got jaundice. But what pluck! He said he
thought of going to Madeira in February with a nephew. I said,
'Dorothy wouldn't like you to go off without her.' He said, 'Oh, I
think it will do Dorothy good to get rid of me for a bit. I've been
such a nuisance to her lately, and I get cross sometimes.' I nearly
cried. I had to get up and look out of the window. Then I came
downstairs and met Mary,[2] and said how cruel and wrong it was
that a person like her father should get attacked like this. Why, why,
why, when there are such nasty people in the world? And she said,
'Oh, Vita, there are things one can't understand—there is something
beyond our understanding, and one must just accept it as best one
can', and I felt there was something so fine about those good, simple
people with their direct and courageous attitude towards life and
death, and their trustful faith.

I thought the other day, in the night, that you were the only
person I have ever really loved. I thought this out rather carefully,
and analysed my feelings, and came to that conclusion. I won't say
that I haven't been *in love* with other people, but you are the only
person that I have ever deeply and painfully loved. That is true.
You know me well enough to know that people don't count very
much with me. I love places (Sissinghurst, the Dordogne, Florence)
far more than I care for people, and Rollo[3] probably means more to
me than any of my friends. And of course Knole . . . but that is a
separate thing I can't speak about. That goes too deep.

Darling, how silly of me to go on scribbling to you like this
when I ought to be writing about Cardinal Richelieu and you ought

[1] A. O. R. Beale, the tenant-farmer of Sissinghurst Castle Farm. He died on
29th January, 1957.
[2] Mary Stearns, daughter of Oswald and Dorothy Beale.
[3] Her Alsatian dog.

to be thinking about the Suez Canal and our poor Niggs who has got himself into such trouble. I will stop now, because all this will bore you (you hate emotional expressions), only I did get rather upset seeing Ozzie, whom I know to be a dying man, and who knows himself to be a dying man, but who pretends not to know it.

H.N. TO V.S-W.   *6th December, 1956*
                                                C.1 Albany, W.1

Such a sweet letter from you today about Ozzie and the problems of life and death. If I had died at Ava Waverley's luncheon yesterday, you would have thought that I had never known how much you loved me. But that would be a false thought. I do know, and it lightens my heart always.

You will have seen in the newspapers that Nigel's Association have passed by a large majority a Resolution instructing the Executive to adopt another candidate for the next Election.[1] I am sad indeed.

DIARY   *14th December, 1956*

Eden returns from Jamaica and makes a sturdy speech at the airport saying how united they all are and how confident he is that he did right in stopping the Russians entering Syria. This is a new excuse. What decent Tories mind is that he has placed them in a false position by obliging them to say things in their constituencies which they now know to have been untrue. Whatever the public may think, most M.P.s do not like telling lies.

DIARY   *15th December, 1956*

Looking back on this Suez crisis, it seems strange to me that at the age of seventy I should have been so passionately moved by the whole business. Of course there was a personal interest in its effect on Nigel. But apart from that, the moral issue affected me as much as anything since Munich. My admiration for the Hungarians and my

[1] The Resolution read: 'This meeting regrets that it has no further confidence in the intention of Mr Nigel Nicolson adequately to represent in Parliament the political views of Bournemouth East and Christchurch Conservatives, and instructs the Executive Council to take steps to obtain a Prospective Conservative candidate to contest the constituency at the next Parliamentary Election.' The Resolution was carried by 298 votes to 92.

realisation of the immense importance of Russia suppressing by force a movement which was patently a working-class movement, were nothing like so intense as the shame and sorrow of the Suez episode. It meant much to me that a Prime Minister who had made his reputation by his moral courage should out of exasperation have violated his principles and told his country a series of shameful lies. It was a disappointment also to realise that my countrymen, in whose political good sense I had firmly believed, could prove as gullible and emotional as the Germans.

DIARY   *22nd December, 1956*

The last of our troops withdraw from Port Said. Thus ends a squalid and most humiliating episode. Eden says that if he were back again in October, he would repeat the operation. He must have lost the power of thought.

H.N. TO PHILIPPA NICOLSON   *26th December, 1956*
                                                        Sissinghurst

I hope Mrs Runningsore[1] listened to Her Majesty's piece about dismissing anger from the soul and thinking only in terms of sweetness and light.

I see there is a revolution in Sumatra. The head-hunters will get busy and we shall be decapitated. Oh dear, I do not wish to have my head cut off and compressed and ligamented till it shrinks to the size of an orange and dangles thereafter from some Indonesian watch-chain. I want to live to see my flowers grow, and Juliet become a grown-up, and the St Paul's precincts rebuilt, and Nigel Minister of State, and Vanessa a teacher of the violin in Bologna, and all my friends rich and happy and successful.

---

[1] H.N.'s name for one of the leaders of my Bournemouth critics.

1957

Harold Macmillan becomes Prime Minister – 'Journey to Java'
– a disappointing luncheon in Singapore – Hugh Gaitskell
on the Atom-bomb – deputation to Harold Macmillan on
Cyprus – H.N.'s letter to Lord Esher on his stroke – the
tower at Sissinghurst repaired – birth of Adam – V.S-W.
distressed by the success of her 'Observer' articles – the first
Russian artificial satellite – 'The Age of Reason' – un-
welcomed adulation of 'Journey to Java' – V.S-W. falls ill
on the 'Reina del Mar' – she recovers in the West Indies

From 15th January until 17th March, Harold Nicolson and V. Sackville-West went on the first of six successive winter voyages. The ship was the Dutch liner 'Willem Ruys', and she sailed from Southampton to Java and back, calling at Cape Town, Colombo, Sumatra, Singapore and Java, where she remained for a week. The return journey was by the same route (for the Suez Canal was still blocked), with an additional call at Las Palmas in the Canary Islands. During this voyage V. Sackville-West wrote a large part of 'Daughter of France', and Harold Nicolson, besides writing a chain of articles which he posted back to England, kept the diary which later in the year he published under the title 'Journey to Java'. On his return he extensively revised the diary, and incorporated in it his reflections on his reading, chiefly on the theme of contentment and melancholy. While the book was a great popular success, he felt that he had lost repute with the critics for having introduced so many personal passages about V. Sackville-West and other fellow-passengers. The sympathetic but teasing portrait of her which he drew in the book is the only published account of her which he wrote.

There were three motives for these winter cruises. Neither of them had ever been to the Far East or Latin America; both needed freedom from interruption in order to write; and both wished to escape the English winter for the sake of their health. But on the second voyage, to the Caribbean and through the Panama Canal to the west coast of South America, V. Sackville-West fell ill on 6th December, 1957, the second day out from Liverpool. For three weeks her temperature fluctuated and she could scarcely leave her cabin. After Christmas her health and spirits revived.

This was the year when Harold Macmillan succeeded Anthony Eden as Prime Minister, and when the Russians launched the first artificial satellite. Harold Nicolson published his 'Sainte-Beuve' on 6th June; and his grandson, Adam, was born on 12th September. Having published two books in this, his 71st year, he embarked on another, 'The Age of Reason'.

V.S-W. TO H.N.   *2nd January, 1957*
Sissinghurst

Your proofs [of *Sainte-Beuve*] came this morning, and I have read them all through—*so* good, as good as your best, which is saying a lot; so human, so penetrating; amusing too, of course. Oh poor little pink Sainte-Beuve! I wish he could read it (but only if all touchiness has been purged away in after-life). It is wonderful how you contrive to arouse one's compassionate affection in spite of everything.

DIARY   *9th January, 1957*

I dine at the Beefsteak, and as I drive there, my taxi-man says, 'Here's a pretty mess, the Prime Minister resigning like that'. It seems that Horace Evans made a thorough examination of him, and decreed that he could not live if he carried on. My only feeling is one of profound compassion.

DIARY   *10th January, 1957*

I go to the B.B.C., and the woman who works the lift says, 'Well, Macmillan is our new Prime Minister'. The Queen had seen Winston and Bobbety [Salisbury], and come to this decision. It is sad for the left wing of the Tory Party, since Butler was the leader of young conservatism, but I daresay that in the circumstances it is right.

H.N. TO PHILIPPA NICOLSON   *13th January, 1957*
Sissinghurst

If I die in Java, think only this of me, that my last thought as I am placed in my 'heavy-shotted hammock-shroud'[1] will be that Nigel was right, not morally only, but also from the eventual expediency of his protest. I believe that if Rab [Butler] had not been so weak about Munich and Harold Macmillan had not been so strong, Winston would have given different advice to the Queen. All my love to the three of you, and cable if something awful happens.

N.N. TO H.N. & V.S-W. (*in Cape Town*)   *22nd January, 1957*
House of Commons

I suppose you know that Eden left on Saturday to go to New Zealand the other way round, via the Panama Canal, because, for

[1] From Tennyson's *In Memoriam*.

some reason, the Suez Canal was not open. He left in a battered New Zealand ship from the Port of London. Gérard André was in the customs shed to see them off, and stepped forward to give Clarissa a bunch of red roses from the French Government. And then they got into the ship and hooted off down the Thames. Oh dear! Everybody feels such a load of depression about it. It is partly because an ill man was led by illness into folly; and partly because his successors have had to pretend that it wasn't folly at all. Everyone as a result is confused. Nobody is acknowledged to have emerged well out of this business. There are no heroes. Only different sorts of traitor.

I've just come back from Church House after the election of the new Leader of our Party. First we had Salisbury on Anthony Eden —too fulsome for that audience. He said that Eden's reputation had never stood higher 'in this country or abroad' than at the moment when ill-health struck him down. Walter Elliot, who followed, was much better. Without going so far as to say that it was a tragedy that a man whose reputation for integrity and diplomatic skill was unchallenged should have resigned in circumstances which threw doubt on both qualities, he almost said it. He said, 'A man's reputation depends on everything he has done, not simply on this phase or that of his career.' But then an idiot had to spoil it all by saying that the world acknowledged the Suez adventure to have been right, and history had already delivered its favourable verdict. You could feel the nervous stirring in the chairs. The group of women candidates who murmured 'Hear, hear!' looked foolish.

Then Rab [Butler] introduced the motion proposing Macmillan's election as leader. I think that the quality I most like about Rab is his melancholy. It wasn't the melancholy of personal disappointment, but the melancholy that right had not triumphed and that he was being obliged to contribute to a grotesque legend. The general feeling in the House is that he has mismanaged his attitude during the past two months. He should have been one thing or the other, not a reluctant apologist. Ah, if only he had come out into the open, what devotion I should have felt towards him! But today he played his part well. He proposed his supplanter gracefully, and then the doors opened and in walked Harold Macmillan and Lady Dorothy in a new red hat. He made a speech. He allowed himself a

329

few felicitous expressions, because it was not quite so necessary in front of this audience to pretend that he was a plain man. He said that the broad stream of Conservative thought was fed by many tributaries which we must not allow to dissolve into a shapeless delta. 'We have always been a tolerant party. We do not expel those who disagree with us. If we had, I should not be here myself.' I thought of Bournemouth. And then he said that unless we permit the strong to flourish, we shall not be in a position to help the weak. This was good Conservative doctrine. 'All this nonsense about Left and Right. I stick by the Middle Way, and I shall have my companions with me, arm in arm, some on my left arm and some on my right.' There was an acclamation, and I jostled out with the others into Dean's Yard.

Later: I've just come back from the House. Tributes were paid to Eden and Macmillan by Gaitskell and Jo Grimond. Macmillan described these tributes as 'stylised preliminaries to inevitable combat, the salutes before a duel'. Gaitskell was good about Eden. He dismissed the events of the last two months, and concentrated on the virtues of the preceding thirty years. There was a lot to say, and he said it well, but the House is still in a touchy mood. When Gaitskell remarked incidentally that illness had struck at Eden before he had finished his work, a Tory shouted, 'Whose fault was that?' There is no doubt that the anger of November is still there. One of the Brigadiers on my side had boasted a few weeks ago that if Edward Boyle[1] were given a job in the new Government, he (the Brigadier) would resign from the Party. This story got around, and I had great pleasure in saying to him today that he was a lucky fellow to be free of the Whips. 'What do you mean?' he asked. 'Oh, I thought you had left the Party because Edward Boyle got a job?' 'Well, for the sake of the Party. . . .' And so it goes on.

H.N. TO N.N. & P.N.   *26th January, 1957*
M.V. Willem Ruys, Approaching Cape Town

Touch wood (and indulging in all forms of sympathetic magic) everything has been perfect. It is a revelation to us to realise that

[1] He had been Economic Secretary to the Treasury since 1955, resigned from the Eden Government in protest against Suez, and was now reappointed to the Macmillan Government as Parliamentary Secretary, Ministry of Education.

there really does exist such a phenomenon as spare time. In this blessed void it doesn't matter one hoot whether today is yesterday or tomorrow. I feel that my nerves have acquired a new casing and that impatience is a vice that is slipping away from me. Women can pause for quite a long time chatting in gangways, and I remain immune from the spasms of rage which assail me in London. But I have not been idle. I have read and annotated several books, and have written an 8,000 word article upon the purpose of life. It is a Halcyon existence, and I render thanks to those friends who made it possible.

N.N. TO H.N. & V.S-W. (*in Singapore*)   *9th February, 1957*
                                    Shirley House, Bransgore, Hampshire

I must tell you about Harold Macmillan's speech to the 1922 Committee at the Savoy on Wednesday. It was superb. His whole speech turned upon the distinction between pride and vanity in the conduct of international relations, and there was not much doubt what he had in mind—*you* will understand, but I mustn't forget that this letter might be opened by the Afro-Asian group. He said that the greatest moments in our history have not been those when we have conquered, but when we have led. You see the subtle change? I was delighted. I said to the Chief Whip[1] as we were going out, 'What a pity it is that now we have the most intelligent Prime Minister of the century, he has to conceal his intelligence from the public for fear that they will suspect it, and that only we, on such occasions as this, can be given the full quality of his mind.' 'Yes', said the Chief Whip. 'Yes.'

H.N. TO N.N. & P.N.   *21st February, 1957*
                                          M.V. Willem Ruys,
                                          Sumatra–Colombo

I got Nigel's letter of February 9 at Singapore, and had only time to dash off an acknowledgement, since Vita's frightful Chinese friend had been observed waving frantically from the dockside, and thereafter clambering up the gangway with an expression of happy expectation on her face. We had believed her safely absent in Hong Kong. Vita is a fly-paper for bores. Not only does she attract the

[1] Edward Heath.

homely flies of Kent, the bumble-bees of Sussex and the dragon-flies of Surrey, but exotic insects wend their way towards the fly-paper from distant Borneo or Cathay. Chop-Suey (as I call her) is the worst of all the bores, since she does not really understand or speak the English language. She insisted on taking us in the steaming heat of a Singapore afternoon to what she called 'a dear little Chinese restaurant'. Vita loves native taverns, and her eyes brightened. But when we got there, it was on the top floor of a modern apartment house. The lift was made of pink plastic, and when we reached the restaurant, it was like that of the Carlton Hotel in Bournemouth, with endless napkins tastefully displayed, air-conditioning and enamel walls and chromium plate. Vita's face fell, but brightened again when she found beside her plate a tissue-paper envelope containing chop-sticks of ivory or bone. I firmly asked for a fork and spoon.

We drank beer, and were given food that was so disgusting that I felt ill. The conversation was equally sticky. 'Tell me', Vita began brightly, 'is there a canteen at the University where you teach?' 'Beautiful flowers', replied Chop-Suey, 'beautiful flowers.' 'Do you teach your pupils English?' I enquired with malice. 'I know one shop near Raffles Place', she answered, 'which has many of them.' 'Has your husband joined you', asked Vita at dictation-speed, 'or is he still in Formosa?' 'Most beautiful flowers', she answered, 'all green and blue and—how do you say—ponk.' 'Pink', said Vita, and the conversation languished.

DIARY   17th March, 1957

Slowly we tie up at Southampton. We then leave the *Willem Ruys* and step on the shore of our native land through the same covered and illumined gangway that we traversed on January 15. Since then we have travelled 25,650 miles. V. has written 40,000 words of *La Grande Mademoiselle* and I 60,000 of this diary with its inserts.

DIARY   31st March, 1957

I start on *Journey to Java* and type out my diary in revised and publishable form. In bed I read Catullus. It passes my comprehension why Tennyson could have called him 'tender'. He is vindictive, venomous and full of obscene malice. He is only tender about his brother and Lesbia, and in the end she gets it hot as well.

DIARY   *2nd April, 1957*

Frank Giles[1] and Kitty and Diana [De La Warr] come over for a drink. Frank makes one point that had not occurred to me. He says that we over here do not understand the Algerian situation. There are one million French settlers in Algeria who have lived there for generations. In proportion to the population, they represent what 42 million English settlers in India would have represented to us. Could we have given independence to India with such a vast white minority prepared to resist it with their lives?

At the dinner-party at Buckingham Palace tonight I talk to Hugh Gaitskell. He says that his Party is split over the atom-bomb question. He must not commit them to any definite rejection, since he may soon be responsible for the decision himself. It is always the difficulty of the Leader of the Opposition that his Party wish to oppose always and do not realise that the leader has to consider what policy he would himself adopt if he were to become Prime Minister tomorrow.

DIARY   *1st May, 1957*

I go to the House to take part in a deputation to the Prime Minister about Cyprus. We ask that Makarios should be brought to London or elsewhere for negotiation, and that meanwhile no executions shall be carried out. The P.M. says that Harding must decide matters concerned with internal security and that the Government do not wish to tie his hands. Blatant murder must be punished by death. But he would be 'surprised' if Harding felt it necessary to execute people for technical breaches of the curfew etc. He says that the NATO solution[2] is the only solution, that the Greek Government were insane to reject Ismay's proposal in so off-hand a way, and that if we can get Makarios to indicate that a NATO settlement is the only alternative to partition, then we shall have made a real contribution.

[1] He was then *The Times* correspondent in Paris.
[2] The proposal by Lord Ismay, the Secretary-General of NATO, that NATO should mediate in the Cyprus dispute. It was accepted by Britain and Turkey, but rejected by Greece.

The deputation consists of Attlee, Clement Davies, Listowel and Kenneth Robinson.[1] Young Zulueta[2] sits there like a child taking notes. The Prime Minister looks weary, and passes a tired hand over his face. He gives the impression that he is economising his expenditure of nerve-force. Only occasionally is there a glint in his eye of the old vivacious Macmillan. But he does say emphatically that the Cyprus situation has drifted on too long, and that when he gets back from his visit to Germany, he will give it top priority. We are satisfied by our interview.

I attend the Royal Academy banquet. When Winston arrives, the crowd in the courtyard cheers loudly. Winston is given a little chair at the entrance to the main room where he sits looking rather childish. On the wall in one of the rooms there is a monstrous caricature of him by Ruskin Spear R.A. which makes him look like a village dotard from the Auvergne. The dinner is far better than last time, and there is unstinted champagne, port and brandy. Winston sits there looking very old, and there is a hint of dribble about his lips.

DIARY   10th June, 1957

Go on with Chapter XIII and finish it and the book [Journey to Java] at 11.50 this morning. I am relieved, since if I die, the book can be published.

H.N. TO V.S-W.   13th June, 1957
                                                             C.1 Albany, W.1

The B.B.C. Overseas people want me to take part in a broadcast justifying the West. I agreed to do so. The whole of modern civilisation, including the hydrogen bomb, derives from the Mediterranean basin, and the East is no good at all except at poetry and art. I despise everything east of Suez (including Suez itself), with the exception of the Chinese, for whom I have a deep respect. My word, some of their carvings I saw at Spinks yesterday were magnificent!

---

[1] Labour M.P. for St Pancras, North, who became Minister of Health in 1964.
[2] (Sir) Philip de Zulueta, Private Secretary to the Prime Minister, 1955–64.

H.N. TO V.S-W.   *26th June, 1957*
                                                    C.1 Albany, W.1

Nigel's dining-club had the Prime Minister as their guest last night.
The P.M. was very frank with them and said that he could not think
out any message to give the people. The masses now took prosperity
for granted and did not realise that in the whole of history prosperity
and full employment made for a rise in the standard, and therefore
in the cost, of living. The country simply did not understand that
we were living beyond our income, and would have to pay for it
sooner or later. Nigel was entranced by his intelligence and wisdom.
He was greatly encouraged. The P.M. went out of his way to be
nice to him, but Bournemouth was not mentioned between them.

H.N. TO LORD ESHER[1]   *25th July, 1957*
                                                       Sissinghurst

I am terribly sorry to hear that you have had a stroke. I had two
strokes in 1955 within eight weeks of each other, and therefore I
consider myself an expert on the subject. What worried me at first
was the unpredictability of the whole business. One stretches up
to get a book from a shelf, or one leans down to pick up a piece of
paper from the floor, and the next thing one realises is that 'Where
am I?' and 'What happened?' feeling. One is always convinced that
the thing will happen to one at the most awkward moments. One
may, like Catherine the Great, be stricken when sitting alone in an
empty house upon a lavatory seat. On the other hand, one may be
knocked over when receiving from the hands of Her Majesty the
Queen the insignia of a Knight of the Bath. Or one may (and this
is my special terror) be assailed when on the top step of the longest
escalator in the Underground, which would entail much tumbling
and embarrassment.

My doctor told me that the thing to do was to rest in the afternoon
and to go to bed early. I have followed this advice whenever
possible, with the result that although I am conscious of a certain
waning of my physical powers, in the sense that the thought of
climbing to the top of Broadcasting House is distressing to me, I do
not notice so far any marked decline in my mental powers. After

[1] Viscount Esher, who was Chairman of many voluntary committees connected
with the arts, was then aged 76.

all, since I had my two strokes in March and May of 1955, I have written two books and some hundred articles.

Some of my friends fear that I may pop off suddenly without having made my peace with God. But if God is aware when a sparrow falls to the ground, he must also be aware when an elderly writer tumbles from the top of an escalator to the bottom. He must be prepared for the event, and must be sufficiently tolerant to excuse the fact that while tumbling I had no time to confess my sins. Even if Hell exists (which I doubt), and even if Heaven is a reality (which I sincerely hope is not true), we shall surely be judged by the amount of good we have done in the world. By that standard your wings and harp are absolute certainties, whereas even I may be accorded a gold triangle, which I could beat at intervals of praising the Deity, and one rather fluffy little wing.

DIARY   *12th August, 1957*

Elvira [Niggeman] telephones to say that there is a letter from David Astor [Editor of the *Observer*] saying that my Table Talk piece is too much like an article, and will I please vary it? What they really want is 'personalities', but that I refuse to give them. But I do an extra piece about Gilbert Harding's[1] visit here. Why should the public be more excited by Gilbert Harding than they would be by Tom Eliot or even by Harold Macmillan? I am sure I am right in thinking that it is because the English enjoy the pleasure of recognition more than they enjoy any other pleasure.

H.N. TO V.S-W.   *21st August, 1957*
                                                         C.1 Albany, W.1

I got such a lovely little poem from you this morning about me flashing my torch beneath the tower. Life may be precarious, but love is in and out of time, and stands there like a fortress for each of us. I feel so sorry for the survivor, since the only comforter would be the cause of his or her distress. I simply cannot contemplate life without you, and I just dismiss the thought from my mind, although it comes to tease and excruciate me sometimes. But not even Robert

[1] As the leading participant in many current television and radio programmes, he was one of the best known and most loved Englishmen of his times. A few days earlier, he had visited the garden at Sissinghurst.

Browning received such a moving poem, and I cherish it much. When I feel something deeply, I am totally unable to express it. You understand that, but who will understand anything when you are gone? I know that I shall be surrounded by affection and even love. But that will be just on the fringe, and the whole centre of life will be an aching gap.

H.N. TO PHILIPPA NICOLSON   *2nd September, 1957*
Sissinghurst

Sissinghurst is passing through a nervous strain. Vita realised that the old barn was in need of repair, and had the idea that Tommy Lascelles, Chairman of the Historic Buildings Council, might repair it out of public funds. So he sent his inspectors to have a look. They reported that the barn was indeed tumbling down, but that it could not be classed as 'an historic building' within the meaning of the Act. But while they were down here, they also noticed that the front porch and the tower were themselves in urgent need of repair, and since they could be classed as historic buildings, they agreed to mend them. So this morning two lorries arrived with scaffolding of iron connected together by neat clamps. This vast Meccano set was flung upon the lawn with great noise. Another set then arrived and was flung upon the paving between the yews with even greater clamour.

Some of the tubular supports are already raised this evening, and Vita is wringing her hands in fear that they will ruin for ever a fine bush of *Rosa wilmottiae*, to say nothing of a *Camellia californica*. Then, when they have erected the scaffolding, they will climb up it and go chip, chip upon the brickwork, which will drive poor Vita insane.

'It is all very well for you', she says in indignation, as if it were my fault. 'I wish I had never told Tommy anything about it', she says, knowing that Tommy is one of my oldest friends and therefore that it must be indirectly my fault. 'You wouldn't like it if they made noises outside your room in the Albany', indicating thereby my indifference to her suffering. So, you see, I am in disgrace more or less, and unjustly—poor me, who wouldn't hurt a fly. 'You are so *mild!*' she says, wishing that I also would give vent to imprecations.

H.N. TO V.S-W.   *4th September, 1957*
                                                    C.1 Albany, W.1

I have been busy all morning doing my proofs of *Journey to Java* and
have now finished them. They leave me in a mood of blue seas and
flying fish, and have recalled to me that calm lake of happiness
which that expedition meant to you and me. I do not think that I
have really made a mock of you, and any sensible person reading
the diary will detect that deep devotion which underlies what I
say. But it is sad in a way to read the last chapter and to put a rubber
band round that little fid of print, and to feel that all this is over.

I, of course, regard the sections on melancholy as the most interesting, but others may feel that so deep a subject should not have been
dealt with from a deck-chair. Anyhow, I have been kind to our
fellow-passengers. I suppose that some people may suggest that I
was paid by the Rotterdam Lloyd to boost their wares. But that is not
true.

DIARY   *12th September, 1957*
                                                    C.1 Albany, W.1

I get up. I shave and wash and dress. I enter the sitting-room, and
help myself to a sausage and a cup of coffee. The telephone rings.
'Yes?' I answer. A very young voice reaches me from the distance,
saying, 'Harold, I have got a brother'. Then Niggs intervenes, and
explains that Philippa had a boy at 6.30 this morning. My delight
at this news shows me how really worried I had been. It appears that
it is an enormous child with a vast mouth. I am so happy that I find
myself singing. Colin [Fenton] is amused. Elvira, when she arrives,
is ecstatic. I telephone to Ben and Eric and Gwen. God be praised.
This is in truth a majestic benefit. I had arranged to record a piece
for the B.B.C. about the London Library, and had intended to
indulge in a stinging invective against the Westminster City
Council;[1] but I feel that any cross words would be out of place, and
so just coo like a turtle dove into the microphone. To think that this
howling morsel of flesh is the heir to the lairds of Skye![2]

[1] For imposing a crippling rate-burden on the Library, of which H.N. was still
Chairman.
[2] Adam now lay in the succession for the Barony of Carnock, which had been
conferred upon his great-grandfather, a descendant of the 16th-century
Nicolsons of Scorrybreck, Isle of Skye.

AN UNDESIRED SUCCESS

V.S-W. TO H.N.   *1st October, 1957*
                                                    Sissinghurst

I am filled with loathing for my *Observer* articles, but must now finish
arranging the latest lot for publication in a fourth book—but what
on earth am I to call it?[1] It makes me rather cross to have had this
(may I say?) success with those wretched articles, and to have gained
a reputation of a kind I never desired or deserved. You will understand this, so I needn't enlarge.

H.N. TO V.S-W.   *2nd October, 1957*
                                                    C.1 Albany, W.1

I don't think that you will really go down to posterity as a writer of
gardening articles, and if you do, I shall clamour aloud in the Hall of
Fame. You will be remembered as a poet, and as the author of many
excellent books on many varied subjects. *The Edwardians* will surely
survive, and *Pepita* and *Knole and the Sackvilles*, and all your literary
and historical books. Then *The Land* and *The Garden* are enduring
classics. So your gardening things will be regarded as a mere
parergon ['a bye-work'], like the flute-playing of Frederick the Great.

DIARY   *5th October, 1957*

I am woken up by V. bringing her portable wireless into my room,
and saying I must listen to the 8 o'clock news. It was announced
before midnight that the Russians have released a satellite which is
now circling the earth at tremendous speeds, giving out signals. The
B.B.C. have managed to record the signals, and play them over to
us—just ping, ping, ping, ping. I am annoyed that the Russians
should have been the first to get away with this.

H.N. TO V.S-W.   *9th October, 1957*
                                                    C.1 Albany, W.1

Mr Barker, an executive editor in Doubleday & Co., lunched with
me yesterday. They are proposing a series of world histories or
'portraits of epochs', and want me to do the eighteenth century. I
said I was too old and ill for that sort of thing, and turned it down.
But this morning, being woken up at the ghastly hour of 7.45 by

[1] It was called *Even More for Your Garden*. It followed vol. I, *In Your Garden;*
vol. II, *In Your Garden Again;* and vol. III, *More for Your Garden*.

339

John [Sparrow] saying goodbye to me, I reflected (a) that in any case I would like to have a book on the stocks; (b) that the portrait of the eighteenth century would be far more interesting than reading the poems of James Bailey;[1] (c) that it is physical, and not mental, effort which is bad for me; (d) that I am not quite as gaga as all that; and (e) that I might as well say yes. So I telephoned to Mr Barker and said that I had reconsidered my attitude.

DIARY   *3rd November, 1957*

The Russians have launched a better and bigger satellite with a dog inside it. The British public will mind more about the dog than the satellite. There is a suggestion that Our Dumb Friends League should stand outside the Soviet Embassy and celebrate a two-minutes' silence.

DIARY   *21st November, 1957*

My birthday. I am 71. Fancy that. I dine at the Diner Molière. I sit between the French Ambassador [M. Jean Chauvel] and Raymond [Mortimer]. I can see that the latter did not really like *Journey to Java*. It is published today, and I doubt whether it will be well reviewed.

DIARY   *24th November, 1957*

I do my review of Clough's correspondence and read the *Journals* of Jean Cocteau. There is a rather meaningless review of *Journey to Java* in the *Observer,* and a rather nasty one in the *Sunday Times.* I detect in both of them a feeling that the book is based on rather strained, and even false, merriment. I can see that in its intimacy and family allusions it may seem embarrassing to many, and it is certainly this that explains Raymond's reticence·on the subject.

DIARY   *6th December, 1957*
                                                              S.S. Reina del Mar,
                                                              Off the Cornish Coast

I am reading in my bunk when the telephone buzzes. It is Vita, who says that she has a high temperature and can I fetch the doctor? I dash

---

[1] H.N. had been contemplating a book on the minor poets of the nineteenth century. Bailey was the author of *Festus* (1839), an epic poem in blank verse.

round to her cabin and find she has a temperature of 102. I stop an officer in the passage and ask him to fetch the ship's doctor. The latter takes V.'s temperature, which has dropped, as she has taken aspirin. He examines her, while I retire delicately and wait in agony, leaning against the handrail of the corridor. He makes a long examination and then at last he comes out. We sit on the sofa in the entrance hall. The doctor agrees that it is not 'flu, but must be some 'local infection', probably from her tooth.[1] He gives her a sleeping pill. He says it isn't anything serious, and that I need not feel alarmed. But I do feel alarmed, and it is difficult to get to sleep.

H.N. TO N.N. & P.N.   *17th December, 1957*
                                             S.S. Reina del Mar,
                                             Approaching Nassau

Vita is really better, and in fact I think she is on the mend. I do not want to boast about it, since in the last twelve days she has at one moment been free from fever, and then it has begun again. But she has now been free for 48 hours and her pulse is at last better. Moreover she is beginning to feel impatient to get down to work. A different person from four days ago. It will be heaven for me to feel that she is safe again, and then I shall be able to turn to the delights of marine voyaging.

H.N. TO P.N.   *24th December, 1957*
                                             S.S. Reina del Mar,
                                             Approaching Venezuela

This is a marvellous ship—really just like a luxury hotel. Vita has had most of her meals in her cabin, as until a few days ago she had this recurrent fever and feels too limp to dress. She was up all yesterday without ill effects. But she has not been able to touch *La Grande Mademoiselle* or to do any sightseeing. Had it not been for the constant anxiety I have been through, and for my loneliness, I would already have got much out of the journey—doing steady reading, taking notes for my book on the eighteenth century [*The Age of Reason*], bathing in the delicious swimming-pool, gazing at the mountains of Jamaica and Cuba, and talking to Lady Magnus-

[1] She had had several teeth extracted in mid-November, including a badly impacted wisdom tooth.

341

Allcroft. The latter is married to Philip Magnus, a clever Oxonian and an excellent writer.[1] She is a real person—obstinate and kind, and has been a friend to me during these dark days. I shall always be grateful to her.

H.N. TO N.N. & P.N.   *26th December, 1957*
                                           S.S. Reina del Mar,
                                           Cartagena, Colombia

We got your telegram for Christmas Day. We listened to the Queen on the wireless, and in spite of the long wash of the Caribbean seas she came across quite clear and with a vigour unknown in pre-Altrincham days.[2] Then at the end they played *God Save the Queen*, and all the old English boys scrubbed up on their crutches and I stood to attention, giving the impression that I had served in not one, but two, European wars. In the evening it was hell on earth. We all had to wear paper caps and be merry with balloons. My cap was in the semblance of an academic mortar-board and was not ill-suited to a Doctor of five universities.[3] But Vita was given the *képi* of an Austrian cavalry officer of 1904, and carried it bravely. Then we went on deck while the others danced, and there was a soft breeze and a new moon and a white star and great solemn waves beside us.

I have done a lot of dull drudgery work, and now that Vita is really better, I am beginning to enjoy the trip hugely. I watch my fellow-passengers reading *Journey to Java*; they eye me with deep suspicion.

[1] Author of biographies of Edmund Burke, Gladstone, Kitchener, King Edward VII etc.
[2] In the August issue of the *National Review*, Lord Altrincham (John Grigg) had published an article about the Monarchy, in which he criticised the Queen's style and manner, and the conventionality of her speeches and entourage. The article had aroused fury in some quarters, delight in others.
[3] Athens, Grenoble, Glasgow, Dublin and Durham.

1958

*Visit to Peru, Chile and Venezuela – V.S-W. depressed by
'La Grande Mademoiselle' – H.N. replies to the charge of
urbanity – the Torrington bye-election – C. P. Snow on
American food – decline of British power in the world – de
Gaulle again leads France – the American way of life – H.N.
disturbed by V.S-W.'s worries – crisis in the Lebanon –
visit to Strawberry Hill – H.N. is given a German decora-
tion – the guilty conscience of Doctor Samuel Johnson – the
Queen Mother at Morley College – H.N. on V.S-W.'s
gardening articles – enthronement of Pope John XXIII – the
Wolfenden Report – Igor Stravinsky – controversy over
'Lolita'*

1958

When the year opened they were together on the 'Reina del Mar' in harbour at Lima, Peru. They continued to Valparaiso, Chile, and then returned by the same route, via the Panama Canal and calling at several ports in the West Indies before disembarking at Plymouth on 9th February. Harold Nicolson had made good progress with the research for his 'The Age of Reason', and V. Sackville-West was at last in sight of the end of 'La Grande Mademoiselle' ('Daughter of France'), which she finished at Sissinghurst in August. Throughout the voyage each of them regularly posted back their weekly article to the 'Observer'.

Three international crises dominated the year: in Algeria, which led to de Gaulle's return to power in France; in the Lebanon, where the American and British intervened to protect the Lebanese Government from a communist threat; and in the Far East, where the United States upheld Chiang Kai-Shek's claim on the Chinese off-shore islands. At home, Harold Nicolson was most preoccupied with my own political problems, for I was attempting to retain my seat against the hostility of the Bournemouth East Conservative Association, who had adopted a new candidate to replace me when the General Election came. At the end of the year the situation was further complicated by the proposed publication by Weidenfeld & Nicolson of the controversial novel 'Lolita'.

H.N. TO N.N. & P.N.   *11th January, 1958*
S.S. Reina del Mar,
At sea between
Valparaiso and Antofagasta (Chile)

Vita has really recovered. Yesterday, for instance, she got up at 6 am. to finish an *Observer* article, then motored in the blazing heat for 90 miles, then visited a *hacienda*, then drove along the coast, then climbed on board, unpacked and said farewell to the Ambassador[1]

---

[1] Sir Charles Empson, British Ambassador to Chile, 1955–58. They had stayed three nights at the Embassy in Santiago.

and his delightful staff who had come to see us off, then arranged her bouquets in vases in her cabin, then unpacked, then dined, and then sat up till 11 watching a film of Don Camillo, and then retired at last to rest without any sign at all of having had a full day. So our enjoyment of the cruise is now intense. We really loved Chile and the Chileans. This part of the world must be an archaeologist's dream. You have merely to scratch the sand, and out come robes of feather-embroidery and necklaces of green and gold dating from before the building of the Parthenon.

H.N. TO N.N.

24th January, 1958
S.S. Reina del Mar,
At sea between
Venezuela and Jamaica

We reached La Guaira in Venezuela early yesterday morning, and we had decided to motor up the super-road to Caracas and see that amazing oil-rich capital, constructed almost entirely of brand-new skyscrapers in marble and gold. But when we went on deck, we first observed aeroplanes flying low over the harbour and then naval frigates with their guns trained, circling round and round outside the harbour. We could also see on the wide boulevard that runs behind the dock-entrance lorries packed with workmen dashing about waving banners on which was inscribed 'LIBERTAD'. We went downstairs to breakfast assuming that there was a general strike, but then the cool calm voice of the captain came over the loudspeakers to say that it was a revolution, and that no passengers could be allowed on shore.[1] Anyhow, I settled down and wrote a review of Winston's really lamentable vol. IV of the History of the English Speaking Peoples.

We much enjoyed Curaçao the night before last—a southern Amsterdam, with barges bursting with fruit and Dutch houses and canals. Little lights beside the lagoons and a swing bridge, and all spacious and tiny at the same time.

V.S-W. TO H.N.

26th February, 1958
Sissinghurst

Oh Hadji, my book [*Daughter of France*] is so bad. It really is. I am

---

[1] This was the military revolution which deposed President Jimenez of Venezuela.

not imagining this: I *know* it is bad. I did take trouble over that book. I read a lot, but I haven't been able to synthesise or compress it as I had hoped. It is just a mess. I had a clear picture when I started, but now it has all got muddled up with detail and the outline has got lost. I write this to you because I know you will understand, and I do feel so dejected that I had to tell somebody, and nobody else will do.

DIARY   *2nd March, 1958*

I take notes from the Cambridge Modern History and from Stirling Taylor's biography of Robert Walpole. The Cambridge History is really too scrappy and specialised for my present outline purpose. It keeps on jumping all over the place and provides me with no continuous narrative. But I am beginning to see my general line. It will be continuous in the sense that it will begin in 1700 and end in 1799, but I shall not tell stories of wars and battles, or even of spinning-wheels and machines, but about people, their adventures and ideas. There are so many fascinating strains to be followed up from Wesley to Casanova.

DIARY   *18th March, 1958*

I write an article for the *Spectator* on the subject of Urbanity. In a Beaverbrook periodical called *Books and Art* a young man writing under the name of Humphry Clinker has accused me in two successive articles of being cultured, snobbish and urbane. I rather like having the chance to answer him, although I do not understand what his real grievance is. He says that *'virtuosi'* such as Cyril Connolly and myself live in ivory towers and do not possess the common touch nor understand the dust and roar of life. We should treat literature as a smart columnist treats life, and should not discuss general ideas but concentrate on personalities and be more newsy. I say in my article that I am writing for an educated public, and that it would be absurd for me to put on a proletarian tone.

DIARY   *28th March, 1958*

John Wyndham and Philip Zulueta[1] are at luncheon, and the latter dashes out to get the result of the Torrington bye-election. He

[1] Private Secretaries to the Prime Minister, Harold Macmillan.

returns looking rather grim. 'They are having a recount', he says. This means that it is pretty close. When I get home Vita tells me that Mark Bonham Carter is in by a small majority. This is a most important political event, since all those who dislike both Tory and Labour will in future feel that it is not wasting a vote to vote Liberal. At 10.15 Violet [Bonham Carter] appears on television, being interviewed by three journalists. Considering that she is not a young woman, has been electioneering for a fortnight, and has had an exciting and strained day, this is pretty sporting of her. She is excellent, and makes not one single foolish remark.

H.N. TO V.S-W.   *10th April, 1958*
                                                                C.1 Albany, W.1

What a shame and humiliation it is for me to find that I get more letters about *Journey to Java* than about any other of my books! Of all my books it is the one that cost me least trouble. Hell!

DIARY   *21st April, 1958*

I review Professor Gordon Ray's admirable biography of Thackeray. Plant out polyanthus and pick flowers for tomorrow. Read Vansittart's book.[1] Also Ben's splendid study of Terbrugghen.[2]

DIARY   *1st May, 1958*

I dine with Kenneth Rose[3] at his flat to meet C. P. Snow and his wife. An excellent and amusing dinner. The Snows are just back from America and tell us that the food there is now so sterilised, dehydrated, pasteurised and frigidaired that it has lost all taste. That is what we shall come to—a tasteless, common-man age.

H.N. TO V.S-W.   *14th May, 1958*
                                                                C.1 Albany, W.1

What a world we live in! The sense of authority has decayed, and the young revolt against the old and the irresponsible against the

[1] Lord Vansittart's autobiography, *The Mist Procession*, Hutchinson, 1958.
[2] *Hendrick Terbrugghen* (the Dutch painter, 1588–1629) by Benedict Nicolson. Lund Humphries, 1958.
[3] The journalist, who was then contributing to the Peterborough column in the *Daily Telegraph*.

responsible. I suppose that something of the same sort occurred after the French Revolution, but people were then mainly uneducated and could not be driven to violence by propaganda. But now, simultaneously, we have the Lebanon on the verge of rebellion, the French Algerians setting up a separate Government, and the Venezuelans spitting at Mrs Nixon. The Americans are so deeply hurt when they discover that they are not loved, and in truth I feel that the students of Lima and Caracas have behaved rudely and wildly. It is all, I suppose, due to the fact that the use of force is now prohibited, and that agitators like Nasser and his myrmidons can lash any crowd into rage and excitement.

Niggs appeared yesterday. He is writing the last chapter of his book,[1] and produces a chapter daily which he flings at Elvira [Niggeman], expecting her to type it in an afternoon. She is good and patient.

H.N. TO V.S-W.   *15th May, 1958*
                                                        C.1 Albany, W.1

I dined last night at the Club. A small gathering, which is always preferable to a large gathering. Halifax, Salisbury, Swinton, Goddard and Tedder. Halifax says that the difficulty of the Government is that they are tied by their local Conservatives, who do not yet realise that we are no longer a Great Power, and that the days are past when we could assert our authority with a Maxim gun. Thus the Government cannot make wise concessions to Ghana, Malta, Cyprus etc. Anyhow, we have not got into a muddle comparable to that which afflicts poor France.

DIARY   *2nd June, 1958*

De Gaulle obtained a 105 majority in the Chamber, and will now establish a dictatorship for six months, and thereafter introduce a reform of the Constitution. He has appointed Couve de Murville as his Foreign Minister, which makes me laugh.[2]

I read James [Pope-Hennessy's] life of Queen Mary. It is a really

---

[1] *People and Parliament.* Weidenfeld & Nicolson, 1958.
[2] M. Couve de Murville had been engaged by H.N. as tutor to his sons during the summer holidays of 1928, when he was aged 21.

remarkable work, dexterously combining factual narrative with imagination, humour with sympathy.

DIARY   *18th June, 1958*

I am very worried about the Lebanon situation, fearing it may prove a repetition of Suez. The difference is that (1) we have NATO backing; (2) we are in touch with UNO, and Hammarskjöld is flying out to Beirut to examine the situation on the spot; (3) if we intervene, it will be at the invitation of the Lebanese Government; (4) we have America with us. This differentiates the situation totally from Suez. Nonetheless, I think it a pity that we should intervene. Hugh Thomas comes in. He has a friend in the Lebanon who assures him that the Lebanese Government is a minority Government. If that is so, our intervention differs little from that of the Soviet in Budapest.

DIARY   *15th July, 1958*

Nigel telephones from the House to say that Selwyn Lloyd's announcement of the American landings at Beirut produced a storm on the Labour benches, with yells of 'Suez!' and 'Budapest!' Our own troops are not committed, but I suppose that if Jordan appeals for help we shall send some. William Clark says to me that the American action was inevitable, but that it should be so, is a condemnation of our diplomacy since 1953.

H.N. TO V.S-W.   *17th July, 1958*
                                                         C.1 Albany, W.1

I had a funny day. Jessica[1] picked me up in her car and drove me down to Strawberry Hill,[2] which is now a Catholic college. They have added to the original building but left the main rooms untouched. It confirmed what I have always said, that one must see a place oneself in order to get any idea of it. I had had the impression that Strawberry Hill was a somewhat gimcrack affair with heavy eighteenth-century Gothick. Not at all. It is a well-built house and the Gothick traceries which Horace Walpole introduced are copied from various chapels and churches and are of the utmost grace and

[1] Mrs Patrick Koppel, H.N.'s niece.
[2] The villa near Twickenham which Horace Walpole bought in 1747.

delicacy. It really is a very pretty house with wide lawns, which in his day sloped down to the river. While we were there a terrific thunderstorm descended and the lightning flashed through the armorial panes in the Gothick windows—just as old Horace would most have desired. I enjoyed it enormously.

V.S-W. TO H.N.   *13th August, 1958*
                                                        Sissinghurst

Do you know what happened at 9.30 last night? La Grande Mademoiselle died, aged 63. This does not mean that I have not still got a lot to do, but the book is so to speak finished, and another month should clear it up. Ouf!

H.N. TO V.S-W.   *10th September, 1958*
                                                    C.1 Albany, W.1

James [Pope-Hennessy] came in having had an interview with his Bank Manager which had depressed him, and thereafter an interview with the United Press who are handling the serial rights of *Queen Mary*, and by this he was elated. Nobody could say that James is ordinary, but, my word, how varied and *vivace* and *verde* is the life he leads! I told him that you had been shocked by the Windsor ménage. I said that you and I might differ in political opinions, but that we saw as one about *vulgarity*. Rich vulgarity is worse than poor vulgarity. In fact, when the latter descends to hop-picker level, it is not vulgarity at all. I said that what had shocked us was that he had half-admired the luxury of the Windsor mill. He said that we had 'feudal' conceptions and were class-conscious, whereas he had no class-consciousness at all. I said it was not snobbishness but fastidious-ness. I think he was slightly impressed, as he listens to what we say.

V.S-W. TO H.N.   *23rd September, 1958*
                                                    Sissinghurst

I am sorry I was tiresome to you, getting upset about Edie[1] yesterday morning. I know you hate emotional manifestations, and shy away. But sometimes one's feelings overcome one, and one bursts out.

[1] Mrs Lamont, a neighbour and a close friend of V.S-W. during her last years. She was widowed in 1960, and had a great interest in gardening, painting and books.

You see, if Edie died, I should really feel rather desolate. For one thing, she is about the only person who understands how much I love you, and would know what I would feel if you got ill or died. She is my only close friend. I haven't got many friends, and I don't want them, but it is nice to have one friend to whom one can talk openly, and if I lost Edie, I should have nobody left.

H.N. TO V.S-W.   *8th October, 1958*
                                                        C.1 Albany, W.1

How can you say that I never pay any attention to your worries and troubles? I devote more time to thinking about wasps which might sting you than I do to thinking about Voltaire or Diderot. Only I keep quiet about it. With half your heart and mind you must know that you are always at the centre of my thoughts. But I don't know how I can take any of the burden off you. I can just see you allowing me to discuss rents with Winch![1] Even when I go to get the Sunday papers from the library, I am restrained and scolded. A crushed life is what I lead, similar to that of the hen you ran over the other day. But I love you more than anyone has ever been loved.

H.N. TO V.S-W.   *16th October, 1958*
                                                        C.1 Albany, W.1

At noon I took a taxi to the German Embassy. I was waiting for the driver to give me change, when the portals of the house were flung open and out rushed a neat secretary who bowed low to me. The taximan must have been impressed. Then up I went to the Ambassador's private flat and the secretary bowed me in and left me alone. I started making amicable conversation, but the Ambassador said that he must first make an allocution and present me with my citation or *Verleihungsurkunde*. Then he made a set speech while I stood sufficiently stiffly to attune with my *visage de circonstance* but not exactly at attention, which might have seemed too military a pose. He then handed me a box containing *Das Grosse Verdienstkreuz mit Stern*. I then relaxed and we sat down and had a glass of excellent, indeed super, *Moselwein*. The Order consists of an enamelled dingle-dangle and a brass star. The *Verdienstkreuz* is awarded to distinguished men who have rendered services to Germany. I went away clasping

[1] Winch & Sons, the land-agents in Cranbrook.

my *Verleihungsurkunde* and my blue box with the star against my chest, thinking how you would have turned on the gramophone record about, 'I can't understand how you can possibly accept Orders from those horrible people who tried to destroy us.' But I was pleased.

V.S-W. TO H.N.   *21st October, 1958*
                                                    Sissinghurst

I've just got home from my Romney Marsh meeting.[1] It was really one of the best meetings I have ever attended. You know when everything goes right from the start to the end; everybody passionately interested; everybody in a good temper and prepared to be amused; everybody prepared to contribute what they wanted to say; and all the speakers real experts in their subjects—such nice men, speaking about trees, hedges, soil, birds, plants, drainage, badgers, foxes, pheasants—oh I wish you had been there! I wish you shared my Kentish interests instead of shaking the blood-stained hands of Germans in London. I gather from *The Times'* description of the drive from Victoria to the Palace[2] that the crowds were polite but not enthusiastic. I liked that bit about the buildings in Whitehall being 'dutifully' beflagged.

DIARY   *28th October, 1958*

There is an absurd article by Henry Fairlie in the *Daily Mail* attacking John Sparrow, Violet Bonham Carter and Sir William Haley as 'cardinals' of the Establishment. Three more disparate people I cannot conceive, and I suppose 'Establishment' means scholarship as opposed to red-brick technology.

H.N. TO V.S-W.   *30th October, 1958*
                                                    C.1 Albany, W.1

I had the American Professor Clifford[3] to luncheon yesterday. He was the man who wrote that really excellent book on the young Samuel Johnson. He was like all American professors I have ever

[1] A meeting called by the Council for the Preservation of Rural Kent.
[2] The State visit of President Heuss of the Federal Republic of Germany.
[3] Professor James L. Clifford, Professor of English at Columbia University since 1946. His *Young Samuel Johnson* was published in 1955.

known, from President Wilson downwards. They are affable and arid with wide smiles and stiff politeness. I asked the Professor if he had ever discovered what was the deep dark sin that weighed so heavily on Johnson's conscience. He said that the Doctor was certainly a masochist and enjoyed being tied up in chains by Mrs Thrale. That particular vice always strikes me as the most comic and unenjoyable of all. But Clifford thinks that he never went very far, and that it was not this that weighed on his conscience. He thinks that he always reproached himself for having deserted his wife when he came to London. He would go out to the coffee-house and spend hours with Garrick and Reynolds while she remained alone in Gough Square, and therefore took to tippling and died a miserable alcoholic. Johnson was so fundamentally good and loving that it may well have been that which poisoned him with remorse.

I went to Morley College for the opening of the new buildings by the Queen Mother. She was in her best mood and spirits. She has that astonishing gift of being sincerely interested in dull people and dull occasions. Really, the woodwork, the pottery and the drawings with which these Morley students occupy themselves in the evening are horrible objects. But the Queen Mother seemed really interested and spoke to almost all of them, putting them instantly at their ease. She asked after you, and I said that you had just finished your book and were planting bulbs. You know how much I like people who are good at their jobs (like Sidney[1] clipping the hedge in the herb-garden or indeed the limes), and she is superb at *her* job. Somehow she creates such an impression (indeed a radiance) of goodwill and good behaviour that no ill feelings could live or breed in such an atmosphere.

H.N. TO V.S-W.   *2nd November, 1958*
                                                     C.1 Albany, W.1

I am glad Edie [Lamont] is doing an index of your gardening articles. There is always the danger of writing about the same theme twice, with the added danger that one may say exactly the opposite the second time. Thus in March 1947 you may have said that those who plant *Esquilogia palpitans* must remember that they detest lime, and in July 1958 you will write: 'As all gardeners know, *Esquilogia*

---
[1] Sidney Neve, one of the gardeners at Sissinghurst.

palpitans only thrive if given a thick top-dressing (six inches deep at the very least—that does sound a lot, doesn't it, but I believe, don't you?, in doing things thoroughly or not at all) of quick (not slow, remember) lime.'

DIARY   *4th November, 1958*

I watch the enthronement of Pope John XXIII on television. The ceremony is badly rehearsed and conducted. Acolytes rush about making signs at other acolytes or whispering in the ear of the Vicar of God what he is expected to do next. It is a great technical achievement to be able to send this living photograph from St Peter's to Sissinghurst, but I get into the train feeling all my anti-Catholic and anti-priesthood sentiments very active.

DIARY   *11th November, 1958*

Nigel and I lunch together. He is worried what to do in the debate on the Wolfenden Report.[1] The mere fact that if he supports it he will seal his fate at Bournemouth makes him all the more eager to express his views openly and defy the consequences. All this is noble but inexpedient. Unfortunately Freddy Ayer[2] joins us, and Nigel asks him whether he thinks that the Government should lead or follow public opinion. Ayer is very positive—Government and Parliament must always be in advance of public opinion. That means a gulf fixed between the Member for Bournemouth East and his electors.

DIARY   *4th December, 1958*

I lunch in a private room at the Connaught at a luncheon given by David Astor for Igor Stravinsky.[3] He greeted me warmly. He tells me how much he enjoyed *Some People*, and what a delight *Journey to Java* had been to him and his wife. I groan inwardly. 'But of course', he adds, putting his hand on my shoulder, 'your best book is your life of your father.' I was overjoyed by that. He said that as a composer he admired technique, and that he felt my technique was

[1] Sir John Wolfenden's Report, which proposed, among other changes in the law, to legalise sexual relations between consenting male adults in private.
[2] A. J. Ayer, Professor of Philosophy in the University of London, 1946–59.
[3] The Russian composer (naturalised American in 1945) was then aged 76.

superb. I swelled with pride. He said how much he envied us writers, who had finished our work when the book was published. It was so different for a composer. His compositions, when played at Buenos Aires or Melbourne, were often entirely different from anything he had composed or intended.

Raymond [Mortimer] says that *Lolita*[1] is a work of literature and a cautionary tale with a moral purpose. but that the public would not see it as that, and would regard it as corrupting and obscene. I wish to God that Weidenfeld's were not publishing it.

V.S-W. TO N.N.   *29th December, 1958*

I did not intend to bother you about *Lolita*, knowing how bothered and badgered you have already been, but now that I have read it myself, I cannot refrain from adding my word to the chorus. I am afraid that I have been horrified and appalled by the thought that you might publish it.

You see, I was led to believe that it was

(a) a sort of cautionary tale and a warning
(b) a tragic story of an otherwise decent man suddenly overcome by a passion for a very young girl
(c) a work of literary value.

I now find that although (a) might in some sense be arguable, (b) and (c) could not possibly be sustained.

To take (b) and (c) in order:

(b) The man is not primarily a decent man at all. I know you will reply that the whole book is a study of a queer and unusual type of perversion. Had the author kept to that, and treated it as such in the sense of an otherwise normal and virile though possibly over-sexed man suddenly finding himself overwhelmingly attracted by his young step-daughter, it might have been tragically convincing. But it is not like that at all, as he constantly describes his feelings for other 'nymphets', and what shocked me above all was his speculation about the possibility of Lolita's daughter and even grand-

[1] The novel by Vladimir Nabokov, which had already become a matter of acute controversy in Britain and other countries. The main theme is the seduction of a girl of 12 by a middle-aged man, Humbert Humbert. In Britain it was published by Weidenfeld & Nicolson in 1959, and there was no prosecution of the book.

daughter succeeding to Lolita. This seemed to me a refinement of cynical vice.

It seemed to me also that it destroyed entirely what ought to have been the central theme of the book: his genuine, though to our minds revolting, passion for Lolita, and shows it up for what it was, merely physical lust unsupported by any intention of lasting affection. Even at the height of his desire for her, he can stop to wonder how to get rid of her as soon as she had ceased to be a 'nymphet'.

And of course the physical details, both in lascivious description and by implication, are (to my mind at least) disgusting.

(c) As to its literary value, I know that some critics have praised it. I can see none, except in one or two passages such as the survey of their journeyings across America. Surely the style alone condemns it? I don't know what language it was originally written in, nor whether this Olympia edition[1] is a translation into something which is not even bad American and certainly is not good English. You would probably reply that you would get a better translation made.

From what I have said, it must be clear how greatly I should deplore your firm publishing this book. It will do you infinite harm in Bournemouth, and possibly in any future constituency, and surely it will tarnish the bright name of Weidenfeld & Nicolson.

N.N. TO V.S-W.   *31st December, 1958*
                                 House of Commons, S.W.1

Thank you so much for your letter about *Lolita*. It was good of you to take so much trouble, and to give me so firm a warning. I have taken it to heart.

I agree that Humbert Humbert is a horrible man—horrible all through the book. That was one of the arguments in favour of publication. The reader is never on his side. If he had been a decent man, it might have suggested to another decent man that love of nymphets was an unfortunate but not wholly disreputable lapse. It suggests the opposite. I don't think you would say that a book about an immoral person is necessarily itself immoral. Some of the greatest tragedies in literature, like the *Agamemnon*, have dealt with horrible people and horrible perversions. So 'corrupting' is really the wrong

[1] *Lolita* had already been published in an English edition in Paris by the Olympia Press.

word. *Lolita* would not corrupt anyone except the already corrupted. What it might do is to shock and revolt them, and I think that this is the real case to be made against publication. It is your own main objection, and I think it very important. Even though the law does not permit the charge of 'shocking' to be brought against a publisher, it is one to which any publisher must obviously give great weight.

You don't think it a work of any literary value. (Incidentally, it was written in English, exactly as you read it: it is not a translation.) If it had no literary merit, the case for *Lolita* would collapse at once. I am rather surprised that you think it has so little. Quite a lot of people whose opinion you would respect think it a novel of outstanding quality. If you have the October (or possibly September) number of *Encounter*, read Lionel Trilling's article about it. Many other leading critics in England and America have praised it highly. So there is a conflict of respectable literary opinion about it. If we abandon publication, we will be accused of great cowardice and of having betrayed a principle. Obviously one must be prepared to face such a charge if necessary, but it is not a pleasant one.

I am as worried as you about it, and was most grateful for your advice.

V.S-W. TO H.N.   *31st December, 1958*
                                                    Sissinghurst

Tomorrow another folder will be added to the many folders containing your letters, which are kept in a special steel file. I hope that some day Niggs may publish a selection.

358

1959

Journey to the Far East – Port Said – Nigel's crisis in Bournemouth – H.N. in Saigon – his dislike of Japan and his pleasure at Macao – a distressing interview in Colombo about Guy Burgess – Nigel loses the Bournemouth poll – V.S-W.'s renewed illness – luncheon at No. 10 for Monsieur Michel Debré – Publication of 'Daughter of France' – H.N. on why he supports the Labour Party – his pleasure in the beauty of nature – the first moon-rocket – H.N.'s dislike of music – a letter from V.S-W. to H.N. about their marriage – James Bond – a world broadcast from Sissinghurst

1959

On 5th January they began their third winter-voyage, this time on the French ship 'Cambodge', which sailed from Marseilles through the Suez Canal to Aden, Bombay, Colombo, Singapore, Hong Kong, Tokyo and Saigon. Harold Nicolson wrote on board 40,000 words of 'The Age of Reason', and V. Sackville-West started her last novel, 'No Signposts in the Sea'.

It was during this voyage that my conflict with Bournemouth reached its climax. The Conservative candidate who had been adopted to replace me resigned in January, and Randolph Churchill suggested himself as a possible compromise candidate. Lord Hailsham, Chairman of the Conservative Party, intervened at this stage and persuaded the local Conservatives to agree to a postal ballot to decide the issue. Members of the Bournemouth East and Christchurch Conservative Association were asked to reply Yes or No to the question, 'Do you wish Mr Nicolson to be your official Conservative candidate at the next Election?' It was, in effect, the first primary election ever held in British political history. The votes were counted on 27th February, and I lost the ballot by 91 votes out of the 7,433 cast. I immediately offered to resign my seat, but I was asked to remain in Parliament until the General Election, which took place on 8th October.

For Harold Nicolson the year was also clouded by the virus pneumonia which V. Sackville-West contracted soon after her return from abroad. She remained bedridden for two months, April to June, but recovered fully, and at the end of the year embarked with Harold Nicolson on a fourth voyage—to South Africa.

DIARY

5th January, 1959
Paris

As we leave Boulogne, I wave at it, and Vita says, 'Who are you waving at?' I reply, 'I am greeting Sainte-Beuve.' The waiter is pleased at this, and smiles delightedly. What English waiter would understand an analogous greeting to Wordsworth? We reach the Gare du Nord an hour late, and then dawdle round the *ceinture*. The train slides past the lighted windows of tenements, and for a flash we see brass chandeliers with red shades and the evening meal below them. Unknown lives. We dine and then go to bed.

DIARY   *8th January, 1959*
                                              'Cambodge', in the Mediterranean

A happy day at sea, and I start on Chapter I of my book on the eighteenth century, doing Saint-Simon, Louis XIV and the beginning of the War of the Spanish Succession. At 4 we pass Gavdos, the island off Crete. It has the peculiar Greek look of crinkled tissue-paper.

DIARY   *9th January, 1959*
                                                          'Cambodge', Port Said

At 3.30 the houses of Port Said rise suddenly *anadyomenai*.[1] After hanging about for the pilot we enter the harbour. As we pass the mole I see the truncated plinth where once rose the statue of de Lesseps.[2] The base remains with its laurel-wreath and the words 'de Lesseps', but the statue has been torn away. It is curious to see the sky-signs intact, advertising Craven A for your throat's sake, and Johnnie Walker and Perrier water.

When I was last in Port Said in 1937, it was still oriental. Not a soul without a turban or tarboosh, and the waterfront men in the long pink and blue *djelabs*. Now they wear western clothes and cloth caps, and the glamour of the East has gone. I sit in the smoking-room reading Diderot, and then a newsvendor squirms in and I buy the *Progrès Egyptien*. It sneers at Macmillan for employing Mr [Eugene] Black, the American President of the World Bank, as negotiator of the Anglo-Egyptian agreement on compensation, on the grounds that it is too humiliating for an Englishman to admit that the invasion of Egypt was a wanton aggression.

We remain at Port Said until midnight, when we make our leisurely way down the Canal, our life-line.

[1] Greek for 'rising from the sea'.
[2] Ferdinand de Lesseps, the French engineer who built the Suez Canal between 1859 and 1869.

H.N. TO N.N.   *17th January, 1959*
                                              'Cambodge', Bombay

A pearly grey morning today, and I was leaning out of my balcony
as the ship slid into this harbour, with the fishing boats putting out
for an early, pearly swim and strange marine birds circling. Then
we were given your cable, saying that Friend[1] had resigned and
Randolph [Churchill] was a candidate for the succession. I fail to
see how Major Grant, having sacked you for opposing Suez, can
admit Randolph whose attack on the Eden policy was ten times
more vehement. The result will be to expose the Executive to
ridicule, and I always felt that ridicule was your best weapon.

By the post we got a long article by Taper[2] on *Lolita*. These
articles in support of the book only make your position more awkward, since you will now have to publish it. But I remain convinced
that the book will be regarded as corrupting and obscene by 99
per cent of the public, and that your firm will lose in repute. I
rather wish I was in England while all this is going on. It has been
my custom hitherto to pat little girls on the head when I find them
playing on deck. Since *Lolita* I avert my gaze, not wishing to be
suspected of *libido senilis*. I am sure that the publication of that book
will ruin your political prospects.

DIARY   *26th January, 1959*
                                                          Saigon

We steam up the delta to Saigon with mangrove swamps on either
hand. It is very hot, and I write about Peter the Great. We get to
Saigon at 3. What the stewardess calls *les misérables* clamber on
board, jabbering and pushing. The sun sets at 6, and Viti and I find
ourselves almost alone on board, and we watch the moon rise over
the Mekong. Some little tonkinoises come on board with their
babies. Viti waves to the little girls in yellow coats and neat white
trousers, and they come up to our chairs, cross their arms and bow
low. It is very pretty. Philip and Jewell [Magnus-Allcroft] get back
for dinner and we sit out in the slight breeze under the full moon.
Little sampans pass and repass with a single light at the bow. It is
all very beautiful. My enjoyment is intense.

[1] Major James Friend, the official Conservative candidate.
[2] Pseudonym for Bernard Levin.

6th February, 1959
                                                                Tokyo, Japan

We take the train from Kobe to Kyoto. It is like the Underground, and we have to stand as far as Osaka. The countryside is hideous beyond belief—pylons, factories constructed in dirty grey cement, endless electric cables and telegraph poles, shanties, dumps—worse than anything I have seen. The Japanese, for all their exquisite social etiquette, are bad-mannered corporately. There are lots of young men sitting down, but not one of them offers Vita a seat. What an ugly, loathsome race! At Kyoto we go round the temples and the shrine garden. Nothing seems to date here. A 1200 A.D. temple is exactly the same as an 800 A.D. temple or a 1867 temple. Ugly Etruscan red columns and shabby pine-trees. The garden is large and very Japanese. Cherries trained carefully over bamboo baskets like wistaria, and masses of azalea which must be a blaze of ill-matching colour when in flower. Get back to the ship and go to bed early, having found Kyoto a terrible disappointment.

13th February, 1959
                                                                      Macao

We drive to the gate which separates Macao[1] from China, a sort of triumphal arch with the Portuguese flag flying. We are not allowed within 100 yards of the barrier, but can see the lines of barbed wire and some Chinese Communist sentries beyond. What fascinates us about Macao is that it is on the one hand exactly like some small Mediterranean port, with houses in the Portuguese style and faint baroque plasterwork with old shutters. Then the streets are arcaded and vivid Chinese shop-signs hang over them and the pillars of the arcades are painted in Chinese characters in red and blue. We find it unlike anything we have ever seen before for the mingling of two traditions. The Chinese junks of the fishing-fleet sail out with their bat wings and the horizon is lined by sailing boats exactly like an eighteenth-century water-colour. Only Viti could share my appreciation and love of this sort of odd mixture.

---

[1] The Portuguese colony opposite Hong Kong island.

DIARY   *25th February, 1959*
                                                                    Colombo

The happiness of the day is clouded by a distressing episode. A
Cingalese newspaper-man rushed up to me. 'Oh Sir Harold', he said,
'I have been waiting for you for four hours. I have a cable to discuss
with you.' I took him to my cabin and he undid his telegram. It ran
something as follows: 'Our Moscow correspondent reports that at
Press Conference Guy Burgess stated that he had asked Prime
Minister for safe conduct to England and back to Russia to see his
mother who is seriously ill. Macmillan, when asked, said it was not
for him to intervene: the Law must take its course. In subsequent
conversation Burgess said that the only one of his former friends who
had kept in touch with him was Harold Nicolson, who had written
regularly. Please get in touch with Nicolson, passenger Cambodge,
arriving Colombo February 25, and ask him to confirm.' I replied
that certainly I had written to Guy since I felt sorry for him, as he
had acted on impulse, and that my principle was not to desert friends
in distress. But that I had written not one word which could not be
published in any newspaper. I made him repeat this, since I do not
trust the accuracy of Cingalese reporters when faced with a scoop.
God knows what he will say.

My first thought was, of course, of its effect on Niggs. If this
tasty bit of news had come out ten days ago, it would have dished
his chances, small though they are. But luckily the ballot is now
closed, and the result may be announced today or tomorrow. Yet,
all the same, if he is turned down by Bournemouth, this news may
make other Associations hesitate to adopt him. I am wretched about
this. What gremlins dog his every step—*Lolita*, and now his father!

I am so upset that when I get to my cabin, I am sick. I seldom
vomit; but now I do, good and proper.

N.N. TO H.N. (*cable to 'Cambodge'*)   *26th February, 1959*
                                                                    London

Votes for me 3671. Against 3762. Lost by 91.

H.N. TO N.N.   *27th February, 1959*
                                       'Cambodge', approaching Bombay

At twenty to eight this morning there came a knock on my cabin door. It was my steward, with a telegram in his hand. I guessed it was the result of the Bournemouth ballot, but I had resolved not to open the cable except when Mummy was there. So I put it on my little table, with a watch on top of it to keep it in place. Then I went and bathed in the waters of the Indian Ocean, had my fresh-water shower, shaved, dressed, and went to Mummy's cabin across the way. She was just up and in her dressing-gown. It was 8.20 am. She slit open the envelope with her paper-cutter and read the contents. 'He has lost', she said sadly.

Our first reaction was emotional. We were enraged that you should have lost. Although you had repeatedly warned us to anticipate defeat, and although we had never really expected victory, the emotional shock when it came was distressing. Then blessed reason came to our aid. In the first place, the figures were nothing like a moral defeat and justified the whole battle. In the second place, if you had got a *majority* of only 91, it would have been difficult for you to carry on. You would have felt that almost half your constituents were bitterly opposed. In the third place, such disappointments are very transient, provided that one has done nothing either dishonourable or foolish.

N.N. TO H.N. (*at Suez*)   *27th February, 1959*
                                                      House of Commons

I went to the smoking-room late last night, and was surrounded by Members who commiserated with me. The Chief Whip, Ted Heath, came up to me, and I told him that I feared that if my immediate resignation were not accepted, my position in the House for the remainder of this Parliament might be a difficult one. 'Don't believe that for a moment', he said. 'Nobody feels anything but respect for your attitude. You have done well, and served the Party most creditably.' I was delighted by this, as he was quite clearly speaking with real conviction, and not as a formal condolence. Maurice Macmillan was particularly generous in his sympathy, and many others, of both Parties, some of whom I had scarcely spoken to in my life, laid a hand on my shoulder as they passed, and said,

'I am so sorry'. That was much the best way of expressing what they felt. There were no histrionics, and I loved the House more than I have ever loved it before.

DIARY
9th March, 1959
'Cambodge', in the Mediterranean

Vita's birthday.[1] I wake up at 7, and there outside my balcony are the Cretan mountains, with on my right the red ball of the sun rising above the tumbled waters and just illuminating the snow-crests. I go along to Vita's cabin. She is as entranced as I knew she would be, and it was a nice birthday present for God to have given her.

H.N. TO V.S-W.
13th April, 1959
C.1 Albany, W.1

I do so hate your being ill. Not that I am as worried as I was in the *Reina del Mar*, since I have more confidence in our local doctor than I had in the ship's doctor, and we have better means of testing here than we had on the wide, wide Atlantic. But I am confirmed in my previous impression that nothing is interesting or beautiful or amus-ing unless you share it with me. Even this wonderful spring and the splendour of the spring-border is meaningless without you:

From you have I been absent in the spring,
When proud-pied April, dress'd in all his trim,
Hath put a spirit of youth in everything.
Nor did I wonder at the lilies white,
Nor praise the deep vermilion in the rose[2]

although even the proudest-pied April could scarcely have flaunted a rose, vermilion or other.

Oh my darling, how I hate you suffering, even as you would hate me to suffer. How deep is our devotion to each other! But I am not jealous, and do not mind how many of your friends visit you, so long as they do not tire you out. You say that jealousy is the symp-tom and concomitant of true love. But I disagree. It is an emerald-eyed lizard.

[1] She was 67.
[2] Shakespeare. Sonnet 98.

367

V.S-W. TO H.N.   *14th April, 1959*
                                                          Sissinghurst

It is not glandular fever, as I suspected, but virus pneumonia. That sounded very odd to me, as I associated pneumonia with a cough and a pain in the lungs; but it seems that I was wrong. I think our doctor must be rather clever, because he suspected it on Saturday and the blood-test confirms it. It is not dangerous unless one does something silly, which I am afraid would include going to look at the spring-border. I asked him.

H.N. TO V.S-W.   *14th April, 1959*
                                                          C.1 Albany, W.1

I had a charming lunch at No 10. Delicious food and wine. We discussed what books had first influenced us. Debré[1] (who is a nice *Ecole Normale* type) said it had been *Le Livre de la Jungle* by Kipling. Nye Bevan said it had been *Le Rouge et le Noir*. So that was a fine interchange of Anglo-French compliments. Couve de Murville was polite, and sent his compliments to Madame. He is so dry and plain, like a biscuit. I like the way we invite the Opposition leaders on such occasions. Both Gaitskell and Nye were there.

V.S-W.'S DIARY   *17th April, 1959*

100. It seems such a small temperature, but I do feel very ill.

H.N. TO V.S-W.   *13th May, 1959*
                                                          C.1 Albany, W.1

A bookseller told me that *Mademoiselle* was selling like hot cakes. I don't know how hot cakes sell, and in fact I have never witnessed the process. But I thanked God that she was well launched before this horrible illness descended on you.

DIARY   *31st May, 1959*

I start working on my American chapter [of *The Age of Reason*], but am badly interrupted. Christopher Hussey comes with Osbert

---

[1] The Prime Minister's luncheon was in honour of Michel Debré, Prime Minister of France, 1959–62.

Lancaster: then Joan Lascelles. Then Victor Mallet[1] with two Americans. Vita stays in bed for luncheon, but gets up afterwards. She minds terribly being *la prisonnière*, and actually sobbed with rage at having missed Osbert and Joan. It is now eight weeks since she was bed-ridden and I do absolutely understand her rage. But I can do little. She regards me as so incompetent in practical matters that she has no confidence in anything except my love.

DIARY   *24th June, 1959*

I go to Transport House and record this flash for the Labour Party to broadcast:

'Why should I, who have had a luxury education and lived a luxury life, vote Labour? Because I believe that they will do more than any other Party to secure equality of opportunity and to solve without violence the African problem, which may become the central problem of the next fifty years.'

H.N. TO V.S-W.   *30th June, 1959*
                                                            C.1 Albany, W.1

My Party no longer really believes in nationalisation. How can they say that private enterprise is a failure, when it has rescued us from a serious slump? But Niggs agrees with me that the problem of the future is not that, nor even the atom-bomb, but Africa. There may be civil war in South Africa and that will spread to Nyasaland and Kenya. We cannot suppress the darkies by shooting them. In fact the rule of Empire is over, and I fear that the Tories will not face the fact. Niggs is worried about his own attitude, not wishing again to dissent from his Party on a major issue.

DIARY   *7th August, 1959*

The Queen is to have another baby in January or February. What a sentimental hold the monarchy has over the middle classes! All the solicitors, actors and publishers at the Garrick were beaming as if they had acquired some personal benefit.

---

[1] British Ambassador in Rome, 1947–53.

H.N. TO V.S-W.   *8th September, 1959*
                                                  C.1 Albany, W.1

What a lovely morning! Sun coming through mist. It was pleasant sitting with you on the bench under the catalpa discussing why so many of our friends were discontented or unhappy. I still maintain that it is worse to muck up one's life by one's own fault than through an act of God or someone else's fault. It adds self-reproach and guilt-feelings to misfortune. You and I can at least feel that we have got the most out of such talents as God gave us. But I believe that the gift I most appreciate is the gift of seeing beauty. Why should I experience such a spurt of pleasure at seeing the tower of Staplehurst church catch the sun through fog? And why should that pleasure be doubled if you are there to share it? Oh bless you, my saint, for giving me such a happy life.

H.N. TO V.S-W.   *14th September, 1959*
                                                  C.1 Albany, W.1

I hate the lunik for having bumped into the radiant moon.[1] 'With how sad steps, O Moon, thou clim'st the skies!'[2]—and then bump, crash, comes a metal projectile from Russia. I should like to feel that Selene would respond by killing Khrushchev and his scientists. Nothing remains inviolate, and no longer shall we enjoy the illusion that that great shining globe represents the unattainable. They will hit Hesperus next—'Hesperus, thou dear jewel of the dark blue night', as Simonides wrote, never foreseeing that one day it would be bumped by Soviet bombs. Moreover, I think it ostentatious for Khrushchev to have achieved this feat on the eve of his visit to the U.S.A. It is as if one were about to visit the Bishop of Peterborough and sent down a French chef in advance. I call it bad manners.

H.N. TO V.S-W.   *3rd November, 1959*
                                                  C.1 Albany, W.1

Niggs tells me that Vladimir Nabokov said to him that all his life he has been fighting against the influence of *Some People*. 'The style of that book', he said, 'is like a drug.' Well, I can assure him that

[1] This was the first Soviet moon-rocket.
[2] Sir Philip Sidney (1554–86). Sonnet 31.

Lolita is not likely to influence me. Nigel has taken a liking to Nabokov, and above all to Madame Nabokov. They have not yet heard a word from the Attorney-General.[1]

H.N. TO V.S-W.   *18th November, 1959*
                                            C.1 Albany, W.1

I lunched with the Swiss Ambassador, and his Cultural Attaché talked to me about the great conductors of the world and how the Philharmonic was about the best orchestra in the world and the Festival Hall without doubt the best theatre. I said I never went to a concert. He looked as if he could not believe his ears, as if I had said, 'It's no use talking to me about books: I haven't read a book for fifteen years.' I suppose my dislike of music must strike the cultured foreigner as an astonishing lack of taste and education.

DIARY   *21st November, 1959*

My birthday. I don't feel a day over 73.[2]

DIARY   *22nd November, 1959*

As I was forced yesterday to spend the whole day reading about Napoleon, I gave myself a treat, or what I expected to be a treat, by reading Ian Fleming's adventure story about James Bond, called *Goldfinger*. I had been told that it was as good as Simenon. This is nonsense, since Simenon always manages to convince one of the truth of his stories, whereas Fleming is so fantastic as to arouse disbelief. This story is too improbable to arouse interest, nor do I like the underlying atmosphere of violence, luxury and lust. I regard it as an obscene book, 'liable to corrupt'.

V.S-W. TO H.N.   *24th November, 1959*
                                            Sissinghurst

You've gone away again, into the different life you lead in London. It is an odd sort of life we have evolved for ourselves—me here, and you in London, and then both of us in our real home over the ends

---

[1] There was still acute controversy over the book. My firm sent the Director of Public Prosecutions an advance copy, so that if he chose to prosecute, he could do so before the book became generally available to the public.

[2] He was 73.

Nov. 24.
1959

V. Sackville-West,
Sissinghurst Castle, Kent.

My Hadji
    You've gone away again, into the
different life you lead in London.
It is an odd sort of life we have
evolved for ourselves — me here,
and you in London, and ten both of
us in our real home over the ends of
the week, so happy and quiet and
busy. Few people would understand
it, in fact people often think that
we are on the verge of divorce.
    How wrong they are.
    How wrong!
        Your Mar

of the week, so happy and quiet and busy. Few people would understand it, in fact people often think that we are on the verge of
divorce.

How wrong they are.

How wrong!

H.N. TO V.S-W.   *27th November, 1959*
                                         C.1 Albany, W.1

I had the Keats-Shelley Committee. They mumble, and I am deaf.
I ought never to have been chosen as Chairman in my dotage, as
I really do not hear properly and can never recognise people. In fact,
I am like an old discarded motor-car, fit only to be thrown on the
dump outside Cleveland Oh! Hi! Oh!—or an old horse like Fox-
hunter fit only for munching and staring over the hedge at passing
trains.

V.S-W. TO H.N.   *9th December, 1959*
                                         Sissinghurst

It always makes me cross when Max [Beerbohm] is called 'The
Incomparable Max'. He is not incomparable at all, and in fact com-
pares very poorly with Harold Nicolson, as a stylist, a wit, and an
observer of human nature. He is a shallow, affected, self-conscious
fribble—so there.

DIARY   *26th December, 1959*
                                         Sissinghurst

In the afternoon vans arrive bearing Mr Maclure of the Columbia
Broadcasting System, two French electricians and three others,
together with vast trunks and suitcases. They establish their apparatus
in the kitchen and dining-room and store-cupboard. I am sat down
in a chair by the fire and lights are adjusted. It takes from 5 pm. to
7 pm.[1] Viti is enraged. I talk to Ed Murrow at St Moritz, to Mrs
Luce in (I think) Los Angeles, and to Chip Bohlen[2] in New York. I
do not see their faces, since the television pictures are put together
later, but I do hear their voices, and we indulge in a three-cornered

[1] This was one of Ed Murrow's *Small World* hook-ups.
[2] Charles E. Bohlen, American Ambassador to the U.S.S.R., 1953–57, and Assistant to the Secretary of State, 1959–62.

discussion on the function of diplomacy. It seems to me to go rather well, but Viti is so angry that she gets bored. At the end they take a final shot of me, pack their many trunks, and sloop off into the night, while the wind howls across the fields and woods. Viti feels that I have been exploited, put-upon, taken advantage of, and maybe made a fool of.

1960

A journey to South Africa – Zanzibar – Apartheid – Harold Macmillan's 'wind of change' speech in Cape Town – Princess Margaret marries Antony Armstrong-Jones – the Prime Minister elected Chancellor of Oxford University – H.N. on snobbishness – meets the Prime Minister at the American Embassy – V.S-W. on the award of the O.M. – 'The Age of Reason' finished – break-down of the Summit Conference in Paris – 'Monarchy' – death of Aneurin Bevan – the Congo crisis – the character of bores – conflict within the Labour Party on Britain's atomic weapons – 'No Signposts in the Sea' – election of President Kennedy – dedication of a Memorial to Duff Cooper – the problem of Guy Burgess' return to England – 'I know that I am going gaga'

The 1960 journey (on the Lloyd-Triestino liner 'Europa') was from Venice, through the Suez Canal, down the East coast of Africa to Zanzibar, Durban and Cape Town, and back by the same route. V. Sackville-West wrote much of 'No Signposts in the Sea' on this voyage, and Harold Nicolson of 'The Age of Reason'. The latter was published in December and the former early in 1961. He then contemplated a book on Goethe, but abandoned it for his last book, 'Monarchy', on which he was well launched by the year's end.

For each of them the weekly article for the 'Observer' acted like a metronome, and there were few events to upset the long established rhythm of their lives, except a recurrence of V. Sackville-West's virus pneumonia, which immobilised her for two months in mid-summer.

It was the year of Harold Macmillan's 'Wind of Change' speech in South Africa, of the abortive Summit Conference in Paris, of the United Nations' intervention in the Congo, and of J. F. Kennedy's emergence on the world stage as President of the United States.

H.N. TO P.N. & N.N.   *3rd January, 1960*
                                              S.S. 'Europa', Suez Canal

I shall post this from Suez, or preferably Aden, since I do not wish to add even the value of a stamp to the exchequer of the U.A.R.

All goes well so far—touch wood, hard and frequently as if it were a xylophone. Vita is wonderfully well. It is a lovely ship, as clean as a new pin, very fast, very steady. The waiters are on the look-out to please. The food is like that of a good Italian restaurant. The band plays Puccini all afternoon and evening, and there is an excellent cinema after dinner. I work hard. Vita has started again on her novel, which takes place on a ship, so she can absorb local colour.

12th January, 1960
S.S. 'Europa', Zanzibar

We leave Mombasa at 5 am. We get to Zanzibar at 2 pm. We go
ashore in a launch. We take a rickshaw pulled by a bowed old dotard
and pushed by his aged son from behind. We creep along at ½ a
mile an hour, but it is a good plan, as the streets are so narrow that
no taxi could pass through them. There are Moorish-looking
houses and doors, but it shows one what miles ahead the Moors were
artistically, since all the Slave Trade carvings are ill-shaped and
crude. We go to the site of the old slave market on which now
rises a cathedral of unusual ugliness. The flowering trees here are far
better than in Ceylon. We have never seen so many or such bril-
liantly blooming flamboyants before. We see a clove-tree growing
like an unhappy olive-tree; we see cloves drying on mats: but the
story that the whole island smells of cloves and apple-tart is a legend.

H.N. TO N.N. & P.N.   *24th January, 1960*
S.S. 'Europa', Port Elizabeth

I cannot describe to you the horrors of Apartheid. I asked an Englishman how one pronounced the word, and he said 'Apart'—pause—
'hate'. And by God, hate it is! It is far, far worse than anything I
had supposed. I was shocked when first landing at Durban to observe
that all the seats along the esplanade (*all* of them, literally) were
marked 'For whites only'. I was shocked when I found that in the
vast Post Office at Cape Town there are counters for the whites and
separate counters for the Negroes. In fury, I queued up behind three
Negroes, but when my turn came, the clerk said to me, 'Sorry, sir,
you are at the wrong desk'. The clerk was himself black. So my
demonstration was fruitless.

At Cape Town I met John Maud, the High Commissioner. He
was discreet, of course, and loyal to the Government to which he
is accredited, but he evidently feels it bitterly. 'Injustice hangs in the
air', he murmured as I was praising the beauty of his house and
garden. But when we got to this little port, the flavour of it hit us
in the face. The Press came to see us as usual, and on this occasion it
consisted of two women and a man who represented a liberal
evening newspaper. What they told us was startling. Their letters
are opened, their visitors noted, their telephones are tapped and

microphones are concealed in their office. The girl was arrested for talking to a coloured fellow-student, and now she won't be able to go abroad as they will refuse her a passport. They told us that many of the white settlers of English origin were just as extreme on Apartheid as the native white South Africans. It is almost certain that the Union will declare itself a Republic and leave the Commonwealth. They want to provoke a Zulu rising and then shoot the Negroes down. They fear that this will shock U.N. opinion and that we will not support them. So they want to be clear of our 'governessy' supervision. These journalists are anxious to see what Harold Macmillan will say when he addresses the Legislature in Cape Town.[1] He is bound to offend somebody, even by his omissions. They want him to say, 'Well, leave the Commonwealth if you want to! You are a moral liability to us. But realise that if you do, you will become a foreign country and will lose all the benefits of Empire preference.'

You know how I hate Negroes and how Tory Vita is. But I do hate injustice more than I hate Negroes, and Vita screams with rage. Fists of execration are raised on high. But truly, you have no conception how shocking it all is. The complete police state. How happy we are with our freedom and Parliamentary Questions! I could not live in this Nazi country in constant fear of the Gestapo. *Fieri sentio, et excrucior*.[2] God bless our little island! God bless her as a jewel of justice!

DIARY   *4th February, 1960*
                                             S.S. 'Europa', Somaliland

We are sliding along the coast of Somaliland. The radio news says that Macmillan made it absolutely clear at Cape Town that we disapprove of their racial policy. That was a courageous thing to do, and I am delighted.

I finish the fourth volume of Hill's edition of Boswell while watching the endless line of Somali scrub. I detect four camels plodding along the beach. At 6.15 we get to Mogadishu, where the port and town-lights are lovely against the remains of a sunset. People come aboard, and we are told that the poverty of Somaliland

[1] On 3rd February. This was his 'Wind of Change' speech.
[2] 'I feel that it is happening, and I am in agony.' *Catullus*.

is heart-breaking, and that the Somalis will never be able to run the country themselves. It is madness to say that they are ripe for self-government. It merely means corruption, impoverishment and cruelty. But the moment one is not prepared to shoot people for disobedience, one simply has to let them have their independence.

DIARY   28th February, 1960
                                                    Sissinghurst

The 6 pm. news announces the engagement of Princess Margaret to Antony Armstrong-Jones. What a sell for the Press who missed the scoop! I am glad, as I did not want that gay girl to be condemned to perpetual maidenhood.

DIARY   3rd March, 1960
                                                       Oxford

I go up to Oxford to vote in the election for the Chancellorship of the University. It is between Harold Macmillan and Oliver Franks. Kenneth Rose comes with me. There are many people on the train intent on the same purpose.[1] John [Sparrow] lends me a cap and gown, and I walk across to the Divinity Schools to record my vote for Macmillan. It is all very quiet and dignified, but no precautions seem to have been taken to prevent people voting twice and I see no system by which they check qualifications. But there must be a register in the background. How I love the Oxford manner! No fuss, no pompousness, but everything easy-going and dignified, and, I hope, efficient. I then go to Balliol, where I sit in the garden quad for a bit and observe as many as three heavily bearded undergraduates, like young apostles. They are redoing the College library.

DIARY   8th March, 1960

John Wyndham says that the Prime Minister was much amused by my statement that after his Cape Town speech I would have voted for him even if he had been, not at Balliol, but at Merton.

---

[1] All graduates of the University were entitled to vote. The Prime Minister won the Election by a comfortable majority.

DIARY   *13th March, 1960*

Go on checking my chapters [of *The Age of Reason*]. It is a rotten book, and it saddens me. A happy quiet day. The girls [1] really have, by their energy and reliability, added much to Vita's contentment with the garden. They are splendid girls.

H.N. TO V.S-W.   *17th March, 1960*
                                         C.1 Albany, W.1

I had some American television men who interviewed me for a feature they are doing on Piccadilly. They asked me whether I do not feel embarrassed by the fact that the porters here wear tail-coats and top-hats. I said that I should feel much more embarrassed if they didn't, since people might mistake me for a porter on the way out. I could see that they thought me very snobbish and old-fashioned. They asked whether the Albany was not 'a privileged sanctuary'. I said, Yes, it was. I added that highly developed civilisations specialise in variety, whereas lower civilisations impose uniformity. That was not a welcome remark.

DIARY   *21st March, 1960*

I dine at the American Embassy. A small party—the Queen Mother, the Prime Minister and Lady Dorothy [Macmillan], the Chancellor of the Exchequer,[2] the Profumos[3] and Jeremy Tree.[4] I sit between Mrs Whitney, the Ambassadress, and Mrs Profumo, but as the P.M. is on Mrs Whitney's other side, we talk across.

He was delighted at having won the Oxford election. He said he regretted the Summit Conference being called 'the' and not 'a'. He quoted me as having said somewhere that the greatest diplomatic asset was the passage of time, and that a regular series of summit conferences, held, say, every four years, would prevent a breach and allow time to flow. He foresaw that in thirty years, if there was

[1] Pamela Schwerdt and Sibylle Kreutzberger, who came to Sissinghurst as head-gardeners in October 1959.
[2] Derick Heathcoat Amory, created Viscount Amory later in 1960.
[3] John Profumo, then Minister of State for Foreign Affairs. He became Secretary of State for War in July 1960. His wife was Valerie Hobson, the actress.
[4] The son of H.N.'s old friend, Ronald Tree. His mother, Nancy Tree, was American.

no war, Russia would become more bourgeois and the gap would narrow. He said that he hoped that Khrushchev would remain in power, as he was personally pledged to peace. He said that he had found de Gaulle much mellowed and very sensible. He had found the bloody Boers of Cape Town 'very nice and friendly'. As he was saying this, they were shooting Bantus in Johannesburg. I thought him in wonderful form—wise and gay. I have seldom enjoyed a dinner more.

V.S-W. TO H.N.   *23rd March, 1960*
                                                 Sissinghurst

I have been thinking over what you said about the award of the O.M. Look, you know that I am not a mean-minded or envious person, and I think I could quite objectively rejoice in this award to Edith [Sitwell] if I thought she deserved it. But I don't. I feel that Edith has built up her personality in many fortuitous ways—her strange appearance, her lovely hands, her Dantesque headdress, and all the Sitwellian legend. But I cannot feel that she is a great poet. A great personality, yes; a true eccentric; but not a major poet. Not worthy of the O.M. She has not the stature. But the worst of it is that I cannot think of *anybody* worthy of the O.M. What an awful reflection on English literature today! Cecil Day Lewis? No. David Cecil? No. Stephen Spender? No. Wystan Auden? No. But then who? I think on the whole I would vote for Kenneth Clark, who combines literature and the arts. He does write so well—like his book on Leonardo and *The Nude*. He would be my candidate.

Prince Andrew looks a nice baby.[1] He looks a person already, not like a poached-egg, like most new-born babies. And did you notice what a startling resemblance he bears to his grandfather George VI?

H.N. TO JULIET NICOLSON (*aged 5*)   *16th April, 1960*
                                                 Sissinghurst

Your mother says that you have started to read, and so I shall ask Messrs. Hatchard to send you a book. I do beg you to acquire the reading habit when young. It is mainly a habit, and once you get it,

---

[1] Prince Andrew was born on 19th February, 1960, and the first photographs of him had just been published.

382

you never lose it, like bicycling or riding or eating jelly cleanly or blowing your nose or being polite to the girls in post-offices or not interrupting one's parents or grandparents when they are writing newspaper articles or making a sauce for *quenelles de brochet*.

Oh my darling Juliet, I am so looking forward to your visit here! Shall I see you dressed as a bridesmaid? 'A happy bridesmaid makes a happy bride.' That was written by the poet Tennyson, and, my word, he really did marry the bridesmaid and lived happily ever after. She was a delicate woman and spent most of her day lying on the sofa under a huge cashmere shawl sent by her son in India. And (since you enjoy stories about the deaths of other people) he died in India, or rather on the boat coming back to England, and he was buried in the Dead Sea, I mean the Red Sea, in a 'heavy-shotted hammock shroud'.[1] Splash, he went, and there were no more shawls for his delicate mother.

H.N. TO V.S-W.   *10th May, 1960*
                                           C.1 Albany, W.1

I am relieved that I have finished *The Age of Reason*; relieved, but not elated. It is certainly a monument, but not *aere perennius*.[2] I fear it is very dull, and so second-hand that it is second-rate. Poor old Hadji. Decline and fall, that's what it is. But I did not feel so exhausted after our walk through the woods as I expected. And I did so love that walk—you, bluebells, blossom, a rainbow and a cuckoo's song.[3]

H.N. TO V.S-W.   *19th May, 1960*
                                           C.1 Albany, W.1

Jim [Lees-Milne] and I sat in Albany listening to Khrushchev howling

[1] '*His heavy-shotted hammock-shroud*
   Drops in his vast and wandering grave.'
      Tennyson's *In Memoriam*, **vi**.
[2] *Exegi monumentum aere perennius*. Horace, *Odes*. 'My work is done, a memorial more enduring than brass.'
[3] '*A rainbow and a cuckoo's song*
   May never come together again.'
      W. H. Davies (1870-1940)

in the Palais Chaillot.[1] I heard the boos with pleasure. He sounded a little mad, I thought, and Miss Macmillan[2] says he was 'like a school-boy searching for rude words', which was true. But truly the Ukrain-ian moujik surpassed himself, and as an old diplomatist I became confirmed in my view that the exchange of insults is not the best method of conducting negotiations between sovereign states. I find great sympathy and affection expressed here for Ike Eisenhower. I confess that I am shocked that so old and dignified a man should be held up to ridicule and abuse.

DIARY   20th May, 1960

I was worried last night about my budget. At breakfast I told Niggs that I must get a job as a hack-writer who wrote the history of City Companies, and that I should have to ask for a fee of £5,000; otherwise I should have to give up living in the Albany. He said, 'Well, I must see what can be done about it.' He goes off to his office and returns in an hour to put a proposal to me from George Weidenfeld. It is that I should write a book on Monarchy. I may take two years on it, do only 70,000 words, and I am to get £1,500 on signature of contract, £1,500 next year, and £2,000 on delivery of the manuscript—£5,000 in all. Thus my dread of having to leave the Albany and alter my whole way of life is removed in 1½ hours.

DIARY   6th July, 1960

Nye Bevan dies at 4.15 in the afternoon.[3] I regret the loss of this splendid coloured figure and a great parliamentarian and patriot. When I was once being scolded for being malicious in my descrip-tions of people, Nye protested, 'Harold is not malicious at all. He is the angel of pity.'

DIARY   15th July, 1960

Khrushchev has announced that the Monroe Doctrine is dead, that

[1] The Summit Conference in Paris, between Macmillan, Eisenhower and Khrush-chev, had ended scarcely before it had properly begun, on the Russian pretext that American U.2 'spy-planes' over Soviet territory had rendered negotiation between them futile.
[2] H.N.'s housekeeper at Albany.
[3] Aneurin Bevan was 62.

he will back Fidel Castro if necessary by force, and that UNO's attempt to prevent massacres in the Belgian Congo is a capitalist plot. Hammarskjöld has mobilised a UNO force from Tunis, Abyssinia and so on. Black will meet black. It was an ingenious thing to do.

H.N. TO V.S-W.   *22nd September, 1960*
C.1 Albany, W.1

Oh God, I had to lunch with such a bore today! I can't think why he likes me, as we have not a single idea in common. He said quite seriously that Queen Victoria would never have consented to give a knighthood to Gordon Richards, the jockey. That they ought to have struck John Gielgud's name off the roll of knights when he got into trouble. Then he said that it was an outrage that the Prime Minister should have to pay court to niggers like Nkrumah. But I am not really annoyed, as he is a museum piece; it is like seeing a railway-engine of 1854. But I have come to the conclusion that the worst bores are those who are in some ways rather intelligent. Thus this man is good at higher mathematics. Utterly stupid and uneducated people are not so dull. But I wish he would not refer to you as 'your dear lady'. He wanted me to inform my dear lady that his quinces have done very well this year.

DIARY   *22nd October, 1960*
The row between Gaitskell and the unilateralists continues.[1] Harold Wilson has come out in opposition to his leader. I cannot but feel that Gaitskell is taking the patriotic point of view and his opponents merely the Party point of view. It would be a bad thing for Labour if Gaitskell is turned out of the leadership, and I for one would never vote Labour again.

DIARY   *29th October, 1960*
In the evening we listen to a broadcast by Vita on the Home Service. She is furious because they introduce her as 'V. Sackville-West, the

[1] The policy of unilateral renunciation by Britain of the atomic bomb had been advocated by Bevan, but he had become reconciled with Gaitskell before his death. The Labour Party Conference had voted by a majority for unilateralism, and Gaitskell continued to fight the decision, and eventually won.

well-known authoress.' She had managed to persuade them not to call her 'Lady Nicolson' or 'Miss Sackville-West' or 'Miss Victoria Sackville-West', but had omitted to warn them not to put 'author' in the feminine. Imagine her rage, therefore, when she gets a letter from the Sevenoaks Urban District Council asking whether they may christen one of their new roads 'Nicolson Road'. That is well enough in Stornoway or Edinburgh, but not in Sevenoaks.

H.N. TO V.S-W.   *1st November, 1960*
                                                 C.1 Albany, W.1

I did like your book[1] so much. It seemed to me of such a lovely texture and so moving. It is such a *decent* book, and all three characters are ennobling. This will make the reviewers think it old-fashioned and upper-class. But you and I prefer the upper to the middle class, even as we prefer distinction to vulgarity. I do congratulate you. What a clever family I have got, what with Adam[2] and you!

V.S-W. TO H.N.   *2nd November, 1960*
                                                 Sissinghurst

I am of course glad that you approved of my book. No approval could please me better than yours. And I thought how odd it was, you and I writing away in our little cabins, not knowing what the other was writing about, and then discovering it in print months later. What one writes is a revelation of what one is.

V.S-W. TO H.N.   *8th November 1960*
                                                 Sissinghurst

I was always well-trained not to manage you. I scarcely dare to arrange the collar of your greatcoat, unless you ask me to. I think that is really the basis of our marriage, apart from our deep love for each other, for we have never interfered with each other and, strangely enough, never been jealous of each other And now, in our advancing age, we love each other more deeply than ever, and also more agonisingly, since we see the inevitable end. It is not nice to know that one of us must die before the other.

---

[1] *No Signposts in the Sea.*   [2] Then aged 3.

H.N. TO V.S-W.   *9th November, 1960*
                                                C.1 Albany, W.1

Did you listen to Nixon conceding defeat in the foyer of a Los Angeles hotel?[1] I am ambivalent about this. On the one hand I have some prejudice against Kennedy because of his father, I don't like candlesticks [Roman Catholics] in high positions, he reminds me of Lindbergh, and I suspect him of wishing to have a tough foreign policy and to worry about prestige. On the other hand, he is on the left, will be nicer to Negroes than to Big Business, and has promised to appoint Adlai Stevenson as Secretary of State.[2] So it works out 50/50 by me.

H.N. TO V.S-W.   *8th December, 1960*
                                                C.1 Albany, W.1

I lunched yesterday at the Café Royal with John Julius[3], Rupert Hart-Davis, Isaiah Berlin and Maurice Bowra. John Julius is a really charming man, and I should imagine, very able. We discussed whom to have as our successors on the Duff Cooper Committee. They asked me to approach Raymond [Mortimer].

In the evening came the ceremony of the unveiling of the tablet to Duff in the crypt of St Paul's. There were about 100 people there. Massigli and Chauvel and Gladwyn [Jebb], and the F.O. and the Grenadiers were represented as well as Eton and New College. I unveiled the thing, and it didn't stick as I had feared. Then turning to the audience, I started, 'I have been asked to say a few words . . .' But it was at the wrong stage of the proceedings, and the Dean tugged at my coat whispering, 'I come first. . . .' So I stopped and returned foolish-looking to my seat. Then the Dean said his bit, and I returned to the tablet and again faced the congregation. 'I have been asked', I said again, 'to say a few words.' And this time my words went uninterrupted. My speech went well enough. Diana

---

[1] Richard Nixon, the Republican candidate, was defeated by J. F. Kennedy by less than 120,000 votes out of nearly 69 million cast.

[2] In fact Kennedy (according to Sorensen) never seriously considered Adlai Stevenson for the job. It went to Dean Rusk. Stevenson was appointed U.S. Ambassador to the U N.

[3] The Second Viscount Norwich, son of Duff Cooper. He was serving in the Foreign Office. He was then aged 31.

387

[Cooper] remained unmoved but trembling. 'Duff would have hated it', she said to me afterwards, 'if I had blubbed in public.'

H.N. TO V.S-W.   *29th December, 1960*
       C.1 Albany, W.1

I got a long, long letter from Guy Burgess. He says that there is no reason at all why he should not come back to London, and that he would come were it not that he fears that he might not be allowed back to Russia. On the other hand, M.I.5 have let it be known that the moment he lands on the tarmac he will be arrested. It may be that they are bluffing. If he does come, the papers will clamour that he should be tried as a traitor, and M.I.5 will look silly if at the trial they can produce no evidence at all. Purely selfishly, I hope he doesn't come. I should be called on to give evidence in his favour, and what could I say? I knew of his drunken habits and sexual promiscuity. 'Do you mean to tell the Court', the Attorney-General would thunder at me, 'that although you knew what sort of man he was, you continued to see him?' As a matter of fact, I had rather dropped him because he was a bore with his drunken habits, but I couldn't say that in court.

DIARY   *31st December, 1960*

Let 1960 go. It has been a beastly year. The rainfall between July and the end of the year has been heavier than for a century. The communist world has gained over the liberal world in every quarter of the globe from Laos to Cuba. The African situation is dreadful. Our own economic situation is only precariously prosperous. My *Age of Reason* has been criticised for misprints, misspellings, repetitions and careless writing. I know that it is because I am going gaga.

1961

A trip to South America – Rio de Janeiro –Montevideo – a self-conscious little girl – interviews with Kenneth Harris – luncheon with the King and Queen of Greece – 'The New English Bible' – Churchill in extreme old age – the Bay of Pigs incident – V.S-W. on opening the garden to the public – H.N. fears his social powers are declining – Yuri Gagarin – V.S-W. visits Knole for the first time in thirty-one years – the Koran – 'Monarchy' finished – H.N. starts on 'The Age of Romance' – American influences on B.B.C. programmes – death of Dag Hammarskjöld – 'Il faut cultiver notre jardin' – Nigel finds fault with 'Monarchy' and H.N. revises it – dinner in the Middle Temple – a toast to the Queen – H.N. attacks the Conservatives – Lord Home on British policy in the Congo

On 8th January they embarked at Genoa on the Italian liner 'Augustus' for a cruise to South America, calling at Barcelona, Lisbon, Rio de Janeiro, Buenos Aires and Montevideo. The books which occupied them were 'Monarchy' and V. Sackville-West's little photograph-album about dogs, which, under the title 'Faces', was her last published work in book form. On her return in February she ceased writing her gardening articles for the 'Observer'.

Harold Nicolson's 'Monarchy' was also his last book, and the first for very many years that he published under any other imprint than Constable's. As soon as it was finished in August, he signed a contract for 'The Age of Romance', but my reluctant letter of 20th September, the only critical comment which he had ever received from a publisher, obliged him to revise 'Monarchy' extensively and caused him genuine concern that his literary powers were failing. In November he was 75.

For V. Sackville-West it was a good year She was free from serious illness, 'No Signposts' had an excellent reception, and she was contemplating a new novel. With the death of Lady Sackville in January she felt able to revisit Knole after an absence of 31 years, and went there four times during the course of the year.

DIARY   20th January, 1961
                                             S.S. 'Augustus', Rio de Janeiro

Viti wakes me up at 5.45, and from my portal I can see the strange pinnacles of Rio harbour sliding past. We go on deck, and it is in truth a wonderful sight. There is a slight mist over the town and the lower hills, but the distant mountains glow with sunshine. It is even more dramatic than we expected, and certainly one of the most beautiful harbours in the world.

We go in the Embassy car to the Botanical Gardens. Wide avenues of tall thin palms with all manner of flowering trees and shrubs, against a background of jungle-covered mountains descending almost into the town. We drive to the Embassy, which is a magnificent white building with porticos and colonnades. Lady

Wallinger[1] was a Miss Zilliacus and writes novels. She is an attractive woman. We have an excellent luncheon. Lady Wallinger then takes us up to one of the peaks from where we get an astonishing bird's-eye view of the bays and harbours. Michael Conolly[2] joins us. 'I have never met an Ambassadress before', he says to Vita. 'Are they all as nice as that?' 'No', she replies resolutely, 'they are *not*.' We leave Rio at 6, and before we lose sight of the harbour, the necklace of lights comes out round the several bays and the great figure of Christ on the Corcovado is floodlit. A memorable visit.

Today young Kennedy takes over from dear old Ike.

DIARY   23rd January, 1961
                                      S.S. 'Augustus', Montevideo

We creep into the harbour of Montevideo at 2. The Uruguayan flag of blue stripes is most attractive. On the quay are clergymen dancing with joy at the sight of our nuns. [Sir] Malcolm Henderson, our Ambassador, comes on board. A nice, diffident man. We get into the Embassy Rolls and are driven to a distant hill where there is a Portuguese fort and a fine view of the town. There is a slaughter-house below us and an acrid smell. Viti is distressed at the sight of a herd of cows waiting outside the slaughter-house unconscious of their doom. Henderson shows us the spot where the *Graf Spee* was scuttled. He said it was not due entirely to Hitler's orders, as some supposed, but because the crew mutinied rather than go out to face certain death in the estuary outside. We then drive to the Embassy. A nice house. Lady Henderson is American and kind. We walk in the garden, which is very pleasant indeed, with green lawns of esparto grass and flowering trees—azaleas and avocado pears and verbena. Malcolm Henderson is interesting on the subject of Uruguay. They have a welfare state with a right-wing government. There is no gulf between rich and poor, and the people are contented. He loves them, and says that they are badly-organised, but gay and friendly.

[1] The British Ambassador in Brazil, 1958–63, was Sir Geoffrey Wallinger.
[2] A young fellow-passenger on the *Augustus*.

H.N. TO N.N. & P.N.   *29th January, 1961*
                                    S.S. 'Augustus', Rio de Janeiro

There is an Argentinian girl on board, aged about twelve, to whom
Vita and I have taken a fierce dislike and whose antics we watch with
horror. She comes into the saloon doing the act, 'Little girl in pink
dress enters saloon of luxury liner'. She then sits down and does the
act, 'Little girl, with finger on her chin, listens attentively to her
mother'. That merges into the act, 'Little girl listens to band with
attentive appreciation'. Then comes, 'Little girl claps to show
appreciation, nodding her head gracefully in the direction of the
band-leader'. Then we play Bingo, and there are several acts dis-
playing little girl in expectation, little girl in disappointment, little
girl in ecstasy of triumph, little girl, cheated of victory, indicates
indifference to the triumphs of this world. Vita and I watch revolted
by self-consciousness reaching such atrocious lengths.

About my book.[1] I could kick myself for not having brought
more works of reference. I find that I shall have to do a chapter on
les rois fainéants, but my knowledge of the Merovingians is frail and
scanty. Anyhow, I have done Chapter VIII, and ought to finish
Chapters IX and X by the time we return. The further I go, the
wider the gap becomes between the actual book and the synopsis.

DIARY   *4th February, 1961*
                                       S.S. 'Augustus', Mid-Atlantic

Vita finds this long Atlantic trip monotonous. She would like to
pass islands all the time. I rather enjoy the great emptiness of space
and time. I get a cable from the *New York Times* asking me to do
2,500 words on public-speaking with special reference to Kennedy's
speeches. But how can I do this without having the speeches in
front of me? I send them a negative reply.

H.N. TO V.S-W.   *9th March, 1961*
                                               C.1 Albany, W.1

I had Kenneth Harris, my interviewer, yesterday.[2] He is an excellent
interrogator, as good as John Freeman, since he makes one think

[1] *Monarchy.*
[2] H.N. was recording four interviews on his life and opinions which were published in the *Observer* later in the year.

about oneself. 'Why are you a member of the Labour Party?' Why indeed? I told him that I was a 'liberal socialist' and that is true. I am sure that the vast outlay on the Health Service would not have been accomplished except under state socialism. But then I also believe in individualism. I fear my Labour side is due all too much to hatred of the Tories, and this hatred has had bottles of real venom poured into it by the Bournemouth episode.

DIARY   16th March, 1961

Kenneth Harris comes for the last of the interviews. We discuss the nature and purpose of culture. I lunch at the Greek Embassy. It is a luncheon of intellectuals to meet the King and Queen of Greece. Henry Moore with his wife are there, and Freddy Ayer also with wife, and Graham Greene and John Lehmann and Rosamond Lehmann, and Jock and Diana Murray, and Lord Adrian and Maurice Bowra and Noel Annan. After luncheon we go into the drawing-room. The Queen instals herself on the sofa and we are made to group our chairs in a semicircle around her. She then delivers a lecture on metaphysics, most of which I cannot hear, catching only such words as 'electrons', 'brotherhood of man', 'objective and subjective', 'materialism' and 'atom-bomb'. Freddy Ayer, with his exquisite manners, tries to intervene from time to time, but she sweeps him aside with a queenly gesture She does not cease until 4.15, and then says goodbye with a kind word for each of her exhausted audience.

Henry Moore tells me that Ben has not only saved the *Burlington*, but much increased its prestige internationally. I liked that.

H.N. TO V S-W.   22nd March, 1961
                                                        C.1 Albany, W.1

Raymond [Mortimer] defends the Bible.[1] He says that nobody knows what the original was really like, that it was written in Aramaic, and that we do not have Christ's actual words. He says that the present version, in that it avoids all poetry and mystery, gives us a clearer view of the original and conveys to us better than before how arrogant and obstinate Christ sometimes appears, if

[1] *The New English Bible* had just been published by the Oxford and Cambridge University Presses.

we accept every statement in the Gospels, however inconsistent with his usual teaching. I can't agree with Raymond's passion for precision. I was quite ruffled by his defence of this *Hansard* type of Bible. I think we should be allowed to keep our legends and illusions. Nothing will make me believe that Christ possessed a harsh character, and it is beastly to make him out as a sort of Lumumba agitator.

H.N. TO V.S-W.   *27th April 1961*
C.1 Albany, W.1

I went to the Academy Banquet and enjoyed it very much. There were several speeches, but I couldn't hear them. Macmillan delivered his very well, but I couldn't catch a word Field-Marshal Montgomery was there with his Garter, and many friends such as Tom Eliot, Tommy Lascelles, Oliver Esher, and so on and so on. I watched Winston leaving. The President [Sir Charles Wheeler] took one arm and an attendant another, and they almost carried the old boy down the steps. He is frightfully old. His eyes are bleary and immobile. I watched his huge bald head descending the staircase, and I blessed it as it disappeared. 'We may never see that again', said a voice behind me. It was Attlee.

H.N. TO V.S-W.   *1st June, 1961*
C 1 Albany, W.1

I had a really interesting dinner with Harold Caccia.[1] He says that the great white soul of America is still blushing scarlet over Cuba.[2] He says he personally has great confidence in Dean Rusk and Kennedy, but that Kennedy 'must run himself in' before he can inspire confidence. He says that it is not true to say that Kennedy inherited the plan for dealing with the Cuban situation as it was carried out. He wanted to show from the outset that he was a strong man determined to defend the Monroe Doctrine, and plunged into the Cuban adventure on false information. He says that the Americans do not blame Kennedy, who is still their red-headed boy, but that they put it all down to the 'diplomatists', meaning thereby their intelligence services. 'Why can't we put a foot right?' they wail.

[1] British Ambassador in Washington, 1956-61.
[2] The abortive invasion of the Bay of Pigs by Cuban exiles on 17th April.

V.S-W. TO H.N. *20th June, 1961*
Sissinghurst

It has been a heavenly day. Lots of people came over the garden, but nobody I knew. I cleaned up Fantin Latour and Tour de Malakoff and some others. I find that if I hide in the jungle of roses, people don't see me, and don't come to ask, 'I wonder if you could tell me the name of a shrub . . . in a different part of the garden. . . . I can't quite remember where . . . nor what it looked like . . . but no doubt you will know what I mean?'

H.N. TO V.S-W. *21st June, 1961*
C.1 Albany, W.1

I lunched with Ann Fleming yesterday. The Kenneth Clarks were there, Diana Cooper, Richard Wollheim,[1] Sir Solly Zuckerman.[2] But I am getting so deaf that I feel embarrassed at parties and become completely inarticulate. I fear that the sun is setting in the west, and that I have ceased to be a social asset and become a liability. Moreover, not only have I ceased to hear, but I have ceased to speak. The old chatterbox has been shut down and the clasp been set upon it. In fact I did not shine or sparkle, and I feel diminished.[3] But I enjoyed my luncheon all the same, and my word, it was good. Scrambled eggs, cold sole, strawberries—but all of such quality that they were set high above most foods. Diana was very sweet.

DIARY *14th July, 1961*

We watch an interview with Gagarin[4] on TV He certainly possesses great propaganda charm, and will personify Holy Russia for many millions. How can a country be a menace when it has as its hero a man with so entrancing a smile?

---

[1] Reader (later Professor) of Philosophy in the University of London.
[2] Scientific Adviser to the Ministry of Defence.
[3] H.N. exaggerated his deafness. He never needed a hearing aid, and it was only when the room had an echo or there were many people in it that he could not follow ordinary conversation with ease.
[4] Major Yuri Gagarin, the Russian astronaut, was the first man to circle the earth in an artificial satellite, on 12th April, 1961. He was visiting Britain in July.

DIARY   *15th July, 1961*

Viti and I go to Knole for luncheon. The Japanese deer are all around. They have much increased. We go to the house and meet Jacobine[1] on the way. We visit the interior and the garden. The sunk-garden and pool are much improved. The rock-garden has wisely been swept away and the little orchard squares have been levelled out. Altogether it is more lovely than ever, and Vita is happy there. We lunch. Charlie [Lord Sackville] is very frail but perfectly compos.

H.N. TO V.S-W.   *9th August, 1961*
                                                            C.1 Albany, W.1

I went to the London Library and got a translation of the Koran. It passes my comprehension how so diffuse, repetitive and superficial a book can be compared to the Bible. It is because of the thinness of the teaching of Mohammed that I deride Moslem thought and despise Christians (and they are few) who become converts to Islam.

H.N. TO V.S-W.   *24th August, 1961*
                                                            C.1 Albany, W.1

At exactly 12.15 yesterday morning I finished my book on Kingship, and now I start on *The Age of Romance*. It will take me three years to do it, and I doubt whether I shall live so long. But it is a fascinating subject, and I look forward to it.

I met Harman Grisewood[2] at luncheon and tackled him about American films and plays and accents. He is very sensible about it and hates it as much as you do. He regrets that the public should rather like American accents, and says that they never get letters of protest about it. What does arouse public rage is the upper-class or 'U' accent. They even complain that the News announcers all speak 'la-di-da'. He assures me that, at least as far as the News is concerned, the B.B.C. will stick to their guns. I asked him about American films, and he said it was almost wholly a matter of finance. There is a vast T.V. audience in America, and when the films have gone the rounds of the United States, they are sent over here and

---

[1] Jacobine Hichens, the novelist, who married Lionel Sackville-West (6th and present Lord Sackville) in 1953.
[2] Chief Assistant to the Director-General of the B.B.C.

sold cheaply to the B.B.C. Thus Perry Mason is cheaper than any English film series and is much liked by the public. 'Personally', said Harman, 'I cannot follow it and always get lost after five minutes.'

My dear old friend Charles Webster[1] has died. He was exactly my age. We flop and drop like the apples in the orchard.

V.S-W. TO H.N.   *19th September, 1961*
                                                        Sissinghurst

It's so hot, and I think of you in London and of poor Mr Hammarskjöld dead in Katanga,[2] and of all the poor people in the U.N. who must be so upset and worried. Meanwhile I go on with my futile little occupations. I've put 400 bulbs in the orchard (fritillaries which you despise, *Narcissus cyclamineus* which you like, *Ornithogalum* which is supposed to naturalise itself but which I have never yet induced to grow, and *Narcissus* 'La Riante'). It sometimes seems rather silly, but as Voltaire wisely remarked, *Il faut cultiver notre jardin*. It is really better to have created a *jardin* which gives pleasure to us as well as to many other people, than for me to go and sit down in Trafalgar Square.[3]

N.N. TO V.S-W.   *20th September, 1961*
                                            Weidenfeld & Nicolson Ltd.
                                               20 New Bond Street, W.1

I'm worried, and I want your help. It's about Daddy's book on Monarchy. I don't know whether you have read any of the typescript, but if you have, I am sure you would agree that it is well below his normal level, and I fear that it will do his reputation harm if it is published in its present form. On the other hand, he loathes criticisms from publishers and hates returning to a book which he has finished, when he has already started on the next.

I can explain what is wrong with it very shortly. The original intention, which he put in the form of a synopsis for us to show to foreign publishers, was that each chapter would deal with a different

[1] The author and Professor of International History at the London School of Economics.
[2] Dag Hammarskjöld died in the air-crash at Ndola on 18th September.
[3] This was the period of the mass sit-down demonstrations by the Campaign for Nuclear Disarmament.

aspect of kingship: thus, the King as a Magician, the Warrior-King, the Feudal King, the Constitutional King, and so on. In each chapter he intended to draw his examples from all ages and all countries, comparing Alexander the Great to Napoleon and Jenghiz Khan in the Warrior-King chapter; and in the Feudal chapter, dealing with the French, German, Spanish and other medieval monarchs side by side.

This was an excellent idea. But after the first two chapters he abandons it for a strictly narrative history. In the Warrior chapter, for example, nobody is mentioned except Alexander the Great, and in the next four chapters (all about the Romans) we get a rather shop-soiled narrative of the events in the reigns of the more unpleasant Emperors. It is no longer a discussion of the theme of Monarchy.

But that is not all. For a book on this subject, surely we should have more than a passing reference to Napoleon, something about the Czars, about the Court of Spain, about the French Revolution, about the Holy Roman Empire after Charlemagne, even something about the great kings of Poland and Scandinavia? But there is nothing about any of these. It does seem to me a little out of proportion to devote a quarter of the book to the Roman Emperors, and leave out all these other monarchs completely.

Of course the easiest thing to do would be to let the book pass as it is, and trouble him no more. But if we do that, the French, German, Italian and American publishers will cancel their contracts. They have all read the typescript, and that is what they say. They insist on having the gaps filled.

I know that he didn't enjoy writing the book, certainly in the later stages, and will hate having to return to it. But I have written to him today telling him what the foreign publishers say (and that I agree with them), and asking him if he would at least make some additions to bring in Napoleon, the Spaniards and the Czars.

We would do this with any author, and so a publisher should. He thinks that a publisher who causes bother to his authors is a bad publisher: I think they are bad publishers if they don't. I hate doing this to him. But if I felt that you would support me, I would be much relieved. He is almost certain to raise the subject with you during this coming weekend.

DIARY   *21st September, 1961*

A letter from Nigel saying that I must recast my Monarchy book since the foreign publishers refuse to take it in its present form, in that it omits so much of importance and varies between commentary and history. What they really mean is that I am getting gaga, and cannot really do this sort of book at my age. Poor Niggs! It must have been an unpleasant letter for him to write. It made me feel quite giddy at the prospect of the work of revision entailed.

DIARY   *22nd September, 1961*

I am still feeling distressed at the obvious waning of my powers. I fear I have not been the same since I had my two strokes, and I am living on the fat of my former reputation. Vita consoles me, as always. She is not in the least annoyed with Nigel for ticking me off, and agrees that he is perfectly right.

H.N. TO V.S-W.   *8th November, 1961*
                                               C.1 Albany, W.1

I dined as John [Sparrow's] guest in the Middle Temple. It is years since that dreadful play *Twelfth Night* was first performed there.[1] We had an excellent dinner with delicious champagne. They do themselves proud. There were many elderly judges who sat there looking benign and clean, whereas I felt that they had all sentenced men to be hanged by the neck. The barrister opposite me told me a horrible story. Some years ago he had defended a man charged with murder and had secured his acquittal. The man wrote to him later saying that he had in fact committed the murder and would have been hanged but for the forensic skill of his counsel. That was a nasty one, but it was even worse when he learnt that the man had committed another murder in Switzerland and had been sentenced to penal servitude for life. He said, 'I had felt so triumphant about my success in court, and then I felt like a criminal who had let loose this Dracula on society.' He was a nice man.

[1] In 1602.

On ss Augustus, *February 1961*

Harold Nicolson with his son Nigel and grandson Adam on 20 June 1962

H.N. TO V.S-W. *9th November, 1961*
C.1 Albany, W.1

A busy day yesterday rummaging in the London Library and taking notes on the history of Poland.[1] Then in the evening I dined with Louis Spears.[2] A posh dinner. The American Ambassador and his wife; Lord and Lady Chandos;[3] the Minister of Defence and Mrs Harold Watkinson. Watkinson told us that the Cabinet had many doubts about deciding to advise the Queen to go to Ghana, but off she goes as I write this. All of us expressed anxiety and distress at the decision, and suddenly the American Ambassador said, 'Gentlemen, let us rise and drink a health unto Her Majesty'. So we all rose in our seats and raised our glasses, looking terribly self-conscious. It wasn't a false sentiment, since we all felt sympathy and admiration for the Queen. But the British, bless them, do hate emotion. I confess that I got a lump in my throat myself. But I do not like sentimental drama. Wasn't that an odd thing to occur?

Madame Mendoza, the Brazilian Ambassadress, said to me, 'Do you live in London?' To which I replied, 'No, my home is in the country'. 'Where in the country?', and past my eyes swam a picture of golden trees and pink brick and Sissinghurst at her loveliest.

DIARY *27th November, 1961*

Iain Macleod in the *Observer* replies to my attack on the Tories.[4] Coals of fire his remarks are. I feel ashamed. Finish my Holy Roman Empire chapter.

---

[1] For the revision of *Monarchy*.
[2] Major General Sir Edward Spears, the author, soldier, diplomatist and ex-M.P.
[3] Formerly Oliver Lyttelton.
[4] In the *Observer* of 12th November, H.N.'s last interview with Kenneth Harris was published, in which he charged the Conservatives with 'cruelty, indifference and selfishness'. Iain Macleod, then leader of the House of Commons and Chairman of the Conservative Party, replied in another interview with Harris by saying: 'Harold Nicolson doesn't hate anybody. He's far too nice a person. Anyway, in the same interview, he seemed to think the world of Harold Macmillan.'

H.N. TO V.S-W. *6th December, 1961*
C.1 Albany, W.1

I lunched with the Birkenheads[1] yesterday. The Foreign Secretary and Lady Home were there. He is very bitter about O'Brien[2] having accused us of intriguing against him in the Congo. My word, I am glad I am not Prime Minister! One worry after another, and lies all around. I told the Foreign Secretary that he ought to make it crystal clear to the country what our Congo policy is. 'But I have made it clear', he said. 'Not crystal clear', I persisted. 'It is a very confused situation', he said. It is indeed.

DIARY *29th December, 1961*

The revise of *Monarchy* is now finished, and I shall do a final revise over the weekend and never think of the book again. No book has ever given me so much distress or trouble. It is due to my waning powers rather than to any lack of interest.

DIARY *31st December, 1961*

The year is dying. Let it die, and please not come back. But Vita has been well and seems far stronger.

---

[1] The second Earl of Birkenhead.
[2] Dr Conor Cruise O'Brien, the Irishman, had been the chief United Nations representative in Katanga since June 1961. He resigned in November, and published a statement charging Britain and France with having obstructed the U.N.'s mandate in the Congo and pressed for his own removal.

1962

A journey to the West Indies – V.S-W. has a haemorrhage –
H.N.'s anxiety for her – visit to Barbados and Jamaica –
her appreciation of 'Monarchy' – she enters hospital for a
serious operation – her life in danger – she returns to Sis-
singhurst and slowly recovers her strength – she has a relapse
and dies at Sissinghurst on 2nd June – her funeral

On 2nd June V. Sackville-West died at Sissinghurst of abdominal cancer. The first indication of it was a haemorrhage which overcame her in the train between London and Southampton, on their way to join the 'Antilles' for a cruise to the West Indies. For over a month she concealed from Harold Nicolson the fact of her haemorrhage, but she told her friend, Edith Lamont, who fortunately accompanied them. To him she explained her tiredness and fluctuating temperature during the voyage as due to lumbago and bronchitis, which simultaneously afflicted her.

On their return home on 15th February, blood-tests were taken, and she was told that she must enter hospital for an operation on 1st March. It revealed beyond doubt that she was suffering from advanced cancer. Harold Nicolson was told, but it is not certain that she ever knew it herself, for her diary stops on 25th February, and from her letter of 26th April it appears that she was satisfied by the explanation that she was suffering from anaemia. She nearly died in hospital, but she insisted on returning to Sissinghurst on 6th April and seemed slowly to regain her strength. She was in no pain. She was able to walk round parts of the garden, and the hand-writing of her letters to Harold Nicolson, which in April was almost undecipherable, returned to normal by the third week of May. Then came a relapse. She was sent for deep-ray treatment to Pembury Hospital, but the effort exhausted her. Immediately on her return from her second treatment on 31st May, she went to bed in the first-floor bedroom of the Priest's House at Sissinghurst. Next evening she fell into the coma from which she never awoke. She died peacefully at 1.15 pm. on Saturday, 2nd June.

DIARY   *19th January, 1962*

Called at 6.45. We leave the Albany and drive to Waterloo through dark, empty streets. The lamps shine on wet pavements. We enter our Pullman and start reading the newspapers, and there, suddenly, is Ben holding Vanessa by the hand and Vanessa clasping her teddy-bear by the other hand. The train leaves at 8.5 and we get to

Southampton Docks at 10.40. Pass through passport and Customs easily. Go aboard the *Antilles*. I unpack and have a nap. Viti also has a nap.

v.s-w.'s DIARY   *19th January, 1962*

Leave Albany at 7.15 and get the 8.5 at Waterloo. Edie [Lamont] meets us there, and we all have breakfast on the train. Ben and Vanessa surprised us by appearing at Waterloo to see us off. *Disastrous* journey. I am very worried and confide in E.

DIARY   *20th January, 1962*
                                                              S.S. 'Antilles'

We are off Bordeaux. It is already warmer. Viti sleeps or lies in her bunk most of the day because of her lumbago.

DIARY   *27th January, 1962*
                                                              S.S. 'Antilles',
                                                                  Martinique

Viti says she is better, but still has a slight temperature and stays in bed. I stay on board. In the evening, her temperature goes up to over 100. I am, as always, sick with worry.

DIARY   *28th January, 1962*
                                                              S.S. 'Antilles',
                                                         Barbados, West Indies

Vita's temperature is down to normal, and the ship's doctor says that she can go ashore. I could not have believed it. We drive to Ronnie Tree's villa.[1] It is one of the loveliest villas I have ever seen, constructed of fine local coral on the lines of Malcontenta or Maser.[2] There is a terrace shaded by thick trees, and only twenty yards away the sea laps gently on a silver beach. Ronnie shows us over the house, which has a fine central room and two wings. We lunch under the trees. We then drive back. It is a monstrously ugly island, like the Isle of Wight covered with decaying sugar-cane. There are signposts and football-fields as at Shanklin. When we get back, Vita is exhausted and her temperature is up to 101. I am worried again, but the doctor tells me to keep calm. '*Ne vous inquiétez pas, Monsieur.*'

[1] Heron Bay, Barbados.   [2] Two Palladian villas near Venice.

V. SACKVILLE-WEST'S ILLNESS

DIARY
1st February, 1962
S.S. 'Antilles',
Between Venezuela and Jamaica

At sea. Vita's temperature is down and her bronchitis is clearing up, but she is terribly weak and ill with all these injections they are giving her. She gets up for luncheon, but goes to bed almost immediately afterwards.

DIARY
8th February, 1962
S.S. 'Antilles',
mid-Atlantic

I watch a film of American college girls flirting with college boys, but cannot stand it long. I suspect that the French[1] show us these films of campus merriment in order to display American culture in all its horror. I talk to Margaret Waugh[2]—a charming girl, intelligent and lovely. She is a fine antidote to Hollywood necking and petting. There is a gala dinner in the evening. Viti has a slight temperature again at night.

V.S-W.'S DIARY
15th February, 1962
Sissinghurst

Thankful to be home. The orchard is misty-mauve with *tomasinianus; parrotia* flowering as never before. Witch-hazel *arboreus* still out; a few *specie crocuses.* I feel really ill, and try to hide it from Hadji. The sooner I see the doctor the better.

DIARY
18th February, 1962

I think Viti is better, but she never lets me know.

V.S-W. TO H.N.
20th February, 1962
Sissinghurst

I did enjoy reading your chapters.[3] When I say 'enjoy', I mean the true enjoyment one gets from reading good writing, quite apart from the mass of information beautifully organised and conveyed. And the gift you have of suddenly startling one by the use of an

[1] The *Antilles* was a liner of the French Line.
[2] Evelyn Waugh, the novelist, and his daughter had joined the ship at Trinidad.
[3] The first page-proofs of *Monarchy.*

unexpected though utterly *right* word, or by a little scene sharply described with the utmost economy. I feel so proud of you, and long to read more.

There is no news here. Oh yes, by the way, the doctor came. I am not anaemic. I never thought I was. But he thinks I ought to see a consultant if I don't get over this tiresome tiredness, and I said, 'All right. I'll think it over'. Perhaps I will. There must be some explanation. Anyhow, don't worry.

H.N. TO V.S-W.   *22nd February, 1962*
C.1 Albany, W.1

We must get at the cause of this exhaustion. It cannot be only the effects of m. & b., and it isn't Anne Aemia. Oh dear, what a worry life is!

I am sorry that Glenn has gone off on his orbit.[1] It was rather an achievement, but immensely expensive. The Americans seem to treat millions of pounds as if they were a few pennies. I do not really see the point of this space-travel, and refuse to believe that information about weather is worth the price of a thousand hospitals and a thousand universities. I am against space-travel, and I don't mind the world knowing it. I am a *square* in these respects.

DIARY   *23rd February, 1962*

When I reach home, Viti tells me to prepare myself for a blow. She has had a haemorrhage and went up to London yesterday to consult a gynaecologist, who said she must go into hospital and be examined. I can see that Viti thinks it is cancer, and faces it with her usual courage. She is really heroic. The haemorrhage occurred in the train from Waterloo to Southampton on 19th January. Her bronchitis was subsequent and incidental. She did tell Edie, but she never told me, as she knew it would worry me. Her unselfishness is phenomenal.

The shock has a strange effect on me. It seems to sunder my life in two—the past being radiant with sunshine, and the present and future dark as night. Familiar objects (my pipe, my sponge, the book I have been reading) all seem like voices from the past. 'Last time I handled you, all was sunlit.'

---

[1] Colonel John Glenn, the American astronaut, had just completed his five-hour, three-orbit, trip through outer space.

DIARY   *28th February, 1962*

Viti leaves home by the morning train. A car takes her from London Bridge to the Royal Free Hospital in Liverpool Road, Canonbury. Edie comes with her. The surgeon comes in while I am there. She says that until she opens things up, she cannot be sure whether it will be a 'minor' or a 'major' operation. If it is a major operation, Viti's life will be in danger for forty-eight hours. She is so gay and calm, seeking to ease my dread.

DIARY   *1st March, 1962*

Dies irae. At 1.30 they telephone to say that Vita is 'still in the theatre', and this fills me with horror. Then at 2.45 the surgeon telephones. 'Lady Nicolson is now back in her bed and having a blood-transfusion. She stood the operation fairly well.' 'Did you do the major operation?' 'Yes.' 'Did you find cancer?' 'Yes.' I feel like fainting, but drink some sherry.

During the afternoon there is a loud rap on the door. When Elvira opens it, she is confronted by a Grenadier in full uniform who hands her a letter. It is from Michael Adeane sending me a message of 'sympathy and encouragement' from the Queen. This makes me feel better. At 6.30 I go to the hospital. V. had felt some pain, and they had given her dope and she was fast asleep. I go away with the picture of the oxygen and blood-transfusion apparatus hanging like gallows in my mind.

DIARY   *3rd March, 1962*

Vita is more conscious than she was this morning. She asks me whether I came to the hospital by car, and when I say 'Yes', she murmurs, 'Good boy.' Then a few minutes later she says, 'Have I been talking nonsense?' I sit beside her and read my book.

DIARY   *6th March, 1962*

The sister assures me that she is slowly recovering her strength. But she is desperately ill, poor darling, and is aware of it. But she does seem what the nurses call 'brighter', and she talks. I read Coleridge's Notebooks. James [Pope-Hennessy] takes me out to dine at the Beefsteak. He is gay and affectionate and does me good.

409

DIARY   *13th March, 1962*

Her terrible weakness seems to continue, and she cannot read or sleep.

DIARY   *20th March, 1962*

It is odd. Two weeks ago I loathed going to the hospital, as it was a *via dolorosa* and horrible to see her so weak and ill. But now every day she seems a little better, and it is a visit I look forward to. But she is still unable to read or eat or sleep.

DIARY   *30th March, 1962*

She had a fair night and is more cheerful this morning. But when she sits up for her meals, her beloved head droops like a narcissus. She is tired again in the evening, but I think the prospect of going home is good for her morale. But I cannot rid myself of my constant anxiety about her.

DIARY   *6th April, 1962*

Viti leaves the hospital at 10 and has a lovely drive in the Daimler ambulance down home. She is met by Edie, the doctor, Ursula[1] and the household. She is not tired.

DIARY   *13th April, 1962*

I find her very weak still. They make her come down for luncheon, and that exhausts her. I am worried again, and go to bed heavy and sad.

DIARY   *23rd April, 1962*

Easter Sunday. Philippa and Nigel appear unexpectedly with the children. He says that I sounded so miserable on the telephone when he rang up last night, that they decided to come down. Juliet and Adam see Vita, and dance the twist in front of her. That amuses her. Then we go round the garden and Juliet dances about picking daffodils. She has such graceful movements. Altogether a successful day, and for the first time since 1st March, I feel almost happy.

[1] Miss Ursula Codrington, who had been secretary at Sissinghurst since 1959.

V.S-W. TO H.N.   *26th April, 1962*
                                                            Sissinghurst

The doctor has just rung up. He has heard from the specialist that I
am anaemic. This is a great relief, because it is what [*illegible*] hoped
for and it explains much. It means that I must have five injections,
which he warns me are very painful. He is coming to give me the
first one himself.

    Later. It is now over, and it was no more painful than all those
piqûres I had on the *Antilles*. When I said so, he laughed and said
that he always believed in being gloomy in advance. He *is* a good
psychologist.

    I must get up now. I am feeling much better, but I can't control
my writing. Can you read it?

DIARY   *28th April, 1962*

Viti is really much better. In fact, the Pembury specialist who visited
her this morning says that if she continues as well as this, no further
treatment may be needed. I am immensely relieved.

V.S-W. TO H.N.   *2nd May, 1962*
                                                            Sissinghurst

I am going to get up and go into the garden. It is quite warm. My
writing is better, don't you think? I hope to go as far as the spring
garden today, and I shall put on clothes to make me feel a little
more human. What I find one grudges is the appalling waste of time,
and not seeing the things that one wants to see. I won't write any
more, but just send you all the love which you know is yours.

DIARY   *8th May, 1962*

Jacobine [Sackville-West] telephones in the morning to say that
Charlie is dead.[1] No pain, no anxiety, no suffering, and ninety-one
years of age. I have Elizabeth Bowen and Philip Toynbee to lunch,
and we discuss the W. H. Smith Prize.

V.S-W. TO H.N.   *16th May, 1962*
                                                            Sissinghurst

Oh God the boredom of being ill! The days seem endless. Of course

[1] Lord Sackville died at Knole.

411

I could get people to come and see me, but it tires me too much.
Edie doesn't tire me, because I don't have to talk. I can even go to
sleep if I like. People keep saying that I look better: I only wish I
felt it. I don't seem to get any strength back.

H.N. TO V.S-W.   *17th May, 1962*
                                                              C.1 Albany, W.1

I had a young man from Oxford[1] to see me about the Munich
crisis and let him have my diary for 1938. He is writing a book
about it, and wanted all the material he could get. I do not think
my diary will be of much use to him, but he is welcome to read it.
I seem to have played a greater part in affairs that year than I did
subsequently. There is no reason why I should have retired to a
second place in the struggle, nor was I aware of it at the time. But I
did. Modesty, I suppose, but I am not sure. I certainly could have
played a more leading role in the crisis had I desired to do so. But I
regret nothing.

V.S-W. TO H.N.[2]   *23rd May, 1962*
                                                              Sissinghurst

Glen[3] slept in my room and was quite quiet until 6 am., when he
got up on my bed and became inconveniently affectionate—huge
rough paws whacking me.

Alvilde [Lees-Milne] is coming down this afternoon to collect
the plants she has ordered. She was very considerate, and said that
she could not come till 4.30, as she was sure that I slept after lunch.

I think sadly of Chelsea,[4] and still more of Stokesay.[5] I hate letting
Philip down, and I was really looking forward to it, and to seeing
Miss Murrell's roses.[6] It may still be all right, but I doubt it.

---

[1] Martin Gilbert. His book (written in collaboration with Richard Gott) was
published by Weidenfeld & Nicolson in 1963 under the title *The Appeasers*.
[2] This letter and the next were the last two letters that they wrote to each other.
[3] A young Golden Retriever.
[4] The spring-show of the Royal Horticultural Society.
[5] Sir Philip Magnus-Allcroft's house in Shropshire, where they had been invited
to stay.
[6] At Shrewsbury, V.S-W.'s favourite rose-nursery.

H.N. TO V.S-W.   *24th May, 1962*
                                                  C.1 Albany, W.1

I hope it is all right about Philippa, Niggs and the children coming
to luncheon on Sunday. I shall see to it that they do not trouble you
too much. Oh my sweet, how I long for the day when you get well
again! I don't like the idea of that vast dog keeping you awake. He
means so well, but he can't reduce his size, nor does he understand
how ill invalids can feel.

I am reading the letters of Oscar Wilde, excellently edited by
Rupert Hart-Davis. He really is a scholar, that man. He has taken
immense trouble in his editing. The book is not out for a month, so
I can take it slowly.

I lunched with Baba [Lady Alexandra Metcalfe] yesterday. I
walked all the way back to Albany, as it was a lovely afternoon. I
sniffed the spring air and the scent of tar. A man came to see me who
is writing a book about Tom Mosley. He had seen Tom. He brought
a recording machine with him on which to record my replies to his
questions. I didn't care for that very much, and then Kenneth Rose
appeared and scoffed at the machinery turning and churning on the
floor. The man detected Kenneth's irony, and packed up and left.
'Do you often submit yourself to such humiliating ordeals?' asked
Kenneth. 'Very frequently', I replied. I like Kenneth, since he is
amused by the publicity to which, from time to time, I am exposed.
I do not like being taken too seriously, and enjoy being teased.

Oh my darling, I shall see you tomorrow and shall be down a
whole week. That will be agreeable indeed.

DIARY   *25th May, 1962*

Go to the *Observer* to get books. Lunch at the Beefsteak. Down
home. Viti is certainly looking better and more cheerful. The
garden is looking lovely, but it is still cold and grey. The nurse has
her dinner in the kitchen, and I am alone with Dr Kildare.[1]

DIARY   *26th May, 1962*

I read the proofs of *Monarchy* and start on the index. It is a cloudy
day and drizzles. What a May to have! But the garden does not
seem to mind in the least, and the flowers are romping out.

[1] The television programme.

413

DIARY   *27th May, 1962*

Philippa and the children come down for luncheon. They are as sweet as can be, and Viti, I think, enjoyed having them. I think she is getting better, but it is a slow process.

DIARY   *28th May, 1962*

Vita is down, I fear—mostly depression. Watch *Panorama* after dinner.

DIARY   *29th May, 1962*

The doctor comes to see Vita. He is worried about the slowness of her recovery, and feels that she really must undergo the deep-ray treatment at Pembury. It will make her feel low and miserable, but it must be done. I am miserable and worried again. What a cursed year this is! Vita is depressed in the evening, and so, by God, am I!

DIARY   *30th May, 1962*

Viti goes off in the car to Pembury to have her treatment. She is to go every day except weekends for five weeks. Edie goes with her. Ursula [Codrington] comes to supper, bless her. Not a happy day.

DIARY   *31st May, 1962*

Viti goes off in an ambulance to Pembury. She is there for a long time and emerges exhausted. She returns about lunch-time, but refuses everything but a bowl of soup. She sleeps soundly after luncheon, but she is miserable, and so am I. It is a lovely day, which makes it all the more intolerable.

DIARY   *1st June, 1962*

Viti is so weak this morning that she is not strong enough to go to Pembury. The doctor comes after breakfast. He says that I must face the fact that there is little hope. He does not think she will suffer much. I return to my room in a haze of fear. Niggs comes down late at night.

DIARY   *2nd June, 1962*

It is a lovely morning. I get up early and walk round the garden. V. is asleep, and I do not disturb her. Glen dances on the lawn with his brother, Brandy. I breakfast with Niggs, and then I force myself to do my review of the composite book *Companion to Homer*. I finish it about 12.30, and start reading the newspaper. Ursula is with Vita. At about 1.5 she observes that Vita is breathing heavily, and then suddenly is silent. She dies without fear or self-reproach at 1.15. Ursula comes to tell me. I pick some of her favourite flowers and lay them on the bed.

N.N.'S DIARY   *5th June, 1962*

The funeral was at Sissinghurst village church at 11.30 this morning. Ben and Philippa and I saw the vicar two days ago, and said that we did not want an address, but merely that she should be mentioned by name at an appropriate point in the service. I had proposed 'V. Sackville-West, wife of Harold Nicolson', but when I told Daddy this, he said that his name was not to be mentioned at all. Philippa explained this to the vicar who, although a little puzzled, did as we wanted. I had the idea of printing a passage from 'The Land' on the back of the service-sheet and Ben suggested the 'island' passage.[1] We cast around for something suitable in which to put her ashes, and decided to hollow out the little sarcophagus of pink Italian marble, which has held the two ink-wells on her writing-table for as long as I can remember. Bunny [Drummond] did the necessary work on it—rough but suitable. We will place it in the Sackville crypt at Withyham.

Just after 11.15 the hearse arrived, and the men carried the coffin out of the Big Room to the front entrance. We set off in a slow procession up the lane. The church was crowded when we arrived, and there were masses of flowers inside (mostly from our own garden), and outside on the grass by the door of the church. In the front pew were Daddy, Ben, Philippa, Luisa and myself. The children were too young to come. The coffin was brought in and put on trestles by the altar steps. At the end of the service Daddy went up to the Bishop of Dover and shook his hand affectionately, and the same with one or two other friends whom he saw in the church as he walked down the aisle— such an unexpected and touching gesture.

[1] The passage begins:
> *She walks among the loveliness she made,*
> *Between the apple-blossom and the water—*
> *She walks among the patterned pied brocade,*
> *Each flower her son and every tree her daughter.*

Then we followed the coffin in our car, driven by Copper, through the lanes and villages of the Weald to Charing crematorium. It was a lovely summer's day, and it cheered us all up. The service at Charing lasted only a very short time. The coffin was placed on a sort of altar which had a lift let in to it. After five minutes of prayer, the coffin slowly sank out of sight. We drove back to Sissinghurst.

Harold Nicolson in 1967

*Philippa Nicolson and Rebecca
in 1967*

Here lived
V. SACKVILLE-WEST
who made this garden
Born at Knole 9 March 1892
Died at Sissinghurst 2 June 1962

Memorial to V. Sackville-West under the tower arch at Sissinghurst, designed by Reynolds Stone

Appendix

HAROLD NICOLSON'S PUBLISHED BOOKS

BIOGRAPHY (POLITICAL AND DIPLOMATIC)
Lord Carnock. 1930 (Constable)
Curzon, The Last Phase. 1934 (Constable)
Dwight Morrow. 1935 (Constable)
Helen's Tower (Lord Dufferin). 1937 (Constable)
The Desire to Please (Hamilton Rowan). 1943 (Constable)
King George V: His Life and Reign. 1952 (Constable)

BIOGRAPHY (LITERARY)
Paul Verlaine. 1921 (Constable)
Tennyson. 1923 (Constable)
Byron, The Last Journey. 1924 (Constable)
Swinburne. 1926 (English Men of Letters Series. Macmillan)
Benjamin Constant. 1949 (Constable)
Sainte-Beuve. 1957 (Constable)

POLITICAL AND SOCIAL HISTORY
Peacemaking 1919. 1933 (Constable), revised edition 1943 (Constable), new edition 1964 (Methuen)
The Congress of Vienna. 1946 (Constable)
Good Behaviour. 1955 (Constable)
The Age of Reason. 1960 (Constable)
Monarchy. 1962 (Weidenfeld & Nicolson)

H.N.D.   417   2D

POLITICS AND DIPLOMACY

The Meaning of Prestige (Rede Lecture). 1937 (Cambridge University Press)

Diplomacy. 1939 (Home University Library, Thornton Butterworth), 2nd edition, 1950, and 3rd edition, 1963, (Oxford University Press)

Why Britain is at War. 1939 (Penguin Books)

The Evolution of Diplomatic Method (Chichele Lectures, Oxford, 1953), 1954 (Constable)

LITERARY CRITICISM, ESSAYS ETC.

Some People. 1927 (Constable), new edition 1959 (Constable)

The Development of English Biography. 1927 (Hogarth Press)

People and Things (wireless talks). 1931 (Constable)

Small Talk (collected essays). 1937 (Constable)

Marginal Comment. 1939
Friday Mornings. 1944
Comments. 1948
} (Constable. Reprints of articles in the *Spectator*)

The English Sense of Humour. 1946 (Dropmore Press, limited edition)

The English Sense of Humour and Other Essays. 1956 (Constable)

FICTION

Sweet Waters. 1921 (Constable)

Public Faces. 1932 (Constable)

TRAVEL

Journey to Java. 1957 (Constable)

ANTHOLOGY (with V. Sackville-West)

Another World Than This . . . 1945 (Michael Joseph)

DIARIES AND LETTERS (edited by Nigel Nicolson)

1930–39. 1966 (Collins)

1939–45. 1967 (Collins)

1945–62. 1968 (Collins)

V. SACKVILLE-WEST'S PUBLISHED BOOKS

POETRY

Chatterton (A drama in blank verse). 1909 (privately printed by
J. Salmon, Sevenoaks)

Constantinople: Eight Poems. 1915 (privately printed by the Complete Press, London)

Poems of West and East. 1917 (John Lane, the Bodley Head)

Orchard and Vineyard. 1921 (John Lane, the Bodley Head)

The Land. 1926 (Heinemann)

King's Daughter. 1929 (Hogarth Press)

Sissinghurst. 1931 (Hogarth Press)

Invitation to Cast out Care. 1931 (Faber & Faber)

Solitude. 1938 (Hogarth Press)

The Garden. 1946 (Michael Joseph)

Collected Poems. Vol. I. 1933 (Hogarth Press)

Selected Poems. 1941 (Hogarth Press)

ANTHOLOGY (with Harold Nicolson)

Another World Than This . . . 1945 (Michael Joseph)

FICTION

Heritage. 1919 (Collins)

The Dragon in Shallow Waters. 1921 (Collins)

The Heir. 1922 (Heinemann. Reissued in 1949 by the Richards
Press)

Challenge. 1923 (published only in the United States by George H.
Doran Co.)

Grey Wethers. 1923 (Heinemann)

Seducers in Ecuador. 1924 (Hogarth Press)

The Edwardians. 1930 (Hogarth Press)

All Passion Spent. 1931 (Hogarth Press)

The Death of Noble Godavary and *Gottfried Künstler.* 1932 (Ernest
Benn)

Thirty Clocks Strike the Hour and other stories. 1932 (Doubleday, New York)
Family History. 1932 (Hogarth Press)
The Dark Island. 1934 (Hogarth Press)
Grand Canyon. 1942 (Michael Joseph)
Devil at Westease. 1947 (published only in the United States by Doubleday)
The Easter Party. 1953 (Michael Joseph)
No Signposts in the Sea. 1961 (Michael Joseph)

HISTORY, BIOGRAPHY AND LITERARY CRITICISM

Knole and the Sackvilles. 1922 (Heinemann. New edition by Lindsay Drummond, 1947)
The Diary of Lady Anne Clifford. 1923 (Heinemann)
Aphra Behn. 1927 (Gerald Howe)
Andrew Marvell. 1929 (Faber & Faber)
Saint Joan of Arc. 1936 (Cobden-Sanderson. New edition by Michael Joseph, 1948)
Pepita. 1937 (Hogarth Press)
The Eagle and the Dove (St Teresa of Avila and St Thérèse of Lisieux). 1943 (Michael Joseph).
Nursery Rhymes. 1947 (The Dropmore Press, limited edition. Michael Joseph, 1950)
Daughter of France ('La Grande Mademoiselle'). 1959 (Michael Joseph)

GARDENS, COUNTRY LIFE ETC.

Some Flowers. 1937 (Cobden-Sanderson)
Country Notes (articles reprinted from the *New Statesman*). 1939 (Michael Joseph)
Country Notes in Wartime (articles reprinted from the *New Statesman*). 1940 (Michael Joseph)
English Country Houses. 1941 (Collins. Britain in Pictures series)
The Women's Land Army. 1944 (Michael Joseph)

In Your Garden. 1951
In Your Garden Again. 1953
More for Your Garden. 1955
Even More for Your Garden. 1958

(Michael Joseph. Articles reprinted from the *Observer*)

A Joy of Gardening. 1958 (published only in the United States by Harpers, New York)
Faces (profiles of dogs). 1961 (Harvill Press)
V. Sackville-West's Garden Book. Posthumously, 1968. Edited by Philippa Nicolson (Michael Joseph)

TRAVEL

Passenger to Teheran. 1926 (Hogarth Press)
Twelve Days. 1928 (Hogarth Press)

APPENDIX

A Joy of Guernsey, 1935 (published only in the United States by Harper, New York.)
Paris (prefiere of dogs), 1907 (Harvill Press)
V. Sackville-West's Garden Book. Posthumously, 1968. Edited by Philippa Nicolson (Michael Joseph)

TRAVEL

Passenger to Teheran, 1926 (Hogarth Press)
Twelve Days, 1928 (Hogarth Press)

Index

423

Betjeman, John 243
Bevan, Aneurin: V.S-W. loathes 93;
at U.S. Embassy 138; resigns from
Government 205; not dictatorially-
minded 210; 'a charming, dangerous
man' 222; should have become
Labour leader 292; accuses Eden of
weakness 305; influenced by Stendhal
368; in atom-bomb controversy
385n; death and H.N.'s assessment
of 384
Beveridge Report 49
Bevin, Ernest: Foreign Office delighted
with 31; refuses to impose govern-
ment on Greece 42; will not appoint
H.N. Chairman of British Council
43; on Azerbaijan crisis 54; at 1946
Paris Conference 70; talks to H.N.
about progress of Conference 75-6;
H.N.'s admiration for 76; growing
physical weakness 78 90; talks to
H.N. about Russian aims 115-16;
H.N. begins to lose faith in over
Israeli war 140; his optimism and
social discourtesy 145; and Berlin
blockade 146; in 1950 Election 186
Beynac 261 264
Bibesco, Prince Antoine 177
Bibesco, Princess Marthe 77
Bidault, Georges 36 70 76 101 115
Biddle, Judge 62
Birkenhead, 2nd Earl of 402
Birkett, Sir Norman (Lord Birkett) 60
62 63 249
Birley, Dr Robert 267-8
Black, Eugene 362
Blum, Léon 68 189
Blunt, Sir Anthony 81n
Bodnant (N. Wales) 73 227
Bohlen, Charles E. 373
Bologna 324
Bombay 363
Bond, James 371
Bonham Carter, Mark 348
Bonham Carter, Lady Violet (Baroness
Asquith) 56 111-12 138 170 348 353

Bonn 275
Bonnard, Pierre 90
Boothby, Sir Robert (Lord Boothby)
128-9 212 247 256 305 317
Bordeaux 262
Bos, Charles du 97
Boulogne 361
Bournemouth East & Christchurch:
N.N. adopted as Conservative candi-
date 213-4; elected M.P. 219-20;
re-elected in 1955 Election 282 283;
capital punishment issue 295 298-9;
attitude to Suez crisis 306 315 319;
N.N.'s speech on Suez 318; dis-
owned by Conservatives 323; fights
back 345; Wolfenden Report 355;
climax of N.N.'s controversy with
361; result of poll 365-6
Bowen, Elizabeth 68 411
Bowra, Sir Maurice 101 313 387 394
Boyle, Sir Edward 176-7 330
Bracken, Brendan (Viscount Bracken):
defeat in 1945 Election 30n; hears
Election results with Churchill 32;
Tory reaction against 36; N.N. suc-
ceeds as M.P. for Bournemouth
East 213n
Bradley Manor 104
Brain, Sir Russell (Lord Brain) 321
Brains Trust 87 170 230 238 248
Brandy (dog) 415
Brazil 391-2 393
Brentano, Dr Heinrich von 276
Brisson, Pierre 197
British Council 30 43-4 124 161
Brooke, Henry (Lord Brooke) 284
Brown, George 300
Brown, Ivor 137
Bruce-Lockhart, Sir Robert 165
Bryant, Sir Arthur 113 268
Buccleuch, Duke of 100
Budapest 315 316
Budberg, Baroness 174
Buenos Aires 391
Bulganin, Nikolai 300 318
Bulgaria 66

Communism: in Britain 49 89 130
187n 188; in France 115 301-2; in
Germany 55-6 89 116; in Greece 40
42 89; in India 89; in Western
Europe 55 74 89 238; Bertrand
Russell on 202
Conant, James B. 276
Congo 377 385 398 402
Connolly, Cyril 43 99 101 291 347
Conolly, Michael 392
Conservative Party: H.N.'s attitude to
17 394 401n; defeat in 1945 Election
30; Churchill calls young Tories
'pink pansies' 45; 'embarrassed' by
Churchill 63; Smuts on 65; in 1950
Election 187; policy in 1951 Election
210; wins 1951 Election 211; gives
impression of wobbling 224; on
Cyprus 261; in Suez crisis 306-7 309
312 316; anti-Eden Tories 317;
Macmillan becomes leader 329-30;
failure to reconcile to loss of Empire
349; on decolonisation 369
Constant, Benjamin 97 107-8
Contact, Magazine 56 82 173
Contact Publications Ltd. 87
Cooper, Lady Diana 255 313 320 321
387-8 396
Cooper, Duff (Viscount Norwich): at
French Embassy 36; H.N. to succeed
as Ambassador in Paris? 65; reviews
King George V 226; dies 255;
memorial service 256; H.N. writes
article on for D.N.B. 276; Duff
Cooper Memorial Prize 313 321;
H.N. unveils memorial tablet in
St. Paul's 387-8
Copenhagen 218 221
Copper, J. 90 416
Copper, Mrs 238
Coppet (Mme de Staël's house) 108
Cornwall 103 190
Coronation of Queen Elizabeth II 241-2
Corsham Court 105
Costello, John 152-3
Cotehele, Cornwall 103

Council of Europe 310 311
Coward, Noel 119
Cowley, Arthur 219
Cranborne, Viscount 222
Cranbrook 77
Crete 362 367
Cripps, Sir Stafford 96 111 120 166
Cromer, 2nd Earl of 147
Crossman, R. H. S. 129 145 304
Croydon, North: H.N. as Labour
candidate in 1948 bye-election 117-
37; proposed 117; doubts about
acceptance 118; accepts 119; adopted
119-20; conduct of campaign 123-
31; result 132; H.N.'s Marginal
Comment on 133-7 186; Attlee on
138; H.N.'s subsequent reflections
on 157 172; loses him a peerage 186;
'made a mess of it' 18
Cuba 385 388; Bay of Pigs 395
Cunard, Lady (Emerald) 76 95
Cunard, Victor 32 80
Curaçao 346
Curzon, Marquess 162 267-8
Cyprus 261 295 303-4 311 333-4 349
Czechoslovakia 311

Daily Herald 126
Daily Mail 140 353
Daily Telegraph 113 163 226 260
Daily Worker 71
Dalton, Hugh 36 102 111 178 191
Dalton, Canon John 167
Damaskinos, Archbishop 39 41-2
Danube, River 76 79
Dardanelles, the 76 116
Dartmoor 105
Dashwood, Sir John 103
Davies, Clement 194 303 334
Davies, W. H. 383
Day-Lewis, Cecil 236 268 296 382
Deakin, F. W. 164
Debré, Michel 368
Deedes, William 211
de Gaulle, see Gaulle, President Charles
de

428

De La Warr, Countess (Diana) 333
De La Warr, Earl 34
Delbos, Yvon 76
Demosthenes 41
Denmark: H.N. visits in 1952 218
Desborough, Lady 225
De Valera, President Eamon 152-3
Devon Loch (racehorse) 299
Devonshire, 11th Duke of 299
Dewey, Thomas E. 154
Diplomacy 42-3 71 101 374
Dix, Dr (at Nuremberg trial) 59 62
Dixon, Sir Pierson 43
Don, Rev. A. C. 194 220 260
Donne, John 260
Dordogne (France) 21 23 261-2 264 288 322
Doubleday, Doran 339-40
Douglas, Lewis W. (U.S. Ambassador) 258-9 283
Dover, Bishop of 415
Driberg, Tom 303
Drummond, Cynthia 109 139-40 235 415
Drummond, Lindsay 109n 139-40
Dublin 152-3 235
Duclos, M. 77
Duff, Lady Juliet 286-7
Duff Cooper Memorial Prize 313 321
Dufferin, 1st Marquess of 176n 277n
Dulles, John Foster: in 1948 Election 154; 'deeply anti-British' 231; 'inferiority complex' 283; in Suez crisis 307 309n; taken ill 315
Durban 378
Dyrham Park 103

Eccles, David (Viscount Eccles) 210 295
Eden, Anthony (Earl of Avon): 'too weak' to lead Conservatives? 36; desires to help Bevin 63; defends H.N. for joining Labour Party 95; on his visit to Berlin in 1948 147; presumed heir to Churchill 224; at Anglo-German dinner 229-30; on Egypt and Iranian oil problem 258;

succeeds Churchill as Prime Minister 281; Bevan and others accuse him of weakness 305; in Suez crisis 305-19 passim; returns from Jamaica 323; resigns 328; sails for New Zealand 328-9; feeling in Party about him 329; Gaitskell's tribute to 330
Eden, Clarissa (Countess of Avon) 230 329
Edinburgh, Prince Philip, Duke of 102
Edward VII 155 174n 175
Egypt: Sudan agreement 236; Nasser's struggle for power 258; in Suez crisis 306-19 passim; H.N. visits 362
Eire 152-4
Eisenhower, President Dwight D.: President-Elect 230; out on a limb in Korea 230-1; in Suez crisis 311; at Paris Summit Meeting 384; succeeded by Kennedy 387 392
Elections, General: of 1945 30; of 1950 183 185-8; of 1951 201 209 210-12; of 1955 282-3; of 1959 361
Eliot, T. S.: V.S-W. feels out of touch with his poetry 38; talks to H.N. about his lectures in Germany 174-5; President of London Library 211n; lectures on The Three Voices of Poetry 249; at dinner for Massigli 269; at Academy Banquet 395; mentioned 43
Elizabeth II, Queen: her engagement announced 102; H.N. meets 188; becomes Queen 219; 'this sweet girl' 220; congratulates H.N. on King George V 229; her radiance 230; invests H.N. with K.C.V.O. 237; her Coronation 241-2; offers Churchill dukedom 287; at first night of film 291; Christmas broadcast 342; birth of Prince Andrew 369 382; visit to Ghana 401; sends H.N. message of sympathy on V.S-W.'s illness 409
Elizabeth, Queen (The Queen Mother): at Buckingham Palace reception 115; welcomes H.N. as biographer of

India: threat of communism in 89; independence 100; a Republic within Commonwealth 170; letter from British intellectuals to Nehru 203; a gloomy forecast for 281-2; comparison with Algeria 333
Indo-China 247
Inverewe 244
Iran: see Persia
Iraq 314
Ireland: see Eire and Ulster
Irun 278
Islam 397
Ismailia 319
Ismay, General Sir Hastings (Lord Ismay) 89 163-4 333n
Israel: birth of the State 139; Arabs attack Jerusalem 140; anti-semitism in England 140; Bevin says problem settling itself 145; murder of Count Bernadotte by Stern gang 148-9; Weizmann as President 173-4; in 1956 crisis 311 312 314
Italian campaign of 1943-5 89
Italy 66-7 73-4 220-1 355

Jacob, General Sir Ian 88-9
Jamaica 323 341
James, Henry 154
Janner, Sir Barnett 183 187
Jansenism 291 301
Japan: attacked by atom-bomb 31; surrenders 32; H.N. visits 364
Jarvis, W. B. 91 93
Jay, Douglas 229
Jebb, Cynthia (Lady Gladwyn) 300-1
Jebb, Sir Gladwyn (Lord Gladwyn): at 1946 Paris Peace Conference 68n 70 72; on negotiations about future of Germany 100-1; in despair about the United Nations 151-2; Ambassador in Paris 277; on French situation in 1956 301-2; supports H.N.'s 70th birthday present 320; at unveiling of memorial to Duff Cooper 387
Jeger, Mrs Lena 304

Jerusalem 140
Jews, the 17 139 145 149; see also Israel
Jewsbury, Geraldine 184
Jimenez, President of Venezuela 346n
Joad, Dr C. E. M. 97-8 154 174 189
Jodl, General 59 64
Johnson, Dr Samuel 353-4
Jones, Enid (Enid Bagnold) 111 320 321
Jones, L. E. 320
Jordan 299 311 314 350
Jordan, Philip 163 186
Jowitt, Sir William (Earl Jowitt): Lord Chancellor 36 37-8; advises H.N. to fight as Independent 49-50; H.N. agrees to take Labour Whip 56-7; speech to Haldane Society 96; 'histrionic capacity' 178; mentioned 195 292
Judd, Charles 317

Katanga 398
K.C.V.O.: offered to H.N. 228; accepted 229; announced 235; his misgivings about 229 235-6 284; invested by Queen Elizabeth II 237
Keats, John 221 259 373
Keir, Sir David Lindsay 231
Keitel, Field Marshal Wilhelm 58-9 61
Kennedy, President John F.: H.N.'s opinion of 17 387; becomes President 377 387 392; H.N. invited to write about his speeches 393; Bay of Pigs crisis 395
Kent, William 228
Kenya 369
Keyes, Admiral Sir Roger 289
Keynes, J. M. (Lord Keynes) 53n 202
Khrushchev, Nikita: H.N.'s opinion of 17; conflict with George Brown 300; moon-rocket 370; Macmillan on 382; at 1960 Summit Conference 383-4; and Cuba 384-5; see Russia
Kildare, Dr 413
Killearn, Lord 307
Killerton (Devon) 103

Nicolson, Harold (cont.)
244 328; his mother's death 204; distress at his brother's death 225 231; his grand-children 259 308 338 383 410
Health: his vigour at sixty 80; physical but not mental decline 178-9 189; reaction to old age 190 224 274; sciatica 273 279; first stroke 279; second stroke 282; effect of the two strokes 20-1 284 295; letter to Lord Esher on having strokes 335-6; deafness 266 274 373 396; not frightened of death 286 302; feeling his age 373 400; third stroke 24
Books: bibliography, *Appendix;* his own estimate of his best books 287; his literary reputation 81 212; his literary style 37 155 192; V.S-W. on his writing 191 287 327; *Age of Reason, The* 339-40 341 361 377 381 ('rotten book') 383 388; *Age of Romance, The* (unfinished) 21 24 391 397; *Another World Than This* 29; *Benjamin Constant* 96 107 108-9 141 146 147-8 170; *Congress of Vienna, The* 20 31 51 212; *English Sense of Humour, The* 54 56 81 283; *Good Behaviour* 210 229 249 255 256 257 260 269 280 287; *Journey to Java* 21 22 319-20 327 332 334 338 340 342 348 355; *King George V: His Life and Reign,* see separate index-heading; *Lord Carnock* 212 287 355; *Monarchy* 21 384 393 397 398-400 402 407-8 413; *Peacemaking* 212; *Public Faces* 31 212; *Sainte-Beuve* 283 291 304 310 328; *Some People* 267-8 287 355 370
Diary: continued to October 1964 23; H.N. considers Pepys's diary 113; thinks his own superficial 138; abbreviated while writing *King George V* 192 201; 'too boring for words' 236; not right to record gossip 236; conveys 'the time-table mood' 248; 'a pitiable little engage-

ment-book' 321; shows 1938 diary to Martin Gilbert 412
Nicolson, Juliet (H.N.'s grand-daughter) 259 260-1 280n 320-1 324 338 382-3 410
Nicolson, Luisa (*née* Vertova, Ben's wife): works with Bernard Berenson 193; engaged to Ben 281; married in Florence 273 285; V.S-W.'s affection for 286; may find Sissinghurst dull 286; expecting baby 302n; Vanessa born 308; at V.S-W.'s funeral 415
Nicolson, Nigel: succeeds father as candidate in Leicester 33; joins George Weidenfeld 87; reaction to H.N. joining Labour Party 92; encourages H.N. to fight N. Croydon 119; not allowed to visit him during bye-election 127-8; on *King George V* 145; profile of H.N. for *Observer* 165n; becomes trustee of Knole 176; fights 1950 Election in Leicester 183 185-7; adopted for Falmouth 183 190; fights 1951 Election there 210 211-12; adopted for Bournemouth East 213-14; elected 219-20; first debates 222; engaged to be married 238; married 244; Juliet born 259; suggests offering Sissinghurst to National Trust 268; re-elected for Bournemouth in 1955 282 283; disagrees with Bournemouth on capital punishment 295 298; in Suez crisis 19 306-17 *passim;* member of Council of Europe 310; publicly protests against Suez policy 318; vote of no confidence passed against him by Bournemouth Conservatives 323; admiration for Macmillan 329-30 331; writes *People and Parliament* 19 349; supports Wolfenden Report 355; *Lolita* 356-8 363; climax of Bournemouth controversy 361; defeated in poll 365-6; criticises H.N.'s book *Monarchy* 398-400; last visits to V.S-W. 410 414; at her

Sackville-West, Victoria Mary (cont.)
attends Queen Mary's funeral 238;
at N.N.'s wedding 244; in Scotland
244; in France with H.N. 261-4;
writes guide to Berkeley Castle 266;
refuses to offer Sissinghurst to
National Trust 268; reads *The Land*
in public 268-9; broadcasts on
Virginia Woolf 274; talks to Churchill 276 286-7; distressed by H.N.'s
stroke 279; damages spine 280; in
Florence for Ben's wedding 285;
welcome to Luisa 286; in France
again 288-9; gets R.H.S. Gold Medal
290; on H.N. standing for Oxford
Chair of Poetry 296; first sees
Vanessa Nicolson 308; to Spain with
H.N. and Philippa 310; attitude to
Suez crisis 313; with H.N. to Java
327; in Singapore 332; Sissinghurst
repaired 337; illness on journey to
South America 340-1; recovers 345-
6; despairs over *Daughter of France*
346-7; finishes it 351; enjoys
C.P.R.K. meeting 353; corresponds
with N.N. about *Lolita*; 356-8 to
Far East 361; at Saigon 363; in Japan
364; Macao 364; off Crete 367; gets
virus pneumonia 367-8; facsimile of
letter from 372; broadcast from
Sissinghurst 373-4; to South Africa
377; on Apartheid 379; on award of
O.M. 382; *No Signposts in the Sea*
386; to Rio de Janeiro 391-2;
Montevideo 392; returns to Knole
after thirty-one years 397; N.N.
appeals for help over *Monarchy* 398-
400; taken ill in train 405-6; last
journey 405-7; 'I feel really ill' on
return 407; advised to have operation
408; operation reveals cancer 409;
returns to Sissinghurst 410; improves
411; last letter to H.N. 412; has
relapse 414; dies at Sissinghurst 2nd
June 1962 415; her funeral and
cremation 415-16

Characteristics and tastes: romanticism
82 241; love of writing poetry 38
195; and reading it 236 266; feeling
for Knole 110-11 176 196 268;
privacy 259; few friends 322 352;
finds profit-motive disgusting 264-5;
sense of ownership 268 352; religion
265 277-8; happiness at Sissinghurst
149; the garden 82 257-8 398; opening it to public 396; fondness for
dogs 138 201-2 322; and for rabbits
264-5; angered by stag-hunting 156;
loves country things 353; terrified in
London 308; clothes 189n 238; extreme Conservative 22 93; but indifferent to politics 38 266; never
forgave Germany 265 353; on Suez
crisis 313; and Apartheid 379; and
capital punishment 298; portrait of
her in *Journey to Java* 327 338
Family: the profundity of her relationship with H.N. 22 264 322-3
372 386; would kill herself if he died
279; but dislike of married status 37
71 308 386; excludes him from running Sissinghurst 352; thinks him
too mild 337; and exploited 374;
affection for her son 185; and
daughter-in-law 286; the chances
that make a family 287-8
Health: summary of her illnesses 23;
eye-trouble 152; 'flu in Spain 165
178; her nerves 178; arthritis 273 274
279 280; damages her spine 280 281;
fluctuating fever 341; virus pneumonia 361 367-8 377; seems stronger
402; haemorrhage in train 405 406;
illness on board ship 406-7; cancer
discovered 409; 'anaemia' 411; relapse 414; death 415
Books: bibliography, *Appendix*; her
writing methods 291; H.N.'s assessment of her reputation 339; *Another
World Than This* 29; *Daughter of
France* ('La Grande Mademoiselle'):
idea of the book 88; temporarily

abandons 107; resumes 237 255 258; progress 274; Steegmuller's book on same subject 291 297; new progress 327 332 345 346-7 ('so bad'); finished 351; sells well 368; *The Easter Party* 140*n* 183*n* 195 201 230 236; *The Edwardians* 212; *Faces* 391; *The Garden* 29 38 43-4 183; *The Land* 268-9 415; *No Signposts in the Sea* 22 361 377 386; *Nursery Rhymes* 183*n*; gardening books 339*n* (see *Observer*); her diary 235; extracts from 236 237 244 247 274 279 284 286 290 297 298 368 406 407
Saigon 363
St Aubyn, Giles 260
St Levan, Lady (Gwen, H.N.'s sister) 204 338
St Levan, Lord 304
Sainte-Beuve, Charles Augustin 283 291 301 361
Saint Pierre and Miquelon Islands 289
Salamanca 278
Salisbury, 5th Marquess of: H.N. shares secretary with 99; possibly advised on biography of King George V 142; at Duff Cooper's memorial service 256; defends Government on Suez 318; advises on choice of Eden's successor 328; farewell speech on Eden 329; mentioned 349
Salter, Sir Arthur (Lord Salter) 34
Samuel, Viscount 156 202 227 248
Sandringham 174 175-6 219*n*
Sands, Ethel 177
Sandys, Duncan 30*n*
San Francisco 69
Sargent, Sir Malcolm 239
Sargent, Sir Orme 80
Sassoon, Sir Philip 228
Sauckel, Fritz 61
Saurat, Prof. Denis 98
Saxe, Marshal Maurice de 263
Saxe-Meiningen, Prince Frederick 167
Schacht, Dr Hjalmar 58 59 60
Schifanoia 280

Schirach, Baldur von 59
Schlange-Schoeningen, Dr Hans 229
Schleicher, General Kurt von 61
Schwerdt, Miss Pamela 381
Scorrybreck (Skye) 338*n*
Scotland 244 297-8 338
Scott, Sir David 31
Scott, Geoffrey 172
Scott, Sir Giles Gilbert 194*n*
Sencourt, Robert 107*n*
Senhouse, Roger 128
Sevenoaks 386
Seyss-Inquart, Dr Arthur 59
Shakespeare, William 106 112 139 208 266 297 367
Shanganagh Castle 153-4
Shaw, George Bernard: decline in his reputation 154; Joad's book on 174; death, and H.N.'s visit to Shaw's Corner 196-7; Vivien Leigh on acting Shaw 297
Shelley, P. B. 221 259
Shepherd, Frank 119-20
Sherwood, Lord (Hugh Seely) 42
Shiant Islands, (Outer Hebrides) 244
Shinwell, Emanuel 87 93
Shirley House (Hampshire) 259 260*n* 316
Silverman, Sydney 295 304-5
Simenon, Georges 223-4 371
Simon, Viscount 237 256
Simonides 370
Sinai 314 (*see* Suez crisis)
Singapore 331
Sissinghurst Castle: no guest-room 113*n*; on the night of Bernadotte's murder 149; H.N.'s summing-up of its serenity 152; the garden at 82-3 168-9 171 207 257-8 381 398; open to the public 396; 'very mellow and English' 239; V.S-W. refuses to offer it to National Trust 24 268; proposal to televise 300; repair of porch and tower 337; world broadcast from 373-4; V.S-W. dies at 415; passes to the National Trust 24

Sissinghurst Place 139-40
Sitwell, Dame Edith 382
Sitwell, Sacheverell 119
Skye 338
Smith, W. H., Prize 411
Smithers, Peter 256
Smuts, Field Marshal Jan Christian 63-5
Smyth, Rev. Charles 194
Snow, C. P. (Lord Snow) 348
Snowdon, Earl of 380 (see Margaret, Princess)
Socrates 221
Soheily, Mme 276
Somaliland 379-80
Soraya, Queen 276
South Africa: Smuts on 64
Southampton, 207 332 405
South Bank, Exhibition of 1951 206
Spaak, Paul-Henri 54
Space-flight: American satellites 284; Russian sputniks 339 340; first moon-shot 370; first manned flight 396; American astronaut 408; H.N. 'against space-travel' 408
Spain 161 164 165 245 278 286 302-3 310
Spain, Queen Ena of (Victoria Eugenie) 240
Sparrow, John: shares Albany with H.N. 224n 255; Warden of All Souls 226; 'a stimulating companion' 256; epitaph on Lord Simon 256; supports H.N.'s candidature for Oxford Chair of Poetry 296 298; co-sponsors H.N.'s 'Java' present 320; accused of belonging to Establishment 353; mentioned 292 340 380 400
Spear, Ruskin 334
Spearman, Sir Alexander 316 317
Spears, General Sir Edward 401
Spectator, The: 'Marginal Comment' 66 113 193; series ends 217 231; article on Croydon bye-election 18 133-7 (in full) 186; on opening of new Chamber 195; obituary of King George VI 209; on Lady Desborough 225; on moving house 226

Spender, Stephen 38 382
Staël, Mme de 108-9
Stalin, Joseph: 'ceased to count' 54; utter ignorance of the West 101; a tiger to Attlee's mouse 186; Shaw has portraits of 197; dies 237
Stalingrad 116
Stamfordham, Lord (Sir Arthur Bigge) 162 204
Stanley, Oliver 55
Stansgate, Viscount 145
Staplehurst (Kent) 152 370
Staples, Mrs (Mrs Hayter) 36 126 282
Starkie, Enid 296
Stearns, Mary 322
Steegmuller, Francis 291 297
Stephen, Leslie 209n
Stern Gang (Israel) 148-9
Stevenson, Adlai: defeated by Eisenhower in 1952 230; and again in 1956 311n; H.N. meets 243; not appointed Secretary of State by Kennedy 387
Stokesay (Shropshire) 412
Stourhead (Wilts.) 103
Strachey, John 303
Strachey, Lytton 319
Strasbourg 310-11
Stratford-on-Avon 106
Stravinsky, Igor 355-6
Strawberry Hill 350-1
Sudan 145 236-7
Suez Crisis of 1956: summary 305-6; H.N.'s attitude to 19 323-4; passim 305-19; Anglo-French ultimatum to Egypt and Israel 312; collusion suspected 314 319; landings at Port Said 316; cease-fire 318; withdrawal 324; anti-Eden Conservatives 317; see Israel, Eden, United Nations
Sumatra 324
Sunday Express 94n 292
Sunday Times 45n 227 296 340
Sutherland, Graham 269
Swinton, Lord 349